D1502895

AMERICAN ROULETTE

American

The History and Dilemma of the Vice Presidency

Roulette

By Donald Young
Introduction by
Senator Birch Bayh

Holt, Rinehart and Winston
New York Chicago San Francisco

Published simultaneously in Canada by Holt, Rinehart and Winston of Canada, Limited.

ISBN: 0-03-091294-6

Library of Congress Catalog Card Number: 78-179943

Designed by Ernst Reichl

Printed in the United States of America

ACKNOWLEDGMENTS Grateful acknowledgment is made to the following publishers, authors, and other copyright holders for permission to quote from their published and private materials as follows:

The Bobbs-Merrill Company: RECOLLECTIONS OF THOMAS R. MARSHALL, VICE-PRESIDENT AND HOOSIER PHILOSOPHER by Thomas R. Marshall; copyright 1925; copyright renewed 1953 by Mrs. Thomas R. Marshall; MY MEMOIR by Edith Bolling Wilson, Indianapolis, The Bobbs-Merrill Company; copyright 1938, 1939; GODS AND LITTLE FISHES by Alfred Pearce Dennis; copyright 1931 by Alfred P. Dennis; copyright renewed © 1958 by Mrs. Mary Value Clark.

Doubleday and Company: THAT REMINDS ME by Alben W. Barkley; copyright 1954; SIX CRISES by Richard M. Nixon; copyright © 1962.

Harcourt Brace Jovanovich, Inc.: JOHN KENNEDY: A POLITICAL PROFILE, copyright © 1959 by James MacGregor Burns; DEMOCRACY REBORN by Henry A. Wallace, copyright, 1944, by Harcourt Brace Jovanovich, Inc.; THE AMERICAN CHOICE, copyright, 1940, by Henry A. Wallace; NEW FRONTIERS, copyright, 1934, 1962, by Henry A. Wallace.

Harper & Row: ALL IN ONE LIFETIME by James Byrnes; THE PUBLIC PAPERS AND ADDRESSES OF FRANKLIN D. ROOSEVELT and WORKING WITH ROOSEVELT by Samuel I. Rosenman; GARNER OF TEXAS: A PERSONAL HISTORY by Bascom Timmons.

Houghton Mifflin Company: THE WALLACES OF IOWA by Russell Lord; THE COMING OF THE NEW DEAL by Arthur Schlesinger.

J. P. Lippincott Company: THE MAN OF INDEPENDENCE by Jonathan Daniels; copyright 1950 by Jonathan Daniels.

William Morrow and Company, Inc.: HUMPHREY: A CANDID BIOGRAPHY by Winthrop Griffith; copyright © 1965.

G. P. Putnam's Sons: FROM HARRISON TO HARDING by Arthur W. Dunn; copyright 1922.

Random House, Inc.: MR. SAM by C. Douglas Dorough; copyright © 1962.

Charles Scribner's Sons: AN AUTOBIOGRAPHY by Theodore Roosevelt, originally published by The Macmillan Company, 1913; FDR: MY BOSS by Grace Tully; copyright 1949.

Simon and Schuster: PRESIDENTS WHO HAVE KNOWN ME by George E. Allen; copyright 1950.

Time Inc.: THE TRUMAN MEMOIRS by Harry S. Truman.

Viking Press: THE ROOSEVELT I KNEW by Frances Perkins; copyright 1946; AN AMERICAN MELODRAMA by Lewis Chester, Godfrey Hodgson, and Bruce Page; copyright © 1969.

James Farley: JIM FARLEY'S STORY: THE ROOSEVELT YEARS, originally published by McGraw-Hill Book Company, 1948.

Raymond Moley: 27 MASTERS OF POLITICS, originally published by Funk & Wagnalls Company, Inc.

To My Father

INTRODUCTION

American Roulette dramatizes one of the most disturbing aspects of the history of the Vice Presidency—our Constitution failed to provide a clear definition of Presidential succession and disability.

As early as 1787, at the Constitutional Convention in Philadelphia, Delaware delegate John Dickinson asked, "What is the extent of the term 'disability' and who is to be the judge of it?"

For almost one hundred eighty years Congress struggled with various proposals attempting to answer the question of Presidential disability and succession. It was not that suggestions, ideas, and legislative proposals were scarce, but rather that there were so many that it was virtually impossible to obtain a consensus.

When a stunned nation mourned the tragedy of President Kennedy's assassination in 1963, questions were again raised about Presidential succession and national stability. What if the Vice President had also been struck down? What if the President had been critically disabled with no mechanism available for the transfer of Presidential leadership?

More than two hundred articles, columns, and editorials appeared stressing the gravity of the situation and urging Congress to insure the continuity of national leadership.

This editorial outcry pointed out that this was the sixteenth time in our country's history that we had no Vice President. Nothing existed in our Constitutional law or among our judicial precedents to solve the problem of Vice Presidential selection or overcome the difficulty in deciding when a President was truly incapacitated.

Many instances come to mind when Presidential authority languished in the hands of a President who was seriously ill. President James Garfield lay between life and death for eighty days before dying. Woodrow Wilson lay paralyzed and disabled for sixteen months while our nation struggled with the tragedies brought by war. We also remember Dwight Eisenhower's heart attacks and national concern over Lyndon Johnson's heart condition. In all these situations there was no legal, Constitutional means of transferring, even temporarily, the power which only rests with the President.

As chairman of the Senate Subcommittee on Constitutional Amendments, I decided to seek the enactment of legislation that would guarantee national stability during a Presidential crisis. But before a plan approved by the Senate Subcommittee could be written into the Constitution, it had to be approved by the full Judiciary Committee, adopted by a two-thirds vote in both Houses of Congress and ratified by at least thirty-eight states. A long road. Finally, on February 23, 1967, with the ratification of the Amendment, an answer was provided to John Dickinson's question on disability.

President Lyndon Johnson witnessed the signing of the Twenty-fifth Amendment to the United States Constitution.

It reads as follows:

> Section 1. In case of the removal of the President from office or of his death or resignation, the Vice President shall become President.
>
> Section 2. Whenever there is a vacancy in the office of the Vice President, the President shall nominate a Vice President who shall take the office upon confirmation by a majority vote of both houses of Congress.
>
> Section 3. Whenever the President transmits to the President pro tempore of the Senate and the Speaker of the House of Representatives his written declaration that he is unable to discharge the powers and duties of his office, and until he

> transmits to them a written declaration to the contrary, such powers and duties shall be discharged by the Vice President as Acting President.
>
> Section 4. Whenever the Vice President and a majority of either the principal officers of the executive departments or of such other body as Congress may by law provide, transmit to the President pro tempore of the Senate and the Speaker of the House of Representatives their written declaration that the President is unable to discharge the powers and duties of his office, the Vice President shall immediately assume the powers and duties of the office as Acting President.
>
> Thereafter, when the President transmits to the President pro tempore of the Senate and the Speaker of the House of Representatives his written declaration that no inability exists, he shall resume the powers and duties of his office unless the Vice President and a majority of either the principal officers of the executive department or of such other body as Congress may by law provide, transmit within four days to the President pro tempore of the Senate and the Speaker of the House of Representatives their written declaration that the President is unable to discharge the powers and duties of his office. Thereupon Congress shall decide the issue, assembling within forty-eight hours for that purpose if not in session. If the Congress within twenty-one days after receipt of the latter written declaration, or, if Congress is not in session, within twenty-one days after Congress is required to assemble, determines by two-thirds vote of both Houses that the President is unable to discharge the powers and duties of his office, the Vice President shall continue to discharge the same as Acting President; otherwise, the President shall resume the powers and duties of his office.

Although no plan is perfect, the Twenty-fifth Amendment represents the best of our efforts. It deals with the problem of vacancy in the office of the Vice Presidency. Under the Amendment, the President may select a Vice President, subject to the approval of a majority vote of the two branches of Congress. In addition, the Amendment provides a positive means of determining if the President is unable to perform the duties and responsibilities of his office. If a President becomes unable to fulfill his responsibilities, he can certify his disability and the Vice President can step in. If the President were disabled and could not or would not ask the Vice President to take over, the Vice President could assume the powers with the Cabinet's consent. In case of a dispute between the Vice President and the President, Congress would make the decision. A two-thirds vote would be required to overrule the President. As we did not wish a President to lose his power by usurpation, we felt that by granting the Cabinet a concurrent role with the Vice President, it would give the President and those who are appointed to office by him equal power with the Vice President.

When Mr. Young's stimulating book on the Vice Presidency first appeared, it shed light on the men who were Vice Presidents and potentially Presidents. Mr. Young illustrated the need to insure a wise rather than expedient selection of a Vice Presidential running mate.

This volume was a timely and enlightening addition to the literature at the time the states were ratifying the Twenty-fifth Constitutional Amendment on Presidential succession and disability. It vividly pointed out the need for the Amendment, and it had the fresh viewpoint that every Vice President may well become the Chief Executive of the most powerful nation on earth.

In this new edition of *American Roulette*, Young adds the most recent chapters to his history of the American Vice Presidency. Written in the same lively style, the new chapters record the tragedies of recent years that propelled the Twenty-fifth Amendment through the Congress. In his analysis of the Presidential campaigns of the sixties, Young provides valuable insights into the selection of the Vice Presidential candidates and how their roles developed in the administrations they served.

The role of the Vice President proves to be delineated by his President, the experience, background, and personality of the Vice President himself, plus the interplay of personalities and events.

Young believes there has been a great development of the Vice Presidency over the last few years. No longer is the Vice Presidency a one-way ticket to oblivion. The Vice President now has numerous tasks assigned to him including a seat on the National Security Council, a role in space and aeronautics, and the chairmanship of the Equal Employment Opportunity Commission. The Vice President can be the President's ambassador to Congress and his foremost ambassador abroad.

Most important, the Vice President is one heartbeat away from the Presidency. In this regard, the Vice Presidency gives a unique opportunity to a man other than the President to gain experience with the major problems facing the nation. It also permits the Vice President to gain a broad perspective on the workings of government, which will be of great assistance to him should he have to assume the office of President. Young sees the developing responsibility of the office as a sign that it will increasingly become a training ground for the Presidency. As the author notes, the "year 1968 marked the only time other than 1800 that each major party nominated a man who had been Vice President."

By examining the past, Young makes us reflect on the future. Now that Presidential succession and procedures for Presidential disability are secured, hopefully we will choose men for Vice President who we feel are qualified to serve as the President of the United States. To that worthy end, this book makes a valuable contribution.

BIRCH BAYH
United States Senator from Indiana

CONTENTS

INTRODUCTION BY SENATOR BIRCH BAYH vii

PREFACE 3

1 JOHN ADAMS—THOMAS JEFFERSON—AARON BURR 5
"Is not my election to this office . . . a curse rather than a blessing?"

2 JOHN C. CALHOUN—MARTIN VAN BUREN 24
"It is an advantage to a public man to be the subject of an outrage."

3 JOHN TYLER 42
"And we'll vote for Tyler, therefore,
Without a why or wherefore."

4 MILLARD FILLMORE 55
". . . willing to offer himself upon the altar of his country. . . ."

5 ANDREW JOHNSON 66
"I am for the Union, the whole Union and nothing but the Union."

6 CHESTER ALAN ARTHUR 89
"The President's tragic death was a sad necessity. . . ."

7 THEODORE ROOSEVELT 111
"We have done the best we could. Now it is up to you to live."

8 THOMAS R. MARSHALL 125
"I could throw this country into civil war, but I won't."

9 CALVIN COOLIDGE 145
"O, we ain' gwine steal no mo,
We ain' gwine steal no mo."

10 JOHN NANCE GARNER 163
"Mr. President, you know you've got to let the cattle graze."

11 HENRY A. WALLACE 174
". . . the century which will come out of this war—can be and must be the century of the common man."

12 HARRY S. TRUMAN 196
"Why this awful fight over the Vice-Presidency? . . . [Are they] gambling . . . that he is going to die . . . ?"

13 HARRY S. TRUMAN (Concluded) 239
"God raises up leaders. We do not know the process. . . ."

14 RICHARD M. NIXON 252
"I told him he would have to chart his own course. . . ."

15 LYNDON B. JOHNSON 286
"this grandson of a 'federate soldier. . . ."

16 HUBERT H. HUMPHREY 317
". . . when the gap between rhetoric and reality becomes too wide."

17 SPIRO AGNEW 340
". . . not exactly the exercise of raw power."

18 THE VICE PRESIDENT'S JOB 372
". . . it's a kind iv a disgrace. It's like writin' anonymous letters."

19 PRESIDENTIAL SUCCESSION AND INABILITY 384
"God looks after fools, drunkards, and the United States."

BIBLIOGRAPHY 397

INDEX 413

AMERICAN ROULETTE

PREFACE

The President of the United States was dead. The incredible news from the South had struck the Capital with the force of a thunderclap, but now one sensed only a hush, an emptiness, a despair. Those who had admired him so greatly and those who had disliked him so intensely somehow discovered an affinity in the common, unexpected loss.

For many, there was no time for tears during that memorable weekend. The Presidential transition must be effected as swiftly as possible. Arrangements must be completed for the funeral—the passage of the caisson through the streets of Washington, the simple service at the White House, the burial. Not since the assassination of Lincoln had the city felt such grief.

Lyndon Johnson, who owed his own position to the late President, had felt the shock as greatly as anyone. But he had regained his composure more quickly than most. He encountered one of his secretaries, who was almost weeping.

"I feel so lost," she exclaimed. "Who is there now? Who is there for the country?"

Johnson smiled faintly. "Why, honey," said the tall Texas Congressman, "there's Truman."

And so, in April, 1945—after the death of Franklin Roosevelt—all thoughts turned to Harry S. Truman, who had been the thirty-fourth Vice President of the United States, and who was now the thirty-third President. In many ways he had been a typical Vice President. He had been nominated in 1944 to "balance the ticket" and to unify the party. As a Senator, he had been competent and hard-working. He had not been a party leader. To the public, he was a nonentity. With all his predecessors, he had dwelt in a constitutional limbo somewhere between the legislative and executive branches of our government. Roosevelt's vigorous exercise of the Presidential power had served only to underscore the limitations of the second office in the land—the Vice President is authorized by the Constitution to do no more than to preside over the Senate and to cast a vote in the event of a tie.

And with six of the Vice Presidents who had preceded him, Harry Truman shared a very special distinction. He had been summoned suddenly under tragic circumstances to assume the Presidency itself.

The Vice Presidency, which has been ignored or ridiculed throughout our history, gains the attention of all of us about once every twenty years when the President we elect dies in office in one of those disconcerting coincidences for which we have no explanation. The assassination of President Kennedy reminded us of our failure to come to grips with the constitutional problems of Presidential inability, of the Presidential succession, of nominating and electing our Vice Presidents, and of finding some useful jobs for them to perform.

Those serving as Vice President have included men who were targets of derision similar to that directed at the legendary Alexander Throttlebottom. Several others were tragic and heroic figures, shackled first by the very impotence of their office, and then overwhelmed by awesome responsibilities suddenly thrust upon them at critical times in our history.

The adoption in 1967 of the Twenty-fifth Amendment to the U.S. Constitution permits the Vice President to act as President under certain circumstances when it appears that the President is disabled. The amendment also provides for an immediate election of a Vice President when that office falls vacant. But the office is still a hollow one, yet controversial as well. The activities of Vice Presidents Hubert Humphrey and Spiro Agnew, among others, stirred strong debates concerning the proper use of the office. Even the ablest men, political leaders and political scientists alike, have been unable to solve the continuing dilemma of the Vice Presidency.

—D.Y.

★

JOHN ADAMS — THOMAS JEFFERSON — AARON BURR

"Is not my election to this office . . . a curse rather than a blessing?"

Gentlemen, suppose each of you had just been elected Vice President of the United States. Please give us your reaction.

JOHN ADAMS: "My country has in its wisdom contrived for me the most insignificant office that ever the invention of man contrived or his imagination conceived."

THOMAS JEFFERSON: "The second office of this Government is honorable and easy, the first is but a splendid misery."

THOMAS R. MARSHALL: The Vice President is "like a man in a cataleptic state; he cannot speak; he cannot move; he suffers no pain; and yet he is perfectly conscious of everything that is going on about him."

JOHN NANCE GARNER: "The vice-presidency isn't worth a pitcher of warm spit."

HARRY TRUMAN: "Look at all the Vice Presidents in history. Where are they? They were about as useful as a cow's fifth teat."

If our Vice Presidents could not take their job seriously, it was not surprising that the country went along with the gags. But three of the men quoted above later became President, and Marshall could have seized the White House had he chosen to do so.

In the face of statistics that would discourage any insurance company, we have become more thoughtful in our attitudes toward our two highest offices.

No President since Ulysses S. Grant has served two full consecutive terms and returned to private life with his health unimpaired.

Six of the eight men who entered the White House by election from 1897 to 1961 died or were seriously incapacitated while in office. The exceptions were two single-term Presidents.

Five of the Presidents who have been in office since 1900 were targets of assassins at some time during their public careers. These five assassination attempts resulted in a total of fifteen casualties—six dead (including two Presidents) and nine wounded (including an ex-President).

In recent years we have been sending older men to the White House, John Kennedy being an exception. Elements of the peace negotiations during or after both World Wars were in the hands of ailing if not dying men.

Only twenty-two of our first thirty-eight Vice Presidents served out the terms for which they were elected. Seven Vice Presidents died in office, another resigned, and eight were promoted by tragedy.

Our eight "accidental" Presidents—the men who succeeded to that office by death—served 24 of the 32 years for which their deceased predecessors had been chosen. Six of the eight were nominated for Vice President at conventions where little if any consideration was given to the possibility that they might become President.

Perhaps with all this in mind, columnists Rowland Evans and Robert Novak concluded on February 2, 1964: "The man picked by the Democrats for the No. 2 spot [in 1964] will be the odds-on choice to succeed President Johnson, either through death . . . or by normal inheritance. . . ."

That phrase "or by normal inheritance . . ." might be challenged. Only three Vice Presidents have been elected directly to the Presidency. And the three—Adams, Jefferson, and Martin Van Buren—all were regarded as Presidential prospects before they became Vice President. But Richard Nixon achieved his nomination in 1960 only after eight busy and controversial years in the No. 2 job.

Since about 1941, each Vice President has been given an

opportunity to perform useful tasks for the President. Yet as recently as 1960, when both Vice-Presidential nominations were offered to the men who had been the leading rivals of the successful Presidential nominees, Nelson Rockefeller refused to run and Lyndon Johnson accepted only with reluctance and against the advice of his friends.

So it is that able men often hesitate to become running mates. They still doubt that the "normal inheritance" will pass to them and, in fact, they fear that they may be forgotten for four years. We still remember the rhetorical question that drew loud laughs on the New Frontier: "What ever became of Lyndon Johnson?"

How may we guard against the choice of Vice-Presidential candidates on the basis of expediency—because of geography, a need to balance the ticket, or for any other reason except the fitness of the man to take over the Presidency?

How may we enlarge the duties of the Vice President, so that he may better prepare himself for the Presidency?

Should the office of Vice President be filled immediately when it falls vacant between elections? And should the present order of Presidential succession be changed?

How shall we ascertain when Presidential inability exists due to illness or injury, and by what procedure may the Vice President assume Presidential powers in such a crisis?

Too many of these questions went unanswered for too many years. Not until 1964 and 1965 did Congress mount a serious effort to prepare, for ratification by the states, a constitutional amendment dealing with Presidential succession and disability. The sequence of perilous events that finally stirred Congress to action can be traced back across the two centuries of United States history.

Representatives from twelve of the thirteen states met in Philadelphia in 1787 to consider revision or replacement of the Articles of Confederation, which had failed to provide for a strong central government. The need for one had become apparent.

During that hot summer the delegates prepared and ratified an entirely new document that, with the addition of the Bill of Rights four years later, stands in essentially the same form today. The Revolutionary statesmen who had cast aside a foreign monarchy, and who feared the establishment of one in this country, unwittingly created an elective kingship and placed within the reach of one man more authority than George III of England had ever hoped to grasp.

Their intention, of course, had been to provide for a separation and a balance of powers among the legislative, executive, and judicial branches of the Government. But the delicate balance has been lost, and the President has gained ascendancy—as the spokesman for the United States in international affairs, as the head of a vast array of executive departments and independent regulatory agencies, and as the Commander in Chief of the Army and Navy, with great emergency powers in time of war.

"The Buck Stops Here," said a sign on Harry Truman's desk, a sign that illustrates another reason for the unique position enjoyed by the man in the White House. The Constitution provides: "The executive Power shall be invested in a President"—one man only. Questions, crises, and entreaties stream upward from the public and the Federal bureaucracy to that single office; outward and downward from the White House flow decisions, edicts, and policies that on one occasion or another have had an impact on every person living on this planet.

And so it is that the executive "branch" speaks with one powerful voice, not with the babble of the 535 voices heard at the other end of Pennsylvania Avenue.

Having created this magnificent office, the convention sought to provide for a successor should the President die. But their invention, the Vice President, was assigned only one duty—to preside over the Senate, and to break tie votes in that body. Technically, then, he was to be a member of the legislative branch. But he is now elected on a national party ticket with a Presidential candidate. In truth, the Vice President is an orphan in the Washington storm. He is constitutionally prohibited from sharing the "executive Power," and he generally has been received with indifference on Capitol Hill.

The Vice President's meager duties have been increased by statute. He may make a few appointments to the military academies; he now has a seat on the National Security Council; and he is a member of the board of regents of the Smithsonian

Institution. He is chairman of the National Aeronautics and Space Council, and he supervises the work of the Office of Intergovernmental Relations.

In view of the unappealing aspects of this office, the writers of the Constitution hastened to insure that the Vice President would always be an able man. How? By providing that the Vice Presidency should be the consolation prize for the man who ran second in the Presidential race. Under this original system, the Presidential electors were permitted to vote for two persons, "of whom one at least shall not be an Inhabitant of the same State with themselves." The elector was not allowed to indicate which of his choices was for President, and which was for Vice President. It was considered likely that the elector would cast one of his votes for a favorite son, but that his second vote would be given to some person of national reputation, and that such a man would be the winner when both the votes of all the electors were counted. The runner up —the Vice President—would be a person of somewhat lesser national renown or, at worst, the favorite son of some large state. As we shall see, this system worked better in theory than in practice.

"Is not my election to this office, in the scurvy manner in which it was done, a curse rather than a blessing? Is this justice? Is there common sense or decency in this business? Is it not an indelible stain on our Country, Countrymen and Constitution? I assure you I think it so, and nothing but an apprehension of great Mischief, and final failure of the Government from my Refusal . . . prevented me from Spurning it."

The writer: John Adams, signer of the Declaration of Independence, diplomat, and in 1789 first Vice President of the United States.

The target of Adams' anger: Alexander Hamilton, brilliant, imperial, energetic, never himself a President or a Vice President, but a man whose life and fate were bound up in the contests for those two offices.

All 69 members of that first Electoral College had cast one of their two ballots for George Washington. Their second votes had been widely scattered, Adams receiving 34, with 10 other men dividing the rest. Hamilton and Adams, like Washington, were Federalists. Adams was generally regarded as the

Federalist choice for Vice President in 1789. However, Hamilton called on some of the electors not to vote for Adams, contending that it would not be appropriate for Adams' vote to approach too closely the total received by the great Washington. But Hamilton himself wanted to succeed Washington, and he hoped that a small vote for Adams would reflect poorly on the latter's popularity.[1] One report was heard that a New York elector planned not to vote for Washington. Had he so acted, and had *all* the electors given one of their votes to Adams, then he would have been the first President. Thus, Hamilton was perhaps justified in seeking to reduce Adams' vote.

This first election marked the beginning of maneuvers by Hamilton, against Adams, that continued until the latter left public office. Adams came to believe that Hamilton sought to defeat him outright in 1789; years later he wrote to a friend:

"Hamilton had insinuated . . . that I should not harmonize with Washington, and (would you believe it?) that John Adams was a man of too much influence to be so near Washington! In this dark and insidious manner did this intriguer lay schemes in secret against me, and like the worm at the root of the peach, did he labor for twelve years, underground and in darkness."

Adams made the best of his job as Vice President. The Senate membership was small, and he had no less than twenty-nine opportunities to break tie votes—still a record. On one occasion, his vote upheld the right of the President to remove appointees without the consent of the Senate.

At first, the Vice President joined frequently in debate, but in later years he lapsed more into the passive role traditionally expected of a presiding officer. Adams did not fail to recognize the potential importance of his position:

"I am Vice President. In this I am nothing, but I may be everything."

President Washington pledged that he would treat his Vice President with "perfect sincerity . . . greatest candour" and with "full confidence." Adams was re-elected with Washington in 1792, despite some reservations concerning his stiff, reserved manners, his coach, and his servants in livery.

[1] In these early elections, most electors were chosen by the state legislatures, rather than by popular votes.

Political parties began to take form during Washington's Presidency. The principal Federalist spokesman was Hamilton, the Secretary of the Treasury. The leader of the anti-Federalists, or Republicans, was Thomas Jefferson, Secretary of State. The Federalists were conservative and prosperous. They championed a strong national government as a safeguard against an "excess of democracy." The Republicans, while loyal to the Constitution, interpreted that document as providing for a "beautiful equilibrium" between the Federal Government and the states.

The emergence of these parties soon bared inadequacies in the means prescribed for selecting the President and the Vice President. In 1796, Washington chose not to seek a third term. The Federalist mantle passed to Adams, and Thomas Pinckney of South Carolina became the Federalist choice for Vice President. The Republicans offered Thomas Jefferson and Aaron Burr as their team. The Federalist electors clearly held a majority, but they were confronted with a problem: although they could vote for both men, they were not permitted to designate which of the two was their Presidential choice. Hamilton had first spotted this constitutional flaw in 1789, and now he saw an opportunity to circumvent the will of the people. He urged South Carolina electors to support Pinckney, and at the same time to throw away their second votes on some candidate other than Adams. Meanwhile, he urged Federalist electors in the North to support Adams and Pinckney equally. Hamilton, who considered Adams too old and stubborn to take orders, hoped to become the gray eminence in a Pinckney administration. He anticipated that the latter would be more receptive to "guidance." Furthermore, if Pinckney were elected, he would be in Hamilton's debt.

The Adams men became aware of the scheme and counterattacked by having a number of Federalist electors in New England hand *their* second votes to some candidate other than Pinckney. The Federalists loyal to Adams achieved their purpose, and more. Not only did Pinckney finish safely behind Adams; the luckless running mate was dropped by so many in his own party that his vote also fell below the total given to the Republican candidate for President, Thomas Jefferson, who thus became Vice President.

The Hamiltonians were abashed by the turn of events that

had placed Jefferson in the second office of the land. Secretary of the Treasury Oliver Wolcott grumbled that Jefferson's very willingness to accept the position was "sufficient proof of some defect of character."

For the first time—but not the last—the United States had men of differing political views in the two highest positions. The danger inherent in this situation was soon revealed. Adams asked his Vice President to undertake a diplomatic mission to France. Jefferson, a former Minister to that country, might have averted the drift toward undeclared war with the revolutionary regime in Paris, but he refused Adams' request. His theoretical reason was that such an assignment lay outside his constitutional duties. As a practical matter, he had no intention of aiding a political opponent. Nearly 150 years would pass before a Vice President would travel abroad in an official capacity, or undertake any other important responsibilities. In the meantime, the office was allowed to fall back into its constitutional strait jacket.

We have never waged a civil war over the right of any man to occupy the White House, although on more than one occasion a calculated or unthinking act at just the wrong time could have provoked a serious crisis. In its history free of civil strife relating directly to the question of who should head the government, the United States is unique, or nearly so. But we almost came to blows in 1800.

The brilliant and erratic Aaron Burr fills a unique niche among our Vice Presidents. He was a member of a family distinguished in theology and scholarship. A Revolutionary War hero at twenty-one, he later became Hamilton's leading political rival in New York. He served for a term in the United States Senate. In 1800, Jefferson ran again for President and Burr, then forty-four years old, became a candidate for Vice President for the second time. The Republicans won, but the electors failed to provide for the difficulty that had threatened Adams in 1796: the possibility that the party choice for Vice President might run even with—or ahead of—the intended Presidential candidate. Jefferson and Burr each received 73 votes. The decision was thrown into the lame-duck House of Representatives, with each state entitled to cast one ballot, and a majority of all sixteen states required to win. The Republicans controlled eight states, and the Federalists six. Two delegations were equally divided.

Firm action by Burr to remove his name from consideration would have averted an impasse. At first, he disclaimed any desire for the Presidency, but then he fell silent, yielding to a reckless ambition that could have sent him to the White House only under conditions so chaotic that his administration would have been doomed to failure.

The deadlock provided an opening for the American Machiavelli, Alexander Hamilton. He saw an opportunity to split the Republican party between the two men who had just been candidates on the same ticket. Hamilton wrote to Oliver Wolcott that it might be wise "to throw out a lure for him [Burr], in order to tempt him to start for the plate, and then lay the foundation of dissention between the two camps." It was not Hamilton's intention to elect Burr, whom he regarded as a demagogue, unfit and dangerous, and utterly unprincipled. Although Hamilton disliked Jefferson, he conceded that the Virginian had some "pretensions to character." He hoped to extract conditions from Jefferson, including a promise to accept the Hamiltonian financial program if he became President.

Ironically, Hamilton succeeded only in splitting his own party. The Federalists were largely prisoners of their own propaganda and they saw, or professed to see, that the election of Jefferson would result in a "Jacobin" revolution. Therefore, they made a serious effort to win the election for Burr, and the balloting in the House droned on for a week. That they were defying the will of the people, the state legislatures, and the electors seems to have meant nothing to the Federalist Congressmen.

The supporters of Jefferson were not unaware of these developments. Reports came to Washington that militias from the Republican states were prepared to march on the Capital. The Federalists were warned that "ten thousand republican swords will instantly leap from their scabbards" should Jefferson be cheated out of the Presidency. The wife of Representative William Craik of Maryland threatened to divorce him if he did not vote for Jefferson. The Virginian refused any compromise with Hamilton, assuring James Monroe: "I would not receive the government on capitulation . . . I would not go into it with my hands tied."

A few of the Federalist Congressmen grew tired of the business. Yet how could they switch their votes to Jefferson, a man they had called "a ravening wolf, preparing to enter your peaceful fold, and glut his deadly appetite on the vitals of your country"? On the thirty-sixth ballot, the Federalists yielded as ungracefully as possible; a few abstained and Jefferson was elected, scarcely two weeks before the inauguration. Burr became Vice President, but under conditions hardly conducive to harmony with his President.

For all his faults, Aaron Burr possessed great dignity and charm. He presided over the Senate with ease and fairness. Among the women of Washington he commanded much attention. He was still young, and he was spoken of widely for the Presidency itself. Yet for Burr, as for many men after him, the Vice Presidency was to be a dead-end street.

Jefferson's supporters became convinced that Burr had conspired against them in the election of 1800. The President passed over Burr in the distribution of Federal patronage, and he failed to bring the Vice President into the councils of the Administration. Burr broke a tie vote to defeat a judiciary bill that Jefferson favored. The President worked assiduously to undermine the position of the New Yorker, and he termed Burr "a crooked gun . . . whose aim or shot you could never be sure of."

The Vice President knew that he would not be renominated, and cast about for another base of political power. His eyes fell on the governorship of New York. In January, 1804, he called on Jefferson, and asked the President's backing in the gubernatorial race. In what must have been a pathetic scene for so proud a man, Burr pleaded that he had run for Vice President four years before with a view to promoting Jefferson's fame and advancement. Such flattery failed to win the support of Jefferson.

In February, 1804, Burr was nominated for Governor, but not on the regular Republican ticket; that party would not have him. He ran as an independent with Federalist support. Burr was a conspirator by nature. His candidacy for Governor was linked with a scheme by certain Federalists to secede from the union and form a Northern confederacy "free of the corrupting influence and oppression of the aristocratic Democrats of the South," as Senator Timothy Pickering of Massachusetts phrased it. The purchase of the Louisiana Territory from France in 1803 had prompted fears in New England that the opening of the West would depress land values in the Northeast. The disunionists believed that a Northern confederacy would succeed only with the support of New York. Although Burr refused to commit himself on disunion, he was nonetheless the instrument by which the rebels might win the Empire State to their cause. As early as 1801, Burr had proposed a toast "to the union of all honest men," a thinly veiled slap at Virginia and Virginians.

Of course, not all Federalists supported the scheme. Hamilton was appalled that a Vice President of the United States would permit himself to be drawn into such a plot. But Hamilton, in the wake of several political defeats, could no longer command the allegiance of his own party. In fact, the year 1804 marked the last hurrahs for both Hamilton and Burr. The Vice President was bankrupt, and in imminent danger of losing his home at Richmond Hill to his creditors.

In an age when virulent political attacks were the rule, this election was notorious. Anonymous pamphlets slandered Burr as "a man destitute of moral virtue, and bent solely on the gratification of his passions, regardless of the public good." Hamilton's own public pronouncements were less personal, but he was recognized as Burr's leading foe.

The Vice President lost the election. Bitter, defeated, discredited, and penniless, he was gripped by frustration.

For fifteen years, Alexander Hamilton had filled his private correspondence with abuse of Aaron Burr. In the winter of 1803, at a private dinner, Hamilton was unusually sharp in his criticism. Another dinner guest, hoping to use Hamilton's broadsides as ammunition against Burr, wrote two letters telling of Hamilton's unguarded remarks. Both letters appeared in the columns of the Albany *Register*. Hamilton was quoted as having called Burr dangerous and untrustworthy. Vague reference was made to "a still more despicable opinion" that Hamilton had expressed of Burr.

In his agitated state, Burr saw the correspondence. After the election, the Vice President wrote a letter of his own which he asked a friend to deliver to Hamilton. He included a copy of

Hamilton's critical statements. Burr's own remarks were short, concise, and laconic, and couched in the polite terms gentlemen used in addressing one another in those days.

Sir,

I send for your perusal a letter signed Charles D. Cooper, which, though apparently published some time ago, has but very recently come to my knowledge. Mr. Van Ness, who does me the favour to deliver this, will point out to you that clause of the letter to which I particularly request your attention. You must perceive, sir, the necessity of a prompt and unqualified acknowledgement or denial of the use of any expression which would warrant the assertions of Mr. Cooper. I have the honour to be

Your obedient servant,
A. Burr

Thus began a remarkable correspondence between the two men that would continue for about two weeks. From the first, Hamilton must have realized that he was trapped. A man of great intellect, he had led the fight for the adoption of the United States Constitution by writing a series of essays collected in *The Federalist.* He had founded our national financial system. He had written many of Washington's state papers and part of the first President's Farewell Address. He had formed and led a political party dedicated to the maintenance of a strong national government. He had been a genuine kingmaker, a manipulator behind the scenes in all four of our national elections. Now he vacillated, he equivocated. He remembered his son, Philip, killed in a duel three years before. If Hamilton admitted the accuracy of the statements carried by the newspaper, Burr would immediately challenge him to a duel. If he denied the statements, he would not only be calling Cooper a liar, but he would also dash his own hopes for a political comeback.

Two days passed before Hamilton replied to Burr. Then, he attempted to discount the statements attributed to him as political oratory. He said he hoped that "on more reflection," Burr would see the matter in the same light. "If not, I can only regret the circumstance, and must abide the consequence."

That last sentence cut off Hamilton's means of escape. Burr, in his next letter, increased the pressure:

"Political opposition," wrote the Vice President, "can never absolve gentlemen from the necessity of a rigid adherence to the laws of honour and the rules of decorum. I neither claim such privilege or indulge it in others."

Hamilton, a man of many words, was now at a loss to find any adequate for his predicament. The correspondence continued until abruptly terminated by Burr's challenge to a duel—which was accepted.

The two men met under the Weehawken heights on the west bank of the Hudson, opposite Manhattan's Forty-second Street, at seven o'clock on the morning of July 11, 1804. The amenities were observed, the requisite number of paces were stepped off, and two shots rang out. Hamilton fell, mortally wounded. Burr approached his prostrate victim, made a gesture as if expressing regret, and then withdrew.

A doctor, waiting nearby, was summoned. As he hurried forward in the bright morning sunlight, he encountered a fleeing man partially hidden behind an umbrella. The umbrella concealed the face of the Vice President of the United States.

Hamilton died the next day, and his political party would soon be dead too. The Federalists praised the man whose popularity had been in decline even in their own ranks. Now he was a hero. The Frederickstown *Herald* lamented:

> The tears of the aged burst forth—the withered hand trembles in grief—the youthful patriots mourn— Their Chief is fallen! Haste! Even now he bleeds! He dies! Catch the stream that flows from his mighty heart, and pour it in thy veins. . . .

Burr was indicted for murder in New York, where the duel had been arranged, and in New Jersey, where it had taken place. An outcast, he fled southward, then returned to Washington where—incredibly—he resumed his duties as presiding officer of the Senate.

Senator William Plumer of New Hampshire wrote to a friend that it was the first time "(God grant that it be the last) that ever a man indicted for murder presided in the American

Senate. We are indeed fallen on evil times. . . . The high office of President is filled by an *infidel,* that of Vice President by a *Murderer.*"

But Senator Robert Wright of Maryland said on the floor of the Senate: "Our little David of the Republicans has killed the Goliath of Federalism, and for this I am willing to reward him."

Burr's term would expire in a few weeks, but not without a final bit of irony.

For several years, President Jefferson had been seeking a means of striking back at the judiciary, which was largely in the hands of the opposition Federalists. In 1803, in *Marbury vs. Madison,* the Supreme Court had asserted that it had the power to declare an act of Congress unconstitutional. Jefferson had always insisted that the states had this right. Now he was confronted by the Court making the same claim, in its own behalf. Jefferson wanted to remove Chief Justice John Marshall, but could find no grounds. However, the President thought that a case might be made against Associate Justice Samuel Chase, a man of violent Federalist principles. Both on the bench and in public, Chase spoke of republicanism as the forerunner of atheism and anarchy. In 1803 he had warned of "mobocracy" and forecast the loss of freedom and property under the Jeffersonians. Such attacks gave the President the opening he sought. He had his chance to make the first move toward neutralization of the Federal judiciary. He secured from the House of Representatives the necessary articles of impeachment against Chase. Since the Justice would be tried in the Senate, its presiding officer would be in a favorable position to grease the skids for Chase, or to hamstring the efforts of the prosecution.

Abruptly, Aaron Burr's stepson was appointed to a judgeship in New Orleans, and his brother-in-law was named Secretary of the Louisiana Territory. Jefferson invited the Vice President to call on him. Other Republicans showered courtesies on the slayer of Hamilton. Burr, of course, was not fooled by these attentions.

The Vice President would soon leave office, but in those last days he restored in some small degree the prestige of his position by presiding with dignity and fairness at the impeachment trial of Chase. He won the admiration of even his severest critics. Chase, as it happened, was found not guilty.

On March 2, 1805, Burr appeared for the last time before the assembled Senators. The doors of the chamber were closed and the galleries were empty as the Senate convened in executive session. Burr delivered a farewell address unmatched in poignancy by any words ever uttered by a Vice President. The legislators listened attentively as Burr apologized for any offense which his conduct might have caused any individual member. He exhorted them to observe always the rules of decorum which had always dignified their debate.

And this most complicated man, this most misunderstood man, cautioned his listeners: ". . . this House, I need not remind you, is a sanctuary; a citadel of law, of order and of liberty; and . . . here . . . will resistance be made to the storms of political frenzy and the silent acts of corruption; and if the Constitution be destined ever to perish by the sacrilegious hands of the demagogue or the usurper, which God avert, its expiring agonies will be witnessed on this floor." Then, bidding the Senators farewell, he strode from the dais, walked to the door, and shut it behind him with firmness and finality.

For the Senators, the experience had been an emotional drain. What the future held for Burr, no one could imagine. Senator Samuel Mitchell of New York wrote: "He is a most uncommon man, and I regret more deeply than ever the sad series of events which have removed him from public usefulness and confidence. . . . Burr is one of the best presiding officers that ever presided over a deliberative assembly. Where he is going or how he is to get through with his difficulties I know not."

The former Vice President vanished into the wilderness to embark on a new career of conquest and treason. He gathered about him a small band of adventurers and concocted some wild scheme to seize New Orleans and then to conquer Mexico. However, he was betrayed, captured, and brought before Chief Justice Marshall in 1807. Tried for treason, Burr was found not guilty on technical grounds.

Languishing part of the time in abject poverty, Burr spent the next three decades pursuing adventure and romance on two continents, with varied success. On September 14, 1836, his second wife obtained a final decree of divorce, and on that same day the third Vice President of the United States died, at the age of eighty.

In 1804, Congress had moved to guarantee that never again would a man like Burr get one foot in the White House, at least not by legal means. An amendment to the Constitution—the twelfth—was hastily ratified. It provided that Presidential electors should ballot separately for the offices of President and Vice President. In effect, Congress conceded what had already become apparent—that the emergence of political parties had rendered less effective the original electoral system. With opposing parties fielding two-man teams, the likelihood of the Vice Presidency going to a defeated Presidential candidate had been reduced. Burr had demonstrated in 1800 that the Presidency itself might be won by a man who wasn't even a candidate for that office.

For the next century, few outstanding men would be elected Vice President. The duties were not sufficiently challenging to attract first-rate public servants, or men seeking to gain the political spotlight. The second office in the land became a sinecure for which men bartered at political caucuses and conventions in return for a handful of votes.

A Vice Presidential candidate would serve to "balance the ticket," a lead weight so to speak. If one nominee were a young liberal governor from the Northeast, his running mate would be an aging conservative senator from the Midwest. From now on both parties would endeavor to face two ways at the same time. Each ticket would offer consolation for the defeated faction. The parties would become all things to all men, and the platforms would be broad enough to accommodate two candidates of divergent viewpoints and appeal. The No. 2 man would be expected to carry his own state and to keep his mouth shut. Provocative men like Burr would not be permitted to run.

These trends probably would have developed even without the Twelfth Amendment. In any case, both parties would have competed vigorously for the support of voters from all over the political spectrum. Certainly, we wouldn't want all the liberals on one side and all the conservatives on the other, with the pendulum swinging 180 degrees every time we turned a party out of office. But the failure of this amendment lay in the reduction of the Vice Presidency to an insignificant office sought only by insignificant men.

The experience with Burr persuaded the ruling Republicans that the Vice Presidency should be given to elderly and less ambitious politicians. George Clinton, who had been Governor of New York for more than twenty years, and who was well past his prime, was chosen to serve with Jefferson during the latter's second term, beginning in 1805.

Clinton had been happier in New York. He was remembered in that state as a great Revolutionary War governor. He had been an outspoken champion of state sovereignty and a critic of the Federal Constitution. Clinton, in fact, hoped to see New York become a separate nation; he accurately foresaw the area's pre-eminence in finance and commerce. He was, as well, the first modern political boss. A man of strong character, he imposed his will on the party, and at the same time enjoyed the confidence and admiration of the public.

But as Vice President, Clinton preferred warming himself by the fire to presiding over the Senate. He lived in a Washington boardinghouse with his daughter and a servant. Now bumbling and a bit cantankerous, he fumbled parliamentary procedure in the Senate to the extent of miscounting votes and appointing duplicate committees.

Jefferson declined to run for a third term in 1808, and Clinton indicated that he was available for the Presidency. However, he was passed over by the Republicans, partly because he was considered "too old," and partly because the party had a much better choice in Secretary of State James Madison. But Clinton was offered and accepted a second term as Vice President. He was not "too old" to be a potential President, and he was the first of many Vice Presidents who were not obliged to meet the same high standards as the men whom they might succeed. Clinton and Madison were elected. Clinton held the President in contempt, and by 1809 he had become openly hostile to him.

Clinton died in office in 1812 at the age of seventy-two, and for the first time the Vice Presidential chair was vacant. He was replaced at Madison's second election with Elbridge

Gerry, another aging Revolutionary statesman. Gerry, a delegate to the Philadelphia convention in 1787, had refused to sign the Constitution. Curiously, one clause to which he had objected provided that the Vice President would preside over the Senate, a situation seen by Gerry as a threat to the independence of the legislative branch.

Gerry could point to a long and creditable record of public service. However, as Governor of Massachusetts in 1812 he had gained his greatest fame with the creation of his "gerrymander," a grotesque salamander-shaped legislative district designed to insure that Federalist pluralities in eleven small towns would be smothered by a large Republican margin in Marblehead. Thanks in part to the gerrymander, the Republicans captured a big majority of the Massachusetts Senate seats at stake in 1812, although the total state-wide Federalist vote was greater. Gerry himself lost a bid for another term in the April gubernatorial election. Two months later he was nominated for Vice President.

Gerry died in 1814 at the age of seventy, and Madison thus became the only Chief Executive to lose two running mates in this manner. Twice during the War of 1812, the United States was without a Vice President. Madison took part in the defense of Washington against the British, and was himself in danger of being captured or killed.

Somewhat sobered by the deaths of two Vice Presidents, the Republicans turned to a younger man to serve under James Monroe. Their choice was forty-two-year-old Daniel D. Tompkins, the Governor of New York, whom they fully expected would restore some prestige to the Vice Presidency. Alas, the men elected to that office seemed to travel under a cloud.

Tompkins' terms as Governor had seen the enactment of liberal reform measures. During the War of 1812, Tompkins had taken command of the Third Military District, comprising southern New York and eastern New Jersey. He put 25,000 men in the field, and to pay the soldiers borrowed considerable sums of money, partly on his own credit. But the overzealous Tompkins failed to keep satisfactory records of his prodigious expenditures. He was unable to produce vouchers for the money he had withdrawn from the state treasury, and during his eight years as Vice President he spent much time in attempts to clear his name in his home state. He was absent from Washington for extended periods. He sought—while Vice President—to regain the governorship of New York, in the hope of winning vindication. However, Tompkins was defeated, and was left broken in spirit and in health. He died at fifty, only three months after his second term ended.

In the course of a few years, a hex had fallen on the office once filled with distinction by Adams and Jefferson. Beginning in 1825, however, the Vice Presidency enjoyed a brief but spectacular renaissance. The next two Vice Presidents so dominated the Capital scene that the history of the United States for several years is in large measure the story of their unremitting contest for national leadership.

★ ★

JOHN C. CALHOUN — MARTIN VAN BUREN

"It is an advantage to a public man to be the subject of an outrage."

President James Monroe was re-elected without opposition in 1820, but the so-called Era of Good Feelings came to an abrupt end with the fragmentation of the Republican (later, Democratic) party. The debates leading to the Missouri Compromise in 1821 were marked by a polarizing of opinion along sectional lines. Great men came to the fore as spokesmen for the regions that they represented: Clay and Jackson from the West, Webster from the North, and Calhoun from the South. They spoke also for the preservation of the Union, and they coveted the Presidency that only the people of a united nation could bestow.

One among them chose to follow the Vice Presidential path to the White House, but he succeeded only in discrediting the office that he sought to exploit. John C. Calhoun wanted to run for President in 1824, but the field was crowded. Instead he bargained separately with two of the candidates, John Quincy Adams and Andrew Jackson. Each agreed to support Calhoun for Vice President, in return for Calhoun's support in their race for President. Calhoun anticipated that the Presidential contest might be deadlocked, with both the Electoral College and the House of Representatives unable to choose anyone, and that as Vice President he might capture the prize by default. The election was in fact a deadlock; it did go to the House, but Adams was quickly chosen President.

Calhoun undertook his duties as Vice President on March 4, 1825. He held that office for eight years, less two months, and when he pounded his gavel, he called an age to order. This was, in fact, the Senate's Silver Age. The Vice President looked out on an assemblage that from time to time contained the faces of four future Presidents—Jackson, Van Buren, Harrison, and Tyler—and three great men who would never be President, Webster, Clay, and Benton. And not far behind them—in stature and in time—would come still others who would fight the nation's battles on that floor for thirty-five years before military hostilities began at Fort Sumter in 1861.

Jackson had received more popular votes than any other candidate in 1824, but he had lost the election in the House to a coalition of the supporters of Adams and Clay. When Adams appointed Clay Secretary of State, the Jackson supporters raised cries of "bargain" and "corruption." Calhoun soon saw that a growing tide of sentiment would sweep Jackson into the White House in 1828 and he smoothly shifted his allegiance to the old general. He and Adams quarreled bitterly, and the Vice President presided impassively as Senator John Randolph of Virginia indulged in long, virulent attacks on the President.

The Jackson men recognized that Calhoun could claim support throughout the country, and that he was the only other possible rallying point for the opponents of President Adams. They allowed Calhoun to hear that Jackson was in poor health, might not live more than a year, and in any case planned to serve as President for only one term. Consequently Calhoun was satisfied to run with Jackson in 1828 as a candidate for a second term as Vice President.

At first glance, it might seem that Jackson and Calhoun would make a successful executive team. Both had been born in South Carolina. Both possessed great courage and energy. Calhoun had been an eloquent champion of the War of 1812, and had served with distinction as Secretary of War under Monroe. Jackson's military exploits during and after the war with England accounted for much of his popularity. Both men were tall, gaunt, erect, and outspoken. Yet there were differences. Jackson, an uncompromising champion of pure democracy, was clearly marked as a man of the frontier. Calhoun was a graduate of Yale University, an intellectual, a member of the old South Carolina aristocracy.

The two soon parted company because Calhoun stayed on as Vice President not to serve Jackson but to serve himself. In a Jackson administration there could be but one leader and but one loyalty. Calhoun was not prepared to bow to the will of any man.

Calhoun was fifteen years younger than the general and could afford to wait a little longer. Jackson entered the White House a sick man, mourning the death of his wife two months before. Yet he was to gain in vigor during his Presidency, and Calhoun was to fade in health and in prestige in the face of a series of jarring rebuffs and frustrations that he could not possibly have foreseen. Calhoun tumbled from his commanding position as the heir apparent before the challenge of a man he seems to have grossly underestimated.

Martin Van Buren, Jackson's choice for Secretary of State, appeared at first to be an unlikely threat. Against the towering, menacing, popular Calhoun, Van Buren stood barely five and a half feet tall; he had exaggerated features, red sideburns, yellow curly hair, and was a dandified dresser. His rivals called him the Little Magician and the Red Fox of Kinderhook. He was from New York and of Dutch descent, and he had been trained well in the devious ways of Empire State politics. By the time he joined Jackson's Cabinet he had mastered all the skills involved in winning votes and elections, in winning and retaining influence with others, and in undermining and destroying political opponents. Self-discipline was his strongest weapon, and urbanity and serenity his means of disarming rivals. He did not excel at frontal assault, but in guerrilla action. Randolph observed that Van Buren "rowed to his object with muffled oars." He was a leader in the Jackson campaign in New York in 1828, and he resigned as governor of that state early the next year to become the general's Secretary of State.

Van Buren and Calhoun each wished to dominate the Cabinet, as a means of winning influence with the President. The Magician, arriving late in Washington, discovered that three of his five colleagues—the secretaries of the Navy and Treasury, and the Attorney General—could be counted as firm Calhoun supporters. The Postmaster General was of negligible influence. The remaining Cabinet member—Secretary of War

John Eaton—proved to be the pivotal member of Jackson's official family.

Eaton was from Tennessee and was a longtime friend and admirer of Jackson. His first wife, Myra Lewis, had been a ward of the general. In 1817, Eaton completed a dull, fawning biography of Jackson, of the type certain to win the subject's undying admiration. In 1818, Eaton was appointed to the United States Senate from Tennessee, where he was joined five years later by Jackson himself. Eaton's first wife had died, and both Tennessee Senators lodged for a time at O'Neill's Tavern in Washington. One of the principal attractions of that establishment was the proprietor's daughter, Peggy O'Neill Timberlake, wife of a Navy purser, who spent much of his time at sea.

Timberlake died in 1828 during a Mediterranean cruise. Officially, he died of a pulmonary disease. Unofficially, he committed suicide after hearing rumors of Peggy's extramarital activities with Senator Eaton. Upset by a rapidly spreading scandal, Eaton sought the advice of Jackson, who was by that time the President-elect. Jackson expressed the view that marriage would end the gossip. Eaton and Peggy were married on January 1, 1829, a step that failed to silence the critics. Van Buren, writing with more discretion than most, described Peggy as "a young widow of much beauty and considerable smartness in respect to whose relations with [Eaton] before marriage, and whilst she was the wife of another, there had been unfavourable reports."

Jackson's determination to name Eaton his Secretary of War set off fresh shock waves in the Capital. Calhoun warned Jackson that "public opinion" would not permit Eaton's appointment, and Jackson surmised correctly that opposition to Peggy came largely from society women.

"Do you suppose," he shouted at Calhoun, "that I have been sent here by the people to consult the ladies of Washington as to the proper persons to compose my Cabinet?"

Eaton was appointed, and his wife was thrust simultaneously into the top ranks of Washington society. In observance of protocol, Mrs. Eaton called on Mrs. Calhoun, but the visit was not a pleasant one. The wife of the Vice President later informed her husband that she had no intention of returning the call, and the Cabinet wives followed her lead. Whatever the evidence of Peggy's adultery, it was clear that she had been convicted of other crimes—the crime of being vivacious and attractive to men, and the crime of having risen above her origins.

Jackson, an unflinching man who could hang British spies and kill an opponent in a duel, stood firmly in support of the Eatons. The general's own wife, Rachel, had died after the campaign of 1828, during which the validity of her marriage to Jackson had been questioned by political enemies. Jackson, bitterly angry, now saw the abuse of Mrs. Eaton as the beginning of a calumny that could bring grief to another marriage. He pleaded with Calhoun to persuade his wife to call on Mrs. Eaton, but Calhoun, knowing what his wife's reaction would be, refused to comply with the President's request.

Van Buren's wife had died some years earlier, and he was not placed in the awkward position of the other Cabinet officers. The Secretary of State showered all the proper considerations on Mrs. Eaton. He won not only the loyalty of the Secretary of War, but also the admiration of the President. Van Buren's poise and social skills were a steadying influence during the tense 1829-30 social season; Peggy insisted on attending the full round of functions and was repeatedly snubbed in public by her feminine counterparts. The Eaton affair rapidly became a political nightmare for Jackson, and administration programs across the board were jeopardized by the lacerating dissension in the Cabinet.

Even Jackson's own household was upset. His official hostess was the glamorous, aristocratic, titian-haired Emily Donelson, wife of his nephew and private secretary. Emily also opposed Peggy, and correctly identified Van Buren as a source of comfort and support for Mrs. Eaton. Now Van Buren found himself in a delicate situation. He could not afford to be arrayed publicly against devoted members of Jackson's own family, even if his position in this particular matter was identical to that of the President.

But Van Buren was unsuccessful in avoiding a confrontation with Jackson's niece concerning Mrs. Eaton. Calling at the White House one day, he unintentionally encountered the redoubtable Mrs. Donelson. She promptly skewered him to the wall with the observation (according to Van Buren's later account) that "whilst almost every tongue in the city was canvassing that lady's merits and demerits she had never heard me say anything upon the subject . . ." Van Buren, always a diplomat, later described that saber thrust as "a remark the tone of which rather than the substance conveyed, tho' gently, a complaint of my reserve."

The Secretary of State attempted to evade the issue by pleading a previous appointment, but Emily insisted on discussing the matter at some later date. Van Buren could only comply. The two met again in the sitting room of the White House. Mrs. Donelson declared that she opposed Peggy, and the conversation began to warm rapidly. Emily's cousin, Mary Eastin, listened for a while, then retreated to a nearby window and began to sob heavily. Van Buren was frantic for fear Jackson might happen onto the scene. The New Yorker pleaded with Emily to use restraint. He urged her to consider how a quarrel in Jackson's own home would bring grief and great strain to her uncle. Van Buren managed at long last to calm both women and exacted from Emily a promise that they would never discuss Mrs. Eaton again.

Although Van Buren had succeeded in extricating himself from a potential catastrophe, he was unable to prevent a division between Jackson and his relatives. Jackson gave Mrs. Donelson the choice of calling on Peggy or leaving the White House. The Donelsons packed their bags and returned to Tennessee.

Jackson also called in Calhoun's three supporters in the Cabinet, and read to them a long paper containing the assertion: "I will not part with Major Eaton from my cabinet and those of my cabinet who cannot harmonize with it had better withdraw, for harmony I must and will have." The three evidently accepted Jackson's point of view, since no resignations were forthcoming at that time. The President would have welcomed an opportunity to get rid of that trio, but he could not abide the embarrassment of disrupting the Government because of a woman.

The general, in any event, was perfectly aware of the differing positions of Calhoun and Van Buren in the matter. His trust in the Vice President had eroded, although their relations were not yet beyond repair. A larger issue would force a break.

By Jackson's time the South was perceptibly drifting free from the mainstream of American life. The alienation was related more closely to economics than to any moral aspects of the slavery problem. The South's economy came increasingly to depend on the export of tobacco, rice, cotton, and other products. But their sale was jeopardized by the European duties imposed in retaliation for high tariffs passed by Northern interests in the United States in 1824 and 1828. The South cast about for some means of circumventing the tariff, and South Carolina struck upon the doctrine of nullification.

In 1828, Calhoun wrote—in secret—*The South Carolina Exposition*, a document that became a rallying point for the disaffected South. He said that the United States "is not a union of the people, but a league or compact between sovereign states, any of which has the right to judge when the compact is broken and to pronounce any law to be null and void which violates its conditions." Calhoun, while obliged to work for the interests of South Carolina, sought at the same time to prevent a move toward outright secession that would doom his own Presidential hopes. He hoped nullification would become the middle course. Like Aaron Burr before him, here was a Vice President of the United States, sworn to uphold the Constitution and at the same time associating himself with a revolt against the Federal Government.

Calhoun's authorship of the *Exposition* was not yet generally known in January, 1830, when the issue of nullification was argued on the Senate floor in the famous debate between Daniel Webster and South Carolina's Robert Hayne. Calhoun by then must have realized the helplessness of his position, his utter inability to carry his views before the Senate or the people in any official capacity. Reportedly, he was reduced to scribbling suggestions on pieces of paper and passing them stealthily to Hayne. He was forced to listen to Webster's epic four-hour rebuttal, and to his cogent, considered arguments that laid bare the futility of nullification, and that ended with the peroration: "Liberty *and* Union, now and forever, one and inseparable." The Vice President could only pound his gavel petulantly as a thunderclap of cheers echoed the oratorical efforts of the Senator from Massachusetts.

What stand would President Jackson take on nullification? Men everywhere were asking that question. Calhoun's supporters decided to smoke out the old general, and the Jefferson Day dinner in April, 1830, provided an opportunity to do so. Jefferson had been the leading exponent of states' rights, and Calhoun hoped to do no less than to turn the whole party to his standard at this very dinner.

The President knew that political enemies hoped to use the dinner to embarrass him, but he did not hesitate to attend. One hundred politicians gathered at Brown's Indian Queen Hotel amid growing tension. Late arrivals found the guests in animated conversation. Twenty-four printed toasts had been distributed; these toasts "savored of the new doctrine of nullification," according to Senator Thomas Hart Benton. The Pennsylvania delegation walked out after reading the toasts, and a few other delegates followed. Jackson and Calhoun sat at opposite ends of a table, eying each other suspiciously. The proceedings dragged on for hours. When all twenty-four prescribed toasts had been delivered, some eighty volunteer toasts were to be offered. The first would come from the President, who rose from his chair as the throng fell silent. The diminutive Van Buren, his own aspirations tied to the outcome of the confrontation of the giants, scrambled onto a chair for a better look. Jackson and Calhoun glowered at each other. At that moment the general threw down the gauntlet to all the disunionists, and to the Vice President in particular. That night he fired the first shot—only a verbal blast to be sure—that would echo down the years amid developments that would lead inexorably to another confrontation at Appomattox thirty-five years later.

"Our union— *It must be preserved.*"

The crowd was stunned to silence. Isaac Hill, an editor, remarked: "A proclamation of martial law in South Carolina and an order to arrest Calhoun where he sat could not have come with more blinding, staggering force."

Jackson signaled that the toast was to be drunk standing. Calhoun rose slowly; his hand trembled, and a little amber fluid spilled down the side of the glass. "He's going to pour it out; he's going to pour it out," someone whispered. But he didn't. He drank.

And now it was Calhoun's turn to propose a toast:

"The Union—next to our liberty the most dear." He paused, then spoke again. "May we all remember that it can only be preserved by respecting the rights of the States and distributing equally the benefit and burden of the Union."

Jackson soon took leave of the dignitaries, and within a few minutes two thirds of the group had followed him out the door. No more than thirty diners remained for the formal close of the banquet.

With Jackson publicly arrayed against Calhoun, no hope remained for their reconciliation. But Van Buren and his friends moved swiftly to demolish the Vice President's position in the party and to secure the succession for the Little Dutchman.

First, Jackson's attention was called to a letter written by William Crawford, Secretary of the Treasury during the Monroe administration. It stated that Calhoun, then Secretary of War, had opposed General Jackson's invasion of Florida when it was owned by Spain during the first Seminole War in 1818. In fact, Crawford said that Calhoun had favored Jackson's arrest. Heretofore, Jackson had believed he had had Calhoun's support in that action, which had added to his heroic image, but which had been taken without the approval of President Monroe.

Jackson wrote to Vice President Calhoun, demanding an explanation of his position on the invasion of Florida. In a reply covering 52 pages, Calhoun admitted Crawford's charge and defended his stand. He emphasized: "I neither questioned your patriotism nor your motives." The Vice President received a sharp rebuke from Jackson:

"I had a right to believe that you were my friend, and, until now never expected to have occasion to say of you . . . *Et tu Brute.*"

Van Buren stayed publicly aloof from the affair, refusing even to read the letter from Calhoun, which Jackson had sent for his inspection. But Van Buren's friends had placed the original letter from Crawford in the President's hands, and now the New Yorker's allies worked overtime fanning the flames of new rumors dealing with the split between Jackson and Calhoun. The Vice President decided to publish not only the correspondence between himself and the President, but also some other letters stating his position during the Seminole campaign. This move also backfired. Publication in February,

1831, of a pamphlet containing the letters brought down the wrath of the President. Now all of the Administration press was trained on Calhoun.

Early in 1831, Jackson revealed that he would seek a second term. Who would be his choice for Vice President to replace the disgraced Calhoun? Attention turned to Van Buren, and the Magician's enemies intensified their criticism of him. The Secretary of State, never ruffled by the political storms raging about him, always maintained his conciliatory bearing and his amiability. These traits were seen by his adversaries as further evidence of his duplicity and intrigue. The prospects for Jackson's re-election—with or without Van Buren on the ticket—were uncertain. The President faced major tests over the bank and nullification issues, he was still saddled with three Cabinet members loyal to Calhoun, and Eaton and his wife were still a source of embarrassment. In the Senate, suspicion grew that Van Buren exercised an inordinate degree of influence in the Administration, and elements of Jackson's legislative program fell into jeopardy.

Van Buren, knowing his position with the President to be secure, but coming under increasing abuse elsewhere, disarmed his opposition with a master stroke. His plan was, in fact, so audacious that he had difficulty finding the courage to broach the subject to Jackson.

After missing many opportunities, Van Buren seized a chance to speak one day as the two were horseback riding near the Capital. The talk had turned to Jackson's problems with the Cabinet.

Suddenly, the Secretary of State blurted out: "General, there is but one thing can give you peace."

"What is that, sir?"

"My resignation."

Jackson was aghast. "Never, sir! Even you know little of Andrew Jackson if you suppose him capable of consenting to such a humiliation of his friend by his enemies."

The ramifications were too many to be explored during one afternoon. The discussion resumed the next morning, and the general was finally convinced that the best interests of the Administration would be served by Van Buren's stepping aside. Their discussion was opened to other party leaders, including Secretary of War Eaton, himself racked by the realization that he was in large measure responsible for Jackson's woes.

Eaton turned to Van Buren and exclaimed, "This is all wrong! I am the one who ought to resign."

The trap was sprung in the moment of silence that followed.

If Eaton expected Van Buren to demur at the thought of such a proposal, he was disappointed. Instead, the awkward silence was broken only by a discreet inquiry from the Red Fox. "What about Mrs. Eaton?"

Taken aback, Eaton could only mumble that he did not suppose she would object.

In fact, the Eatons were not at all happy about the resignation, but the Secretary of War felt that he had no alternative. The resignations of Eaton and Van Buren were announced; with his two closest friends out of the Cabinet, Jackson felt justified in calling for the resignations of the three Calhoun supporters. The remaining bastion of Calhoun strength crumbled, and all the Cabinet posts were quickly filled with men who favored Van Buren as Jackson's successor. Van Buren's close friend, Edward Livingston, succeeded him as Secretary of State. The success of Van Buren's ploy was not lost on the Vice President. Calhoun grudgingly conceded: "He has so surrounded the President with his creatures that his affairs can be safely administered in his absence."

The new, stronger Cabinet marked the onset of success for the Jackson administration, and the elimination of Eaton cleared the way for a joyful reunion between Jackson and the Donelsons, who soon returned to the White House.

To prove to one and all that he had chosen to take the veil, politically speaking, Van Buren obtained a recess appointment (the Senate was not in session) as Minister to England. In the late summer of 1831, he sailed away from the caldron of political factionalism in which he had been embroiled for a quarter of a century. He passed the next few months in a round of London social activities, interrupted only by weekend excursions to Oxford, Blenheim, Warwick Castle, and other such shrines. He found time to help run the United States at long distance, as he and Jackson exchanged letters on a number of important matters.

Now occurred one of the most stupid blunders ever found in all the lore of American politics. After stalling as long as possible, the United States Senate agreed to consider Jackson's nomination of Van Buren to be Minister to England, six months after he had taken up his duties. During the time Van Buren had been whiling away the hours amusing the ladies at diplomatic teas in London, enmity among his many critics had been abuilding on Capitol Hill. His foes included Henry Clay, already the National Republican candidate for President in 1832; Daniel Webster, the leading spokesman for the Union; and John C. Calhoun, nullifier, silent and frustrated on the dais. Such was the unity that men of diverse views found in a hatred of Andrew Jackson and his friends. A head count of Senators revealed enough votes to reject the nomination. But merely defeating Van Buren would not be enough; he must be tried in the court of public opinion and executed. Hence there followed one of the most disgraceful exhibitions of nonstatesmanship ever seen in the Senate chamber. Four reasons were advanced for disapproving the nomination. It was charged that:

1. Van Buren, while Secretary of State, had mismanaged the West Indian trade treaty with Great Britain.

2. He was responsible for the break between Jackson and Calhoun.

3. He had broken up the Cabinet to further his own political ambitions.

4. He had introduced the spoils system into politics.

The merits of these charges were—and are—immaterial. For two days in late January, 1832, they were debated *ad nauseam* on the Senate floor. A dozen set speeches were delivered against Van Buren. Each oration was rushed into print so that the nation might also know of the New Yorker's wickedness. Each Senator stressed that he spoke only from a sense of public duty; all expressed the pain they felt at being obliged to arraign a man whose manners and deportment were so urbane.

Thomas Hart Benton, recalling the scene years later, was moved to paraphrase the famous last words of Madame Roland, just before the blade fell, to wit: "Oh Politics! how much bamboozling is practised in thy game!"

Clay and Webster were among those delivering speeches against Van Buren. But Calhoun would not be denied his right to share in this ritual murder. Since the foes of Van Buren were in a majority, some abstained in order to produce a tie, thus giving Calhoun a rare opportunity to vote, to perform an official act of some significance.

Here were Henry Clay and Daniel Webster and John C. Calhoun—three of the five men chosen in 1957, from among all who ever served in the Senate, as being worthy of having their portraits placed in the Senate reception room—here they were, embroiled in a conspiracy to discredit Jackson and Van Buren for purely political reasons.

The tie vote was announced. Calhoun had his chance. Like some wrathful *deus ex machina* the Vice President shouted No and descended in triumph from the dais. The Senate rang with cheers.

The exultant Calhoun exclaimed: "It will kill him, sir, kill him dead. He will never kick sir, never kick."

But Benton remarked to a fellow Senator, "You have broken a minister, and elected a Vice-President."

News of the vote sent Jackson into one of his celebrated towering rages. Naturally, he took it as a personal rebuke. And while he had favored Van Buren as his running mate and eventual successor, he had not until now been prepared to force Van Buren on the party. The Senate vote was a call to arms.

Van Buren received the news with equanimity. "Altho' I had ardently desired it," wrote a friend, "I could not persuade myself to believe that their passions would drive them into a measure the inevitable results of which might have been seen by a schoolboy."

Lord Aukland's comment on encountering the defrocked Minister was perhaps the most perceptive of all: "It is an advantage to a public man to be the subject of an outrage."

And so it was. Many persons in the United States felt revulsion at such a cynical maneuver. Jackson had little trouble bringing about the selection of Van Buren for Vice President on the 1832 ticket. But the manner of his nomination is important to us today.

Presidential and Vice Presidential nominations had been made in Congressional caucuses until the attempt in 1824 to push through the election of the ailing William Crawford. In 1831 a minor party had called the first nominating convention, the granddaddy of all the hoopla that fills our television screens today. The National Republicans nominated Clay for President at another convention held later that year. In 1832, the Jacksonians also summoned a national convention. For what purpose? Certainly not to renominate Jackson, whose choice was assured; in fact, the President had already been endorsed by many state caucuses and conventions. The title of the official account of this convention tells its purpose:

"Proceedings of a Convention of Republican [now Democratic] Delegates from the several States in the Union for the Purpose of Nominating a Candidate for the Office of Vice-President of the United States."

Jackson recognized that there were elements in the party unreceptive to Van Buren, and that it would be necessary to win ratification of the New Yorker's candidacy on the national level.

Van Buren was chosen over nominal opposition. But what an ironic situation! The need to choose a Vice-Presidential candidate brought about the first Democratic National Convention, yet few men of any real merit would be nominated for Vice President at national conventions until approximately one hundred years had elapsed. Weary delegates would prefer to catch the first train out of town, rather than tarry over the selection of a running mate. All too frequently the No. 2 man would be chosen perfunctorily in hotel rooms filled with the odor of dead smoke and stale coffee.

Circumstances relating to Van Buren's nomination caused the establishment of a significant precedent. At this first convention the Democrats adopted the two-thirds rule. William King of Alabama explained to the delegates that "a nomination made by two-thirds of the whole body would show a more general concurrence of sentiment in favor of a particular individual, would carry with it a greater moral weight and be more favorably received than one made by a smaller number. . . ."

To make a long story short, it was necessary to make Van Buren's nomination look as impressive as possible. In adopting that resolution, the Democrats were writing more history than they imagined.

Later, in 1844, Van Buren himself, after several years of

enforced retirement, sought to make a political comeback and got a majority vote at the convention, but he fell short of the needed two thirds, and lost the nomination.

Likewise, Champ Clark of Missouri had a majority on several early ballots at the 1912 convention, but he failed to get two thirds, and the nomination went to Woodrow Wilson on the forty-sixth ballot.

Because of the two-thirds rule, the Democrats needed a record total of 103 ballots to choose their nominee in 1924.

Because of the two-thirds rule, Franklin Roosevelt almost missed the nomination in Chicago in 1932. After that convention, the rule was finally dropped.

Because of the two-thirds rule, the South for a century exercised a near veto power at Democratic conventions. The abandonment of that rule clearly confirmed a shift toward liberalism for our largest party.

Such was the legacy of the 1832 convention.

In November, the Jackson-Van Buren ticket swept to a great national victory. The Little Magician was chosen to occupy the chair whence had come the tie-breaking vote that had assured his political fortune. Jackson rightly interpreted his victory as support for his positions against nullification and a national bank.

Calhoun, meanwhile, suffered through the few remaining months of his second term, with Administration men taunting him. One day, Senator John Forsyth of Georgia lashed out bitterly, but indirectly, at the Vice President.

Calhoun could stand it no longer: "Does the Senator allude to me?"

In one devastating counterquestion, Forsyth cut the Vice President and the Vice Presidency down to constitutional size, and established the image of the office as one of fumbling impotence.

"By what right," Forsyth demanded, "does the Chair ask that question?"

The assembled Senators reflected on the fact that strict custom required the Vice President to remain silent. Calhoun was humiliated. Since 1825 he had held this dreary office, and the bright hopes with which he had entered upon it had long since vanished. He had abused his limited powers, and his every move had been scrutinized in terms of his unconcealed ambition. He had grown old before his time. The flaming eyes were sinking deeper into the whitening flesh, though the massive shock of gray hair still bristled ferociously. He was becoming, said Harriet Martineau, "the cast-iron man, who looks as if he had never been born, and never could be extinguished." John Randolph, himself near death, observed the Vice President closely. "Calhoun must be in Hell," he wrote. "He is self-mutilated, like the fanatic that emasculated himself."

Rebuffed by Jackson, denied even the privilege of defending himself in debate, and concerned by the growing militancy in South Carolina, Calhoun chose the only course open to him. In December, 1832, he resigned, our only nationally elected official ever to do so. The prestige of the Vice Presidency tumbled again.

In November, a convention in South Carolina had declared the tariff acts of 1828 and 1832 to be null and void, effective February 1, 1833, in the state of South Carolina. Calhoun hastened home. In early December, Jackson alerted the military and naval forces to prepare for any contingency. To the loyalists of South Carolina, he sent assurances of Federal support, and he charged: "The wicked madness and folly of the leaders, the delusion of their followers, in the attempt to destroy themselves and our Union has not its parallel in the history of the world. The Union will be preserved."

While in South Carolina, Calhoun was elected to a new office—United States Senator. As the nation waited for developments, he returned to Washington in January, 1833, to take his place on the floor of the Senate, and to swear once more to uphold and defend the United States Constitution.

Who now would challenge Calhoun's right to speak? He and Webster faced each other in the most significant constitutional discussion yet witnessed in the Congress concerning the nature of the Union. Calhoun reasserted the constitutionality of nullification, while Webster supported Jackson's nationalist views. Jackson won passage of a so-called Force Bill, authorizing him to collect revenues in South Carolina, using the power of the Federal Government if necessary. Hand in hand with this bill came a compromise tariff, proposed by Clay, that gradually reduced rates. The President signed both bills into law. South Carolina repealed its ordinance nullifying the tariff, and saved face by passing another ordinance nullifying the Force Bill.

The South now turned from nullification as the answer to Federal-state problems. When next the issue arose, secession *from* the Union, not nullification *within* the Union, would be the rallying cry of the rebels.

As for Senator Calhoun—no longer a contender for national office—he played a significant role in the Compromise of 1833, a role he could not have played while presiding. Van Buren, of course, moved up to the Presidency in 1837, but not because of any distinction achieved in the No. 2 position. Jackson had already settled on Van Buren as his eventual successor. The latter, furthermore, was the last man ever elected President directly from the Vice Presidency. Political leaders learned well the lesson of the Calhoun fiasco; from now on they would seek to avoid the dubious honor of a Vice-Presidential nomination.

In 1837 the first of three Southerners named Johnson became Vice President. Richard M. Johnson of Kentucky, the running mate of Martin Van Buren,[1] had gained renown as the probable slayer of the Shawnee warrior and statesman, Tecumseh, at the Battle of the Thames in 1813. As a Congressman, he had called for the delivery of mail on Sunday. Johnson had argued that the Government's no-mail policy was an extreme case of Sabbatarianism, and the opening wedge for the establishment of a state religion. The rotund Kentuckian pointed out that a letter from a kinsman or a friend carried a certain spiritual significance of its own by providing a communion of the heart.

Johnson, a bachelor, enjoyed the company of three Negro mistresses, the first of whom was a slave he had inherited from his father. He made no secret of his associations and even sought to introduce into society two daughters born of the first union. The second slave mistress eloped with an Indian.

[1] In 1836, Van Buren won a narrow victory in the Electoral College. For the Vice Presidency, Johnson had a wide lead over his nearest opponent, but he fell just short of the required majority. The choice went to the Senate—the only time this has happened. The Senate elected Johnson over a Whig, Francis Granger, by a vote of 33-16.

The third turned up at social gatherings and addressed the Vice President as "my dear Colonel" in the presence of white guests.

Johnson was considered something of a drag on the Democratic ticket in the Southern states, and he failed to win renomination at the 1840 national convention. The delegates could not find a replacement and adjourned without naming anyone, an event unique in American political history. The Democratic electors were left to their own devices, but their scattered votes were of no consequence, since the Whigs won the election anyway.

One of our more enterprising Vice Presidents, Johnson left the Capital one summer to manage an inn, where he took personal charge of the purchase and sale of food. Of worthier note, he devoted much of his time to the education of Indian youths.

During Johnson's term, the nation marked the fiftieth anniversary of the adoption of the Constitution. No President had yet died in office, or been disabled. But not again would death be absent from the White House for half so long a time.

★ ★ ★ JOHN TYLER

"And we'll vote for Tyler, therefore,

Without a why or wherefore."

"At thirty minutes past midnight, this morning of Palm Sunday, the 4th of April, 1841, died William Henry Harrison, precisely one calendar month President of the United States after his inauguration. . . .

"The influence of this event upon the condition and history of the country can scarcely be seen. It makes the Vice-President of the United States, John Tyler of Virginia, Acting President of the Union for four years less one month. . . . In upwards of half a century, this is the first instance of a Vice-President's being called to act as President of the United States, and brings to the test that provision of the Constitution which places in the Executive chair a man never thought of for it by anybody."

John Quincy Adams looked up from his diary to see the drops of water clinging and sliding against the windowpane.

"This day was in every sense gloomy—rain the whole day."

One searches in vain for any loss sustained by the Presidency in the death of old "Tippecanoe," incumbent and recumbent within thirty days, and succeeded by "and Tyler, Too"—the second half of one of our more prophetic political slogans.

But if Harrison left little mark on the Presidency, Tyler stirred a Constitutional tempest that has never quite settled.

Furthermore, his principal actions as President—while proper in themselves—underscored the cynicism with which Vice-Presidential nominations were being passed around.

The Whig national convention met in Harrisburg in December, 1839, to nominate candidates for the 1840 campaign. The party comprised a number of diverse groups united primarily by their enmity for Jackson and his political heirs. The leading Whigs were Henry Clay and Daniel Webster, both ardent nationalists. Clay sought to aid the growth of industry through an elaborate system of internal transportation improvements, high tariffs, and a national bank. Webster, who stood second to none in his dedication to the Union, generally subscribed to Clay's program. But the Whigs attracted all the opponents of the Jacksonians, both North and South, a conglomerate of politicians related to Clay and Webster only by party label. Calhoun and his Southern rebels enlisted for a while, as did the Anti-Masonic Party from the North, antinullification states' rights Southerners, and some Democratic Conservatives.

The maintenance of some semblance of unity obliged the party to nominate hoary military types with uncomplicated political philosophies. At Harrisburg, Clay was bypassed in favor of William Henry Harrison of Ohio, the aging hero of the War of 1812. The Whigs fully expected that, after Harrison had done his part by getting elected, he would serve as no more than a figurehead controlled by Clay and Webster.

But first Harrison had to be elected, and this seemed to require giving the Southern Whigs a place on the ticket. John Tyler of Virginia, a recent convert from the Democrats, was the choice for Vice President. He had resigned from that party and from his Senate seat as well in 1836 in a dispute with Jackson. In 1838, Tyler had hoped to return to Washington as the winning Whig candidate for the United States Senate from Virginia. But his plans ran counter to the interests of Clay, who had another choice for Senator. Reportedly, Tyler was promised the Vice-Presidential nomination at the Harrisburg convention if he stepped aside in the Senate contest. He lost out on the Senate race, but won his Vice-Presidential nomination.

Tyler was a tall, gaunt, cordial, well-read aristocrat, marked in appearance by an aquiline nose and scarred in character by a streak of vanity and stubbornness. As with so many Vice-

Presidential nominations, the choice of Tyler seemed at first glance to be a good one. The ticket was in geographical balance. Tyler could be counted on to draw a number of his Southern Democratic friends into the Whig column. At the convention he supported Clay, and his own nomination could be expected to placate the disappointed followers of the Kentuckian. But Tyler's regard for Clay was personal and not ideological, and their friendship would not long survive Tyler's inauguration as President. An exponent of states' rights, he was a potential threat to the nationalist Whigs who had hoped to control Harrison.

The party dichotomy was glossed over at the convention. The crowd that nominated Harrison and Tyler declined even to frame a platform, but relied instead on the most prolonged and noisy campaigns of hooey and hogwash that the country has ever seen. Eighteen-forty was the year of political jingleism, and of the Log Cabin and Hard Cider campaign against President Van Buren ("Van, Van . . . is a used-up man"). Tyler figured no more prominently in this campaign than did Vice-Presidential candidates in other elections. But the slogan "Tippecanoe and Tyler, Too" made the name, if not the man, familiar. When the opposition taunted the Whigs with the reminder that Tyler was a renegade Democrat, the Whigs replied with still another jingle that ended:

And we'll vote for Tyler, therefore,
Without a why or wherefore.

Harrison and Tyler were elected. On a chilly, blustery fourth of March, 1841, the sixty-eight-year-old general took the oath as the ninth President. For nearly two hours he stood bareheaded, braving a stiff north wind to deliver the longest inaugural speech on record. He cited the virtues of limited Presidential power, promised to use the veto sparingly, and pledged to serve only one term.

From the day of his inauguration, Harrison's footsteps were dogged by hungry office seekers eager to benefit from the change of administration. They followed Old Tip into the White House and even chased him up the stairs, his pockets bulging with their petitions. The harassment drained away the strength of the President. The public suspected something was wrong when he missed his usual morning trip to market to buy supplies for the White House. Harrison first suffered from chills and a fever, and then contracted pneumonia. Doctors applied suction cups to Harrison's right side in the apparent belief that the infection could be drawn out through the skin. They then administered doses of castor oil, snakeweed root, opium, crude petroleum, brandy, and other remedies to the defenseless patient. A siege of vomiting and diarrhea weakened the President beyond rescue and he died on April 4.

Early on the morning of Monday, April 5, John Tyler was aroused by a frantic pounding on the door of his Williamsburg, Virginia, home. A messenger informed him of Harrison's death, and Tyler prepared immediately for the trip to Washington. He arrived in the Capital at dawn on Tuesday. For fifty-three hours the nation lacked a head of state. In two centuries we have had no longer Presidential hiatus as a result of a death.

Tyler believed that the Presidency had passed to him automatically, as to a crown prince. But he took the Presidential oath as a precaution, thus establishing a precedent observed by seven other accidental Presidents. In an inaugural speech on April 9, Tyler asserted: "For the first time in our history the person elected to the Vice-Presidency of the United States . . . has had devolved upon him the Presidential office." This view has now come to be so generally accepted that we tend to forget the spirited controversy attending Tyler's rather bold interpretation of the Constitution. The pertinent clause (in Article II, Section 1) states: "In Case of the Removal of the President from Office, or of his Death, Resignation or Inability to discharge the Powers and Duties of the said Office, the Same shall devolve on the Vice President. . . ."

A dispute arose in 1841 as to whether "the Same" refers to the words "Powers and Duties" or to the word "Office." Tyler contended that "the Same" modified "Office," and that he was entitled to move into the White House and to draw Presidential pay. John Quincy Adams and other strict constructionists argued that Tyler had inherited only the powers and duties of the office, and not the office itself. Some members of Congress said that communications sent to Tyler should be addressed to the "Acting President." In rebuttal, Representative Henry A. Wise of Virginia declared that Tyler considered himself "by the Constitution, by election, and by the act of God, President of the United States." Efforts to downgrade Tyler's status failed in both houses.

Not all scholars have been reconciled to Tyler's interpretation. Since 1841 the discovery and collation of much original source material has thrown new light on the convention debates in 1787 and on the wording of the preliminary drafts of the Constitution. We now know that the convention's Committee on Style, assigned the task of putting the approved draft into clear and concise language, managed to muddy the meaning of the clause cited above. It is now apparent that the delegates at Philadelphia did not intend that John Tyler should succeed to the Presidency in 1841, or that Lyndon Johnson should become President as a result of the violence in Dallas 122 years later. But the Twenty-fifth Amendment, adopted in 1967, establishes that if the President dies, resigns, or is removed, "the Vice President shall become President."

The acceptance of Tyler's interpretation of the Constitution proved both a blessing as well as a bane. On the one hand, his action helped preserve Presidential prestige. What if Lyndon Johnson had become only Acting Chief Executive in November 1963? Suppose he had been forced to skimp on a Vice-President's salary and to live in some remote section of Washington, denied full honors during any trip abroad. Mischief-makers like De Gaulle and Khrushchev would have surmised that the United States was passing through some sort of prolonged interregnum, and our position as a leader and mover of world events might have been weakened.

But while Tyler solved one problem, he created complications. Suppose Harrison had not died, but lingered on, too ill to run the Government. Suppose that Tyler, using the same reasoning as before, claimed the Presidency on the basis of the same clause in Article II, Section 1. But then suppose Harrison recovered and demanded the return of his office. If Tyler were merely acting as President, he could step aside and Harrison could resume command. But if Tyler were in fact President, there would be no apparent constitutional means by which Harrison could unseat him.

The question of what to do in the case of a Presidential inability that may or may not be permanent is no longer in the realm of the hypothetical. We have indeed had Presidents who were seriously incapacitated. In each case the Vice President declined to take charge, fearing that he could not return the office to the displaced President should the latter recover. The 1967 amendment focused on that problem, too.

But when Tyler took the oath, these crises were still far in the future. Tyler's immediate problem—as he saw it—was to establish himself firmly in control. He rebuffed Secretary of State Daniel Webster, who told him that during Harrison's tenure executive decisions had been reached by a majority vote of the President and the Cabinet members, with each man, including the President, having one vote. Tyler promptly made the Cabinet understand that final authority in all matters lay in his own hands. Webster accepted Tyler's dictum and stayed on as Secretary of State.

But the accession of Tyler threw Clay's future into doubt. Harrison had pledged to serve one term, and it was generally understood within the party that Clay would be given the Presidential nomination in 1844. But now Tyler was the nominal leader of the Whigs, and the expectation grew that he would seek renomination. Clay saw that his hopes turned on isolating the President from the rest of the party, and he submitted a legislative program of his own to the Senate. The proposals, which reflected the views of the nationalist Whigs, included an appeal for a new national bank, the repeal of the independent treasury system, and an increase in tariff rates. Clay knew that he would have the overwhelming support of the Whigs in Congress. His call for the national bank was a direct challenge to the states' rights President to subscribe to the nationalist program. Tyler indicated that he would not sign a bill permitting a national bank to establish branches in the states without their consent.

Even before the bill reached Tyler's desk, the President and Clay parted company. A warm exchange at the White House reportedly culminated with Tyler pointing his finger at the Senator and declaring: "Go you now, then, Mr. Clay, to your end of the avenue, where stands the capitol and there perform your duty to the country as you shall think proper. So help me God, I shall do mine at this end of it as I shall think proper."

Clay returned to Capitol Hill and pushed his bank bill through Congress. The legislation reached Tyler in August, 1841, barely four months after his succession. Quite early in his term he had come to a crossroads. To sign the bill would mean surrendering his principles and merely following the lead of Clay. To veto the bank bill would bring ostracism. Tyler chose to become the President without a party. Back to the Congress on August 16 came the bank bill with a stinging veto and a charge that it was unconstitutional. The Whigs had not the votes to override. All this was gall and wormwood to the men who had waited for power for so long during the Presidencies of Jackson and Van Buren. Victorious at last in the election of 1840, they had seen the glory snatched from them by the succession of a Vice President totally out of sympathy with the aims of the dominant wing of the party. For the first time the nation realized the folly in nominating "balanced" tickets at national conventions.

The Whigs had nobody to blame but themselves. Yet Clay took the Senate floor on August 19 to deliver a lengthy harangue against the President. The Kentucky Senator made an absurd assertion. He said that if the party had known that Harrison would die after one month in office, and that Tyler would veto a bank bill passed by the Whig majority, then Tyler would not have received a single vote at Harrisburg or in the election. But it was well known that Tyler had opposed a national bank in the past. He could be faulted for having accepted the nomination, but most of the responsibility for the dilemma now facing the party lay with those who thought the Vice Presidency should be used as bait to capture a few extra votes. A party, of course, never *could* know that a Presidential nominee would die one month after inauguration, but it was inviting trouble to nominate a Vice-Presidential candidate on any basis other than the possibility that just such a death might occur. In his speech to the Senate, Clay called for the President's resignation, contending that two thirds of the country favored the bill that he had just vetoed. Tyler was under no legal or moral obligation to resign under the circumstances, and he did not do so.

The Whig press and the Whigs in Congress rallied so overwhelmingly behind Clay that the President saw at once that he had lost any hope of winning control of the party. But he said that he might accept an amended version of the bank bill. The Whigs took pains to prepare a measure tailored to what were believed to be his specifications. The bill was passed. Up it went to the White House. Back it came to the Congress. Unconstitutional, said the President. The bill, in his judgment, did not contain proper safeguards for the rights of the states.

After the second veto the Whigs expelled Tyler, though in a somewhat unorthodox fashion. On September 11, some fifty Whig Congressmen massed in Capitol Square, denounced the President and all his works, and declared that the alliance between Tyler and the party was terminated. The Congressmen charged that Tyler was not a true Whig. But since the party had not adopted a platform for the 1840 campaign, who could define the principles of Whiggery? At any rate, the news was well received. It was reported: "The fires of a thousand effigies lighted the streets of the various cities."

Denunciations of Tyler could not save the program of Henry Clay. In the spring of 1842, he resigned from the Senate, ostensibly to retire, but in fact to prepare for another bid for the Presidency in 1844. One of Clay's last vindictive acts was a resolution proposing a constitutional amendment limiting the veto power of the President. The proposal was defeated.

Tyler found himself almost bereft of support. He had not allied himself with the Cabinet that he had inherited from Harrison; he had in fact placed little value on any advice they might be willing to tender. After the second veto all of the Cabinet officers resigned except Webster. He stayed on until 1843 to complete diplomatic negotiations with Great Britain—because he saw no future in following Clay and because he was in debt and needed a job. In four years, twenty-three Cabinet ministers shuffled in and out of the administration, including five Secretaries each in the War and Navy departments. Tyler closed his term with an official family composed mainly of Southerners and Democrats. Old John C. Calhoun was Tyler's last Secretary of State, but the President was not close even to Calhoun. His personal band of supporters dwindled down and most of these were states' rights Virginians.

Throughout his term Tyler piled up ten vetoes, the second highest total by any President to that time. Finally, he was threatened by the ultimate indignity: impeachment. John Minor Botts, a Whig Congressman from Tyler's own Virginia, preferred several charges against the President, and in January, 1843, offered a resolution calling for a committee to investigate the charges. The resolution was defeated, 83-127. If the Whigs were less than unanimous for the resolution, it was only because they feared making a martyr out of a man they considered to be of no importance. As one of their editors put it, the impeachment proceedings "might invest nothingness with consequence."

A similar effort to remove Andrew Johnson in 1868 was to come much closer to succeeding. Both Tyler and Johnson entered the White House after the death of a President. Both had been chosen to balance the ticket, and neither had close ties to the party leaders who had tendered the nominations. In each case, the attempt to remove the President was led by some of the same politicians who had applauded his nomination for Vice President.

Tyler's wife died in 1842, and he remarried in 1844 while still in office. With sixteen children, he ranked first among the Presidents as a family man. With all his excellent personal qualities, he could have been one of our most popular Chief Executives instead of one of the least popular. Any man *elected* to the Presidency usually takes office with the support of a majority of the total population. But Tyler entered the White House as a virtual unknown, and within six months he had been cast out of his own party. No electronic communications system could bring the image of this man into the homes across the nation. The press railed against him almost daily. And he seemed reluctant to venture far from Washington.

In the summer of 1843, Tyler did visit a number of cities in the Middle Atlantic and New England states. He was received warmly almost everywhere. At Stonington, Connecticut, hundreds of young ladies, each carrying a bouquet, greeted him at six thirty in the morning. A girl of sixteen stepped forward. "Allow me, Mr. President, to have the honor to present you with some of the sweetest flowers of Connecticut."

"My dear young lady," said Tyler, "you are one of the sweetest flowers that Connecticut can possibly produce." The writer for the New York *Herald* reported: "He then kissed all the young ladies that were introduced to him, to the amount of several hundred."

But to most of the country the President remained just a cipher, a name in the news, a political accident. Tyler hoped to win a second term. He looked to the Democratic party, but the Jacksonians were not about to welcome back the man who had deserted them in 1836. The President pinned his hopes on a favorable public reaction to his campaign to admit Texas to the Union. Both prospective Presidential nominees in 1844—Clay for the Whigs and Van Buren for the Democrats—were out of step with most voters in their opposition to annexation of Texas. While the Democratic delegates met in Baltimore, approximately one thousand supporters of Tyler rallied elsewhere in the city and nominated the President for re-election. If Tyler expected that the regular Democratic convention would turn to him, he was disappointed. More than likely he intended merely to embarrass Van Buren. The weakness of the Tyler movement was apparent. Most of his supporters at Baltimore were not fighting for principle, but were officeholders hoping somehow to perpetuate their employer in power. The Democrats ignored Tyler, rejected Van Buren, and gave their nomination to James K. Polk, a champion of Texas statehood.

Tyler's candidacy was now superfluous. His only contribution would be to split the pro-Texas vote, thereby throwing the election to Henry Clay. On August 20, 1844, Tyler withdrew from the race, and his supporters melted into the Democratic ranks. The President of the United States had become a political non-person. But Tyler's bitter critic, Clay, missed out on the Presidency again as Polk won the election by a narrow margin.

Tyler's record was not a blank. One cannot write off an administration that saw the reorganization of the Navy, the ending of the second Seminole War, the annexation of Texas, the signing of a treaty with China opening the door to the Orient, and the signing of the Webster-Ashburton Treaty resolving several points at issue with Great Britain.

But the Tyler years were a strong argument for the adoption of a parliamentary form of government on the British pattern, where ministerial responsibility is fixed, and where a Parliament is dissolved upon a vote of no confidence in the Prime Minister's government. Tyler managed to preserve the office thrust on him so unexpectedly, but he failed to strengthen it. He demonstrated that his accidental status did not prevent his full exercise of Presidential prerogatives. Efforts to impeach him and to weaken his veto power failed. But while he exercised that veto power with force, he failed to propose specific legislation of his own. He had never been a national leader, and he seemed unable to build a following as President. He passed four years in the White House almost as isolated as if he had remained Vice President.

Philip Hone, a New York Whig, appraised the ticket that had been nominated and promoted with such fanfare in 1840: "Poor Tippecanoe! It was an evil hour that 'Tyler too' was added to make out the line. There was rhyme but no reason in it."

James K. Polk had hoped to receive the Democratic Vice-Presidential nomination in 1844—a modest ambition—but before the year was out he had won a lot more. Former President Van Buren, who still had wide support within the party, had seemed certain to get the Presidential nomination. Andrew Jackson had endorsed his former protégé. The old general also encouraged his fellow Tennessean, former Governor Polk, to seek the Vice Presidency. Polk was willing, and several of his friends fanned out from Tennessee to promote him.

But before the delegates met, Van Buren wrote a letter declaring his opposition to statehood for Texas. His stand dismayed Jackson, and prompted other party leaders to cast about for another Presidential candidate. At the convention Van Buren obtained a majority, but he needed two thirds. For seven ballots the delegates were deadlocked. On the eighth roll call, Polk received a few votes. On the next ballot, a stampede swept the erstwhile Vice-Presidential contender to a unanimous nomination.

Polk wanted Texas in the Union. Since many Democrats did not, the party resorted to the tried and true means of mollifying the dissidents. The Vice-Presidential nomination went to Senator Silas Wright of New York, a friend and ally of Van Buren, and an opponent of Texas statehood. Wright, however, was not in Baltimore at the time of his nomination. He received the news at the Capitol Building in Washington from Samuel F. B. Morse's newfangled "electromagnetic telegraph." Congressmen who had gathered around the machine in the Capitol basement first got word of Polk's victory. Then out clattered the news of Wright's nomination.

"A Kangaroo ticket, by God!" someone exclaimed. "Strongest in the hind legs."

But Wright turned down the nomination, an action unprecedented in American politics up to that time. He said that it would be hypocrisy for men with differing views on Texas to run together. To his credit, he would not permit the Democrats to repeat the Whig blunder of 1840. Word of Wright's decision was returned to Baltimore on the telegraph. The men in that city thought there had been some mistake. Did Mr. Wright really disdain the prize? Back from Washington came the affirmation: Yes, we have no Vice President.

Disbelieving Democrats dispatched a rider to the Capital to confirm beyond doubt the report carried by Morse's contraption. When Wright could not be dissuaded, the delegates resumed their balloting. Senator Robert J. Walker, a fervent expansionist and a convention official, prevailed on the delegates to nominate his brother-in-law, George M. Dallas of Pennsylvania. Dallas favored Texas statehood, and Walker had large speculative holdings throughout the Southwest. Dallas had a distinguished record, as Vice-Presidential nominees go. He had been Mayor of Philadelphia, District Attorney for Eastern Pennsylvania, United States Senator, and Minister to Russia.

When nominated, Dallas was at his home in Philadelphia, oblivious to the honor that had come his way. At five thirty the next morning he and his wife were awakened by a furious pounding at their door. Half asleep, half dressed, and clutching a shotgun, Dallas opened the door cautiously. There stood his brother-in-law and a coterie of jubilant and soused friends. They whooped into the house and announced his nomination. Dallas and his wife looked on sleepily as Walker and his pals staged an impromptu war dance in the parlor for "Polk, Dallas, and Texas." The second largest city in the Lone Star State today bears the name of the eleventh Vice President.

Dallas, who is looked upon as one of our abler Vice Presidents, kept in close touch with Polk and his policies during their four years in office. In 1846 he put loyalty to the President ahead of his own principles by breaking affirmatively a tie vote on a low-tariff bill opposed by himself but favored by Polk. He at once lost the support of the protectionists from his home state. "Farewell to all Vice-Presidents from Pennsylvania for the future," wrote one editor. "We have had enough of one to last us while all who live now shall continue to breathe. . . ." The hex has been upheld, and no Pennsylvanian has won a major party Vice-Presidential nomination since that day. Dallas himself never again held high elective office.

To run with their candidate, Clay, in 1844, the Whigs had turned to a member of a prominent New Jersey family still represented in Congress. But they were unable to equal the felicity of their 1840 phrasemongering. With bad prophecy and worse poetry, the Whigs proclaimed:

> The country's risin'
> For Clay and Frelinghuysen.

The nominee, Theodore Frelinghuysen, was known for his efforts to apply religious teachings to public issues. He was called the "Christian statesman." Frelinghuysen advocated humane treatment for the American Indian. He was a president of the American Bible Society and an officer in the American Sunday School Union and the American Temperance Union.

Who could sling mud at a record like that!

★ ★ ★ ★ MILLARD FILLMORE

"... willing to offer himself

upon the altar of his country. . . ."

To appreciate the importance of the Vice Presidency, consider first the great debates that have marked the history of our national legislature. What have been the most memorable triumphs and tragedies recorded in the United States Senate? The following could be cited, perhaps to the exclusion of no more than one or two others:

1. The passage of the Compromise of 1850, which gave the North several additional years to mobilize its resources and to strengthen its resolve to preserve the Union at any cost.
2. The implementation of the reconstruction laws, comprising punishments so severe that the South was permanently estranged from the main currents of American life.
3. The adoption of civil-service reform in 1883.
4. The rejection of the Treaty of Versailles.
5. The passage of the Civil Rights Act of 1964, when Northern Senators—disregarding the pressures of election-year politics—won approval of a bill they believed long overdue.

Fate helped decide every one of these momentous issues. In four instances a President died, and in the fifth he was incapacitated. In each case, awful responsibilities were suddenly thrust upon a Vice President whose background muddied the crystal ball for those seeking a solution to the dispute before the country. And in each case the public pondered anew the vagaries of Vice-Presidential nominations, and wondered if the politicians had learned the lessons of history.

The spring and summer of 1850 was a most critical period. Several men of great stature occupied seats on the Senate floor, and on the outcome of their deliberations hung the preservation of the Union. The presiding officer was a tall, slightly stout, moon-faced man from New York. He was to all appearances a mediocrity, and he would be forgotten by history except for his unexpected chance to demonstrate that appearances can be deceiving.

His name was Millard Fillmore. A lawyer from Buffalo, he had been elected to several terms in Congress, serving for a brief time as chairman of the Ways and Means Committee. In 1844 he had run without success for Governor of New York. Two years later he had been elected State Comptroller, not exactly a job one would ordinarily use as a steppingstone to national office.

Henry Clay, who was now past seventy, had failed in his fifth and last try for the Presidency in 1848. He lost the Whig nomination to another general, Zachary Taylor, the hero of Buena Vista. Once again it was time to award the booby prize to one of Clay's followers, who on this occasion were truly disheartened and bitter. Since Taylor was from Louisiana, the Whigs looked north, and to the key state of New York. But who in New York? The Vice-Presidential nominee emerged from the tangled rivalries of Empire State politics. The Whig power structure in New York might have been designed by a nineteenth-century Rube Goldberg. Thurlow Weed—a newspaper publisher and the would-be dictator of New York Whiggery—hoped to push his protégé, William H. Seward, into the Senate or the Vice Presidency, and eventually into the White House. But when the nominations for Vice President were opened, up popped John Collier, who had been temporary chairman of the convention. He placed Fillmore's name in nomination, and somehow conveyed the misleading impression that Fillmore had supported Clay, an impression strengthened by the fact that Weed—who had opposed Clay at the convention—was also a factional foe of Fillmore. Collier hoped to be New York's next Senator, and he considered Seward and Fillmore his leading rivals for that office. The nomination and election of Fillmore to the Vice Presidency would be a rebuff to Weed and Seward, and would at the same time put Fillmore out of circulation. Weed could hardly be counted as a Fillmore fan, but the alternative could be a fatal party split, so he acquiesced in the nomination. Fillmore was chosen. Of such Byzantine maneuverings are Vice Presidents—and Presidents—made.

Once again the Whigs offered a schizophrenic ticket. Taylor owned slaves, while Fillmore opposed slavery. But in an irony of history, Taylor would soon turn against the South, and Fillmore would hold out the olive branch of compromise to that section of the country.

Taylor and Fillmore were elected, and Seward went to the Senate. Fillmore and his New York rivals maintained an uneasy truce during the election, but they soon broke completely over the distribution of patronage. Weed and Seward had worked hard for the ticket, and felt that Taylor owed them a great deal. The bland, amiable Fillmore was no match for the hard-driving Seward when it came to competing for the attention of the President. "We could put up a cow against a Fillmore nominee and defeat him," boasted the Buffalo *Express*. Fillmore's lukewarm friends in New York turned their backs on him, complaining that he should not have forgotten them in the distribution of the spoils. But Fillmore was helpless. Beyond the confines of the Senate chamber the Vice President exercised little influence and no power. Weed and Seward treated him with contempt. His was the usual fate of a Vice President.

The significance of the competition between Seward and Fillmore carried far beyond the distribution of a few jobs to needy New York Whigs. In the great debate that would soon begin in the Senate, Taylor would continue to put his faith in Seward, who was an implacable foe of slavery and compromise. The President would ignore Fillmore, whose early career in the House had been marked by some degree of legislative skill, notably in his successful efforts to pass the tariff of 1842. Seward brought no strength to Taylor that he did not already have. If Fillmore had been enlisted by the Administration during the spring of 1850, he might have helped win the day for the President. But by the time the Vice President had a chance to exercise his influence on behalf of conciliation, Taylor was beyond caring.

After an absence of seven years, Henry Clay returned to the Senate in December, 1849. Simultaneously, the California territory reopened the slavery controversy by asking for admission to the Union as a free state. Although her entry would upset the numerical balance with the slave states, President Taylor urged Congress to approve California's petition. In one of the curious flip-flops in American history, the slaveholding President had become convinced that Southern politicians were hatching treasonable plots against the Union. Southern Congressmen called on the President and urged him to reconsider his position on California. "Old Rough and Ready" not only rebuffed the pleas of his guests, but warned on one occasion that if they contemplated anything so treasonable as seceding from the Union, he would personally take command of the United States Army, track them down, and hang them.

Clay, now seventy-two years old, stepped into this restless malaise with the last of the great compromises for which he will forever be remembered. He offered no new legislation, but merely proposed the passage of several bills submitted by spokesmen from the North and South. He called for the admission of California as a free state, the adoption of a stronger fugitive-slave law, the abolition of slave trade in the District of Columbia, the organization of New Mexico and Utah as territories without restriction as to slavery, and the payment to Texas of an indemnity for the cession of land to New Mexico.

The country held its collective breath as the Senate began the debate on the compromise. Millard Fillmore had the best vantage point. Detached and silent on the Senate dais, he watched the aging supernovae—Clay, Daniel Webster, and John C. Calhoun—as they moved toward their final flashing conjunction in the inner space of the Senate chamber.

Calhoun, a wasted and shrouded figure too near death to talk, but with the spark of life still in his eyes, remained seated while a colleague read his final speech. The South Carolina Senator rejected Clay's plan and accused the North of provoking a disruption of the Union. The South had no compromise to offer, said Calhoun, and no platform but the Constitution. On the seventh of March, Webster rose to speak, "not as a

Massachusetts man, nor as a Northern man, but as an American. . . ." Throwing his support to Clay, Webster abandoned his opposition to a fugitive-slave law and deserted his own followers in the process. Seward of New York, speaking for the President, condemned the compromise and charged that issues based on moral convictions "are impossible of adjustment through bargaining." Extremists on both sides attacked the compromise and each other.

Fillmore spoke only when obliged to admonish the hotheads to observe decorum. His pleas were in vain. Tension rose as the months passed, and the debate dragged on, and the nation's business went unattended. In March, Calhoun died. In April, a bitter quarrel between Missouri's Benton and Mississippi's Henry Foote ended with the latter drawing a pistol on the Senate floor, and Benton screaming, "I have no pistol! Let him fire! Let the assassin fire!" The drain of many years and the strain of long debate began to show in the faces of Clay and Webster.

By early summer, observers in the Senate were tabulating the probable votes for and against Clay's compromise, now in the form of an omnibus bill. The tally was very close. It began to appear that the fate of the compromise could be decided by the solemn, bland-looking man holding the gavel. Speculation on Fillmore's position took into consideration his rivalry with Seward and his known antipathy to slavery. But Fillmore said nothing. And he had presided with such fairness, courtesy, and equanimity that no man could know where he stood. On June 18, Fillmore wrote to a friend: "I think the Compromise Bill will pass the Senate, but it may come to my casting vote—as to that—*Quaere?* I shall wait till I see what shape it assumes before I determine to say yea or nay." And so the man required by our Constitution to speak last and least continued to preside above the battle, sifting the truth from the demagogy, and biding his time.

At the White House, the President was not silent. Taylor, under the influence of Seward and his friends, continued to call for the immediate admission of California. This, said Webster, was "flatly impossible." Patriotic and conscientious, Taylor was at the same time politically inexperienced, and he was envious of the great prestige enjoyed by Clay. While he retained a keen desire to preserve the Union, he clung stubbornly to his position as that Union began to tremble about him. In Nashville, representatives from the Southern states met to discuss secession, should California be admitted. Meanwhile, Taylor rushed troops to New Mexico as a border war loomed in territory claimed by Texas.

Fillmore knew that if he were called upon to vote, his "yea" or "nay" would have great repercussions throughout the country. He decided to attempt to soften in advance an adverse reaction from one source. One day in early July he rode up to the White House to call on President Taylor. The Vice President explained that he might support the compromise in the event of a tie vote. He said that he hoped the President would not regard this as a hostile gesture, but as an action in behalf of the best interests of the country. Having stated his position, Fillmore returned to the Senate. He had prepared for the possibility that he might be obliged to vote. He would soon be called on to do a lot more.

On the Fourth of July, Taylor participated in patriotic ceremonies at the site of the Washington Monument. During the extremely hot afternoon, he drank a large amount of water. He later consumed a quantity of cherries, which he washed down with iced milk. Shortly thereafter he was stricken with cramps, and a doctor diagnosed his condition as cholera morbus. Soon symptoms of typhus appeared. The President, tired and weakened as a result of the criticism engendered by the debate over the compromise, had not the strength to resist the ailment. On the afternoon of July 9, doctors announced that he was dying.

Millard Fillmore was alone with his thoughts that night, his wife and daughter having left the city to escape the heat. Late in the evening came the knock on the Vice President's door. A messenger told him that President Taylor was dead.

Fillmore spent a sleepless night. He was not averse to the honor of the Presidency, but, like accidental Presidents before and after him, he faced immediately a fateful decision that would almost certainly affect his career. Since childhood he had had a prejudice against slavery. The stronger fugitive-slave law incorporated in the compromise was anathema to him. The abolitionists had already marked Webster for defeat, and any Northerner supporting Clay was risking political suicide. At the same time Fillmore feared the approach of a storm that would destroy both himself and the country; some way must be found to end the lacerating acrimony of the slavery debate. Fillmore would write: "The man who can look upon a crisis without being willing to offer himself upon the altar of his country is not fit for public trust."

Widespread grief over the President's death was coupled with speculation as to what the future might hold. On July 10, Fillmore was sworn in before a joint session of Congress. He chose to say nothing about supporting Taylor's policies. But the new President soon declared that he was ready to accept the compromise proposals either in omnibus form or individually. Salmon P. Chase estimated that the President's first message in favor of the compromise swung six New England Senators to his position. Fillmore hoped, if not to unify the country, at least to preserve an uneasy truce. But old wounds were not easily healed, even in a time of transition. Members of the pro-Seward Cabinet immediately submitted their resignations. Fillmore asked them to stay on for a month while he organized his Administration, but they granted him only a week. The President tapped Daniel Webster to return as Secretary of State. He consulted with Clay on other Cabinet posts, and then filled key positions with nationalist Whigs. The grip of Seward and other Northern extremists in the executive departments was broken.

Now Clay redoubled his efforts to achieve passage of the compromise. But like his late antagonist, Taylor, he would not be on hand to see the resolution of the debate. Exhausted by his long struggle, the aging statesman left for Newport, Rhode Island, and a badly needed rest. To a young Senator from Illinois, Stephen A. Douglas, fell the task of pushing the compromise through the Senate. The omnibus approach was abandoned, and Douglas won passage for each bill separately. The Seward faction and the Southern fire-eaters found common cause in opposition, but moderates who were appalled at the alternative to the compromise now held the upper hand. The House of Representatives concurred in the Senate action.

One by one the bills came to Fillmore, and he signed each into law. Only once did he hesitate. The measure requiring the return of fugitive slaves was to him repugnant. Knowing that the bill provoked the wrath of the abolitionists, he was at the same time reconciled to signing it. To avert the appearance of inconsiderate action, he requested the Attorney General to rule on its constitutionality. Reassured as to the bill's legality, Fillmore signed the Fugitive Slave Act into law. Violence attended the enforcement of the law in the North, but Fillmore never balked at implementing the act, and he showed his determination to use force if necessary.

The Compromise of 1850 solved nothing, and no one was satisfied. The Union had been preserved, but the slavery question would soon be revived. However, one cannot discount the action of Fillmore and his associates by saying that they merely postponed the inevitable. Ten years later, when war did come, the North was stronger, militarily and economically. Northerners could then say that every effort had been made in behalf of compromise. And though Fillmore could not see the future, the North would have its greatest leader in the White House in 1861.

As President, Fillmore could afford to be magnanimous with his old rivals, Weed and Seward. But when they failed to reciprocate, out came the patronage ax. Out of office went the semiliterate political hack Weed had named Collector of the Port of Buffalo to humiliate Fillmore. Out went some more Seward-Weed appointees. No one could now doubt who controlled the patronage in the state of New York.

But the power did not rest for long in Fillmore's hands. His support of the Fugitive Slave Act had proved to be his undoing. For their candidate in 1852, many Whigs wanted not a man who stood somewhere in the middle of the political spectrum, but a man who stood nowhere at all. Fillmore drew support for renomination from Southern Whigs, and might have won had not Webster, at the age of seventy, decided to seek the nomination. The administration vote was split, and the choice fell to General Winfield Scott. Fillmore stayed in contention through 53 ballots, but the day had not yet come when an accidental President would be given a nomination to a full term of his own. In the balloting, Fillmore failed to command the support of his own state. Seward and Weed won the last round.

Scott proved to be an inept campaigner as the Whigs went down to their final defeat. Within the year both Clay and Webster were dead, and the party itself soon faded into oblivion. The Whigs were victims of their own internal contradictions, which had become painfully evident when both their successful Presidential candidates were succeeded by Vice Presidents holding opposite views on key issues.

In 1856, Fillmore accepted the Presidential nomination of that sorriest of American third parties—the Know Nothings. As the candidate of this antiforeign, anti-Catholic faction, Fillmore polled 21 per cent of the vote. His candidacy spoke little for the judgment of the man who just six years before had sacrificed his career in the cause of moderation and compromise.

Blizzards and torrential downpours have long been a part of inauguration day folklore. Never will the cherry blossoms bloom when a new President takes up his duties in the Capital. But the inauguration of the thirteenth Vice President of the United States, William King, was indeed unusual. A witness when King took the oath in March, 1853, recalled "the clear sky of the tropics over our heads, the emerald carpet of Cuba beneath our feet, and the delicious sea breeze of these latitudes sprinkling its coolness over all of us."

King, who was in the last stages of consumption, was authorized in a special bill passed by Congress to take the oath in—of all places—Havana, where he had gone for his health. The Vice President was unable to stand unaided during the ceremony. He had been elected with Franklin Pierce in 1852, but he never had a chance to preside over the Senate as Vice President. Ironically, no man ever elected to that office was better prepared to fulfill the one duty prescribed in the Constitution for the Vice President. He had been a Senator for thirty years, had served as President pro tempore during five administrations, and had been chosen to preside over the Senate after the accession of Fillmore in 1850.

A month after taking the oath in Cuba, King returned to his home in Alabama, where he died the next day. With the exception of this brief time, the United States was without a Vice President from 1850 to 1857.

Vice Presidents came and went, and the jinx attending the office seemed unbroken. Even the youngest man to serve was touched by John Adams' curse. John C. Breckinridge of Kentucky was elected at age thirty-five on the winning Democratic ticket with James Buchanan in 1856. Being from a border state, Breckinridge was inevitably caught up in a tug of loyalties during the prewar years.

In 1860, the Democratic party split over the slavery issue and Vice President Breckinridge won the nomination of its Southern proslavery wing.[1] After his inevitable defeat by Lincoln, and after the end of his own term, he was sent back to Capitol Hill as United States Senator from Kentucky. He pledged to seek any compromise to preserve the Union, but his efforts were in vain. When war did come, Kentucky proclaimed its neutrality. Despite his sympathy with the Confederate cause, Breckinridge stayed on in the Senate. He opposed Lincoln's war program, and after Union troops entered Kentucky, the state legislature asked him to resign from the Senate. In November, 1861, in the Federal District Court at Frankfort, Kentucky, the former Vice President was indicted for treason against the United States. A month later the Senate declared Breckinridge to be a traitor, and formally expelled from its ranks the man who had once presided over its deliberations.

Breckinridge hurried South, and as a Confederate general he saw action at Shiloh, Chickamauga, and Murfreesboro. He also served as the Confederate Secretary of War in 1865. At the end of the war, he fled into exile, and did not return to the United States until 1869, when he obtained the special permission of the Federal Government. Even then, he was only forty-eight, but his political career was at an end.

[1] By running in 1860 against Lincoln and Stephen A. Douglas—the Democratic candidate—Breckinridge added his name to the growing list of Vice Presidents who later ran for President as candidates of splinter factions. Fillmore's candidacy with the Know Nothings and Tyler's abortive attempt to win a full term have already been mentioned. Van Buren, whose name had been voted on at four Democratic conventions, accepted the Presidential nomination of the Free-Soil party in 1848. Another former Vice President and President, Theodore Roosevelt, led his celebrated Bull Moose revolt against the Republicans in 1912. And former Vice President Henry A. Wallace ran as the Progressive party candidate for President in 1948. Also, a third party of sorts was formed in 1866 to support Andrew Johnson's policies, but he never stood as a candidate of this group. No single reason explains the propensity of Vice Presidents for casting their lot with third parties, though several were clearly political mavericks.

The new Republican party put up national candidates for the first time in 1856. John C. Frémont was nominated for President. For Vice President, the Republicans chose William L. Dayton of New Jersey. But in the balloting for that office, 110 votes went to a man named Lincoln. When Abraham Lincoln heard the news out in Illinois, he joked with his friends, saying: "I reckon that ain't me." Lincoln, who knew better, added that ". . . there's another great man in Massachusetts named Lincoln and I reckon it's him."

★ ★ ★ ★ ★ ANDREW JOHNSON

"I am for the Union, the whole Union and nothing but the Union."

By midafternoon of this Good Friday, a haze and a hush had fallen across Washington City, and clouds passed under the sun in a harbinger of storm. Secretary of War Stanton had released employees within his jurisdiction to attend church services. Many did so, while others hurried home. The streets were unusually quiet.

During the final hour of the Agony, a man with a mission unrelated to worship strode purposefully through the downtown streets. He wore a black mustache, he had coal-black hair, and he was dressed in black. On his person he had concealed a small brass derringer and a long sheathed knife. He entered the Kirkwood House on Pennsylvania Avenue at 12th Street, and approached the desk clerk.

Was Mr. Atzerodt in?

The clerk said he was not. The man in black went to the hotel bar. While drinking, his rabid mind apparently hit upon a bizarre ploy in an already daring sheme, a twist worthy of the Theater of the Absurd. He returned to the hotel desk.

Was the Vice President in?

He was not, replied the clerk. The man in black asked for a blank card. On it he wrote; "Don't wish to disturb you. Are you at home?" And then he signed his name: "J. Wilkes Booth." The clerk dropped the card into the box of the Vice

President's secretary. The man in black left the hotel. The interlude over, he hastened to make ready for his Last Act.

But later, that interlude would provide an anticlimax to the crime of the century. And Andrew Johnson, on the basis of that cryptic note and other "evidence," would stand accused in the halls of Congress of complicity in the murder of President Lincoln in order to procure that office for himself. The man in black would not live to enjoy Johnson's discomfiture, but perhaps he would be looking up at the scene from a niche in Hell reserved for bad actors.

Abraham Lincoln was twice elected President, and two men served with him as Vice President. The first held the office for four years and is remembered by few. The second served for six weeks, but later secured an honored place on our roster of heroes.

Hannibal Hamlin of Maine was the first of Lincoln's running mates. An outspoken critic of slavery, he left the Democratic party in 1856 and joined the Republicans. He served as governor and United States Senator before accepting the Republican Vice-Presidential nomination in 1860. Hamlin was stocky and muscular, and his swarthy complexion led to suggestions by the opposition that he was part Negro. The imputation carried no apparent weight, and the Lincoln-Hamlin ticket won easily against the divided Democrats.

Lincoln had expressed the hope that he and Hamlin would work together closely, but the Vice President—by his own testimony—did not exercise much influence within the Administration. Hamlin enlisted in the camp of the Congressional Radicals—those who later opposed Lincoln's more conciliatory postwar plans for the defeated South.

By convention time in 1864, several factors weighed against the renomination of Hamlin. The War Between the States was not going well for the North. Criticism of Lincoln was heavy, and he was by no means sure of re-election. Hamlin, from the safe state of Maine, would add nothing to the ticket. The ideal Vice-Presidential nominee would attract the votes of prowar Democrats, avert the charge that Lincoln was a sectional candidate, and discourage recognition of the South by European nations.

Lincoln had long been eying Andrew Johnson of Tennessee.

A tailor by trade, Johnson had been taught to read by his wife. He was a stocky, broad-shouldered, determined-looking man with a mass of thick dark hair. As a spokesman for the people and as an opponent of the slave holding aristocracy, he had built a successful political career in Tennessee. A man of conscience and great perseverance, Johnson had by 1861 overcome his modest beginnings to become one of the most effective and respected members of the United States Senate. As rebellion inundated the South, he alone among the Senators from the Confederate states insisted on remaining in his seat at Washington. Horace Greeley, editor of the New York *Tribune*, was saying that the North should "let the erring sisters depart in peace." Johnson, representing Tennessee but speaking for the Union, denounced secession as treason. He won passage for a Senate resolution declaring that the purposes of the war were not conquest or subjugation, but the preservation of the Union and the defense of the Constitution.

Lincoln, impressed by Johnson's courage, asked him to undertake the task of re-establishing Federal authority in Tennessee. In 1862, Johnson accepted the President's appointment as Military Governor of the Volunteer State. He faced a nearly insuperable task. Some 454 engagements were fought on Tennessee soil between 1861 and 1865. Ironically, the western part of the state, which supported the Confederacy, was cleared of rebel troops first. Here, Johnson set up his government amid almost universal hostility. Pro-Union Eastern Tennessee was not freed from Confederate control until 1863. Governor Johnson, doubling in brass as a brigadier of volunteers, was burdened daily by a multitude of problems large and small. Union armies had to be supplied with arms and reinforcements; grievances of officers, soldiers, and widows of war had to be heard; paper work must be completed, and on and on. By 1864 his work had won wide attention in the North and unmitigating scorn in the South.

During these years, Lincoln and Johnson were in frequent contact, and they shared a common understanding of conditions in the South. But reports came to Lincoln that Johnson had been highhanded in the administration of his office, and in the spring of 1864 the President dispatched General Daniel Sickles to Tennessee to investigate the Governor's record. Sickles reported that Johnson's policies had been no more stringent than called for by the circumstances. Lincoln did not give Sickles any reason for his interest in Johnson.

Strictly speaking, the Republican party did not nominate candidates in 1864, since the name Republican had been dropped in favor of the "National Union" party. This gesture would ease the conscience of Democrats who supported the Union and who wished to vote for Lincoln as the best guarantee of its preservation. Expectations grew that in return for their support, the Democrats would be represented on the ticket. Johnson was a logical choice, but other Democrats were mentioned, and Hamlin himself wanted a second term. Party leaders looked to Lincoln for guidance, but little was forthcoming. The President was publicly noncommittal, but his very silence suggested that he was not opposed to a substitution for Hamlin.

Lincoln, a shrewd politician, could not remain indifferent to the Vice-Presidential nomination. Therefore, we must be skeptical of his note to one of his secretaries in which he said in part: "Wish not to interfere about V.P. Cannot interfere about platform. Convention must judge for itself." In the welter of conflicting reports on Lincoln's role in this nomination, one can only conclude that the President gave at least tacit encouragement to the Tennessee Governor. If his instructions were more specific, he succeeded in covering his trail well.

And so the convention groped its way to a consensus on the Vice Presidency. In addition to Johnson and Hamlin, the contenders included Daniel Dickinson, a War Democrat from New York. His chances faded when Secretary of State William Seward's friends realized that their state would not likely be represented in the Administration by both a Vice President and a Secretary of State; they therefore opposed Dickinson.

Judge Horace Maynard of Tennessee won much sympathy for his state and its Governor when he spoke to the delegates of the courage and suffering of the Southern Unionists. He praised Johnson as a man who "stood in the furnace of treason."

Johnson took a narrow lead over Hamlin and the others on the first ballot, and the convention quickly swung behind the Tennessee man. But the National Union party was not quite united. Representative Thaddeus Stevens of Pennsylvania exclaimed to his colleagues, "Can't you get a candidate for Vice-President without going down into a damned rebel province for one?"

Press reaction was mixed. The New York *World* said: "The age of statesmen is gone; the age of rail splitters and tailors, of buffoons, boors and fanatics has succeeded. . . ." But Greeley's *Tribune* noted that in Johnson the rebels "have no more original, consistent, implacable foe, and not many more effective. His nomination is a pledge to the Unionists of the seceded states that they at least are not deemed outcasts from the pale of our nationality. . . ."

Military victories by the North in the fall of 1864 clinched the election of Lincoln and Johnson. In February, 1865, Congress resolved that no electoral votes from rebel states would be counted. Returns from Tennessee were thrown out, with the apparent implication that the incoming Vice President was something less than a full-fledged citizen of the Union.

Andy Johnson fell ill with typhoid fever early in 1865, and he hoped to be excused from attending the inauguration. But Lincoln insisted that he be present in Washington on March 4. Johnson arrived in the Capital somewhat recovered, but in a weakened condition. On the night before the inauguration, the Vice President-elect attended a party in his honor, a party overflowing with wine and oratory.

At the Capitol the next morning Johnson felt shaky. He sought relief in stimulants. After putting down several drinks, he shuffled forth to take the oath of office. But before Hamlin could swear in his successor, Johnson plunged into his speech. He looked out on a glittering scene. The galleries were filled with women from Washington society, and arrayed before him were the diplomatic corps, the Cabinet, and the Supreme Court. Lincoln entered the chamber during Johnson's speech.

The Vice President spoke for fifteen minutes, but it must have seemed like an hour to others. He did not refer to notes. His theme was "the people," a theme he played over and over. He said that but for the plain people he would not be present on such an occasion. He had risen from humble origins, he reminded everyone. He did not claim to be wise and learned. He admitted he knew little about parliamentary law, and would have to request the Senate's indulgence.

Not content with demeaning only himself, Johnson admonished his auditors that they too owed much to the people. "You, Mr. Secretary Seward, Mr. Secretary Stanton, the Secretary of the Navy, and the others who are your associates . . . derive not your greatness and your power alone from President Lincoln. . . . Humble as I am, Plebeian as I may be deemed, permit me in the presence of this brilliant assemblage to enunciate the truth that courts and Cabinets, the President and his advisers, derive their power and their greatness from the people."

On and on he rambled, while the Republican Senators stared at their desks. Massachusetts' Charles Sumner covered his face with his hands. Attorney General James Speed whispered to Navy Secretary Gideon Welles: "All this is in wretched bad taste." He added later, "This man is certainly deranged." It is said that Abraham Lincoln's head slumped in humiliation. While he was undoubtedly embarrassed, it is not likely that Lincoln felt unkindly toward Johnson. The President, after all, was waiting to speak in his own inaugural address of "malice toward none" and of "charity for all."

Finally Johnson ended his harrangue, took the oath, kissed the Bible noisily, and sat down. Even some of the newspapermen were too embarrassed to report the speech. But Johnson soon became the talk of the town, discussion of his speech eclipsing the attention given to Lincoln's classic address. Some Senators considered asking Johnson to resign. His performance proved to be a sobering experience for the Senate, which passed a resolution excluding forthwith all intoxicating liquors from the Senate portion of the Capitol Building.

Johnson recuperated from his illness and his embarrassment at the suburban Silver Spring home of a friend. A day or two after the inauguration, Lincoln remarked to a Cabinet member: "I have known Andy Johnson for many years; he made a bad slip the other day, but you need not be scared; Andy ain't a drunkard." This was certainly true, and Johnson drank less than most men in those days. But his querulous, intemperate manner would often convey the impression that he was "under the influence" when he was not. Johnson would never live down that day, and the Vice Presidency was tarred again. His critics recited a bit of doggerel that went, in part:

O, was it not a glorious sight,
To see the crowd of black and white,
As well as Andy Johnson tight
At the inauguration.

Other, more important events claimed attention. Lee surrendered at Appomattox on April 9. It was time, in Lincoln's words, to bind up the nation's wounds. But some men concerned themselves with inflicting new wounds. One such individual was George Atzerodt, a native of Prussia and a carriage painter by trade, who lived in Maryland with his common-law wife and child. Short, brawny, and goateed, he had a ferocious look and the heart of a coward. Atzerodt, a Southern sympathizer, seemed pitifully eager to make friends. One of his acquaintances was the actor, John Wilkes Booth, who drew him into the infamous conspiracy to kill the top officers of the Federal Government.

Originally, Booth had contemplated kidnaping the President, not murdering several people, and when he turned toward the more extreme course, Atzerodt wanted out. But being too cowardly to run away, Atzerodt tremulously agreed to register in a room above the one occupied by Vice President Johnson. On the night of April 14, at about ten fifteen, he was supposed to knock on Johnson's door, and when the Vice President opened, he was to shoot him point-blank. Other men would kill Seward in his home, while Booth paid a visit to Ford's Theatre.

Knowing Atzerodt to be a drunkard and a weakling, Booth decided to shore up his colleague's confidence at a last meeting at the Kirkwood on the afternoon of the fourteenth. Atzerodt, who wasn't in, would be hard pressed to account for his own activities during that day. Much of it was spent drinking and asking suspicious questions. The bartender and the customers at the Kirkwood pondered the squirrelly little man who was so eager to learn if Johnson carried firearms, if he was protected by soldiers, and if he often left his room at night.

But Atzerodt didn't look like a man capable of committing murder, and this turned out to be the case. During the early evening he wandered through the city, arranged for a horse, and drank some more. At the appointed hour, he returned to the Kirkwood, but somehow he ended up back at the bar instead of at the door of the Vice President. The opportunity passed. During that night Atzerodt attempted to flee the city, but he was soon captured. Later he would be tried, and hanged.

The Vice President retired early on the evening of the fourteenth, and was nearly asleep when startled by a frenzied pounding on the door at approximately ten thirty. His caller was not an assassin but a friend, former Governor Farwell of Wisconsin. Farwell burst into the room to say that he had run all the way from Ford's Theatre, where Lincoln had just been shot. For a few frightened moments, the two were as little in control of themselves as the frantic citizens even then pouring out into the streets.

Johnson received accounts of Lincoln's condition, then decided to go to the President himself. Friends pleaded that he not do so, for reports now came that Seward had been stabbed, perhaps fatally, and that other Cabinet officers were also marked for death. But the former Military Governor of Tennessee had long since grown accustomed to threats of assassination. He buttoned up his coat, pulled his hat down over his face, hurried past a mob of five hundred in front of the hotel, and plunged forward into a raw, rainswept night. In a few minutes he had covered the three and one half blocks to the home of William Petersen, across from the theater, into which the dying President had been carried. He stood disheveled among the doctors and dignitaries, and stared at Lincoln's face. After a short time he walked back to the hotel.

Late the next morning at the Kirkwood, a few hours after Lincoln's death, Johnson was sworn in as the seventeenth President. On hand were a few Senators, a general, and most members of the Cabinet. He spoke briefly with discretion and true humility, in sharp contrast with his performance at the Capitol just six weeks earlier.

Johnson and his invalid wife, plus their children and grandchildren—eleven persons in all—moved into the White House on June 9, after Mrs. Lincoln finally departed.

Meanwhile, attention turned to the new President's policies toward the South. Before Lincoln's death Johnson had sounded off on occasion about the advisability of hanging Confederate President Jefferson Davis and otherwise meting out severe punishment to the rebels. The Congressional Radicals remembered such talk with pleasure. One of them, Representative George Julian of Indiana, wrote later: ". . . while everybody was shocked at his [Lincoln's] murder, the feeling was nearly universal that the accession of Johnson to the Presidency would prove a godsend to the country. Aside from Mr. Lincoln's known policy of tenderness to the Rebels . . . his . . . views of the subject of reconstruction were as distasteful as possible to the radical Republicans."

And from the Radical press and the Radical pulpits came other voices hailing the assassination as an Act of God that would harden Presidential policy toward the South.

But Johnson himself was of the South, and his late efforts to preserve the Union had not been coupled with any serious wish to wreak vengeance. Soon word was brought to him of a prostrated Confederacy, of torn rail lines, of closed banks, of farms overrun by weeds, of abandoned plantations. When accounts came to the White House of a South now repentant, and of a moderate element gaining the ascendancy, Johnson found a widening rift between himself and the Radicals. Before the end of April, he was telling visitors from Indiana: "If a state is to be nursed until it again gets strength, it must be nursed by its friends, not smothered by its enemies."

So Johnson moved to implement Lincoln's program. His goals were to win pledges of loyalty as quickly as possible, to put the Southern state governments into the hands of responsible whites, and to get the states back into the Union. The President wanted to extend the franchise to the Negroes only as they became fit to exercise that privilege. On May 29, Johnson issued a Proclamation of Pardon and Amnesty that applied to most Southerners. Congress was not in session, and he frankly hoped to restore the South to the Union before that body convened in December. As the year 1865 neared its end, six states had fulfilled the obligations prescribed by the President, and had Congressmen waiting in Washington to take their seats.

Incidental to his apparent success with the South, Johnson seemed on his way to forming a center party composed of Lincoln Republicans, War Democrats, and Southern moderates. Johnson was winning the admiration of a South that once hated him, and the support of men of good will everywhere. He was the first accidental President to bask—even briefly—in the sunshine of public approval. But Lincoln had enjoyed great prestige as a result of his statesmanship in time of war, and he had acted at the same time with great political skill. Johnson, on the other hand, was rigid and stubborn in the application of policies that were themselves conciliatory. And he was no match for the men in Congress who had plans of their own for the South.

Leader of the Radicals in the House was Thaddeus Stevens, an irascible, crippled old man who looked on the Southern states as "conquered provinces." He was determined to devote the last years of his life to the punishment of traitors. The Republicans became alarmed at the speed with which the Confederate states were returning to the Union and electing solid Democratic delegations. With a Democrat in the White House, and with War Democrats and southern sympathizers very much in evidence in the North, it appeared that a coalition was being fashioned to deny national leadership to the party that had been primarily responsible for the prosecution of the war. Congress was also eager to reclaim powers surrendered to the Executive branch during the war.

Congress convened and immediately barred the Southern representatives. A committee of fifteen under the control of Stevens was appointed to fashion a reconstruction program. In February, 1866, Congress passed a bill guaranteeing military protection for freedmen deprived of their rights by state law. Johnson vetoed the bill, criticizing its failure to provide for trial by jury or for any other recognized rules of law. The veto was sustained. Speaking at an impromptu rally at the White House three days after the veto, Johnson denounced the Radicals as traitors. He named Stevens and Sumner. "Does not the blood of Lincoln appease the vengeance and wrath of the opponents of this government?" Johnson shouted.

Next, Congress passed a Civil Rights Act which Johnson said invaded both the legislative and judicial powers of the states. This time moderate Republicans joined the Radicals to override. Johnson never again saw one of his vetoes sustained, and effective control of reconstruction policy passed from the President's hands.

Details of the long running battle between Johnson and Congress need not be recorded here. Johnson was a man of rugged honesty and earnestness who was simply thrust abruptly and without preparation into a delicate situation that he could not control. He reaped a whirlwind of hate, and his accidental status left him more vulnerable to abuse by his enemies. To reduce the threat of Johnson's veto power, the Radicals tried in the Congressional elections of 1866 to win a two-thirds margin in both houses.

Unlike the hesitant John Tyler, Johnson decided to carry his cause to the people. In August, he undertook a cross-country speaking tour—his ill-fated "swing around the circle." His principal argument was that the refusal by the Radicals to permit a normalizing of relations between the states prevented the restoration of the Union for which the war had been fought.

Johnson had reason on his side, and his prepared addresses were effective. In New York, he pointed out that the Southern states had laid down their arms and accepted the terms of the North, and he asked, "Do we want to humiliate them and degrade them and tread them in the dust?" He said he welcomed back a repentant South, even with all its "heresies." "I am for the Union," he said. "I am against all those who are opposed to the Union. I am for the Union, the whole Union and nothing but the Union."

But Johnson, who had been placed on the 1864 ticket as the symbol of one state's return to the fold, never succeeded in projecting himself as a truly national figure who had the concern of all the people at heart. He never outgrew the habits of the stump speech. The tactics that proved effective in Tennessee rough-and-tumble appalled the somewhat more sophisticated citizens in the North. The thin-skinned President allowed hecklers—some planted by the Radicals—to provoke him. Time and time again he interrupted his prepared remarks to quarrel with noisemakers in his audience. He didn't seem to realize that he was President, that he should stand above those who would attempt to tear down that office and the man occupying it.

"Why don't you hang Jeff Davis?" someone would ask, and the yelling and shouting match would begin. On another occasion, the President might ask plaintively, "What is my offense?" and a drunken rowdy would reply, "You ain't a Radical." Easily rattled, the President swung wildly at political opponents, declaring for example that ". . . having fought traitors at the South, I am prepared to fight traitors at the North."

His attempts to engage the people directly in debate brought from one Republican Congressman the observation that Johnson fell into the "error of supposing it possible for him to lay aside his official character and [speak] as a private citizen about public affairs. It is simply *an impossibility*." The embarrassment of the public at this debasement of the Presidency was shared by many politicians who made a point of being elsewhere when Johnson came to town. The Radical Congressmen stayed away, of course, but news reporters sympathetic to their cause came to write distorted accounts of what Johnson was trying to say.

Once, in response to derision from a crowd in Cleveland, Johnson exclaimed, "I say here tonight that if my predecessor had lived, the vials of wrath would have been poured out upon him." Perhaps. But Johnson did his cause no good by inviting comparison with Lincoln.

Like Tyler and Fillmore, Johnson had no firm base of support, and an attempt was made to reactivate the National Union party label. Delegates met at Philadelphia in August to pledge support to Johnson's program, and to attempt to elect Congressmen favorable to him. But the movement foundered in the wake of Johnson's inept "swing around the circle." Johnson's support came from the wrong places. Copperheads and Southern rebels turned away more votes than they could deliver. During the congressional campaign the first intimations were raised that the President was somehow responsible for Lincoln's assassination. The voters gave Johnson's enemies a two-thirds majority in both houses. With the election over, the Radicals threw out the Presidential reconstruction; two years after Lee surrendered, military rule was established throughout the South, and the carpetbag became one of the most odious symbols in American political annals.

With a "mandate" from the people, the more fanatic Congressmen lost all sense of restraint or propriety. Though Johnson no longer had the capacity to thwart their policies, the Radicals could not abide his presence in the White House. Those who recall how the Soviet leaders attempt to rewrite history after every purge are invited to listen to Representative Benjamin F. Loan (R-Mo.) as he speaks in the House chamber on January 24, 1867.

At first, Loan declared, Lincoln's murder "was supposed to

have been the rash act of a reckless young man rendered desperate by the failure of the cause to which he was devoted. But subsequent developments have shown it to have been the result of deliberate plans adopted in the interests of the rebellion. The appeal to arms on the part of the Rebels had failed. The only alternative . . . was fraud and treachery." Lincoln, of course, was incorruptible, but next to him "stood one who by birth, education and association was a Southern man, a lifelong pro-slavery Democrat . . . influenced by all the grossest instincts of his nature, without moral culture or moral restraint, with a towering ambition. . . ."

Loan revealed that the Southern leaders "were quick to understand the advantages offered them by such a person occupying the second office in the government. They readily comprehended the means necessary to reach and use such a subject; but one frail life stood between him and the chief magistracy of the Republic. . . . An assassin's bullet wielded and directed by Rebel hand and paid for by Rebel gold made Andrew Johnson President. . . . The price that he was to pay for his promotion was treachery to the Republicans and fidelity to the party of treason and rebellion."

Representative Robert S. Hale of New York was on his feet to protest this slander. But Speaker Schuyler Colfax explained that he could not restrain the "gentleman from Missouri." Hale demanded that Loan back up his tall tale with proof, and Loan promised that proof would be forthcoming.

A forum for the airing of such charges was already functioning. Earlier in January, Representative James M. Ashley (R-Ohio) stood in the same House chamber and declared, "I charge Andrew Johnson, Vice President and acting President of the United States, with the commission of acts which, in contemplation of the Constitution, are high crimes and misdemeanors, for which, in my judgment, he ought to be impeached." The House authorized its Judiciary Committee to make an inquiry.

The investigation was nothing if not thorough. Navy Secretary Gideon Welles wrote in his diary that the committee examined Johnson's public life, his domestic life, his bank accounts, his speeches, his conversations, and all his other doings as man and President. Johnson's private secretaries, some members of the Cabinet, and some members of his family were quizzed by the zealous investigators.

The committee members listened to a wild melange of charges from witnesses who for one reason or another were prepared to impeach Johnson on any grounds. No testimony was more sensational than that which seemed to tie Johnson to Lincoln's murder. To begin with, of course, there was that mysterious note written by John Wilkes Booth at the Kirkwood House on the afternoon of the murder. Booth's purpose has never been established. Probably, he had anticipated that Atzerodt would fail in his assignment, and that therefore it would be necessary to leave evidence that would kill Johnson politically if not physically. Another theory is that Booth's note was intended for Johnson's secretary, whom Booth knew, and from whom he may have wished to obtain a pass for that night to get by the sentries surrounding the city.

From this rather fragile beginning, the investigators studied other evidence purporting to link Johnson to the conspirators. In doing so, Johnson's enemies blandly overlooked the fact that two years before eight persons had been convicted—and four had been hanged—for conspiring to kill Lincoln, Seward, Grant, and Johnson. Now the Radicals were attempting to prove that Johnson was a part of that same plot, one of the objects of which had been his own murder.

Evidence included a report of a letter written by Johnson to Jefferson Davis during the war in which the Tennessee Governor allegedly revealed military information. The letter was never found. A Rev. Matchett claimed to know two men of "excellent characters" who could testify that Booth had been in touch with Johnson before the assassination. The men were never found. Also, much interest was shown in a diary found on Booth the night he was shot. On later examination, it was discovered that some pages had been cut out, and Congressman Ashley was convinced that the missing pages implicated Johnson. The pages were never found.

Ashley was not a member of the committee, but he was active in rounding up evidence. His star witness was a man named Sanford Conover. What did it matter that Conover himself was then imprisoned on a perjury conviction? Conover, in fact, had been a witness at the original conspiracy trial, at which time he claimed to possess proof that Jefferson Davis had hired Booth to kill Lincoln. When this nonsense was discredited, the prison doors closed behind Conover. Now, in 1867, Ashley paid frequent visits to Conover in jail. If we can believe any accounts of their conversations that have survived, it can be concluded that Ashley offered to obtain a pardon for Conover if the latter would produce evidence linking Johnson to Lincoln's death.

Ashley even explained the type of evidence that Conover was supposed to supply. He was to produce a witness who would testify that Booth's original plan was to kill Lincoln on Inauguration Day, 1865, and that Vice President Johnson was aware of this plot, which in turn explained his shaky condition and weird behavior during his inauguration speech.

Ashley's plans collapsed. When Conover's pardon failed to come through, he wrote a letter to Johnson exposing the scheme.

Other Congressmen were active in the effort to unseat Johnson. According to the *National Intelligencer*, Benjamin F. Butler of Massachusetts admitted paying Mrs. Sanford Conover $50 to produce evidence against the President.

On November 23, Democrats hailed Representative Ashley himself before the committee. What was the big idea, they asked, in promising proof that Johnson was implicated in Lincoln's murder, and then producing none? Unabashed, Ashley replied: "It was not that kind of evidence which would satisfy the great mass of men, especially the men who do not concur with me in my theory about this matter. . . . I have always believed that President Harrison and President Taylor and President Buchanan were poisoned, and poisoned for the express purpose of putting the Vice Presidents in the Presidential office. In the first two instances, it was successful. . . . Then Mr. Lincoln was assassinated, and from my stand-point I could come to a conclusion which impartial men, holding different views, could not come."

The assassination angle was only the most sensational of the charges aimed at Johnson. The others boiled down in the main to the fact that the President disagreed with Congress on the means of reconstructing the South. This, in the judgment of the House, did not constitute high crimes or misdemeanors, and on December 7, 1867, the impeachment resolution was voted down, 57 to 108. The Radicals acted not from lack of desire to impeach, but from an embarrassing lack of evidence. But the enemies of the President would live to fight another day.

In March, 1867, the Radicals passed the Tenure of Office Act, which prohibited the President from removing any official appointed with the advice and consent of the Senate, without first getting the Senate's consent. To his everlasting credit, Johnson did not allow to pass unchallenged this brazen attempt to subordinate the Presidency to the will of Congress. A showdown was not long in coming.

For the most part, Lincoln's Cabinet had transferred its loyalty to Johnson, in striking contrast to the hostility displayed by the official families inherited by Tyler and Fillmore. But Secretary of War Stanton had stayed on to spy for the Radicals. Johnson tolerated him longer than necessary, until finally he asked for his resignation. The Secretary of War refused to quit and promptly barricaded himself in his office. Johnson formally dismissed Stanton without bothering to obtain the Senate's permission. The Radicals did not miss this opportunity. Quickly, eleven articles of impeachment were drawn and approved in the House and sent to the Senate, which would serve as a court to try the charges.

Johnson did not appear in the Senate during his trial, but was represented by some of the ablest legal talent available. His lawyers made quick work of the charges against the President. Of course, the Radicals were not interested in the facts, but only in voting the President out of office. Nonetheless the charade was played out to the end. Ben Butler arraigned Johnson before the Senate as a man who had succeeded to the Presidency "by murder most foul." Butler called Johnson the "elect of an assassin." The circus that followed might be likened to the Moscow show trials of the 1930's, except that the Radicals lacked a confession and—as it turned out—a conviction. Old Thad Stevens attempted to testify against the President, but now his acid tongue produced little more than a death rattle.

At the White House, Johnson awaited his fate. "Bring me in a list of the murderers of Charles I," he said. "I'd like to see how many of them came to an untimely end."

On May 16, 1868, came perhaps the most dramatic vote in

the history of the Senate. All 54 members were present, one arriving on a stretcher. All voted, even Senator Benjamin Wade (R-Ohio), the Senate President pro tempore, who would succeed Johnson if the latter were convicted. Wade voted against Johnson and professed to see no violation of ethics in doing so. He had already selected his Cabinet.

With 19 votes required to acquit, a heroic handful of Republicans joined the Democrats. The count stood 19 for acquittal and 35 for conviction, one short of the needed two thirds. The seven Republicans who deserted the Radicals destroyed their political careers on the spot. None was ever elected to a major office again. Senator Edmund G. Ross was told by telegram: "Kansas repudiates you as she does all perjurers and skunks."

Even now, the Radicals did not give up, because the vote had come on only one of the eleven articles of impeachment, and hope still remained that one of the renegades could be bullied, bribed, or blackmailed into voting for conviction on some other article. The Republican National Convention was at hand, and was used as an excuse to adjourn the trial for ten days.

The Republicans adopted a platform saying in part: "We profoundly deplore the untimely and tragic death of Abraham Lincoln and regret the accession to the Presidency of Andrew Johnson, who has acted treacherously to the people who elected him and the cause he was pledged to support. . . ." The platform conveyed the impression that Johnson had been convicted! It said that he had been "justly impeached for high crimes and misdemeanors, and properly pronounced guilty thereof by the vote of thirty-five Senators."

When the court reconvened on May 26, the Radicals brought two more articles to a vote, but the same 19 senators held firm for acquittal. The prosecution capitulated, and the court adjourned *sine die*.

The most calculated assault ever on the institution of the American Presidency had failed. Stanton resigned as Secretary of War. The Tenure of Office Act was declared unconstitutional by the Supreme Court in 1926, but during the intervening period no President allowed himself to be intimidated by its provisions. Notwithstanding Johnson's personal triumph against great odds, the significance of his victory went beyond one man. Benjamin Curtis, one of his associate counsels at the Senate trial, wrote to the President. "I have not esteemed this proceeding of very great personal importance to you," he said. "But to the country, it was of such importance that it would be difficult to overstate it."

Johnson's last months in office were relatively uneventful. He did receive 65 votes on the first Presidential ballot at the 1868 Democratic convention, but his total declined on succeeding roll calls. Six years after leaving the White House, Johnson was re-elected to his old seat in the United States Senate. When the ex-President first entered the Senate chamber—this room in which he had known both humiliation and triumph—he was received with thunderous applause. Many of his old friends and enemies were dead, and the passage of years had softened the emotions of those still living.

It would be futile to speculate on the course reconstruction would have taken had Lincoln lived, or if someone else had been nominated for Vice President in 1864. All that can be said for certain is that events taking place after that nomination have left a permanent scar on the relations between the Northern and Southern sections of our country. This scar is the legacy of what historians have called The Age of Hate.

Eleven Vice Presidents have advanced to the Presidency, but only one man ever hoped to occupy those two offices in reverse order. Ben Wade fully expected that the Senate would convict Andrew Johnson, in which case Wade would serve out the final ten months of his term. Wade could not command any support for the 1868 Republican Presidential nomination, which was wrapped up for Ulysses S. Grant. But he did hope that if he occupied the White House in advance of the convention, the delegates would honor him with the Vice Presidency. By the time the Republicans convened, however, the Senate Radicals had already lost their first vote in the impeachment trial. Wade's Vice-Presidential stock dropped accordingly.

Lincoln's death had inevitably revived interest in the No. 2 office, and a number of men entered the race. Wade led for four ballots, but on the fifth the convention turned to Schuyler Colfax of Indiana, the Speaker of the House. Colfax had been a newspaper reporter, and then the publisher of the *St. Joseph Valley Register* in South Bend, the leading Whig journal in northern Indiana. He helped organize the Republican party in his state, and served for fourteen years in the United States House, the last six as Speaker. For want of a better term, he can be classified as a moderate Radical. "Smiler" Colfax perpetually wore a frozen grin along with his brown beard. Lincoln had regarded the amiable Hoosier as a friendly rascal. No one doubted his ambition.

Grant, the Republican Presidential candidate, hailed from Galena, Illinois. Noting that the candidates had resided in adjacent states, the New York *Tribune* was no less enthusiastic:

". . . it was wisely felt that no geographical reasons should weigh against the imperative wisdom of putting forward our two best men, both for availability before the people and for capacity and integrity in office."

It would seem that the GOP could have broken the tradition of geographical balance in behalf of abler men than Grant and Colfax. But these were the years when the Republicans succeeded in politics without really trying. The *Tribune* praised Colfax's "valuable training" as a journalist, and observed: "The rail splitter and the tailor were a powerful team, but the tanner and the editor will match them." Horace Greeley, the *Tribune* editor, would sing a different tune as Grant's election opponent four years later.

Colfax carried the burden of the campaign. He stumped the country, while Grant wisely kept his mouth shut. The Democrats, of course, didn't have a chance.

By 1872 many liberal Republicans were tired of the bungling and indifferent ethics of the Grant administration. These idealists broke away to form a third party, which quickly blossomed into a major party when the Democrats accepted their nominees. The anti-Grant coalition had several able Presidential candidates to choose from. But after a long deadlock the delegates handed their nomination to Greeley, an eccentric crusader whose shafts were long since spent. When the Vice-Presidential nomination went to Governor B. Gratz Brown of Missouri, the liberal crusade quickly showed signs of turning into a farce. "Boozy Gratz" Brown—so nicknamed for his lack of temperance—made a fool of himself during the campaign. Speaking at a Yale class reunion, he denounced all things Eastern, and ended his visit by getting drunk. From that day on his candidacy was not taken seriously.

In this, the sorriest year in our political history, the Republicans could do no better than offer four more years of Grantism. There was some confusion over the Republican Vice-Presidential nomination, however, thanks to Schuyler Colfax. In September, 1870, he had announced that he would retire at the end of his term. But the Vice President enjoyed wide popularity within the Republican party, and his statement triggered a small Colfax-for-President boom. If Colfax hoped that Grant would retire after one term, and that the party would then turn to him, he was disappointed. The President concluded correctly that Colfax was after his job, and the general's friends started looking for a substitute for Vice President. Colfax, realizing too late that he might be left out of the picture altogether, passed the word that he would accept a second term if drafted. But he was too late, and the convention nominated Henry Wilson of Massachusetts to run with Grant.

Wilson, the "Cobbler of Natick," was the son of an impoverished day laborer. Largely self-educated, he climbed the ladder from cobbler, shoe manufacturer, teacher, editor, United States Senator, to Vice President. He dedicated his life to the liberation of the slaves and the betterment of the lot of the workingman.

But the country had not heard the last of Colfax. As a lame-duck Vice President, one would expect that he would serve out his term and fade into obscurity. However, the unexpected happened: the Crédit Mobilier scandal broke while the campaign was in full swing.

Some years before, Congress had agreed to pick up the tab for the construction of the Union Pacific Railroad. This was done when the builders were unable to find investors willing to sink money into a line to be built through the sparsely populated West. Oakes Ames, one of the directors of the railroad, was also a member of the House of Representatives. He knew that the line could be built for far less money than Congress had granted. Ames and some of his fellow stockholders schemed to steal the balance. They set up a dummy corporation, the Crédit Mobilier of America, to build the railroad. All the money from the government was turned over to this phony outfit. After building the railroad, Crédit Mobilier had a tidy sum of more than $23 million left over. All this was pure gravy, but the stockholders soon began quarreling over the division of the spoils. Congressmen began to hear rumors, and there was some talk of an investigation. Alarmed, Ames gathered up several hundred shares of Crédit Mobilier stock and passed them out among fellow Congressmen. As Ames put it, he placed the shares "where they will do most good." He offered the stock far below face value, and if a Congressman could not afford to buy the stock, he was allowed to pay for it out of dividends, which were large.

The New York *Sun* obtained the names of the favored Congressmen, and published the list on September 4, 1872, two months before the Presidential election. "Smiler" Colfax's name led all the rest. The Republicans might have congratulated themselves for having dropped Colfax from the ticket, but alas! the list of the accused also contained the name of their new Vice-Presidential candidate, Henry Wilson.

The House of Representatives organized an investigation, which got under way in December. Colfax did not fare too well. Ames told the committee conducting the investigation that Colfax had paid for some stock, although none had been transferred to his name. The Vice President appeared voluntarily before the committee to deny that he had either sought to buy stock, or that he had been offered any. He also denied that he had ever exerted any influence—either as Speaker of the House or as Vice President—in behalf of any legislation in which Crédit Mobilier had an interest. In the course of his testimony, Colfax remarked that he saw nothing morally wrong with the Union Pacific stockholders setting up a dummy corporation to sign contracts with themselves.

Ames resumed his testimony on January 22, 1873. His memory had improved, and he filled in the details of his dealing with Colfax. One transaction he recalled was his payment to Colfax of $1,200 in dividends for twenty shares of stock in June, 1868. But Ames could not produce a receipt for the money. An examination of Colfax's bank account revealed that he had deposited $1,200 in bills in June, 1868.

These puzzling developments helped jog the memory of the Vice President, who now returned to testify again. Yes, he could explain that large bank deposit in June, 1868. One day, he was opening his mail at breakfast, and out popped a $1,000 bill. He remembered the incident because the sudden appearance of the bill had caused some comment at the breakfast table. The $1,000, he said, was a campaign contribution (Colfax had just been nominated for Vice President). The donor was a New Yorker named George F. Nesbitt, who had since died.

Sending a $1,000 bill through the mail is a bit extraordinary in itself; furthermore, Colfax was unable to produce the letter Nesbitt had written and mailed with the bill. Then someone discovered that Nesbitt, a printer, had held a valuable contract from the Post Office Department for the manufacture of envelopes. At the time he allegedly made his campaign donation to Colfax, the latter was chairman of the House Committee on Post Offices and Post Roads. So Colfax's explanation hardly placed him in a better light.

When the House reviewed the evidence gathered by its committee, some mention was made of impeaching Colfax. The judiciary committee decided, however, that this action was not warranted. The committee did not clear Colfax; it simply indicated that his misconduct—if any—occurred before he became Vice President. Impeachment would have been pointless, since Colfax's term would expire in a few weeks. On March 4, 1873, Colfax left office and sank into a deep and well-deserved oblivion.

Henry Wilson survived the scandal relatively unscathed. It turned out that he had taken twenty shares, for which he had paid cash. On thinking the matter over, Wilson had requested permission to return the stock. He did so, and had therefore already disassociated himself from Crédit Mobilier by the time the *Sun* published the list of stock purchasers.

Meanwhile, Grant and Wilson were elected. Greeley's wife died just before the election, and he sank into despondency and died on November 29. His 66 electoral votes were scattered, 18 going to his running mate, Brown. Henry Wilson suffered a fatal stroke while presiding over the Senate in 1875. He was the fourth Vice President to die in office.

More often than not, Vice-Presidential candidates subtract votes from the ticket. Such appeared to be the case at the next Presidential convention in 1876, when the Democrats nominated a supporter of sound money, Samuel J. Tilden, for President. The Vice-Presidential candidate they chose, Thomas A. Hendricks of Indiana, was a spokesman for the inflationary

Western wing of the party. Conservative Democrats worried about Tilden's poor health, and the possibility that a Democratic victory could put Hendricks in the White House. The defection of these sound-money men helped defeat the ticket.

It was time for a change, though, even if just from one Republican to another. After an era of financial panic, corruption, and reconstruction, the country relaxed under the pious leadership of the new Republican President, Rutherford B. Hayes, and his wife, who was unaffectionately known as "Lemonade Lucy." In keeping with the new moral tone at the White House, Vice President William A. Wheeler often joined Hayes and his family for a round of prayer and hymn-singing.

★ ★ ★ ★ ★ ★

CHESTER ALAN ARTHUR

"The President's tragic death was a sad necessity. . . ."

Civil War songs, not hymns, were heard most often when next the Republicans met in Chicago in the summer of 1880. By the thousands they came, to whoop and holler at the longest, noisiest, and gaudiest of all the Republican national conventions. This was the heyday of the Grand Army of the Republic and the waving of the bloody shirt, of a looking backward to past glories.

This convention has been called the last stand of the Old Guard. In truth, it must be said that the Republican Old Guard has been buried many times, but has never died. Then as now, the Republicans had their factions. Today's "conservatives" and "moderates" were the "Stalwarts" and "Half Breeds" of 1880. The party in those years, however, was not divided by ideology, but by personalities.

First of all there was Ulysses S. Grant who, said his nominator, "hails from Appomattox/And its famous apple tree." Aging, discredited, and jobless, he was trying for a comeback. He had served two terms, had left office under a cloud, and had rediscovered his popularity during a triumphant world tour. Many people forgot his sorry record in office, and remembered only the heroics.

Grant's principal rival in 1880 was James G. Blaine of Maine, the "Plumed Knight," a Speaker of the House, a

United States Senator, twice Secretary of State, and five times a Presidential bridesmaid. Scarred by Crédit Mobilier and a smattering of other scandals, he nonetheless was the ablest and most popular Republican of his day.

The nominating arena itself was dominated by the garish, arrogant Senator from New York, Roscoe Conkling. Not a candidate himself, Conkling was the commander of the Stalwart forces and the manager of the Grant campaign. He had been a powerful influence during the general's Presidency. For ten years he had been the absolute boss of the New York Republican party. The policies of the retiring President, Hayes, had jeopardized the flow of Federal patronage to the Conkling machine. But if Grant could be returned to the White House, Conkling would again be secure in his power.

In the words of the journalist Henry Stoddard, Conkling "loved to use words as a prize-fighter loves to use his fists." He was one of the great spread-eagle orators of his time, a politician conscious of his public appearance, a devotee of boxing and body-building exercises. On the platform, the preening Conkling was an unforgettable sight, with his long beard, his cream-colored pantaloons, his moon-colored vest, and his silk scarves. Blaine once sneered at his "haughty disdain, his grandiloquent swell, his majestic supereminent, overpowering, turkey-gobbler strut."

As the convention opened, little attention was paid to two other men. James A. Garfield was a United States Representative from Ohio and floor manager for John Sherman, one of the Presidential dark horses. Chester Alan Arthur, a cog in the New York Stalwart machine, was remembered as the former collector of the spoils for the port of New York. More from them later.

The 1880 convention proved to be the opening scene of a tragic political drama, but there had also been a prologue. In 1877, President Hayes had taken office, pledging to serve only a single term. In his inaugural address he called for a "thorough, radical, and complete" reform of the United States Civil Service. The Jacksonian tradition that "to the victors belong the spoils" was a fact of American political life. Other leading nations had taken steps to strengthen their national bureaucracy through competitive examinations and guarantees of tenure. But in this country the growth of an administrative class, even if chosen on merit, was seen as a menace, a forerunner of the superstate. Anyway, politicians asked, what was wrong with a public employee kicking back a portion of his salary to the party that helped get him elected?

Hayes issued an executive order declaring: "No officer should be required or permitted to take part in the management of political organizations, caucuses, conventions, or election campaigns. . . . No assessment for political purposes, on officers or subordinates, should be allowed. . . ." Congress greeted this announcement with grumbling and indifference. Conkling scoffed at the "snivel service."

But Hayes meant business. His eye fell on the New York Custom House and on its top officials, Chester A. Arthur and Alonzo Cornell. Both were close associates of Senator Conkling. Cornell, in defiance of Hayes's instructions, continued to serve as both naval officer at the Custom House and as chairman of the New York State Republican Committee. Arthur had held the collectorship since 1871, with yearly incomes running as high as $40,000. Hayes ordered an investigation of the Custom House, and found that the 1,011 officials and clerks on Arthur's staff included many members of the Republican state organization. Assessments from their salaries filled the party treasury, and they worked long and hard for the GOP during primary and election campaigns. Employees at the Custom House augmented their salaries with tips, bribes, and petty blackmail from the merchants whose imports they handled. Investigators found an overstaffed and generally lax operation, and many instances of goods being admitted duty free. While Arthur made some effort to carry out Hayes's policies, it was clear that he was unable or unwilling to sever his ties with the Republican party. Hayes decided that Arthur and his assistant, Cornell, would have to go.

Hayes was interested in performance, not personalities. But had he taken a closer look at Chester Arthur, he would have discovered a most unusual man and politician. Arthur was a Phi Beta Kappa graduate of Union College at the age of seventeen. He had taught school and practiced law, and for years had been a valuable ally of Conkling. An honest man himself, Arthur merely diverted his eyes from the gamier side of Custom House politics. In fact, he had little in common with the greedier political animals who scurried about the imperial throne of "Lord Roscoe." Arthur was well-bred and well-read, and lived with his wife and children in discriminating splendor in his Lexington Avenue town house. Here was a machine politician, a spoilsman, who also had good taste and good sense, who could converse with authority on the poetry of Robert Burns while dallying for hours over a gourmet dinner. He was a fastidious dresser, an expert on fishing, and an enthusiastic reader of Dickens and Thackeray. Standing six feet, two inches, large in all his dimensions, with shaven chin and luxuriant side whiskers, Arthur dominated any social gathering.

But not even his friends could have imagined in their wildest dreams that Chester A. Arthur would someday become President of the United States, especially after Hayes finally succeeded in ousting Arthur and Cornell from their jobs at the Custom House. After a bit of foot-dragging, the Senate confirmed a successor to Arthur with the symbolic name of Merritt.

Senator Conkling severed his ties with the national Republican administration. As for his jobless friends, Arthur was made New York Republican state chairman, and Cornell was nominated and elected Governor of the Empire State. So matters stood when the Stalwarts trooped out to Chicago in 1880 to fight and die for General Grant.

For more than thirty ballots the Grant and Blaine forces held firm. The minor candidates clung to their small blocs of votes, preventing a choice. On the thirty-fourth roll call Wisconsin shifted some votes to Ohio's Garfield, who had been very much on the scene for days without antagonizing the various camps. Garfield rose to protest the votes cast for him, was ruled out of order, and within two more ballots was the beneficiary of a band-wagon surge that carried him to the nomination. Blaine's Half Breeds led the switch. The count on the thirty-sixth ballot stood at 399 for Garfield and 306 for Grant, as the Stalwarts stood firm to the bitter end. Conkling was inconsolable and irreconcilable.

For Garfield, the dark horse, a dignified scholar in politics, this was a moment of triumph of which few men dare to dream, and his nomination provided a storybook climax to a memorable convention. But in Stoddard's paraphrase, "his path of glory led shortly to the grave."

Garfield's first task was to find a Vice-Presidential candidate. The Republicans were sure to lose all of the South, and New York's large bloc of electoral votes was essential to victory. The Vice-Presidential bone must therefore be tossed to the Stalwarts. Conkling, aware of the strategy, snapped, "I hope no sincere friend of mine will accept it." Garfield sent an emissary to Levi P. Morton, a wealthy, dignified New York banker, with an offer of the Vice Presidency. Morton sought Conkling's approval. The boss rasped, "If you think the ticket will be elected, if you think you will be happy in the association, accept." Morton thought it over and sent his regrets.

Ohio then left it up to New York to name the running mate, and the Stalwarts met to make the choice. Conkling, sulking, was absent. Incredibly, a boom developed for Arthur, the faithful Stalwart servant who had suffered so much at the hands of the incumbent Ohio Republican President, Rutherford Hayes. Since it was impossible for anyone to be angry at the mild-mannered Arthur, and since the Republican party needed a conciliator, if nothing else, Arthur was the choice of the Stalwart caucus.

But Arthur's selection would have to be approved by Ohio and by Conkling. The men from the Buckeye State were abashed to say the least, but they could reject Arthur only at the risk of shattering the party beyond repair.

Arthur himself sought out the ruthless, domineering leader whose orders he had obeyed so loyally for so many years. He found Conkling in the convention pressroom, deserted, except for one reporter. The round-faced, solemn Arthur, hat in hand so to speak, still showing deference to the New York Senator, said that the Garfield leaders would accept him for Vice President. Conkling might have been amused had he not still been smoldering as a result of Grant's defeat. He told Arthur to decline, that Garfield was sure to lose the election.

But Arthur, with rare assertiveness, would not let the matter lie. "There is something else to be said," he fairly blurted out.

"What, sir, you think of accepting?"

Arthur wavered momentarily and then spoke slowly and with emphasis. "The office of Vice President is a greater honor than I ever dreamed of attaining. A barren nomination would be a great honor. In a calmer moment you will look at this differently."

"If you wish for my favor and my respect you will contemptuously decline it."

Arthur looked the Stalwart leader in the eye. "Senator Conkling, I shall accept the nomination and I shall carry with me the majority of the delegation."

For a brief moment the haughty Conkling stared at his toady-turned-tiger. Then he spun around, strode to the door, and left the room in a cloud of rage. Arthur looked after him regretfully.

Arthur's name was put before the convention, and he won the nomination on the first ballot with nearly two thirds of the votes.

If the convention accepted Arthur, the public was somewhat less enthusiastic. The New Yorker, insofar as his name meant anything to the average voter, was associated with corruption. At a campaign rally, someone asked Secretary of the Treasury John Sherman if Arthur had been removed from his job at the Custom House because of dishonesty. "Oh, no," came Sherman's hardly reassuring reply. "He had not been dishonest, just inefficient."

Independent voters wrote to *The Nation*, inquiring if it were possible to split their ballots for President and Vice President, voting for Garfield while scratching Arthur. E. L. Godkin, the editor, wrote that this was impossible; but he urged his readers to support the Republican ticket. He pointed out that ". . . there is no place in which [Arthur's] powers of mischief will be so small as in the Vice Presidency. . . ." Besides, said Godkin, the chance that the forty-eight-year-old Garfield would die in office was "too unlikely a contingency to be worth making extraordinary provision for."

Garfield traveled east in August to seek a better understanding with the Stalwarts. Conkling, still sulking in his tent, refused to meet the candidate, but Arthur was there. Also present was Thomas Collier Platt, who would soon join Conkling in the Senate. Platt did the hard bargaining with Garfield. The Stalwarts wanted only one guarantee. If elected, Garfield must clear all New York patronage appointees through Conkling. Garfield pointed out that some recognition would have to go to a handful of anti-Conkling delegates from New York who had thrown their support to Garfield at the convention. Platt acquiesced on this point; otherwise, Garfield agreed to "consult" with the Stalwarts in doling out all jobs to New Yorkers. As it turned out, trouble was to develop after the election, when the President-elect and the Stalwarts disagreed on the meaning of the word "consult." Garfield would interpret that word in a very strict sense, and the consequences would prove unfortunate to several persons involved.

For the time being, however, the Republicans were burying only their differences. Conkling gave his support to the ticket, and Garfield and Arthur carried New York. The Republican team led the Democrats by only 10,000 in the national popular vote. Garfield defeated his Democratic opponent, General Winfield S. Hancock, by 214 to 155 in the electoral vote.

Between the election and the inauguration, several developments seemed to bode ill for the new administration. For one thing, Vice President-elect Arthur was behaving like the spoilsman of old. In January, 1881, the New York State Legislature met to elect a United States Senator (the popular election of Senators was not written into the Constitution until 1913). Arthur, oblivious to the dignity of his new position, lobbied in the corridors of the statehouse at Albany in behalf of the Stalwart candidate, Thomas C. Platt, who was chosen.

In February, Arthur spoke at a Republican-party dinner, and was careless enough to refer in passing to the previous fall's campaign in Indiana, where the race had been close and where reports were afoot that the Republicans had bought the election. He mentioned the "secrets of the campaign," but declined to say more, noting that reporters were present and he feared "what they might make of it before the inauguration takes place."

Garfield, meanwhile, was constructing his Cabinet with great difficulty. Blaine was tapped for Secretary of State, and the appointment confirmed Conkling's worst fears. How could he do business with an administration whose dominant figure would be that Half-Breed scoundrel who had likened him to a turkey gobbler? Conkling countered by asking Garfield to appoint Levi Morton Secretary of the Treasury, an office rich in patronage. Garfield was not about to let the Stalwarts get so valuable a prize. Furthermore, he did not want a Wall Street banker to head the Treasury Department. He offered to name Morton to a lesser Cabinet post, but Conkling would not compromise.

As more Garfield appointments were announced, Conkling realized that the President would be scarcely any improvement over Hayes. New York Republicans began to draw the same conclusions, as they recognized the direction in which the new political tides were running. Conkling's iron grip on his home territory began to weaken. On the other hand, Arthur had turned against the new President, remaining loyal to his old Stalwart leader.

The Senate convened in special session after the inauguration to consider Garfield's appointments. On March 20, Conkling called at the White House in one final effort to salvage some jobs for deserving Stalwarts. The President agreed to appoint nine of Conkling's friends to Federal positions. Pressing his luck, Conkling inquired if the President had any plans for a change at the New York Custom House. Garfield brushed aside that subject with the remark that it could wait until another time.

The Senate received the nine Conkling-approved nominations with some surprise. Secretary of State Blaine, who had plans for constructing a political base in New York, hurried to the White House. What words were exchanged by Blaine and Garfield, to what extent the veteran party leader dared to lecture the young President, we cannot be sure. But we do know the results of their meeting. A day or two later, Garfield sent another batch of nominations to the Senate, and this time the news was all bad for Conkling. In the new list, E. A. Merritt, Collector of the New York Custom House, was shifted to a diplomatic post. In his place Garfield proposed the one man guaranteed to curl the hairs on Conkling's beard.

The President's choice, William H. Robertson, had been the very symbol of Republican insurgency in New York State. He had led the band of nineteen anti-Conkling delegates at the 1880 convention who supported first Blaine and then Garfield. His appointment to any position would have outraged the New York Senator. To give him Arthur's old job was the unkindest cut of all.

Garfield's handling of the appointment was most inept. To begin with, he had agreed to "consult" with the Stalwarts, whatever that meant, but he had not even notified Conkling that the Robertson nomination was on the way. Garfield admitted privately that this was an error on his part, though he added that any communication with Conkling would have failed to change the position of either man.

Secondly, Garfield appeared not to be his own man. Blaine's dramatic intercession in the form of his late-evening call at the White House suggested strongly that he was goading the President into a scrap with the Stalwarts.

Thirdly, the appointment of Robertson did not even please the advocates of civil-service reform. Merritt was in every way qualified to continue in the post he had been given by Hayes. The reformers had no wish to see a new machine built out of the crumbling wreckage of the old. Garfield, while he did not share Conkling's cynical contempt for public service, was obviously not a zealous crusader in the tradition of Hayes.

Finally, Garfield was hurling a direct challenge at one of the dearest of Senate traditions, senatorial courtesy. Under this principle a nominee for an office in any given state would not be confirmed without the approval of that state's Senators—assuming that they belonged to the President's party. All Senators benefited from the distribution of jobs to their friends, and Conkling fully expected that they would not permit an undermining of the system. He demanded that the party choose between himself and Garfield, and in doing so he made the first of two grievous miscalculations. The Senate was tired of Conkling's grandiose behavior, of his rule-or-ruin policy, of his open warfare against any President he could not control. And the Republican Senators did not wish to defy a President barely settled in the White House. Conkling soon realized that he would have difficulty stopping Robertson's confirmation.

Garfield, for his part, became as uncompromising as his opponent. He wrote in a letter: "This brings on the contest at once and will settle the question whether the President is registering clerk of the Senate or the Executive of the United States."

Arthur, Conkling, and Platt wrote to the President protesting his failure to "consult" with the Senators. Arthur called on the President and pleaded with him to realize that Robertson's appointment would wreck the party in New York State. More accurately, it would wreck Conkling, a possibility not likely to cause Garfield to lose any sleep.

During this period of tumult and shouting, Arthur asserted: "Garfield has not been square, nor honorable, nor truthful with Conkling. It's a hard thing to say of a President of the United States, but it is, unfortunately, only the truth."

Without great enthusiasm the Republican caucus agreed to support the Robertson nomination. But Conkling, of course, did not. At this point he made his second great miscalculation. He grandly announced that he was resigning from the United States Senate; he would return to Albany, win re-election to his Senate seat, and thereby gain vindication. Platt liked the idea, said he would also resign—and was tagged forever with the nickname "Me, too."

Writing in his journal, Garfield called this "a very weak attempt at the heroic. If I do not mistake, it will be received with guffaws of laughter." He ridiculed their "masquerading as injured innocents." With the malcontents away from the Capital, Robertson was approved by the Senate with only one dissenting vote.

The Senate then adjourned. Its presiding officer, Vice President Arthur, was now free to perform the political duty he seemed to enjoy most. Once again he hastened to Albany to seek out old friends, to urge them to vote for the re-election of Conkling and Platt.

The cartoonist Thomas Nast depicted Arthur as a bootblack for the ex-Senators. A New York *Tribune* editorial said: "The manly figure of the Vice President of the United States still stands at Albany under a sign which reads: 'Political dickering and other dirty work done here.' "

Pathetically, Conkling found that he now had to beg—often in vain—for the support of legislators who once would have fallen in line at the snap of the fingers. His failure to put his own candidate in the White House had led inevitably to a realignment of political loyalties, to a revolt by party moderates willing to come to terms with the National Administration.

The contest was prolonged. Not only were two senatorships at stake, but the minority Democrats cast all their votes for their own men, who had no chance. Thus, the warring Republican factions had all the more difficulty in obtaining a majority of the whole body for any two candidates. From the first, however, it appeared that Conkling and Platt had little chance to win. It is a tribute to Conkling's exaggerated concept of his own power and importance that he failed to realize that his time was past, that his antics were but ludicrous anachronisms.

The American public grew tired of the whole business. After all, what was the purpose of government? Were Presidents and Vice Presidents and Senators sent to Washington merely to engage in a greedy scramble for jobs for their friends, solely to line their own palms with silver and to perpetuate themselves in power? How much could a man like Hayes accomplish in an era of public plunder, when pleas in behalf of ability and honesty were considered the cries of a weakling. All too often, American public opinion must be shocked into action. In the summer of 1881, the Pearl Harbor of civil-service reform was almost at hand.

May turned into June, and the New York senatorial struggle continued. Newspaper editorial writers were freely predicting that the Republican party would be shattered. One by one, the men who were eager to help pick up the pieces saw only the collapse of their own careers.

Thomas Collier Platt, the original Republican "me-tooer," was a tall, thin, cadaverous man, characterized by tenacity, energy, and unswerving loyalty to Roscoe Conkling. Unhampered by principle, skilled in the handling of all the manifold problems involved in building a political organization, he had risen to membership in the United States Senate. Platt was a married man, an elder in the Methodist Episcopal Church, a hymn singer, and collection-plate passer.

While engaged in his efforts to win re-election, Platt was staying at the Delavan Hotel in Albany. One day in June an informal delegation of Half Breed legislators trooped into the hotel and slipped up to Platt's floor. Political enterprise and scruples being what they were in those days, Platt's opponents plunked a stepladder in front of his door, and one by one they climbed it to peek through the transom. They were not disappointed. There for all to see was the ex-junior Senator from New York in the arms of what Conkling's biographer called an "unspeakable female." Mission accomplished, the Half Breeds left the hotel.

This story was too good to keep, and soon all of Albany was filled with accounts of the investigation by the "stepladder committee." How long would the papers keep quiet? Not indefinitely, it seems. Platt did not fail to hear of his undoing, nor did he have any doubt as to his own course. On July 1 he announced his withdrawal as a candidate for re-election. He told friends that he did not wish to embarrass Conkling's chances. The next day, Saturday, July 2, 1881, the Albany *Argos* and the New York *World* carried Platt's withdrawal statement along with a delicate but unmistakable account of his downfall.

During the interminable election contest, Arthur and Conkling customarily spent their weekends in New York City. In this merciless heat they were more eager than usual to escape Albany. Their cause had been reduced to the level of a farce. They had become a laughingstock. The future seemed to offer little to a Vice President at odds with his President and to an ex-Senator deserted or embarrassed by his friends.

Shortly after 10 A.M. on Saturday their Hudson River boat docked in Manhattan. They could expect to find the newspaper reporters on hand with their inevitable harassing questions. But the news awaiting Conkling and Arthur was totally unexpected—incredible, shocking, unbelievable.

Less than an hour before, James A. Garfield had been walking through a Washington train station on his way to deliver an out-of-town commencement address. Without warning, a thin bewhiskered man had stepped up behind the President, pointed a gun at his back, and fired two shots. Garfield had crumpled unconscious to the floor.

The assailant made no effort to escape. He stood there waving his revolver, and shouting, "I did it and I want to be arrested. I am a Stalwart and Arthur is President now."

In their first dazed awareness of this tragedy, Arthur and Conkling must have realized vaguely that their careers were approaching turning points. But probably neither could have seen that day that the turning would be in diametrically opposite directions.

Charles J. Guiteau was a drifter and a ne'er-do-well with a craving for publicity and an egotism that knew no bounds. He was devoid of taste and judgment, and was a failure at everything he ever tried to do except when he tried to kill a President. A religious fanatic, he was once a believer in something called Bible Communism. On another occasion, he claimed to be an employee of a firm called Jesus Christ & Co. He had been a clerk in a law office, an insurance salesman, and a lecturer, and he wanted to publish a newspaper. His wife had divorced him on grounds of adultery.

In 1880 he favored the election of Garfield and campaigned for him with great enthusiasm. He wrote a speech entitled "Garfield against Hancock." He hung around Republican headquarters in New York City, distributing copies of his speech. His immediate objective was to obtain, from the Republicans, a paid assignment as a stump speaker, but all the officials to whom he talked turned him down. They regarded him as a nuisance and a crank, but he couldn't understand this. He talked to Vice-Presidential candidate Arthur about ten times during the summer and fall of 1880. He passed out literature urging Garfield's election. When the returns rolled in, Guiteau became convinced that his efforts had proved decisive in the Republican victory, and he set about to get a job in the Garfield administration.

Nor was he at all bashful about the extent of his capacity to serve the new President. His aspirations shifted a couple of times, but he finally decided that he wanted the Paris consulship. Once, at the White House, he pushed through a crowd of fellow office-seekers to confront Garfield personally. He returned again and again to the Executive Mansion, helping himself to official stationery and sending notes in to Garfield asking why his nomination had not been sent to the Senate. He cornered Grant, Arthur, and Blaine, and made similar demands.

Finally, somehow, his wrinkled brain was penetrated by the concept that he was not going to get the appointment. The realization of his failure coincided with the climax of the patronage brawl between Garfield and Conkling. Guiteau came to identify his own rebuff with the defeat handed to the Stalwarts. He had no trouble finding newspaper material denouncing Garfield. The simple-minded Guiteau read and reread editorials and articles describing the impending collapse of the Republican party. On May 18, the Senate confirmed Robertson's appointment, and at this critical juncture Guiteau believed that God himself intervened. On the evening of the eighteenth, he said later, a message from Heaven told him that if Garfield were "removed," everything would be all right again.

From that day on, Guiteau was convinced that he had been

chosen by God to assassinate the President, thereby putting the Stalwart Arthur in the White House. He set about his task with cool calculation. He purchased a revolver with a fancy handle, one that would look impressive in a future museum display. He practiced firing the weapon in a wood along the Potomac, near the White House. He inspected the District of Columbia jail to see if it were a comfortable place to stay. He stalked Garfield throughout the city and passed up several chances to pull the trigger, once because he felt sorry for the ailing Mrs. Garfield at the President's side.

But when he learned that Garfield would be in the railroad station on the morning of July 2, Guiteau decided the time had finally come. First, he wrote two letters. One was addressed to General William Sherman, asking him to supply troops to protect Guiteau against lynch mobs. Another was addressed to the White House, and read in part:

"The President's tragic death was a sad necessity, but it will unite the Republican party and save the Republic. . . .

"I am a stalwart of the stalwarts.

"I was with General Grant and the rest of our men in New York during the canvass. . . ."

Immediately after carrying out God's will, Guiteau was seized and locked up in jail. One of his bullets had gone astray, but the other had struck the vertebrae of the victim's spinal column and become deeply imbedded in the muscles of the back. The President, who soon regained consciousness, was taken back to the White House.

Arthur hurried to Washington, and called at the White House on the evening of July 3. First he saw Mrs. Garfield, and then went to a room in which the Cabinet members had gathered. He paused at the door, expecting an invitation to enter. Instead, no one moved, and every eye confronted the Vice President in silent hostility. Arthur, confused, was about to withdraw when he was recognized by another visitor who hurried forward, welcomed him, and drew him into the room. The Cabinet officers then stepped forward to shake his hand.

The chill that Arthur had felt that night was settling over the country. If Andrew Johnson had been accused of conspiring to kill Lincoln, imagine the miserable position in which Arthur now found himself. Within hours after Garfield fell, the Baltimore *American*, a Republican paper, proclaimed that Guiteau had been "inspired with the same motives" that had guided Grant's bid for a third term. The Charleston *News and Courier*, a Democratic paper, said that ". . . the intrigues of Conkling and the Slanders of Grant" had "wrought up the miserable assassin to the pitch of regarding the death of the President as a political necessity."

Ex-President Hayes sputtered into his diary: "The death of the President at this time would be a national calamity whose consequences we can not now confidently conjecture. Arthur for President! Conkling the power behind the throne, superior to the throne!"

In an anguished letter, a friend of John Sherman wrote, "How fatal a mistake was made at Chicago in the nomination for the second place. The prayer for poor Garfield is *universal.* There is not popular confidence in the possible succession. . . . Yours very sincerely in this hour of apprehension and sorrow."

A headline in the New York *Tribune* summed up the national sentiment in a few words: MURDERED BY THE SPOILS SYSTEM.

Many citizens had never understood how the quarrel over civil-service reform affected them personally. Now, at long last, they began to realize the tremendous stakes involved, even if only through the senseless act of a deranged man who was not a friend of any of the party leaders. But no apparent means seemed to be available by which public opinion could be brought to bear in behalf of reform. In fact, the impact of Guiteau's bullet had very largely paralyzed the entire Federal Government from the President on down. Garfield was incapacitated, and in great pain. Arthur, too compromised to make any effective gesture, moved to Washington and awaited developments. Secretary of State Blaine acted as a regent of sorts, and kept Arthur informed of the President's condition. The Cabinet members handled only routine matters of the type that did not require the attention of the President. The imprisoned Guiteau, confident that the Stalwarts would allow no harm to come to him, called for pen and paper and settled down to write his memoirs.

Conkling returned to Albany, to watch his political life-blood dribble away in the final ballots for the senatorship. Conkling, not the simpleton Guiteau, was the most hated man in America, the target of vile letters and threats. In mid-July, on the fifty-sixth ballot, a successor was finally chosen. Platt, whose misbehavior had been page-one news for a few hours, was temporarily forgotten.

For eleven weeks the President lingered between life and death. During this time he performed a single official act, signing his name to an extradition paper. With great effort, he wrote a letter to his mother. For the first time Americans gave serious thought to the constitutional provision that in the case of a President's disability, his powers and duties "shall devolve on the Vice-President."

No one as yet could reply to the question first raised by John Dickinson, a delegate to the Constitutional Convention in 1787: "What is the extent of the term 'disability' and who is to be the judge of it?"

Arthur made no move to assume Garfield's duties. All persons concerned kept in mind that John Tyler had claimed the Presidency outright—under the same constitutional clause—after Harrison's death. Although the Cabinet members agreed unanimously that Garfield was not able to function as President, they feared that once the powers and duties (and the office?) devolved upon Arthur, they could not be restored to Garfield, should he recover.

Arthur returned to New York City in August, where he remained in seclusion from all but a few close friends. He could not turn to his wife for comfort; she had died in January, 1880. The strain, compounded by cruel attacks directed at him by some elements of the press, almost broke Arthur's own health. During this period of self-imposed silence, the Vice President had ample opportunity to reflect on his past associations and activities, and on the events that had brought him to the threshold of the Presidency.

On August 27, word came that the patient had developed complications and would surely die. But life ebbed slowly, as Garfield yielded reluctantly to a spreading infection introduced by unsterile attempts to explore the wound.

Garfield loved the sea, and he longed to return to the Atlantic shore. Doctors, with painstaking care, and hoping for a miracle, arranged to have the dying man borne to a house in the seaside town of Elberon, New Jersey. There his family gathered, along with the doctors and members of the Cabinet, all waiting for the end.

Meanwhile, the newspapers began to prepare their readers for the change of command. They now pictured the Vice President in more charitable terms. He was described as a gentleman of good intentions and modest ability. All agreed that the greatest danger to the country lay in his friendship with Roscoe Conkling.

About midnight on September 19, Arthur heard a clamor in front of his Lexington Avenue home. A servant went to the door, but Arthur did not wait for the message to be conveyed in the usual manner. A reporter looked past the Negro at the door, saw Arthur hurrying forward, and shouted to him that Garfield had died.

The worst fears of the country were not realized. Arthur did not open the back door of the White House to Conkling, and the former Senator did not presume to attempt to turn the clock back to the years of Grant. To begin with, Conkling was out of office. Secondly, public opinion would not tolerate a return to the ways of the past, and Conkling knew it. He made little effort even to reply to the abuse directed at him from all sides. Once he exclaimed, "How can I speak into a grave? How can I do battle with a shroud? Silence is a duty and a doom!"

Once, Conkling did come to Washington to ask a favor of the President. He wanted William Robertson removed as Collector of the Port of New York. Arthur could not have missed the irony in the opportunity to expel the official now holding the office from which he had been fired only four short years before. The two old friends conferred at the White House for five hours. After the meeting, a reporter spotted Conkling at a Washington train station. His face seemed almost black with rage, and his eyes flamed with the old-time wrath. Robertson did not lose his job.

Guiteau, meanwhile, was put on trial for his life. The conduct of both the defense and the prosecution was a disgrace. The District Attorney spent days merely proving that

Garfield had been murdered. He offered a section of Garfield's backbone as an exhibit, which even Guiteau was reportedly permitted to pick up and examine.

The slayer said he was present in the courtroom as an agent of the Deity. He said that God knew what He was doing when He inspired him to assassinate the President, and he cited an editorial from the New York *Herald* saying that Arthur's first two months in office had been an improvement over the same period under Garfield. The assassin's defense was conducted by his brother-in-law, who clearly lacked an understanding of criminal law. The defendant was allowed to lecture the court daily and to interrupt the lawyers and the witnesses. Guiteau's lawyer argued that he was insane, and that Garfield had died not as a result of the bullet, but because of his doctors' incompetence. It was all a fine show and drew large crowds.

Guiteau received as many as one hundred favorable letters and telegrams a day during his stay in prison. The defendant, not missing a trick, called on Arthur and others whose careers he felt he had advanced to contribute money to his defense. In a grim foreshadowing of events in Dallas in 1963, Guiteau was shot at twice while in custody. One of his own guards fired at him through the window of his cell, grazing his head. A drunk shot at him while he was being transported through the streets from the courtroom to his cell, but the bullet only nicked his arm.

Guiteau was found to be sane and guilty, and he was sentenced to hang. Arthur refused to grant a reprieve. The pathetic, almost childlike killer went to the scaffold in June, 1882, reciting a poem he had composed, which went in part:

I saved my party and my land;
Glory Hallelujah!
But they have murdered me for it
And that is the reason
I am going to the Lordy.
Glory Hallelujah! Glory Hallelujah!
I am going to the Lordy.

Arthur, it turned out, was not the complete stranger to civil-service reform that most people supposed. As collector at the Custom House he had approved the use of tests to eliminate the unqualified and to discourage others from trying. In accepting the Vice-Presidential nomination, he had endorsed reform. But not until an assassin's bullet lifted him to the Presidency did a somewhat chastened Arthur spell out his proposals on the subject. In his first annual message to Congress he suggested principles that might be incorporated into law: "Original appointments should be based upon ascertained fitness. The tenure of office should be stable. Positions of responsibility should, so far as practicable, be filled by the promotion of worthy and efficient officers. The investigation of all complaints and the punishment of all official misconduct should be prompt and thorough."

For some time the leading exponent of reform had been Senator George H. Pendleton of Ohio.[1] His efforts had gained nothing until Garfield was shot and Arthur took up the cause with energy. Then, in the Congressional elections of 1882, the issue proved decisive in a number of districts.

In his second annual message in December, 1882, Arthur said action could no longer be postponed. A bill was quickly passed and sent to the President. On January 16, 1883, the man who had once been ousted from a job in the name of clean government signed the Pendleton Act into law. The act incorporated the proposals called for by Arthur in his first message to Congress. A Civil Service Commission was established to administer the system. This law protected only a small percentage of the government payroll, but it permitted the President to increase the number of merit employees from time to time. The Pendleton Act is still the cornerstone of the civil-service system.

At the time of Garfield's death, one of Arthur's associates had exclaimed, "Chet Arthur, President of the United States! Good God!" If this attitude was shared by the country, the alarm proved unfounded. In addition to his efforts in behalf of the Pendleton Act, Arthur gave the country honest, efficient leadership in all other respects. He saw to it that the Govern-

[1] Pendleton had been the Democratic Vice-Presidential candidate in 1864 on the ticket with General McClellan. McClellan (thirty-seven) and Pendleton (thirty-nine) were the youngest team of candidates ever to seek national election. They were defeated by Lincoln and Andrew Johnson.

ment pressed its prosecution of some Republicans accused of mail fraud. He fought for tariff revision, preservation of the national forests, Federal aid to education, tax reform, and a stronger Navy. Blaine retired to write history, and Arthur changed all but one of his Cabinet members. Although his new official family was mildly Stalwart in complexion, its balanced composition and quality showed that Arthur wished to follow a moderate course.

Arthur put behind him the anguish he had felt at the time of Garfield's illness and death. His Presidency was marked by the same unruffled amiability that had characterized his previous career. The White House became the scene of glittering social activities and literary chatter. One of Arthur's first acts as President was to supervise personally a renovation of his new home. Twenty-four wagonloads of furniture were hauled away. Many of these items were to be the objects of a nationwide search by Mrs. Jacqueline Kennedy and her committee during another renovation eighty years later.

In advance of the 1884 election, the sympathetic Chicago *Daily News* solicited comments on Arthur's Presidency from prominent citizens. A typical reply came from Henry Ward Beecher, who wrote in part, "I can hardly imagine how he could have done better."

But many in the Republican party still regarded Arthur as a political accident, and their loyalty remained with James G. Blaine. The latter came out of retirement to seek the nomination in 1884, and even Platt conceded that Blaine's turn had come. Arthur hoped to win a nomination that had eluded Tyler, Fillmore, and Andrew Johnson. He ran a close race with the Plumed Knight for four ballots at the Republican convention, but lost. The remnants of the Stalwart organization supported Arthur, simply because they had no one else. But to his disappointment, the President did not receive the votes of the reformers.

Arthur left the White House with the approval of most of the public and the press. Thanks to his judgment, poise, and dignity, the nation had weathered a most difficult period, and the public had gained a greater respect for the national government and the institution of the Presidency. But after leaving office, Arthur had little time to enjoy his new status as a statesman. His overindulgence in food and his generally soft living had taken a toll, and the ex-President died in November, 1886, at the age of fifty-six.

Blaine, meanwhile, had been defeated in the 1884 Presidential race. Conkling, his rival chieftain and great antagonist of but a few short years before, continued to practice law in New York, cloaked in bitter obscurity. In a favorite night spot, surrounded by raconteurs and journalists, he drank away the evenings of his last years. Seemingly willing to defy nature as he had always defied his human opponents, Conkling was among the few who dared to brave Manhattan's famous Blizzard of 1888. With transportation paralyzed during this monstrous storm, Conkling walked the two miles from City Hall to Madison Square, a trek that required from two to three hours. Once again he had been unable to measure the force of his opposition. Trapped in a white wilderness, the old Stalwart boss was overpowered, as Stoddard suggested, by the wrath of the Storm King.

Long after contemporaries had forgotten the mindless babbling of Guiteau and the haughty pronouncements of Conkling, they would remember Blaine's eulogy to Garfield. In February, 1882, before a joint session of Congress, the great orator from Maine reviewed the life of the former President. Many believed that Blaine had precipitated the quarrel between Garfield and the Stalwarts, but in his eulogy he spoke candidly and tastefully of the events leading to the assassination. At this point it seemed to reporters that President Arthur paled slightly and settled a bit deeper into his seat. But the most memorable part of Blaine's address was the peroration, the account of Garfield's final trip from Washington to the house by the sea.

"Gently, silently, the love of a great people bore the pale sufferer to the longed-for healing of the sea, to live or die, as God should will, within sight of its heaving billows, within sound of its manifold voices. With wan, fevered face tenderly lifted to the cooling breeze, he looked out wistfully upon the ocean's changing wonders,—on its far sails, whitening in the morning light; on its restless waves, rolling shoreward to break or die beneath the noonday sun; on the red clouds of evening, arching low to the horizon, on the serene and shining pathway of the stars. Let us think that his dying eyes read a mystic meaning which only the rapt and parting soul may know. Let us believe that in the silence of the receding world he heard the great waves breaking on a farther shore, and felt already on his wasted brow the breath of the eternal morning."

★ ★ ★ ★ ★ ★ ★

THEODORE ROOSEVELT

"We have done the best we could.

Now it is up to you to live."

A liberal professor of mine once conceded grudgingly that Senator Robert Taft was occasionally right, "but for all the wrong reasons."

In 1901, the great Theodore Roosevelt became President of the United States—but for all the wrong reasons. As an Assistant Secretary of the Navy in 1898 he had provoked the peaceable William McKinley and kept the department in a turmoil with his demands for a showdown with Spain. When war did come, he abandoned his job, dashing off to seek fame in a military career that lasted less than four months. His greatest glory came for leading a disorganized, foolhardy charge up Cuba's San Juan Hill, an event so romanticized that we have forgotten the senseless and considerable spilling of blood, and the heroic defense by the outmanned Spaniards. After a term as Governor of New York, he was pushed into the Vice Presidency by political enemies determined to bury him in an office where he could cause them no more trouble. Finally, the assassination of McKinley elevated Roosevelt to the office that had been his ultimate goal.

Yet after succeeding McKinley, Roosevelt needed neither war nor depression, nor any similar crisis, to make his mark as an outstanding President. Our first modern Chief Executive, he seized the reins of power as no predecessor had. He sent the fleet around the world, dug the Panama Canal, mediated one war and helped delay another, joined forces with the more responsible muckrakers to inaugurate the Progressive Era, preserved millions of acres of forest land for future generations, and performed all these feats and many others with a flair and a zest that made his achievements seem larger than life.

At the end of the Spanish War, Teddy believed that he could ride his popularity all the way to the top, but he needed some office in which to hang his hat until McKinley retired. There was, of course, the governorship of New York; the occupant of that office is almost automatically a Presidential contender. Roosevelt was elected governor in 1898 in the first flush of his Cuban heroics, but the term was for only two years, and he would have to run again in 1900. However, he had already gotten into hot water in Albany by advocating laws to bring corporations under public regulation. Businessmen carried their complaints to the New York Republican political boss, who was none other than Thomas Collier Platt, now older, more cadaverous, and a Senator once again. Platt had spent years battling his way back into political power, and now the young rough-riding war hero was causing him trouble. Roosevelt not only angered the businessmen, but he clashed with Platt over the distribution of state patronage.

Platt decided to get Roosevelt out of New York. He hit upon the idea of persuading him to run for Vice President with McKinley in 1900. McKinley's first Vice President, Garret Hobart, had died in office in 1899. In view of the events of 1880 and 1881, it is surprising that Platt still should have regarded the Vice-Presidential nomination as a means of getting rid of anybody. At any rate, he had a large selling job on his hands. Not only did he have to persuade Roosevelt to run, but he had to win the approval of McKinley and the convention delegates. The New York boss began by appealing to Roosevelt's egotism, and was so successful that the Governor did not realize at first what lay behind the suggestion. Roosevelt was already thinking about what course he should follow in 1900. He was aware that he enjoyed tremendous public popularity, and that he could probably win the Vice-Presidential nomination. But he liked being Governor, and knew that he would not be happy as presiding officer of the Senate. He conceded that the second office was an "honorable place," but argued that he was a young man (forty-one) and there would not be much for him to do. Edith Roosevelt sought to discourage her husband from running, pointing out that he would grow restless at being a figurehead.

One of Roosevelt's closest friends, Senator Henry Cabot Lodge, Sr., of Massachusetts, recognized the validity of these objections, but urged Roosevelt to weigh his decision carefully. Lodge wrote to his friend: "It is the tradition of our politics, and a very poor tradition, that the Vice-presidency is a shelf. It ought to be, and there is no reason why it should not be, a stepping-stone. Put there by the popular desire, it would be so to you."

Roosevelt and Lodge were both students and writers of history, and they engaged in a bit of sparring on what the lessons of the past had taught. Roosevelt pointed out that Silas Wright refused the Vice-Presidential nomination in 1844, "came back and ran for Governor and was elected by a larger majority than that by which Polk carried the state." Lodge wrote back: "I have forgotten the incident of Silas Wright but let me call your attention to the fact that he was never President, whereas Van Buren was!"

About this time Roosevelt finally realized the purpose behind Platt's Vice-Presidential talk. The Governor wrote to Platt, saying: "The more I have thought over it, the more I have felt that I would a great deal rather be anything, say professor of history, than Vice-President."

Having decided to stay in New York and fight for a second term as Governor, with or without Platt's support, Roosevelt put a great deal of energy into discouraging talk that he would accept second place on the ticket in 1900. He sent Professor Nicholas Murray Butler of Columbia University to the Capital in March. Butler told the Republican national chairman, Mark Hanna, that Roosevelt didn't want the nomination. Hanna considered Teddy some sort of a wild man and his nightmares were filled with visions of Roosevelt being elected Vice President and then succeeding to the Presidency by accident. Hanna banged his fist on the table and told Butler that he (Hanna) would control the convention, and that Roosevelt would not get the nomination.

Roosevelt hustled to Washington himself and assured every

one who needed to know that he did not want to be Vice President. He was somewhat taken aback when the older hands in the McKinley administration were all too willing to agree with him. "Of course not, Theodore, you're not fit for it," said Secretary of War Elihu Root.

"I think you are unduly alarmed," Secretary of State John Hay chimed in. "There is no instance of an election of a Vice-President by violence."

Lodge warned Roosevelt that if he went to the Philadelphia convention he would be nominated, and that if he really didn't wish to be chosen, he should stay away. Roosevelt went to Philadelphia. Hanna was also on the scene, fulminating against the rising tide of enthusiasm for Roosevelt.

Hanna was a wealthy Ohio banker who had taken up Presidential kingmaking as something of a hobby. In 1888, he had promoted one of John Sherman's several abortive Presidential tries. Hanna then looked around for another prospect, and found one in William McKinley. For years he built up McKinley as a Presidential candidate, spending lavishly in the process. The two men became close friends. Both possessed a large amount of political acumen, and the pay-off came in 1896, with McKinley's nomination and election to the Presidency. Hanna became national chairman and United States Senator from Ohio.

But by the summer of 1900, Hanna had been slowed a bit by age (he was sixty-two), by rheumatism, by a heart ailment, and by a temporary fear of a falling out with McKinley. He also failed to recognize the genuine enthusiasm for Roosevelt among the delegates and in the Republican rank and file. He was skeptical of Roosevelt's insistence that he was not a candidate. Hanna intended to poke around Philadelphia and come up with someone to stop the New York Governor. But many leading possibilities did not want the Vice Presidency, and others were not wanted by the delegates.

Hanna hoped and expected that McKinley would speak up and give some direction to the convention. But the President remained in the Capital, conveying his sentiments in the third person through a chain of secretaries posted in Washington and Philadelphia. The first message from the President came on Sunday night, June 17, two days before the convention would open. Hanna was not cheered to learn: "The President has no choice for Vice-President. Any of the distinguished names suggested would be satisfactory to him. The choice of the convention will be his choice, he has no advice to give. . . ."

Hanna failed to realize that intervention by the President in behalf of someone other than Roosevelt would have been taken by the delegates as an attempt to thwart their will. Such a move by McKinley probably would have failed; at the same time his prestige would have been reduced and the party would have been divided. Roosevelt had a firm hold on many delegates, especially on those from the West, who remembered his early days as a rancher, and his sturdy espousal of Americanism, integrity, and hard work, virtues applauded by the men and women west of the Mississippi. His charge up San Juan Hill had merely been the frosting on the cake for these Roosevelt fans.

McKinley, above the battle, seemed to sense the mood of the convention better than Hanna. He apparently concluded that if Roosevelt were to be nominated, it should be the result of an outpouring of popular sentiment by the delegates, not because Platt wanted to get him out of New York. By remaining neutral, McKinley permitted the enthusiasm of the delegates to take its course.

Ordinarily, Hanna could count on an alliance of state bosses and patronage-hungry Southern delegates to force through any nomination. But New York's Platt was already defying him, and Platt found a convention ally in the Pennsylvania leader, Matthew Quay, who had an old score to settle with Hanna. In 1899, Quay had stood for re-election to the Senate, but the Pennsylvania legislature was unable to choose a Senator. The Governor of Pennsylvania reappointed Quay to the "vacancy." This somewhat unorthodox action was challenged by the Senate itself, and by a narrow margin—Hanna's opposition—Quay was refused his old seat. Quay came to the Philadelphia convention determined to be for any candidate Hanna was against—and that meant Roosevelt.

On Monday, Hanna talked to McKinley by phone from his hotel room in Philadelphia. The national chairman hung up the receiver in despair, just as Wisconsin national committeeman Henry Payne walked into the room to ask about a credentials dispute.

"Do whatever you damn please!" Hanna snapped. "I'm through! I won't have anything more to do with the convention! I won't take charge of the campaign! I won't be chairman of the national committee again!"

"Why, what's the matter?" Payne asked.

"Matter!" Hanna shouted. "Matter! Why, everybody's gone crazy! What is the matter with all of you? Here's this convention going headlong for Roosevelt for Vice President. Don't any of you realize that there's only one life between that madman and the Presidency? Platt and Quay are no better than idiots! What harm can he do as Governor of New York compared to the damage he will do as President if McKinley should die?"

"You control the convention," Payne said. "Why don't you nominate another man?"

"I am not in control!" Hanna exclaimed. "McKinley won't let me use the power of the Administration to defeat Roosevelt. He is blind, or afraid, or something!"

Hanna had asked the President to permit him to threaten officeholders with loss of influence at the White House if they voted for Roosevelt. McKinley rejected such a maneuver.

In desperation Hanna asked Roosevelt himself to say again that he did not want the nomination. The latter issued a rather weak-kneed statement that he thought he could serve the party best by being renominated for Governor of New York. He called on his friends to respect his wishes and judgment.

The next day, Tuesday, June 19, Hanna called the convention to order. Shortly after twelve thirty, Roosevelt strode into the hall and down the aisle toward the New York standard. He wore a wide-brimmed black hat reminiscent of the type he used in the Cuban campaign. Applause and cheers swept the convention and followed him all the way to his seat. He paid no attention, and did not remove his hat. On the platform, a smile faded from Hanna's face.

On Tuesday night, McKinley sent another third-person message to Philadelphia. The Administration, he declared, "has no candidate. The convention must make the nomination; the Administration would not if it could. . . ." McKinley ordered his friends not to dictate to the convention.

Hanna, his fears rising and falling like the line on a fever chart, was heartened by a development in the New York delegation. On Tuesday night, at a caucus, Platt dropped the veil of pretense on why he supported Roosevelt for Vice President. He told the Governor that if he refused to accept the nomination at Philadelphia, he would be beaten for renomination in New York (and it is quite possible that Platt had the votes to back up his threat, notwithstanding Roosevelt's popularity). Roosevelt, in his autobiography, gave his reply to Platt: "I answered that I would accept the challenge, that we would have a straight-out fight on the proposition, and that I would begin it at once by telling the assembled delegates of the threat, and giving fair warning that I intended to fight for the Governorship nomination, and, moreover, that I intended to get it." This, according to Roosevelt, brought Platt to terms. The New York delegation agreed to pledge its Vice-Presidential votes to its lieutenant governor, Timothy Woodruff. Hanna was smiling again, but not for long.

Teddy's Western friends were up in arms. If New York wouldn't support its own Governor, the West would come to his aid. A spontaneous movement swept the city. Now no one could say that Roosevelt was the candidate of the bosses. Platt had backed down. The delegates would decide.

However, it was another boss, Pennsylvania's Quay, who drove the final nail into the coffin of the stop-Roosevelt movement. On Wednesday morning he introduced a resolution providing that in the future state representations at the national convention should be determined not by the whole population of the state, but by the size of the Republican vote in each state. This suggestion panicked the Southern delegations, many of them controlled by Negroes. The Southerners counted few Republican votes on Election Day, but relied on the continued dole of federal patronage from the national committee when the Republicans were in power. Ordinarily, they took orders from Hanna. After Quay sat down, the Southerners milled around in confusion, trying to find out what he was up to. They did not have long to wait. Quay passed the word that if they pledged their votes to Roosevelt, he would forget his resolution. Quay had gained his revenge, had clinched the nomination for Roosevelt, and had destroyed Hanna's iron grip on the Southerners.

After this development, other Vice Presidential hopefuls withdrew. Hanna, one of our most skillful political leaders, had taken the worst licking of his life, and he conceded defeat. He told a press conference on Wednesday night that Roosevelt would be nominated. To make it all official, Teddy bowed to the sentiment of the convention, declaring: "I cannot disappoint my Western friends, if they insist. . . . I cannot seem to be bigger than the party."

Next day, amid the usual parading and waving of banners, McKinley and Roosevelt were nominated unanimously. Unlike the convention of 1880, these Republicans had no further time for bitterness or carping criticism. The country was prosperous, we had just fought a "splendid little war," the American flag was being planted across the Pacific, Republican election prospects were never brighter, and to top it off, a brand-new century was at hand.

The wide-eyed optimism and good humor of the delegates was reflected by Chauncey M. Depew in his speech seconding Roosevelt's nomination. Depew, one of the most popular after-dinner speakers of his time, offered a tongue-in-cheek endorsement of the Roosevelt candidacy. Instead of invoking memories of a birth in a log cabin—hardly appropriate in this case—Depew offered the candidate as "the child of Fifth Avenue," and the "child of the exclusiveness of Harvard." He traced the Rough Rider's career as cowboy, Assistant Secretary of the Navy, and soldier. One paragraph must have made the candidate blush:

"At Santiago, a modest voice was heard, exceedingly polite, addressing a militia regiment laying upon the ground, while the Spanish bullets were flying over them. The voice said: 'Get to one side gentlemen . . . that my men can get out.' And when this polite man got his men out in the open where they could face the bayonet and face the bullet there was a transformation, and the transformation was that the dude had become a cowboy, the cowboy had become a soldier, the soldier had become a hero, and rushing up the hill, pistol in hand, the polite man shouted to the militiamen lying down: 'Give them hell, boys! Give them hell!' "

The crowd roared, and the banners were waved aloft. Hanna was more subdued. "We have done the best we could," he told his friend McKinley. "Now it is up to you to live."

Once nominated, Roosevelt churned all his customary energy into the election campaign. He was "as strong as a bull moose," he told reporters, and he stumped the country with great success. Teddy's flag-waving nationalism, his appeals in behalf of honesty and dedication to principle, and his criticisms directed at corporate wealth helped rally the younger and more progressive voters. He rivaled the Democratic Presidential candidate, William Jennings Bryan, in popularity.

Hanna, the old pro, forgot his threat to quit the campaign. In fact, his national committee was so well organized that he found time to do some campaigning himself. He delivered seventy-two speeches in one week, made a big hit with his audiences, and disproved his caricature by critical cartoonists as a dollar-grabbing plutocrat.

McKinley and Roosevelt were elected. The bands quit playing, the crowds stopped cheering, and the Vice Presidency in all its emptiness closed in on the restless hero of San Juan Hill.

"I fear my bolt is shot," he said.

Roosevelt had attended law school for one year. He thought he might be able to complete his course while Vice President, then take a bar exam and get into a New York firm. He sought advice from Alton B. Parker, then Chief Judge of the Court of Appeals of New York. In one of the quirks of history, Judge Parker would be Roosevelt's Democratic opponent in the Presidential race three years later.

On the afternoon of September 6, 1901, William McKinley held a public reception in the spacious Temple of Music at the Pan-American Exhibition in Buffalo. Hundreds of persons waited in line for hours for the privilege of shaking the President's hand. Among them was a short clean-shaven young anarchist named Leon Czolgosz. The expression on his face was vacant. His right hand was bandaged. At 4 P.M. the reception line began to move, and Czolgosz moved with it. From the hall's great organ, the strains of a Bach sonata carried across the crowd. Czolgosz, bandaged hand and all, shuffled toward the smiling President, past the Secret Service guards, past a squad of Exposition police, past several Buffalo city detectives, past ten artillerymen in full-dress uniform. At 4:07 he stopped in front of the President, who obligingly reached out to shake his unwrapped hand. But Czolgosz raised his right hand instead. Two shots exploded out of the bandage, one of them ripping through the President's stomach.

Later, Czolgosz said simply, "I thought it would be a good thing for the country to kill the President."

That same day, Vice President Roosevelt was speaking at a gathering of the Vermont Fish and Game League on the Isle La Motte in Lake Champlain. When he learned of the shooting, he rushed to Buffalo by special train from Burlington, Vermont. He remained in the city until September 10, when he was told by the doctors that McKinley would recover.

Roosevelt, perhaps to reassure the country, left Buffalo to join his family in the Adirondacks. On Friday, the thirteenth of September, Roosevelt and some friends climbed Mount Marcy. At 2 P.M. they were eating lunch beside a brook when a man came huffing up the trail. He carried a message saying that the President was dying. Roosevelt returned to his base camp early that evening, rested for two hours, and then began his celebrated dash back to civilization by buckboard, down gutted mountain roads and past precipitous cliffs. Relays of horses and drivers brought him to the village of North Creek, thirty-five miles away, where a special train waited.

He arrived in Buffalo at one thirty on the afternoon of the fourteenth. McKinley had died early that morning, his last words being from a favorite hymn, "Nearer, My God, to Thee."

Hanna's grief was augmented by bitterness. "I told William McKinley it was a mistake to nominate that wild man at Philadelphia. . . . Now look, that damned cowboy is President of the United States."

After taking the oath, Roosevelt pledged "to continue, absolutely unbroken, the policy of President McKinley for the peace, the prosperity, and the honor of our beloved country."

But he also told reporters: "I was voted for as vice president, it is true, but the Constitution provides that in the case of the death or inability of the President, the Vice President shall serve as President and, therefore, due to the act of a madman, I am President and shall act in every word and deed precisely as if I and not McKinley had been the candidate for whom the electors cast the vote for President."

Roosevelt actually struck a happy medium somewhere between these two positions. He was wise enough to listen to the advice of Hanna, Hay, Root, and the others, while at the same time he shaped a program far different from McKinley's.

Hanna, although no longer in so powerful a position of influence as he had once been, became something of a statesman during his last years in the Senate. His feeling toward Roosevelt softened considerably. But Hanna, as a symbol of the *ancien regime*, became the rallying point of that element within the Republican party that stopped short at the edge of the twentieth century and refused to advance any further. There was talk of Hanna-for-President-in-1904. The Ohio Senator discouraged such speculation, but he never shut the door firmly enough to suit Roosevelt. The President was well aware of the jinx on accidental Presidents who tried to win terms of their own. What Hanna would have done or could have done to stop Roosevelt in 1904 will never be known, because the National Chairman died in February of that year. No one on the horizon was big enough to challenge Roosevelt, who was renominated and re-elected overwhelmingly.

Nineteen hundred was a watershed year for the Vice Presidency. As Teddy Roosevelt entered the White House, the United States was entering a century and an age from which there was no turning back. Roosevelt, who grasped instantly the meaning of the Spanish War, was well aware of the international role America must play in the years to come. He was uniquely qualified to serve as ringmaster during the exciting years of domestic reform and incipient imperialism. With the advance of United States Presidents to the front ranks of world statesmen, and in the wake of three assassinations in thirty-six years, the importance of the Vice Presidents inevitably increased. While they might still fall short of what potential Chief Executives ideally should be, rarely again would we see nominations given to the likes of "Boozy Gratz" Brown and Schuyler Colfax. But the job itself was still a bore, and means of making the office useful would not readily be found.

The other late-nineteenth-century Vice-Presidential nominees—the winners as well as the losers—have been largely forgotten. They were all prominent men in their own time, but they have left little mark on our history. The Vice Presidency was a dead-end street for almost all who served. Most of the Vice Presidents during this period had little or nothing to do with affairs of state.

Republican Vice-Presidential nominees between 1884 and 1896 were John A. Logan of Illinois, Levi P. Morton of New York, Whitelaw Reid of New York, and Garret A. Hobart of New Jersey. Morton and Hobart were elected. Morton, after passing up a chance to run with Garfield in 1880, ran with Benjamin Harrison eight years later. He was denied renomination, but later served a term as Governor of New York.

Hobart served with McKinley from 1897 to 1899, when he died in office. The President frequently sought his advice on important matters. Had he survived, Hobart might have been renominated in 1900, thereby closing the door to Theodore Roosevelt.

Late-nineteenth-century Democratic candidates for Vice President included Thomas A. Hendricks of Indiana (twice, 1876 and 1884), William H. English of Indiana (1880), Allen G. Thurman of Ohio (1888), Adlai E. Stevenson of Illinois (twice, 1892 and 1900), and Arthur Sewall of Maine (1896).

English had been out of public life for nearly twenty years when placed on the ticket with Hancock. However, he had become the president of a large bank, and it was hoped he would make a generous campaign contribution after being awarded the nomination. The Republicans, meanwhile, made English an issue in the campaign. One of their documents took note of his baldness, his full beard dyed black, the many mortgages he had foreclosed, and the fact that he owned a theater in Indianapolis.

Hendricks, after being defeated for Vice President in 1876, won the second time around with Cleveland in 1884. He died in office in 1885.

Stevenson was an assistant postmaster general during Grover Cleveland's first term, and he had the task of removing 40,000 Republican postmasters to make room for deserving Democrats. Partly in appreciation for this service, he was placed on the ticket with Cleveland in 1892. In 1893, Cleveland underwent a secret operation for the removal of a growth on the roof of his mouth, from which he quickly recovered. Thus, the long-forgotten Adlai Stevenson actually held a higher office and brushed closer to the Presidency than his more famous grandson and namesake who was defeated so badly by Dwight Eisenhower in 1952 and 1956.

For a few years early in this century, party tickets were marked by an "ideology gap." As enthusiasm for the Square Deal, the New Freedom, and the New Nationalism swept convention halls and political rallies, the remnants of orthodoxy clung tenaciously to the Vice Presidency as a consolation prize. Presidential nominees had not yet come to the point of dictating their choices for running mates. Party leaders tended to pick for the Vice Presidency true-blue conservatives more in line with their own thinking, which ran about a generation behind that of the rank and file.

Presidents gradually thought more about putting their Vice Presidents to work. Roosevelt, in 1896, said that he favored giving the Vice President a seat in the Cabinet and a vote in the Senate. However, his own Vice President from 1905 to 1909 was Charles W. Fairbanks of Indiana, a party stalwart out of tune with the times. He and TR drifted apart almost from the first. Finally, Fairbanks allied himself with House Speaker Joe Cannon and others to fight the President's program in Congress.

Roosevelt didn't bother to conceal his low opinion of his Vice President. And when humorist Finley Peter Dunne heard Teddy might take a trip in a submarine, he advised the President: ". . . you really shouldn't do it—unless you take Fairbanks with you."

In 1908, Roosevelt forced the Republicans to nominate William Howard Taft for President, and the surly delegates chose the orthodox James Sherman of New York to run with him. The two failed to get along during an administration when nothing seemed to go right. At the 1912 convention, the party split down the middle between Taft and Roosevelt; when the latter saw that he was beaten, he led his supporters out the door and into the Bull Moose party. The forlorn delegates left behind duly renominated the President. And then, with a one-minute speech and a complete lack of enthusiasm, Sherman was named for a second term. Never before had a major party given a Vice-Presidential nomination to the same person twice in succession. In this most memorable of Presidential years, a shopworn tradition was dropped without notice. Sherman, however, died a few days before the election, and 3,500,000 persons voted for a dead man. Taft himself finished a poor third behind Wilson and Roosevelt.[1]

The Democrats had reached an extreme of sorts in 1904 by nominating eighty-year-old Henry Gassaway Davis of West Virginia for Vice President, but the expectation that the wealthy candidate would appreciate the honor with a large check was not fulfilled. In 1908, the Democrats chose Senator John Kern of Indiana for the second office. Kern had never held any high office, though he later served a term in the Senate. The *Nation* grumbled about the "flippant way" in which the parties were filling out their national tickets.

[1] In Milwaukee, during the 1912 campaign, Roosevelt was shot by a man named John Shrank, who said McKinley's ghost had appeared to him twice, and had asked him to revenge his death at the hands of Roosevelt. The bullet fractured Roosevelt's rib and lodged short of his right lung. The ex-President insisted on delivering his speech before going to a hospital. It is unlikely that the stunned audience remembered much of what he said. Roosevelt recovered.

★ ★ ★ ★ ★ ★ ★ ★

THOMAS R. MARSHALL

"I could throw this country into civil war, but I won't."

Three Vice Presidents have had the opportunity to assume the powers and duties of the Presidency under the constitutional provision dealing with disability.

All three, each under somewhat different circumstances, chose not to act. The first, Chester Arthur, in whose cause Garfield's assassin had pulled the trigger, would have provoked a stormy reaction from the public had he moved a muscle in the direction of the White House before Garfield's death. But no truly urgent problems confronted the nation in 1881.

Such would not be the case thirty-eight years later, when an issue crucial to the future of the world hung in the balance during a President's illness. But a veil of secrecy drawn around the White House obscured the true situation, with perhaps serious consequences for us all.

The sequence of events leading to a most melancholy personal and public tragedy began at the Democratic National Convention at Baltimore in 1912. Woodrow Wilson had been nominated for President after forty-six exhausting ballots. The convention then selected Thomas R. Marshall—Indiana lawyer, philosopher, and governor—for Vice President for all the traditional reasons: the Hoosier balanced the ticket geographically, his state had swung 29 important votes to Wilson during the balloting, he represented a pivotal state, and he had the good fortune of being promoted for national office by a skilled Democratic boss, Tom Taggart of Indiana.

This nomination was the beginning of an unusual relationship between Wilson, the tall, scholarly, college professor, and Marshall, a self-effacing little man who decided that he was too small to look dignified in a Prince Albert coat. Marshall symbolized—if anyone did—the "good old days" to which many political candidates evidently wish to return. A graduate of Wabash College, he studied law in the office of Judge Walter Olds of Fort Wayne, and was admitted to the Indiana bar on his twenty-first birthday. He took up the practice of law in Columbia City, Indiana, and there he remained for one third of a century, whiling away the years of a lazy age when the troubles of Nicholas II and Kaiser Wilhelm seemed as remote as the harvest moon reflected in the waters of the Wabash.

Marshall was a Democrat by birth. His grandfather once said that he was willing to take his chances on Hell, but not on the Republican party. In those days the Democratic creed bore little resemblance to the philosophy that Franklin Roosevelt would espouse in a later generation. Marshall declared that every man had a right to "his chance in life, unhampered and unaided by legislative enactment."

Marshall made his mark in Columbia City, a small town of 3,000. He became an enthusiastic Mason, eventually attaining the thirty-third degree. He was an active church worker, a popular temperance speaker—and a heavy drinker. The young lawyer was as much at ease with local bankers, ditch diggers, the town drunks, and ministers of the gospel as he would someday be with diplomats and kings. At the age of forty-one, Marshall was lulled into matrimony. Three years later, he put down the bottle for the last time, a step apparently taken at the insistence of his wife.

Opportunity knocked for Marshall in 1908, at the Democratic state convention. The fifty-four-year-old lawyer, who had never held political office, allowed his name to be placed in nomination for Governor, and when the leading candidates became deadlocked, the delegates turned on the fifth ballot to the man from Columbia City. Marshall was elected by a narrow margin.

The new Governor found citizens arguing about such issues as reinstatement of Sunday baseball, changes in the liquor laws, stream pollution, and timber conservation. He successfully sponsored an extensive program of labor and social legislation and in short order attained some degree of reputation beyond the borders of his state, a reputation that led to his nomination for Vice President in 1912. Wilson and Marshall won easily, since the Republicans were split by the Bull Moose revolt.

In 1913, President Wilson embarked on his program of domestic reform known as the New Freedom. At first he regarded his Vice President as a "small calibre" man, and although his assessment of the Hoosier grew more favorable in later years, the two were never close and Marshall never had a real part in Wilson's programs.

The new Vice President seemed willing to test his oratorical skills on unfamiliar audiences, though he must have presented a curious picture to people seeing him for the first time. He weighed about 125 pounds, and his most striking feature was a large gray mustache. Kindly, generous, and observant, he nonetheless committed an almost irreparable gaffe in one of his first public appearances as Vice President.

In a speech at a Jefferson Day dinner in New York City in 1913, Marshall startled his well-heeled auditors by warning that the tendency of wealthy men to accumulate vast fortunes must be curbed, or the nation might face socialism or paternalism. He declared that a man's right to inherit property was not a natural right but a mere privilege granted to him by the Government. He asserted that all estates above an exemption limit of $100,000 should revert to the state.

A rumble of protests greeted this assertion by the Hoosier philosopher. The *Literary Digest* remarked: "Amid the crash of precedents that are being broken these days . . . the ancient rule that 'little Vice-Presidents should be seen and not heard' very properly goes down with the rest."

Marshall's criticism of inherited wealth no doubt pleased the folks back home who remembered that as Governor he had refused to bow before the pressure of the corporations and the trusts. The Vice President sought to silence his critics by reducing a social truth to a few well-chosen words: "I believe in vested rights but not in vested wrongs."

The torpedoing of the British liner *Lusitania* by a German submarine in 1915—an attack fatal to more than one hundred Americans—prompted another controversial observation by the Vice President. Marshall declared that anyone taking passage on an English ship was virtually on English soil, and must expect to accept the consequences. The New York *Times* complained: "If Indiana cannot raise men of Presidential calibre, she should at least try to train mediocre men in some of the negative virtues. She should train them to keep silence when they . . . have not the mental equipment to fit them for an understanding of what is required." The *Times* expressed the hope that Marshall would not again "spatter flippant epigrams on an international tragedy."

Marshall weathered these early, harsh judgments to become a great success as a public speaker. Possessed of a dry wit and a small bank account, he supplemented his modest salary by hitting the lecture trail, and in the process, became one of our best-known and most popular Vice Presidents. And he never forgot the advice of William Jennings Bryan, sage of the Chautauqua circuit: "Always get your money before you step onto the platform." Unfortunately, many Americans have never countenanced a mixture of wit and statesmanship, as Adlai Stevenson discovered. While many persons found Marshall amusing, few took him seriously as a public servant.

In presiding over the Senate, Marshall endeavored to be fair to the opposition party, but at the same time he exerted his personal influence in behalf of many bills favored by the President. Inasmuch as Wilson did not see fit to award him any extraconstitutional assignments, Marshall adopted a model philosophy toward his position. He chose "To acknowledge the insignificant influence of the office; to take it in a good-natured way; to be friendly and well disposed to political friend and political foe alike; to be loyal to my chief and at the same time not to be offensive to my associates; and to strive . . . to deal justly with those over whom I was merely nominally presiding."

However, as Vice President, he won the admiration of the Senators. (Admittedly, Marshall ruffled a few traditional feathers. Complaining, for instance, that his feet didn't touch the floor, he replaced the big chair used by his predecessors.) Once, when the Senate paid a moving tribute to its presiding officer, Marshall replied by blaming his presence on an "ignorant electorate." He explained that "those who know nothing are placed in the seats of the mighty. The wise men remain at home and discuss public questions on the ends of street cars and around barber shops."

This man from Indiana was well suited to serve as Vice President during the last of the halcyon years. He appeared to be a relatively simple man while life itself in rural-oriented America was largely unruffled by the long-building crisis across the ocean. But before his terms were over, Marshall—and the United States—would pass through harrowing experiences. The Vice President would draw upon a reservoir of common sense that too few realized he possessed.

The first four years slipped safely by. Wilson kept the European War at arm's length, and he was unanimously renominated at St. Louis in 1916. The convention promised to be so dull that the host city feared few delegates or visitors would stay for the scheduled four days. Reportedly, the city fathers counted on a little excitement over the Vice-Presidential nomination. As it happened, some Democrats were dissatisfied with Marshall, and it seemed a contest might develop. But Wilson praised his Vice President, saying: "He has given me every reason to admire and trust him." The opposition to Marshall collapsed.

The Republican team comprised Charles Evans Hughes and former Vice President Fairbanks, of Indiana, who was making something of a comeback. For the first time in American history, both Vice-Presidential candidates were from the same state. When the Democratic ticket won re-election in one of the closest contests of the century, as California swung to Wilson two days after the voting, Marshall observed: " 'Tis not so deep as a well nor so wide as a church door; but 'tis enough, 'twill serve."

Marshall's hopes for four more quiet years were not realized. World War I brought momentous issues before the Senate. The Vice President spoke frequently in behalf of Liberty Loan campaigns, and he undertook other efforts to rally public opinion in support of the war. Marshall, originally known for his wit, won admiration when the country was sobered by the bloody stalemate in the Western trenches. Even the previously hostile New York *Times* observed: "Thomas R. Marshall, whom the American people have chosen to be their

President in case of any vacancy in that office . . . is an American patriot, and the words he speaks have a sense and sanity that are urgently needed."

With the arrival of peace, precedents began to fall. Wilson went to Paris to fight for his Fourteen Points. Marshall, at Wilson's request and in his absence, became the first Vice President to preside over Cabinet meetings. However, Marshall regarded himself as a member of the legislative branch. He had legal doubts about presiding and he emphasized that he would not be responsible for any consequences. When someone suggested that he might have to take the Presidential oath, Marshall declared that he would not assume the office or any duties thereof (aside from presiding at the Cabinet meetings) unless he received a court order to do so. All went smoothly, however. Wilson returned in triumph from his European trip, and Marshall again concentrated on his Senate duties and on the upcoming debate on the Treaty of Versailles.

In a country that had just fought a war to end all wars, and that was not quite ready to assume its international responsibilities, it was easy to laugh with the wise old Vice President who found it so easy to laugh at himself. Marshall, perceiving that he was being followed by a policeman, once turned on his uninvited protector and assured him: "your labor is in vain. Nobody was ever crazy enough to shoot at a vice-president." Marshall made his most famous statement one day when he was presiding over the Senate. Joe Bristow of Kansas was expounding at length on the many needs of the country. During a pause, Marshall leaned over to one of the Senate secretaries and remarked in a voice that carried to several persons: "What this country needs is a really good five cent cigar."

For Marshall the Vice Presidency had been a lark, a job that had not overtaxed his abilities or added many gray hairs to his mustache. But on September 26, 1919, the smile faded from Marshall's face, and the chuckles of his admirers trailed away into somber thoughtfulness.

Admiral Cary Grayson, Woodrow Wilson's personal physician, had just announced that the President was canceling the remainder of a Western speaking tour, and was returning immediately to Washington. Wilson, said the doctor, had suffered a "complete nervous breakdown." Marshall pondered the terse announcement, and waited for details.

He would wait a long time.

In the spring of 1919 at Paris, Wilson had worked as many as eighteen hours a day while fighting for his League of Nations. He was plagued by headaches, fever, diarrhea, coughing, and lung congestion; at the conference table he became increasingly irritable. He returned to the United States bearing the early symptoms of a physical and mental collapse. On July 10, Wilson placed the treaty and the League covenant before the Senate. Shrewd, bearded Henry Cabot Lodge, Sr., the Republican majority leader, referred the treaty to the Committee on Foreign Relations, of which he was the chairman.

Lodge professed to be in favor of the League—with "reservations." The committee itself was packed with "irreconcilables"—men who would vote against United States entry with or without reservations. Wilson's distrust of Lodge turned to despair when the Massachusetts Senator began his parliamentary delaying tactics by reading the 268-page treaty aloud in the nearly empty hearing room, an effort that required two weeks.

Wilson declared at a Cabinet meeting that he would be willing to give up his life for the League. Although privately admitting that he was at the end of his tether, the President decided to carry his fight over the heads of the Senators and to the American people. He plunged into a Western speaking tour that proved to be too much for a frail and aging man. He traveled eight thousand miles, speaking forty times to cheering crowds while intense heat, severe headaches, and anti-League Senators pursued him. Wilson pressed on, through the Midwest, the Northwest, California. Then he turned eastward. In each city he warned that world peace rested solely with a League of Nations, and with American membership in that League.

At the Pueblo (Colorado) Fairgrounds, on September 25, he delivered perhaps his best speech—and his last. Driving himself unmercifully, almost blinded by the pain in his forehead, the President brought tears to many eyes.

"Mothers who have lost sons in France have come to me,

and taking my hand have not only shed tears upon it, but they have added: 'God bless you, Mr. President.' Why, my fellow citizens, should they pray God to bless me? I ordered their sons overseas. I consented to their sons being put in the most difficult parts of the battle line where death was certain. Why should they weep upon my hand and call down the blessings of God upon me? Because they believe that their boys died for something that vastly transcends any of the immediate and palpable objects of the war. . . ."

The President was near collapse. That night, Doctor Grayson noticed a curious drooping of the left side of his mouth and a trace of saliva trickling out. Grayson knew that the remainder of the trip must be canceled. He won Presidential secretary Joseph Tumulty to this point of view, and together with Mrs. Wilson they pleaded with the President to return to Washington. Wilson feared he would be labeled a quitter, but he finally yielded. The Presidential express, with shades drawn, stopping only to change engines, hurtled fifteen hundred miles across the country to Washington. Grayson announced that the President needed a complete rest.

Wilson disappeared into the White House. For a few days one could catch glimpses of him taking brief afternoon rides through the city. Terse and reassuring medical bulletins came daily from Grayson.

Public concern fell off somewhat, and by October 2 the New York *Times* carried only a three-paragraph item, which reported Grayson's announcement that the President "is feeling somewhat jaded. . . ." Other news clamored for attention. Albert, King of the Belgians, had arrived in New York. The steel strike was on. Nine persons were dead in Arkansas racial violence. The Chicago White Sox, soon to be called the Black Sox, had lost a World Series game to Cincinnati, 9-1.

However the papers failed to report the major event of the day: the President had suffered a cerebral thrombosis, and was near death. Nor would the news be printed the next day, or the next. To be sure, the bulletins grew more ominous. "The President is a very sick man," said Grayson. Yet no details were forthcoming.

From the morning of October 2, when Mrs. Wilson found her husband lying on the floor of the bathroom at the White House, doctors fought a desperate battle to save the President.

The left side of his body was paralyzed. Complications led to another crisis on October 17, when doctors feared than an onset of fatal uremic poisoning would occur at any moment.

Of all this, the public knew nothing. Most Americans believed that the President had suffered only a nervous breakdown, complicated by digestive and prostate trouble. By now four doctors were signing the daily medical bulletins, most of which gave assurances that the patient was making slow but steady progress toward recovery.

One Senator, who was guessing, wrote to a constituent that the President had suffered a "cerebral lesion." Grayson complained about diagnoses by men without medical degrees, but the doctor wasn't giving away any information himself. Inevitably, the vacuum left by the silence of Wilson's doctors was filled by wild rumors. For the first time curiosity seekers noticed bars on some White House windows, and they concluded that the old mansion sheltered a madman. But the bars had been placed there to protect the windows in the days when Theodore Roosevelt's children played ball on the lawn.

Secretary of the Navy Josephus Daniels, one of the few men who knew of Wilson's true condition, urged Grayson to bare the details, in which case, he said, a "wave of sympathy would pour into the White House whereas now there is nothing but uncertainty and criticism." But Wilson's family chose secrecy. The President, a proud man, could not bear to be the object of pity.

What about the country's business? Wasn't this a case of Presidential disability? Should the Vice President take the oath of office? Mrs. Wilson raised the question of her husband's resignation with Francis Dercum, one of the doctors.

Dercum's prescription included a generous dose of politics:

"For Mr. Wilson to resign would have a bad effect on the country, and a serious effect on our patient. He has staked his life and made his promise to the world to do all in his power to get the Treaty ratified and make the League of Nations complete. If he resigns, the greatest incentive to recovery is gone. . . ."

So Mrs. Wilson began her "stewardship," as she called it:

"I studied every paper, sent from the different Secretaries and Senators, and tried to digest and present in tabloid form the things that . . . had to go to the President. I, myself, never made a single decision regarding the disposition of public affairs. The only decision that was mine was what was important and what was not. . . ."

Obviously, merely determining the importance of a document is a major decision. Edith Wilson was a woman of poise, charm, and discretion, but she was totally untrained in the handling of executive business. How could she be expected to "digest" such complex developments as the Senate debate on the Treaty of Versailles?

Men begged to see the President on matters of highest importance. She turned them all away: "I am not interested in the President of the United States. I am interested in my husband and his health."

Republican Senator Albert B. Fall of New Mexico exclaimed: "We have petticoat government! Mrs. Wilson is President!" Senator Lodge complained that "a regency . . . was not contemplated by the constitution."

The President was bedridden for weeks and Mrs. Wilson sheltered him from almost everyone but the doctors. The nation began to drift. Bills passed by Congress became law without the President's signature. Letters addressed to Wilson went unanswered. It was impossible to know who had intercepted them, or whether they had even been read. Beyond the quiet of that bedroom, beyond the purview of the stricken President, postwar convulsions shook the nation. A headline-seeking attorney general sallied forth to save the country from "Communists." Race riots swept major cities north and south. A nationwide steel strike resulted in violence and death. Living costs zoomed. Returning servicemen clamored for jobs.

Secretary of State Robert Lansing was the one member of the Administration bold enough to challenge Mrs. Wilson's regency, but unfortunately his position had been compromised by testimony given in September before the Foreign Relations Committee. William C. Bullitt, who had been attached to the American Peace Commission in a minor capacity, testified that Lansing had privately criticized the League of Nations. He said that the Secretary of State had labeled the League as useless, and had contended that the statesmen in Paris had simply arranged the world to suit themselves. Lansing admitted criticizing the League. A shocked Wilson had received this news while on his Western tour, but he was stricken before he had any opportunity to confront his Secretary of State.

Now, on October 3, Lansing requested a private meeting with Wilson's secretary, Joe Tumulty. The Secretary of State dared to suggest that in view of the incapacity of the President, the Vice President should be summoned to act in Wilson's place. Lansing recited, for Tumulty's benefit, that clause of the Constitution providing that in case of a President's "Inability to discharge the Powers and Duties of the said Office, the Same shall devolve on the Vice President . . ."

Tumulty, loyal to Wilson, retorted coldly: "Mr. Lansing, the Constitution is not a dead letter with the White House. I have read the Constitution and do not find myself in need of any tutoring at your hands of the provision you have just read."

Lansing persisted. He suggested that either Tumulty or Doctor Grayson could certify the President as disabled. In reply, the little Irishman hoisted himself up to full size, and was delivered of one of the most fatuous statements ever carried on waves of sound: "You may rest assured that while Woodrow Wilson is lying in the White House on the broad of his back I will not be a party to ousting him. He has been too kind, too loyal, and too wonderful to me to receive such treatment at my hands."

Could Tumulty have suggested a more appropriate time to implement this clause of the Constitution? At this point in the conversation, according to Tumulty's memoirs, Grayson entered the room. Tumulty exclaimed, "And I am sure that Doctor Grayson *will never* certify to his disability. Will you Grayson?" [Italics added.]

According to Tumulty, Grayson left no doubt in Lansing's mind that the Secretary of State was wasting his time. Tumulty himself added that if anybody outside of the White House circle sought to certify to the President's disability, he and Grayson would stand together and repudiate such a move.

Thus Grayson and Tumulty both were declaring that they would *never* certify the President as disabled, although the patient in question had suffered a cerebral thrombosis the results of which no man could foresee. It might well be argued that this intransigent policy had catastrophic consequences.

Tumulty ends his account of this scene with an absurd statement that lays bare the fallacy of his position. He says that he told Lansing: ". . . *if the President were in a condition to know of this episode* he would, in my opinion, take decisive measures." [Italics added.]

The "decisive measures" undoubtedly would include Lansing's dismissal from the Cabinet. Lansing, under threat of being removed from office for having dared to challenge the regency, was himself spared from that fate because of the very accuracy of his suspicions. Wilson was too ill even to lift a finger to wigwag Lansing out of the Administration.

Lansing next took the seemingly routine step of calling meetings of the Cabinet, to conduct such executive business as was possible in the absence of the President. In the past, other Cabinets had assembled without the President, notably during the period while Garfield lay mortally wounded. Yet Wilson would later point to Lansing's move as further evidence of his disloyalty. Lansing requested that Grayson appear at a Cabinet meeting scheduled for October 6. The doctor blandly told the Secretaries that Wilson was suffering from a nervous breakdown, indigestion, and a depleted system, and that he should be bothered as little as possible.

During the next four months the Cabinet met twenty-one times under Lansing's aegis. Then, in February, 1920, the Secretary of State received a letter signed by Wilson. "Is it true," the President asked, that Lansing had called meetings of the Cabinet? The world knew that the Secretaries had been assembling in a room several hundred feet from Wilson's bed, yet the President now sought confirmation of this fact. (He seems to have been vaguely aware that the Cabinet had been meeting. But when Lansing released this letter to the public, the phrase "Is it true" placed the President in a very poor light.) When Lansing acknowledged the truth of Wilson's "suspicions," the President requested and received his resignation.

In his memoirs, Tumulty quotes Wilson as declaring: ". . . it is never the wrong time to spike disloyalty. When Lansing sought to oust me, I was on my back. I am on my feet now, and I will not have disloyalty about me."

No doubt Wilson would have been loath to surrender even temporarily the powers of the Presidency. But his use of the word "oust" suggests another concern. He apparently believed that if Marshall were sworn in as President, then he (Wilson) would have no Constitutional means of reclaiming the office upon recovering from his illness.

And what did Marshall know of the President's condition? Officially, nothing. On Sunday, October 5, he poured out his anxieties to David Houston, the Secretary of Agriculture. The Vice President complained that he was being kept in the dark and asked Houston for details on Wilson's illness. Houston himself knew little. Marshall asserted that as Vice President, he ought to be informed immediately. Then he exclaimed that it would be a tragedy for himself and for the country, if he had to assume the duties of the President, that many men knew more about the affairs of government than he. It may be questioned whether, if Marshall really held this low opinion of himself, he should have accepted twice, the Vice-Presidential nomination.

Eventually, even those at Wilson's bedside came to believe that Marshall should be informed of the President's condition. But they feared that an official notification might permit the Vice President to mount a campaign to declare Wilson disabled. So Marshall must be told indirectly, unofficially. The regency chose J. Fred Essary, a reporter for the Baltimore *Sun,* to undertake this task. Essary called on Marshall, and presented the facts bluntly. He said that the President might die at any hour. Marshall sat speechless, staring at his hands clasped before him on the desk. Essary hesitated, rose, and walked to the door. He looked back, but Marshall never looked up. Years later, Marshall apologized for his behavior, explaining: "It was the first great shock of my life."

Now began the real ordeal of Thomas R. Marshall. Friends besieged him with advice. Some urged that he declare himself President. Four Republican Senators assured him that he would have the support of the GOP majority in the upper house if he so acted. Many persons assumed that he was in fact already President, or at least acting in that capacity. Foreign statesmen and a few foreign Governments addressed official documents to him. Job hunters badgered him. He received petitions for pardons from Federal prisoners.

The Vice President struggled with the problem. Was it his duty, under the Constitution, to make the first move? He went to the White House in hopes of seeing the President, but Mrs.

Wilson barred the way. He finally decided that he would assume the Presidency only in the event of a resolution by Congress and the approbation in writing of both Mrs. Wilson and the President's physician. Of course, none of these conditions was ever met.

Marshall's secretary, Mark Thistlethwaite, urged him to take more decisive steps. The Vice President replied, "I am not going to seize the place, and then have Wilson, recovered, come around and say, 'Get off, you usurper!' "

And on another occasion, Marshall confided to his wife, "I could throw this country into civil war, but I won't."

On November 23, 1919, while delivering a speech in the civic auditorium in Atlanta, Marshall was interrupted by the whispered news of a phone call. The stunned Vice President faltered slightly, then steadied himself, and a hushed audience heard him say, "I cannot continue my speech. I must leave at once to take up my duties as Chief Executive of this great nation."

He asked the people to pray for him and requested the organist to play "Nearer, My God, to Thee." Then police hustled him off to his hotel.

The phone call was a hoax.

During these months of crisis, Marshall must have recalled many times the cruel jest that a Vice President of the United States has nothing to do except worry about the health of the President.

Marshall missed the Presidency by the narrowest of margins. Wilson did not die, and no one produced medical records proving his incapacity. Once, a Republican Senator did get as far as the sickroom. Senator Fall, a member of the Foreign Relations Committee, took advantage of a temporary United States-Mexican crisis to request a personal conference with the President. Perhaps to his surprise, an audience was scheduled for that very day—December 4, 1919. Fall hoped to find evidence that Wilson was mentally unfit. He was disappointed. True, he found Wilson in a semi-darkened room, flat on his back, covered with a blanket up to his chin. But the President, who had been carefully briefed beforehand, held his own in the discussion of the Mexican problem, and came up with a few bright remarks of his own that threw Fall off balance. At the end of their conversation, Fall exclaimed in his best unctuous manner, "Mr. President, I am praying for you."

"Which way, Senator?"

Fall retreated from the room in disarray.

During his trip overseas, Wilson had been the guest of European royalty. Now some distinguished persons were arriving in America for return visits. It became the Vice President's duty to substitute as our official host to the bluebloods from across the ocean. Marshall fulfilled this assignment with great dignity. The Prince of Wales—the future Edward VIII—came. So did the heroic and idolized King Albert of the Belgians, who brought his queen and his son, the Duke of Brabant. Years later, Marshall wrote of the Belgian prince that although he was born "in the atmosphere of courts and courtiers, he was far more self-conscious than I, a Hoosier, born in the gum-boot district of northern Indiana."

If all this excitement were not enough, the Vice President and his wife were struck by personal tragedy. At a welfare center Mrs. Marshall discovered a sick and delicate child. She pleaded with her husband to agree to take the baby into their own home. Marshall wrote later: "With the brutality which marks the man, I had said to her that she might keep him, provided he did not squall under my feet. He grew out of his crib; but he never walked with as sure a certainty on the streets of Washington, as he walked into my heart . . . he came to be the sun and center of Mrs. Marshall's life and of mine." The little boy was never adopted. He died in February, 1920, of an excess of acid in the blood. The sixty-five-year-old Vice President and his wife fled to Arizona "to get away from the toys."

The grief and worries of one Vice President paled into insignificance beside the greater tragedy Marshall could watch unfolding almost daily from his chair at the front of the Senate chamber. Month after month, the debate on the Treaty of Versailles dragged on. More than eighty Senators professed to favor a League in some form. The public was counted as being overwhelmingly in favor of the League, and yet, the treaty never passed. Wilson, ill and stubborn, failed to gauge the mood of the Senate. He failed to realize that passage without compromise was impossible. Early in the debate he had snubbed an alliance with those who had only mild reservations.

Then Lodge introduced his own "strong reservations." One of these, in Wilson's view, nullified the important Article X, which committed each member to undertake to respect and preserve against aggression the territorial integrity and independence of all the members.

The debate became a personal contest between Wilson and Lodge. Neither would yield, but the struggle was unequal. The isolated President received only falsely optimistic reports from Mrs. Wilson and his secretary, Tumulty, who feared that bad news might kill him. Lodge, at the center of the battle, sensed a slow shift in the mood of the country. He realized that as the memories of war faded, so did the idealism Wilson sought to sustain; as the months slipped by, other problems—strikes, riots, and the high cost of living—held the attention of the country. Lodge and his associates succeeded in planting seeds of doubt in the minds of those who still followed the League debate closely. The fear among nationalists that the United States would surrender its sovereignty to an international body was carefully cultivated. Many who sincerely wished to prevent another war now viewed the League as an instrument by which the United States might be drawn into some future foreign conflict. The great orators of the Senate—notably William E. Borah and Hiram Johnson—led the opposition to the League.

The Senate Democratic leadership was weak, but, more importantly, the man who could have broken the deadlock lay in the White House, refusing the needed compromise with Lodge. For Woodrow Wilson, all the clocks had stopped on that hot afternoon of September 25 in Pueblo. He could still hear the cheers of that crowd roaring approval of a League without reservations. For them, and for the soldiers who had died in battle, there would be no surrender. For Wilson, the honor of the nation was at stake.

Colonel Edward M. House, once the President's closest adviser, wrote letters urging compromise, and reporting that Lodge was willing to co-operate. The letters were never answered. Reports came from overseas that France and England also could accept reservations. This news apparently carried no weight with Wilson either.

On November 19, 1919, the Senate finally acted. First, the Senators voted on adoption with the Lodge reservations. The Democrats had clear instructions from the sickroom to vote No, and they did. The treaty was defeated, 39-55, failing even to win a majority where two thirds were required. Then the Senate voted on the treaty without reservations. This time only one Republican joined the 37 Democrats in favor, and the treaty lost, 38-53.

Incredibly, a nation that had fought a war to make the world safe for democracy couldn't even bring the hostilities to an official end by the necessary vote in its own legislative body, let alone help set up the machinery to prevent future wars.

When the final vote was announced, Senator Swanson of Virginia rushed up to Lodge and exclaimed, "For God's sake, can't something be done to save the treaty?"

"Senator, the door is closed," replied the Republican leader. "You have done it yourselves."

At the White House, Edith Wilson broke the news to her patient as gently as possible. For a few minutes the President remained silent, and then said, "All the more reason I must get well and try again to bring this country to a sense of its great opportunity and greater responsibility."

Fate had been cruel to Wilson. Had he died in Colorado in September, the League would probably have sailed through the Senate as a tribute to a martyr (much as the heart of President Kennedy's program passed Congress in the months after his assassination). On the other hand, had Wilson not been stricken quite so severely, he could have kept in closer touch with his lieutenants, and perhaps could have moved toward some accommodation with the Republicans.

Supporters of the League would not give up. The issue was revived and brought to another vote in March, 1920. Almost every voice—including those of such men as William Howard Taft, William Jennings Bryan, and Herbert Hoover—was raised in behalf of compromise. By now Wilson was presumably in better health, and in a position to see the need for conciliation. But once again, the Democrats had their marching orders: vote No on the treaty with reservations. This time, one half of the Democrats deserted Wilson, and threw their support to Lodge. On the vote to accept the treaty with reservations, the count stood 49 to 35 in favor, just 7 votes short of the needed two thirds.

Again, Wilson accepted the news calmly, and expressed the belief that history would prove him right. The historians have disappointed him. One of his biographers, John M. Blum, has written that Wilson "existed in a demiworld of querulous fantasies." And Thomas A. Bailey, in *Woodrow Wilson and the Great Betrayal,* blames the League defeat on "Wilson and his docile following who delivered the fatal stab."

In 1850, another foe of compromise, crusty old Zachary Taylor, had died during a crucial Senate debate. The succession of Vice President Millard Fillmore had cleared the way for the passage of the measures known collectively as the Compromise of 1850. Had Thomas R. Marshall replaced Wilson in the fall of 1919, as a result of Wilson's disability, history might have repeated itself. Marshall had presided over the Senate for six years; on the basis of his observation of that body, and because of his own amiable nature, he would have sought an agreement with the reservationists. Marshall himself favored a League with reservations. He had told Thistlethwaite that if he became President, he would not consider himself obligated to pledge support to all of Wilson's policies; perhaps he had the League in mind. Few persons believe that as President, Marshall would have scaled the heights of greatness that Wilson attained before 1919. But after his collapse, Wilson was a crippled and nearly helpless man. On this one question of bringing the United States into the League of Nations, it seems almost certain that Marshall would have succeeded where Wilson failed.

A generation later, the nation did not repeat its error after World War I; no effective voice was raised against United States entry into the United Nations. American ambassadors to the United Nations included Henry Cabot Lodge's grandson and namesake, who then advanced to a Vice-Presidential nomination. But the events of 1919–1920 did not lead to a solution of the disability problem. Wilson's collapse brought a flurry of concern in Congress. Four bills dealing with disability were introduced in the House, but none got out of committee. The country never seemed to worry about the problems of Presidential succession and disability except when tragedy struck, and then, inevitably, apathy returned until "the next time."

Wilson never achieved a full recovery. He did not meet with his Cabinet until April, 1920, seven months after his speech in Pueblo. Even then, he was very much a stricken man, pale, with a weak voice and a slack jaw. He still believed that the people would sustain his position on the League in the 1920 election. He evidently permitted himself to hope that the Democrats would give him a third nomination. Doctor Grayson was convinced that further political activity would kill him, and urged Cabinet members not to put Wilson's name forward during the national convention in San Francisco, but Wilson refused to rule himself out of the race. He said that he could not decline to accept a nomination that had not yet been offered.

The new Secretary of State, Bainbridge Colby, enthusiastically telegraphed Wilson from San Francisco that the President must lead the "solemn referendum" on the League, and that he would have the President's name placed in nomination unless Wilson forbade him. Other Cabinet members, whose loyalty to the President now took the form of sparing him a further call to duty, quickly silenced Colby. Wilson's name was never presented. In the 1920 election, the Democratic candidate, James M. Cox, lost by an overwhelming margin. Marshall saw Wilson briefly just before the inauguration ceremonies on March 4, 1921. With that exception, he served out his last year and a half as Vice President without exchanging a word with, or catching a glimpse of, the lonely old man in the White House.

The Vice President was never reimbursed for the expenses he had incurred in entertaining the European royalty. So in his last few months in office, after the 1920 election, he went back on the lecture circuit. One political speech brought him back to his native state of Indiana. Sitting in the smoking car of a train, he pondered what light and cheerful things he could possibly say to the Hoosier Democrats who waited for him that night. A large man entered the car and slumped into the seat beside him.

"Mighty bad day for business," said the stranger, as he looked at the rain falling in sheets outside.

"What's your line?" Marshall asked.

"Automobile accessories. What's yours?"

"Distributing dope."

"I thought they wouldn't let you sell that stuff."

"But I have a special arrangement with the Administration for a short time," replied Marshall.

The old man with the gray mustache was left alone with his thoughts. Had he been a believer in symbolism, Marshall might have likened the office of the Vice Presidency to the train, hurtling in splendid isolation through a rain-swept night toward future calamities no man could see.

★ ★ ★ ★ ★ ★ ★ ★ ★

CALVIN COOLIDGE

"O, we ain' gwine steal no mo,

We ain' gwine steal no mo."

Republicans gathered in Chicago in 1920 to ballot in a building that, prophetically enough, had once served as a prison. The party confidently expected to win over the Democrats in a country tired of war and disenchanted with talk about a League of Nations. The delegates passed over a number of able men, including General Leonard Wood, Illinois Governor Frank Lowden, and California Senator Hiram Johnson, all of whom were considered too progressive or independent by the senatorial cabal that controlled the convention.

At the proper moment, after the leading candidates had become deadlocked, the delegates were offered a way out of their predicament in the form of that darkest of dark horses, Senator Warren G. Harding of Ohio. Harding, an undistinguished Senator, had been presented as a compromise at a meeting of party leaders in the "smoke-filled room" at the Blackstone Hotel at two o'clock in the morning. Later the same day, on the tenth ballot, he was nominated.

It was Saturday afternoon, and the tired delegates were eager to wind up the show and leave town. The party bosses had little time to turn up a Vice-Presidential candidate. Someone approached Senator Hiram Johnson who replied, "We're living in a day of strange events, but none so strange as that I should be considered second to Senator Harding."

The leaders looked elsewhere, made their choice, and word was passed to the delegates that they would nominate Senator Irvine H. Lenroot of Wisconsin for Vice President. Senator Henry Cabot Lodge, the permanent chairman, and his colleagues had no reason to doubt that the delegates would do as they were told. They had already accepted both the prescribed platform and the Presidential nominee, though there was some grumbling about putting another Senator on the ticket, a man who evoked no enthusiasm.

Nonetheless, the delegates seemed disposed to concede the nomination, and many started shuffling and crowding into the exits as Senator Medill McCormick of Illinois began to place Lenroot's name in nomination.

Hardly had McCormick started to speak when someone shouted "Coolidge!" McCormick droned on, only to be interrupted again and again by cries of "Coolidge!" The Senator finished his address, seconding speeches were made for Lenroot, and presumably the next step would be a motion that nominations be closed.

But now someone in the middle of the Oregon delegation was standing on a chair, gesturing frantically for recognition. The acting chairman decided to let the man have his say. Amid the clatter of seats and the scraping of feet, an obscure delegate named Wallace McClamant delivered a nominating speech comprising not more than a hundred words, most of them inaudible. Everyone could see the man, but few knew who he was. Somehow the rising stridency of his voice overcame the subsiding turmoil, and many heard the closing words, ". . . for the exalted office of Vice President Governor Calvin Coolidge, of Massachusetts."

Galleryites and delegates who had already jammed into the exits now hesitated, returned to their seats, and caught the spirit of revolt. The parochial New Englander, Calvin Coolidge, seemed an odd rallying point for the forces of insurgency. But on that stifling afternoon in Chicago, the Massachusetts Governor stood for something positive in the minds of the delegates. As a result of certain events which had occurred not long before the convention, Coolidge was regarded as a man of action in a way that he would seldom, if ever, be regarded again. Coolidge was nominated, 674½ to 146 for Lenroot. The choice was made without deliberation, without in fact all of the delegates present. Yet once again, a nomination for the Vice Presidency would prove to be of great importance.

Coolidge, a native of Plymouth, Vermont, had moved to Massachusetts, where he had entered politics and been elected to a series of public offices, including the governorship. He didn't attend the 1920 covention; he had scarcely ever traveled outside of New England. At the time of his nomination for Vice President he had never even been to Washington. But on a fall day in 1919 Coolidge had gained national prominence. Typically, for a notoriously taciturn man, he hit the national front page with one cogent, incisive statement.

Boston police had formed a union to fight for higher wages. The police commissioner denied the right of the men to organize, and he suspended the unionists early in September, 1919. Practically every member of the force walked off the beat. Within hours the Massachusetts capital seemed headed for the law of the jungle. Hoodlums and idlers—cautiously at first—clustered in the downtown area, and then, with ever-increasing boldness, stormed through the streets, looting and terrorizing. Amateur police were recruited from the ranks of national guardsmen, ex-servicemen, and Harvard students. A nervous nation, already alarmed by a postwar "Red Scare" and the demands by the American Federation of Labor, watched and waited. Samuel Gompers, president of the AFL, called on Governor Coolidge to overrule the police commissioner and reinstate the suspended men. Coolidge chilled Gompers with a telegraphed reply: "There is no right to strike against the public safety by anybody, anywhere, any time." It was an unanswerable declaration. The police commissioner organized a new force, and peace was restored to Boston.

President Wilson and 70,000 others sent messages to the State House in Boston praising Calvin Coolidge. The slim, short, almost faceless Governor was also applauded in the press. Coolidge, one of the shrewdest politicians of his time, did not fail to follow up his advantage. When renominated for Governor in October, 1919, he asserted: "The forces of law and order may be dissipated; they may be defeated; but so long as I am their commander-in-chief, they will not be surrendered." The Governor was re-elected by a wide margin.

Even surprise nominations at national conventions are seldom quite so spontaneous as they seem. The ground for the selection of Coolidge had been prepared well in advance by Frank Stearns, a wealthy Boston merchant and fellow Amherst alumnus of Coolidge. Before the Chicago convention, Stearns distributed nearly 70,000 copies of *Have Faith in Massachusetts*, a collection of the Governor's speeches. The books were sent to prominent Republicans all over the country. Coolidge might have become the Presidential nominee if the convention deadlock had persisted, even if the aristocratic Senator Lodge did grumble that a Massachusetts man who lived in a two-family house was simply impossible.

Despite the haste of its doing, the Coolidge nomination restored some of the faith in the convention process that had been lost with the selection of Harding.

The Governor, meanwhile, was taking his customary stroll across The Boston Common. After returning to his two-room apartment on the fourth floor of the Adams House, he was advised by phone of developments in Chicago. During one call, he turned from the receiver and snapped at his wife, "Nominated for Vice President."

"You're not going to take it, are you?" she asked.

"I suppose I'll have to," he replied. His facial expression, as ever, was grimly unchanged.

Again, congratulations poured in to Boston. Vice President Thomas R. Marshall telegraphed the man who would be his successor, saying, "Please accept my sincere sympathy."

In the fall campaign, Coolidge called on the voters to rely on themselves and to resist government interference in business. He preached frugality, an obsession of his, and boasted that he had not purchased a suit in eighteen months or a pair of shoes in two years.

Harding, sensing that his own nomination had been less well received than that of Coolidge, announced that his running mate would play a major role in establishing communications between the executive and legislative branches of the Government. After their election in November, Harding invited Coolidge to attend meetings of the Cabinet, and the Vice President accepted. Marshall, under protest, had presided over a few meetings of the Cabinet, but the action by Harding and Coolidge marked the first real advance toward enlarging the functions of the Vice President. The payoff was not long in coming, for after Harding died, Coolidge would say, "My experience in the Cabinet was of supreme value to me when I became President." Coolidge had climbed the political ladder by keeping his ears open and his mouth shut. He seldom spoke at the Cabinet meetings except when directly asked to express an opinion.

Coolidge was the perfect Vice President if one measures his performance within the traditional confines of that office. Having had long experience in the Massachusetts Legislature, he was thoroughly familiar with parliamentary procedure. More dynamic men have been bored to tears by the daily droning of oratory in the Senate chamber. But Vice President Coolidge said he found that presiding was "fascinating," and "I was entertained and instructed by the debates." A sympathetic biographer has explained that the calm of the Vice Presidency gave Coolidge a chance "for meditation on the lessons of the past and on the promise for the future. . . . Every statesman requires interludes like these when he can lie fallow and equip himself for further exertions." But had all gone well, Coolidge could have held this office for eight years. It is difficult to imagine a Theodore Roosevelt or a John Kennedy "lying fallow" for eight years while in the prime of political life.

But Coolidge was an unusual breed of political cat. "Mr. Coolidge's genius for inactivity," wrote Walter Lippmann, "is developed to a very high point. It is far from being an indolent inactivity. It is a grim, determined, alert inactivity which keeps Mr. Coolidge occupied constantly. . . . Inactivity is a political philosophy and a party program with Mr. Coolidge."

One could not say that the Vice President ruled the Senate with a heavy hand. Once, when two members were shouting at each other, he was urged to use his gavel to maintain order. "I will if they become really excited," Coolidge replied.

Many anecdotes circulated during the incumbency of Silent Cal. He was asked why he accepted so many dinner invitations. "Got to eat somewhere," he rasped. A society matron sidled up to Coolidge at one affair and said she had placed a bet that she could make him say more than two words. "You lose," came the crisp reply.

Harding ignored the prim example set by his Vice President. He went on his own merry way, playing poker with the boys in the little green house on H Street, meeting his mistress in the coat closet of the big white house on Pennsylvania Avenue, and generally having a great deal of fun at the job of being President.

He had appointed many of his cronies to office and some of them quickly betrayed him. The man he named to head the Veterans Bureau—whose military record included a desertion from the army—proceeded to steal the country blind. His Secretary of the Interior accepted a bribe and leased valuable oil reserves to speculators who expected to make $100 million on the deal. In 1923, Harding began to learn of these and other scandals. The public knew nothing, but Senators began to ask questions. Some top officials resigned. The legal adviser to the Veterans Bureau killed himself in a home he had purchased from Harding. A prominent member of the "Ohio gang" shot himself to death in the apartment of Attorney General Harry Daugherty, who had managed Harding's Presidential campaign.

By the summer of 1923 the burdens of his office were weighing heavily on the shoulders of the President. Harding and some friends planned a trip to Alaska, where he hoped to escape the spreading gossip. But there was no escape. His Western train trip, interrupted by speechmaking and pursued by the heat of the sun, was reminiscent of the tour Wilson had taken four years before. In Kansas City, Harding's anxiety increased after he received private information from the wife of former Interior Secretary Albert B. Fall, who had resigned. Later, the receipt of a coded message from Washington left the President near collapse. Time and time again he asked those accompanying him what a President should do when he is betrayed by his friends. In Seattle the President fell ill, and he was in serious condition on his arrival in San Francisco on July 29. Harding was confined to his bed for a few days, seemed to be recovering, and then died on the evening of August 2, while his wife read to him from a magazine. Cause of death was given as food poisoning, but a heart ailment was probably to blame. Later, there would also be talk of murder and suicide.

About 1 A.M. on August 3, old John Coolidge was awakened by a commotion outside his farm home in Plymouth, Vermont. At the door was W. A. Perkins, who operated a small private telephone line from Boston to nearby Bridgewater. He carried two telegrams, one from the New York *Times* and the other from Harding's secretary. Both of them reported the President's death.

The Coolidge family, including the Vice President and his wife, had gone to bed at 9 P.M., as usual, after hearing word that the ailing Harding was recovering. But now Calvin was awakened by his father, who climbed the stairs and called out his name in a trembling voice. Coolidge got up, and received the news with almost no visible emotion. Soon everyone was up and dressed.

While reporters and townspeople began to gather outside, Coolidge withdrew briefly to write a statement pledging to carry on Harding's policies. A copy of the Presidential oath was located somewhere, and to John Coolidge, a notary public, fell the unique honor of swearing in his son as President of the United States. The ceremony was performed by the faint light of a flickering kerosene lamp, at 2:47 in the morning, in the presence of about six persons, amid the typical furnishings of an old-fashioned New England farm home. The President and his father faced each other across a marble table on which rested a Bible once owned by Calvin Coolidge's mother.

Years later, when asked to recall his first reaction upon learning that he was President, Coolidge replied, "I thought I could swing it."

Before the swearing-in, Coolidge's father had shaved and put on a collar and tie. Now he was so excited that he sat up for the rest of the night. As for the thirtieth President, Calvin Coolidge climbed back into bed and went to sleep.

Coolidge could not have been unaware that something was seriously wrong in the Harding administration. Now that he was President, he resorted to his tested technique of simply letting events take their own course. Congressmen demanded investigations, black headlines filled the papers, and the allegations of wrongdoing muddied the reputations of many men.

An impulsive President might have rushed to disassociate himself from his predecessor, leaping into the front ranks of those clamoring for a full investigation. But publicly, Coolidge confined himself to a press conference statement, a snappish "Let the guilty be punished." He made no move to dismiss the two remaining Cabinet officers who had been implicated. Secretary of the Navy Edwin Denby had co-operated in transferring to the Department of the Interior the oil reserves leased to private speculators. And Attorney General Daugherty, the nation's chief legal officer, was linked to other attempts to defraud the Government.

But for several reasons, Coolidge declined to request the resignations of Denby and Daugherty. Aware that the nation was slow to accept the awful truth about the Harding administration, he avoided the pitfall of getting ahead of public opinion. Even the New York *Times* denounced as character assassins those Democratic Senators who were leading the demands for an investigation. Furthermore, the President was loath to dismiss any officer on the basis of rumor. And as a mere accidental President, the successor of a man who was being genuinely mourned, he dared not anger the nation by any precipitate action.

Finally, he was a shrewd practitioner of what Lippmann called "alert inactivity." Coolidge himself summed up this philosophy one day in a conversation with Secretary of Commerce Herbert Hoover: "If you see ten troubles coming down the road, you can be sure that nine will run into the ditch before they reach you and you have to battle with only one of them."

And so Coolidge timed his non-moves perfectly. The Senate passed a resolution calling on the President to dismiss Denby. Coolidge refused, and issued a statement declaring that the Senate had no constitutional right to tell him to dismiss a Cabinet member. The Senate backed down, but by that time Denby's position had become untenable. The Secretary of the Navy voluntarily resigned in February, 1924, saying that he did not wish to embarrass the President further.

Daugherty was a more difficult problem. He stubbornly refused to quit, arguing that to do so would be to admit his guilt, and Coolidge hesitated to ask for his resignation. Once again, the Senate got Coolidge off the hook, by beginning an investigation of the Department of Justice. When Daugherty said he wouldn't open his department files to the investigators, Coolidge had the needed excuse to call for his resignation. Daugherty was replaced with the able Harlan Fiske Stone, who quickly put the power of the Department of Justice behind the mushrooming investigations of Harding's chums.

Before the fumigation of Daugherty's department had been undertaken, Coolidge had also set up an independent team of special prosecutors. Republican Owen J. Roberts, a Philadelphia lawyer, and Atlee Pomerene, a former Democratic Senator from Ohio, carried the brunt of the Government's case in the manipulation of the oil reserves. The trials were to drag on for years. Several persons, including former Interior Secretary Fall, eventually went to prison. Coolidge, by saying and doing no more than necessary, and by setting his own example of uncompromising honesty, emerged personally and politically unscarred.

During most of his adult life, Calvin Coolidge had held one public office or another. His business was politics, and he plied his trade with great skill in the nominating arena and in the legislative halls. Of course he wanted to be elected to a full four-year term. But whereas Teddy Roosevelt had nearly three years in the White House behind him when he sought a nomination of his own, Coolidge had succeeded to the Presidency only ten months before the 1924 Republican convention opened.

Nonetheless, he had little trouble securing the nomination. Times were generally good, and getting better. Coolidge was free of the taint of the Harding regime, yet was committed to the policies that had first won popularity for the late President. And no one seemed willing or able to challenge the Coolidge leadership. The President defeated Hiram Johnson in Johnson's own California primary, and went on to poll more than 90 per cent of the convention vote.

The Democrats had nothing to lose by pounding away at the corruption theme. They searched the President's background for bits of scandal and found nothing, but the Republican party as a whole was more vulnerable to criticism. A famous cartoon of the 1924 campaign depicted the GOP elephant and the Democratic donkey singing new lyrics to the tune of a familiar song of the day. The elephant led off with a rather quavering, "O, we ain' gwine steal no mo, We ain' gwine steal no mo." And the donkey brayed back, "But How'n the 'ell kin the country tell— 'You ain' gwine steal no mo'?"

In any campaign the Presidential candidate's own character

is important, and nobody believed that Coolidge was a thief. Alice Roosevelt Longworth visited the White House, and found that "the atmosphere was as different as a New England front parlor is from a back room in a speakeasy."

The campaign gave the President an opportunity to talk about his favorite subject. "I am for economy," he said, and "After that I am for more economy." As for the burning domestic issue of the day—prohibition—he said only that the law should be enforced, a perfectly safe position. Insofar as foreign affairs were mentioned during and after the 1924 campaign, Coolidge did little to shake the public free from its belief that the United States lived in splendid isolation from the rest of the world.

But Coolidge's popularity did not rest on his stand on a particular issue. He was the No. 1 tranquilizer during the Aspirin Age. Round and about him Americans lost fortunes in Florida real estate, killed each other in one sensational "Crime of the Century" after another, ignored the constitutional ban on the importation and sale of liquor, cheered their athletic heroes, indulged their flaming youth, and played mah-jongg until dawn. During the Roaring Twenties, Coolidge yielded to only one of its vices. He surrendered to the crossword puzzle craze.

A friend from the President's early days, A. P. Dennis, wrote: "Mr. Coolidge is eighteenth century—frugal, simple, honest, hard-bitten—set down in a twentieth-century age of jazz, extravagance in speech, dress, mad desire for pleasure. As a Nation our craving is to be saved from ourselves. The yearning of the mass mind, whether in religion or politics, is for something to hold to—something to hold us—something to which the poor tentacles of self may cling, as we are carried along by the heedless current of years."

The 1924 election was no contest. The nation voted for four more years of Coolidge and prosperity.

The Republicans had to search twice for their 1924 Vice-Presidential nominee. Ex-Governor Frank Lowden of Illinois, who disagreed with Coolidge on farm policy, said that he wouldn't take it, but the delegates went ahead and nominated him anyway. Lowden sent two telegrams rejecting the nomination, and issued a declination to the Associated Press. For only the second time (Silas Wright being the first in 1844) a Vice-Presidential nominee refused to accept.

After Lowden declined, the Republicans nominated Charles G. Dawes, a man whose personality could not have differed more from that of the President with whom he ran. Unlike Coolidge, Dawes was outspoken, aggressive, and impulsive. His blunt manner angered many. He is regarded as one of the ablest men ever to serve as Vice President, although not because of any achievements in that office itself. Those were the empty years in Dawes's long and honorable public service, but they would be memorable in a negative way.

Charles Gates Dawes was born in Marietta, Ohio, in 1865. He practiced law in Lincoln, Nebraska, then moved to Illinois to enter business and Republican politics. He served as McKinley's campaign manager in Illinois in 1896, and as controller of the currency from 1897 to 1902. Commissioned a major during World War I, he came home from France as a brigadier general. An aftermath of his war service brought him nationwide fame.

The general had headed the supply procurement division, and was drawn into the inevitable postwar investigation of military spending. By taking a close look at how the Democrats had conducted the war, Republican Congressmen hoped to turn up all kinds of graft and corruption. But Dawes went before the committee, not as a guilty-looking Democrat, not as a profiteer, but as a justifiably outraged, hand-waving, shouting ex-general—and a Republican to boot—whose testimony did much to take the heat out of the investigation.

The Congressmen asked him many, many questions, even one concerning the price the United States had paid for mules.

"Sure we paid," roared Dawes. "We didn't dicker. Why, man alive, we had to win the war. We would have paid horse prices for sheep if sheep could have pulled artillery to the front. Oh, it's all right now to say we bought too much vinegar and too many cold chisels, but we saved the civilization of the world. Damn it all, the business of an army is to win the war, not to quibble around with a lot of cheap buying. *Hell and Maria*, we weren't trying to keep a set of books, we were trying to win the war!"

On rolled the thunder. "Long after this committee is dead and gone and forgotten the achievements of the American army will stand as an everlasting blaze of glory. You have tried to make a mountain out of a molehill. The people are tired of war talk and fault finding. The army was American, neither Republican or Democratic."

From that day on, he was known as "Hell and Maria" Dawes.

Harding named him the nation's first director of the budget. Just before being nominated for Vice President, he helped draw up the "Dawes Plan" for the handling of German reparations payments. For this service he received the Nobel Peace Prize. Not since the time of Theodore Roosevelt had such a prominent American been honored with a Vice Presidential nomination. And like Teddy, Dawes worked hard for the election of the ticket.

In 1924, a great many Republicans as well as Democrats were running around nights wearing bed sheets and waving torches. During the campaign Dawes spoke out vigorously against the Ku Klux Klan, to the discomfort of some of the local dignitaries seated behind him on the platform.

After Coolidge and Dawes were elected, but before the inauguration, the impetuous Vice President-elect committed the first of a series of errors that destroyed his usefulness to the Administration. He wrote to Coolidge that he would not accept any invitation from the President to attend Cabinet meetings. Coolidge hadn't tendered an invitation, and Dawes took the initiative away from the officer to whom it belonged. Furthermore, Dawes announced to the press that he had written the letter, thereby delivering a public and totally unwarranted slap at the President. Dawes coupled his refusal to meet with the Cabinet with a declaration of "friendship and high regard" for Coolidge; but he said he feared that the establishment of such a precedent would mean that some future Chief Executive would be obliged to invite into his Cabinet meetings a Vice President whom he might regard as "unsuitable."

Dawes had raised a valid point, and touched upon one of the weaknesses of the Vice-Presidential office as it is still structured: Whereas a President can dismiss a Cabinet officer if conditions so require, he cannot dismiss a Vice President with whom disagreements might arise, and the presence of such a man in Cabinet meetings could not be ended without embarrassment all around.

Nonetheless, Dawes could have settled the matter with the President privately. His failure to exercise restraint foreshadowed a more surprising episode.

On March 4, 1925, Dawes took the Vice-Presidential oath, and promptly stirred up a fuss with his opening remarks. Wasting no time on amenities, he plunged into a frontal attack on certain Senate rules. Standing tall and lean, Dawes put on his best hard-nosed, stiff-collared, patronizing performance, and the Senate didn't like it for a minute. The ninety-six members of the "club" were not accustomed to sitting still for a lecture, least of all from a Vice President!

Dawes took aim at Rule XXII, "the Filibuster rule," which virtually assured unlimited debate, and which, he said, gave "a minority of even one Senator, at times, power to defeat the measure" under consideration. The Vice President demanded to know "Who would dare oppose any changes in the rules necessary to insure that the business of the United States should always be conducted in the interests of the nation. . . ." He warned that failure to change the rules would "lessen the effectiveness, prestige, and dignity of the United States Senate."

Poor Coolidge. This was to have been the big day of his life, his inauguration to a full term as President. He had composed one of his better addresses, a strong appeal for economy in government. But most of the talk in Washington was of Dawes's speech. Not since the time of Andy Johnson had a new Vice President upset the decorum of the inauguration program. The next morning some papers carried eight-column banners telling of the newest challenge to the dilatory rules with which the Senate had lived so long. A few members supported Dawes, but most agreed with Senator Joseph T. Robinson of Arkansas that the Vice President had shown little knowledge of the Senate and little good taste.

The best defense of the *status quo* was delivered by the respected Senator Walter George of Georgia, who conceded: "There are some features of the rules, no doubt, that should be changed, but he defeated any change by the brutal and clownish way in which he went about it. With all its faults, the

Senate is the greatest deliberative body in the world, and the only body in which gag rule has not been applied. Dawes comes in here from the business world, where there is impatience of restraint. Here deliberation is necessary as a check against hasty and ill-considered action, and to prevent the complete domination of executive authority."

Dawes carried his fight to the country, but the issue did not excite the public. The rules change came to a vote in the Senate, and the supporters of the filibuster won. The question remains whether a more tactful approach by Dawes might have succeeded in strengthening the cloture provision—thereby changing the course of later civil-rights debates.

Within a week after his inauguration, another incident brought down laughter and ridicule on the shoulders of the Vice President, and helped undermine his solemn efforts to reform the talkative Senators.

Coolidge sent up to the Senate the name of Charles Warren to succeed Harlan Fiske Stone as Attorney General. Democrats and insurgent Republicans opposed the nomination because of Warren's identification with the sugar trust. It appeared that the vote would be close, and many Senators wished to speak for or against the nomination. On the afternoon of March 10, Dawes asked the Democratic and Republican floor leaders whether a vote would be taken that afternoon. He was informed that a half-dozen Senators still wished to speak, and that consequently no action would be taken that day. Dawes turned over the gavel to a Senator, and headed uptown to the New Willard Hotel for his customary afternoon nap.

While the Vice President dozed, several Senators canceled plans to speak. Quickly Warren's nomination was brought to a vote. As the calling of the roll progressed, it became apparent that the vote might end in a tie. E. Ross Bartley, the Vice President's secretary, rushed to a phone and put in a call to the hotel. Word came that Dawes was on the way. In the Senate chamber, the chief clerk dragged out the roll as slowly as he could, but finally all the senators had been heard, and the count stood 40 for Warren, and 40 against. Republicans used every parliamentary device to stall for time. Others stood on the Capitol ramparts watching for the first sign of the tie-breaking Vice President.

Dawes, it should be noted, was the great-great-grandson of William Dawes, the patriot who rode with Paul Revere on that famous night in '75. William Dawes has been largely forgotten by history, perhaps because Longfellow couldn't rhyme his name as easily as "Revere." At any rate, Charles Dawes's taxi came screaming to a halt in front of the Capitol rotunda. Hardly a man is now alive who remembers seeing the dignified fifty-nine-year-old Vice President scramble up the Capitol steps, sprint down the marble halls, and come panting into the Senate chamber on that March day in 1925. Too late. One Democrat who had originally voted for Warren decided to switch, and Dawes found that he had no tie vote to break. Warren was defeated, 41-39.

Coolidge, of course, was not amused by this exhibition, and thereafter showed little inclination to draw Dawes into the Administration in any capacity. As for the Vice President, after this debacle few persons could take seriously his lectures to the Senators on how they should perform their duties. He endured a great deal of ribbing, as from Senator George Norris of Nebraska who did some of the most effective needling with his rendition from the floor of a parody on "Sheridan's Ride." The last stanza went in part:

And when his statue is placed on high,
Under the dome of the Capitol sky . . .
Be it said, in letters both bold and bright:
O, Hell an' Maria, he has lost us the fight!

In time, Dawes won high regard from the Senators for his ability as a presiding officer, and his early challenge to the Senate procedure was overlooked or forgotten. But he was too involved in the world around him to settle into an impartial role. On his last day as presiding officer he found himself considerably more popular than on his first. But his refusal to attend Cabinet meetings and his differences with Coolidge on farm policy left the office essentially where it had been for 140 years.

Meanwhile, Coolidge on August 2, 1927, had announced: "I do not choose to run for President in 1928." Some skeptics insisted that he wanted another full term, though it is almost certain that he did not. One ramification of his announcement should be mentioned here; Coolidge found himself in a unique situation because of the circumstance under which he had succeeded to the Presidency. He had become President in August 1923, and had served only nineteen of the forty-eight months to which Harding had been elected. He was the first accidental President up to his time who had served less than half of his predecessor's term. Therefore, if he had run for re-election in 1928, would he have violated the two-term tradition? Coolidge himself felt that the time he had filled out for Harding should not be charged against him, and his refusal to run in 1928 was not based on this particular question.

However, most Democratic and some Republican Senators did profess to see a Coolidge candidacy in 1928 as a break with tradition. Furthermore, they doubted that the President meant what he said when he withdrew his name from consideration. So a majority of the Senators, in March, 1928, gratuitously voted for a resolution declaring it to be "the sense of the Senate that the precedent established by Washington and other Presidents of the United States in retiring from the Presidential office after their second term has become, by universal concurrence, a part of our republican system of government, and that any departure from this time-honored custom would be unwise, unpatriotic and fraught with peril to our free institutions. . . ."

All of the prominent Democrats in the Senate solemnly voted for this resolution. Many of them were still in office twelve years later when President Franklin Roosevelt ran for a third full four-year term. Did these Democrats, who trembled at the thought of Calvin Coolidge serving for two and a half terms, stand by their principles when Roosevelt ran a third—and a fourth—time? Does the sun rise in the West?

The passage of the Twenty-second Amendment in 1947 vindicated Coolidge and rebuffed Roosevelt. The amendment limits a President to two terms, except that a former Vice President may be elected twice if he has served less than half the term of a predecessor. Lyndon Johnson, who served only fourteen of the forty-eight months to which John Kennedy had been elected, also retired after one full term. Harding and Kennedy were the only Presidents to die during the second half of their terms.

In 1928, the Republicans nominated Herbert Hoover for President. His humanitarian service during and after World War I placed him almost above politics. Some party stalwarts even regarded him as being soft on liberalism. Senate Majority Leader Charles Curtis of Kansas asked, "Why should we nominate a man for whom we will have to apologize throughout the campaign?" Hoover's chief apologist, as it turned out, was Curtis himself, who received the Vice-Presidential nomination.

Curtis, who was part Kaw Indian, had been in politics since the 1880's. Oswald Garrison Villard, a liberal writer, called him "the apotheosis of mediocrity" and as "faithful and as devoted to his party as he is dull and dumb." But the New York *Times* noted that the Vice-Presidential nomination was bound to go to the farm states, and it was just as well that the experienced Curtis had been chosen. Curtis was nearly seventy years old, and was not about to blaze any trails in the nation's second highest office. He was the last of the "traditional" Vice Presidents, the last of the long gray line of mediocrities who had filled the office so often since the time of George Clinton.

It is appropriate that during Curtis' incumbency the Broadway curtain should rise and fall on the satirical musical play, "Of Thee I Sing," with Victor Moore in the role of Alexander Throttlebottom, the Vice President with the name no one could remember. Poor Throttlebottom was reluctant to accept the nomination because his mother might hear about it. He passed his Vice-Presidential years feeding the pigeons in the park, and trying to find two references so he could obtain a library card.

After the stock-market crash, supporters of both Hoover and Curtis came to believe that GOP chances in 1932 might be improved if the other man were dropped from the ticket. However, both were renominated. Curtis told a heckler in Iowa that the average voter was "too damn dumb to understand" what the Republican candidates were talking about. Unfortunately from the Republican standpoint, the voters would remain in a state of ignorant bliss for the next twenty years.

When Curtis and Throttlebottom shuffled off the stage, an era ended. From 1933 on, the Vice Presidency would never be the same again, and the occupants of that office would be movers and shakers who will loom large in any study of American history.

★ ★ ★ ★ ★ ★ ★ ★ ★ ★

JOHN NANCE GARNER

"Mr. President, you know you've got to let the cattle graze."

Franklin D. Roosevelt, like his cousin Theodore, first ran for national office as a Vice-Presidential candidate. He attended the 1920 Democratic National Convention as a supporter of New York Governor Alfred E. Smith, but Governor James M. Cox of Ohio was nominated. Cox indicated that he preferred the thirty-eight-year-old Roosevelt as his running mate. Cox was not closely identified with the Wilson administration, and the nomination of Roosevelt—the Assistant Secretary of the Navy—would avert the impression that the Democrats were turning their backs on Wilson. Roosevelt lived in pivotal New York, where he had managed to avoid close ties with Tammany Hall. His name was a final recommendation for his nomination; it was hoped he would draw the votes of progressive Republicans who had once supported his cousin. Roosevelt, who received the Vice-Presidential nomination by acclamation, campaigned energetically but in vain; the Democrats lost to Harding and Coolidge. A year later Roosevelt was stricken with polio and dropped temporarily from the political scene.

In 1924 the Democrats seemed driven by a political death wish. They convened in Madison Square Garden with high hopes of riding back into office in the wake of the Harding scandals. Sharply divided over personalities, the Ku Klux Klan, and prohibition, the Democrats answered 103 roll calls before choosing a compromise candidate, John W. Davis of West Virginia. On the first Vice-Presidential ballot, the exhausted delegates scattered their votes among twenty-five men and five women. However, a consensus was quickly reached in behalf of Governor Charles Bryan of Nebraska, the brother of William Jennings Bryan. Charles Bryan, who had made a good record as Governor, brought to the ticket all the advantages—and disadvantages—of his brother. The coupling of Bryan, a symbol of the populist movement, with Davis—a Wall Street lawyer—made little sense.

Four years later, the Democrats nominated Senate Minority Leader Joseph Robinson of Arkansas to run with Presidential nominee Al Smith. The New York Governor opposed prohibition and Robinson favored it, and someone poked fun at "the Democratic donkey with a wet head and wagging a dry tail. . . ." The selection of Robinson also reflected concern about the Solid South. From 1928 to 1960, eight of the nine Democratic Vice-Presidential nominees were from Southern or border states. The strategy failed in 1928, as the Democrats lost part of the South and most of the rest of the country in the Hoover landslide.

John Nance Garner was born in Blossom Prairie, Texas, on November 22, 1868. He began the practice of law in Clarksville at the age of twenty-one. A doctor told him he was suffering from tuberculosis and must move to a drier climate or die. Garner settled in Uvalde, in southwest Texas, shrugged off his ailment, and enjoyed good health for the next three quarters of a century. He didn't spend all of his time in Uvalde, however.

After serving for a while as county judge, Garner was elected to the State Legislature in 1898. When the time came to redraw the boundaries of the state's congressional districts, Garner headed the committee in charge. He carved his own personal district out of the prairie, and proceeded to run for United States representative. Beginning in 1902, he was elected to Congress sixteen times, and might have held a mandate from his fief for half a century had he not accepted a call to national office.

Over the years, Representative Garner won popularity

and respect from his fellow legislators, but he remained almost unknown to the country at large. Garner did little campaigning. He did not fill the mails with transcripts of his speeches, for the simple reason that he made no speeches. After being in Congress for ten years, he admitted that he had never even seen five of the counties in his district. A newspaper announced in 1924 that he had not introduced a bill in the previous eight years. In fact, Garner was to introduce only four major bills during his three decades in the House. Yet in a quiet way he brought great ability and influence to bear in behalf of—or against—almost every significant piece of legislation to come before Congress during his last twenty-five years in Washington.

Garner's philosophy as a legislator might be described as the "Texas idea," to which Sam Rayburn and Lyndon Johnson later subscribed. In Garner's words, "Men who have known how to compromise intelligently have rendered great service to their country. The most constructive laws on our statute books have been put there by intelligent compromise. That does not mean that men have to abandon fundamentals or basic principles."

During the depression, Garner co-operated with Herbert Hoover when he felt that the President was right. He said: "I astonished people here in Washington once by saying I was for the welfare of the country first and that of the Democratic party second. . . . I am still that way, and it's somewhat like accusing a man of treason to say to him, in times like these, that he would try to block any constructive measure simply because it comes from the other side of the political fence."

Early in his Congressional career Garner directed his ambition toward the powerful position of Speaker of the House. It is possible in this country to become a young poet, a young corporation executive, or even a young President, but no one in recent times has found a short cut to leadership in the lower house of Congress. A critic observed that Garner's rise to power was based on the obituary column and on the powers of inertia. Another wrote that the Texan had spent his career with one hand in the pork barrel and the other scratching backs.

But in 1931 the waiting game was over and Garner, now stocky, white-haired, pink-faced, and already sixty-three years old, succeeded to the office that he considered to be second in importance only to the Presidency. But he would serve as Speaker for little more than a year. With great reluctance, he put aside the honor and the power of the speakership to accept the nomination to the most derided office in the land.

As Democratic leader of the House, Garner was regarded almost automatically as a Presidential contender in 1932. He discounted such speculation, observing: "No Democrat from Texas is going to have availability for his party's Presidential nomination except under extraordinary circumstances."

Yet when the convention met in Chicago, Garner had the solid support of delegates from Texas and from California, where he had won the Presidential primary. For three ballots the convention was deadlocked. Franklin Roosevelt, who had succeeded Al Smith as Governor of New York, had a majority but lacked about 100 votes of the required two thirds. The Roosevelt ranks showed signs of cracking, and already talk was heard of a compromise candidate.

Garner regarded his own chances as slim, and he feared a repetition of the 1924 Madison Square Garden fiasco and its 103 ballots. The Texan looked over the voting state by state, and concluded that Roosevelt ought to be nominated. He sent orders to his campaign manager, Representative Sam Rayburn, to turn his delegates over to Roosevelt on the fourth ballot. But his supporters in Texas said that they would not go to FDR unless Garner took second place on the ticket. The Speaker had no desire to be kicked upstairs, but he accepted the Vice Presidency in the cause of party unity. He was determined to help win an election for the National Democratic party, which had been wandering in the wilderness for a dozen years.

Recalling the 1924 deadlock, Garner explained: "If Roosevelt's strength had begun to break up on the fourth ballot, as it would have, I don't think any candidate could have got a two-thirds majority until after so bitter a contest that chances of winning the election would have ceased to exist. I did what I believed was best in the situation." A country in the grip of depression voted for Roosevelt and Garner by a wide margin.[1]

[1] Garner might have succeeded to the Presidency under unique and tragic circumstances. In January, 1933, President-elect Roosevelt was in Miami to make a speech. A man named Giuseppe Zangara fired five

Garner never pretended to enjoy his new job, and it is doubtful if any other Vice President so consistently maligned the office. "A great man may be Vice-President," said Garner, "but he can't be a great Vice-President, because the office in itself is unimportant." Some of his other remarks were less eloquent.

Even from the dais, Garner often spoke his mind, and on one occasion he tossed out a parliamentary decision not covered by Robert's Rules of Order. The noisy, radical Huey Long enjoyed badgering the Vice President, and once, after making himself particularly offensive to the chair, the Louisiana Senator jumped up and spoke in a bantering voice:

"Mr. President, I rise to make a parliamentary inquiry. . . . How should a senator, who is half in favor of this bill and half against it, cast his vote?"

Garner, his beady eyes peering out from under white bushy brows, rendered a decision worthy of Solomon: "Get a saw and saw yourself in two; that's what you ought to do anyhow!"

But Garner was on cordial terms with most Senators. Many a legislative hassle was settled in the Vice President's office, where newsmen and Congressmen gathered periodically to "strike a blow for liberty," as Garner called his bourbon-and-branch-water ceremony.

Drawing on his knowledge of parliamentary procedure and on his great influence on Capitol Hill, Garner helped push Roosevelt's revolutionary New Deal program through Congress. Given the history of the Vice Presidency, and considering Garner's own relatively conservative origins, no one could have been too surprised if the Texan had dragged his feet from the first. But he felt a sense of duty to the President. He recognized the desperate straits in which the country found itself, and he knew that the future of the party hung on the success or failure of the Administration's policies. Furthermore, Garner had yearned for power for so long, and had enjoyed such a brief taste of it as Speaker, that he was unwilling to accept the Vice-Presidential limitations prescribed by tradition.

---

shots at Roosevelt as he rode from the stadium in a car. The Mayor of Chicago was killed and four persons were injured, but Roosevelt was not hit.

During their first term Roosevelt and Garner established what seemed to be a model working relationship. Once again, a Vice President attended Cabinet meetings. Garner became the first Vice President to travel abroad in an official capacity, when he attended the installation of Manuel Quezon as President of the Republic of the Philippines in 1935. The next year he persuaded Roosevelt to establish weekly legislative conferences with Congressional leaders, in which Garner also participated.

At the Cabinet meetings, Garner endeavored to explain the mysteries of Congress to Roosevelt and to his band of professorial brain trusters and other political amateurs. Garner's report on conditions there was sometimes gloomy and betrayed his own wish that he had remained as Speaker. In 1934 he told the Cabinet that he had never seen the House of Representatives in such turmoil. Garner criticized the House leaders who, he said, seemed to have no control over the House and little apparent disposition to get behind Administration legislation.

As long as Garner enjoyed the confidence of both the executive and legislative branches, he could serve very effectively in a liaison role. Perhaps the framers of the Constitution had really conceived this to be the most important function of the Vice President, without spelling it out. But Garner's position was fraught with possibilities for mischief should he have a falling-out with Roosevelt. At first, as we have seen, all went well. As late as 1935, the Vice President told Interior Secretary Harold Ickes that he felt that the Administration had not gone far enough to satisfy the expectations of the public for a liberal government. He said that if FDR were defeated for reelection, he might be succeeded by a reactionary Republican who would open the door to fascism or communism. Ickes noted in his diary that Garner had spoken "with deep feeling and with sadness."

On the other hand, Garner was irritated by the growing use of the term "New Deal." The Texan took his Democratic politics straight. He did not like to hear references to the New Deal Party or to New Deal Democrats, especially from some of Roosevelt's younger, more pragmatic recruits. As the 1930's progressed, and as the country showed signs of climbing out of the depression, Garner gradually concluded that he could best serve his country by restraining the President.

Roosevelt and Garner were renominated at Philadelphia in 1936. The Republicans chose Alfred M. Landon for the Presidency, but passed over Styles Bridges for the second spot, thereby dodging a potential Democratic slogan, "Landon Bridges falling down." Instead the GOP chose a Chicago newspaper publisher for the Vice Presidency, and went into battle with "Off the Rocks with Landon and Knox." And carried two states.

Like Thomas R. Marshall, Garner expected that his second four years would be a breeze. Roosevelt said that he would never again run for public office, and Garner vowed that he wouldn't either. The President, however, saw the 1936 landslide as a call for more liberal legislation. From time to time at Cabinet meetings, Garner would interject the admonition, "Mr. President, you know you've got to let the cattle graze."

FDR's proposed reform of the Federal judiciary—his court-packing bill—brought the Democratic party to the crossroads in the summer of 1937. The President proposed to add one justice to the Supreme Court—up to a total of six—for each justice past seventy who had served at least ten years and who declined to retire. The purpose was to break the conservative control of the Court, which had overturned seven basic New Deal laws.

Instead of consulting with the legislative branch on this most important and controversial bill, Roosevelt called in Congressional leaders—including Garner—and unveiled down to the last comma the heretofore secret bill that he wished passed. Garner was stunned by this procedure.

The Democrats held a lopsided majority in Congress, but many conservatives and a few progressives joined in revolt against Roosevelt's plan. Many Congressmen who disagreed with some of the Court's decisions were opposed to a move that threatened to undermine the independence of the judiciary. Garner himself, in the Senate lobby, held his nose and gave a thumbs-down sign, perhaps his first open display of contempt for a position taken by the President.

In June, with the Senate about to vote on the Court bill, Garner and his wife left Washington for a Texas vacation they had planned five months before. Roosevelt was annoyed at what he regarded as a walkout by the Vice President. Ickes concluded that Garner was "off the reservation." Roosevelt wrote Garner, pleading for him to return to Washington, but Garner remained in Texas.

On July 14, Majority Leader Robinson dropped dead of a heart attack brought on by his struggle to save Roosevelt's Court bill. With Robinson dead, support for the measure melted away. When Garner returned to Washington and told Roosevelt that he was beaten, the President asked the Vice President to arrange the best possible compromise. It is not clear to what extent Garner attempted to salvage any part of the wreckage, but the record shows that the Senate voted to return the bill to committee, in effect killing it.

The Court fight marked the beginning of a breakup of the Grand Coalition which Roosevelt had assembled for his re-election in 1936. Hereafter the Democrats would see a schism opening between their conservative and liberal members. The Vice President held Roosevelt responsible for the split, and a sudden flurry of other developments reinforced this conviction.

Simultaneously with the climax of the Court fight, the Democratic Senators elected a successor to Robinson. Roosevelt and Garner both pledged to keep hands off the majority-leader contest, but then the President intervened—decisively as it turned out—in favor of Senator Alben Barkley of Kentucky. Garner frowned at the intense pressure brought to bear by the President on individual members of the Senate, and he correctly foresaw that Roosevelt's continued indifference toward the prerogatives of the legislative branch would jeopardize his future program.

Earlier in 1937 Roosevelt and Garner had quarreled for the better part of three hours at the White House one afternoon concerning Administration policy toward sit-down strikes. Members of John L. Lewis' CIO Automobile Workers Union had occupied a number of plants and refused to work themselves or to let others work. Garner believed that the strikes were Communist-inspired, and that the seizure by workers of property they did not own was a brazen defiance of law. Garner urged Roosevelt to condemn the tactics as illegal, but the President refused to speak out. When Roosevelt said that he could not get the men out of the plants without bloodshed, Garner replied, "Then John L. Lewis is a bigger man than you are if you can't find some way to cope with this." Garner said later, "We went at it hot and heavy."

Garner, unhappy about a continuing trend toward deficit financing, and concerned about the Administration's attitude toward Congress, labor, and the courts, had not yet seen the worst. In 1938, Roosevelt undertook to purge several Senators who had opposed his Supreme Court bill. He intervened directly in Democratic primaries in all parts of the country. Garner believed that the President had succumbed to pressure from ultra-liberals who wanted to realign the major parties along progressive and conservative lines.

"It is not a question of making the Democratic party the progressive party," said the Vice President. "It has always been the more progressive one. It is a question of the Democratic party or a personal party—a Roosevelt party. It's risky business. When you build around a personality instead of a party program and principles then your party is up Salt Creek when that personality is off the ticket. . . .

"This talk about dividing the country into two political camps—one progressive and the other conservative—is all so much stuff. There will always be agitation [for] this realignment, but in my considered judgment, it will never come. If it did you'd find you'd have a radical and a reactionary party and neither of these could serve the nation."

The voters in the Democratic primaries rebuffed the President by renominating most of the men he had opposed. The Democratic rift helped contribute to heavy party losses in the November election, as the Republicans picked up six Senate seats, eleven governorships, and more than eighty seats in the House.

Charles G. Dawes had warned about the dangers of bringing a Vice President into Cabinet meetings, and his arguments seemed to be borne out by the events during the last two years of Garner's second term, 1939 to 1941.

Garner seemed embarrassed as he sat at one end of the long rectangular table with Roosevelt and the Cabinet officers. The conservative press had applauded him as the principal wrecker of the Court bill, and the Texan symbolized the resistance within the Democratic party to the Roosevelt leadership. The last long private conference between the President and the Vice President took place in December, 1938, and thereafter they confronted each other only in the presence of others.

Their Cabinet exchanges were frequently unpleasant. Roosevelt would often complain about a lack of leadership in Congress, and Garner did not fail to take the hint. Roosevelt tossed out other pointed barbs. Garner, for his part, became morose, and from time to time would interrupt the President with "Well, didn't I tell you so?" or "You remember that I brought that up two or three years ago."

Interior Secretary Ickes told his diary that he found Garner's "old, red, wizened face" a "disgusting sight."

The friction caused a chill and a suspicion to fall across the Cabinet room. The President became convinced that Garner was leaking information about Cabinet talk to his cronies on the outside. The Secretaries didn't want their half-developed ideas and programs discussed at Washington cocktail parties and in the press. Labor Secretary Frances Perkins wrote later of "a drawing in of horns, a limitation on the free and vigorous expression of opinion." Department heads adopted the custom of lingering behind after a Cabinet meeting to talk privately with FDR. Garner called it "staying for prayer meeting."

The culmination of the ideological and personal estrangement between Roosevelt and Garner came in the summer of 1940, when the President stood as a candidate for a third term. The Vice President strenuously opposed a third term, arguing: "A President, any President, weak or strong, is in position to exercise great power from the first breath he draws after taking office until he leaves that office. No man should exercise the great powers of the Presidency too long." And he said on another occasion: "I would be against a third term on principle even if I approved every act of Roosevelt's two terms. I would oppose my own brother for a third term."

Public opinion polls showed that if Roosevelt had not become a candidate again, Garner would have been the overwhelming Presidential choice of rank-and-file Democratic voters. He was by now, by choice or not, the leader of the faction within the party that desired to close the books on the New Deal for good. Although he was past seventy, it may well have been that the Presidential bug was biting. At any rate, Garner announced his candidacy for President. He insisted that his name go before the convention to give Roosevelt's opponents a chance to be heard. The Vice President went down to a crushing defeat before the third term "draft."

Garner left Washington forever in 1941, filled with deep unhappiness, distrust of Roosevelt and his policies, and concern for the welfare of the country. To John L. Lewis he was a "labor-baiting, poker-playing, whisky-drinking, evil old man." His public service had spanned forty-six years, and he was to live still another quarter of a century. He had suffered the fate of all those who live a long life. By the time he reached the Vice Presidency he already seemed to be an anachronism, crowded and hurried by a generation of men grappling with problems unknown and unforeseen by the young Texas legislator of the 1890's.

Men of his own era died, and protégés grown old themselves made occasional pilgrimages to Uvalde to pay their respects to the aged statesman. Newspapermen and friends always took note of his birthdays, especially those milestones ending in "0" or "5." Such a day was November 22, 1963, the end of the ninety-fifth year for the man who had walked this planet simultaneously with Millard Fillmore and perhaps thirty other Presidents past, present, and future. A younger man was campaigning in Texas that day, a President less than half Garner's age. John Kennedy found a few minutes in a crowded morning schedule to call Uvalde and extend birthday greetings. Garner, moved, replied in words at once touching and soon poignant: "God bless you. You're my President and I love you. I hope you stay in there forever."

★ ★ ★ ★ ★
★ ★ ★ ★ ★
★

HENRY A. WALLACE

". . . the century which will come out of this war—can be and must be the century of the common man."

Vice Presidents have been with us almost 200 years. Since 1900 they have been chosen in a somewhat less cavalier fashion than during most of the earlier period. But the concept of the *working* Vice President dates only from about 1941.

Since then, every Vice President has been politically in tune with his President, and has displayed a loyalty to his chief in striking contrast to the circumstances found so often before. Each Vice President during this period (with the exception of Truman, who served only three months) has assumed executive positions of far greater responsibility than those delegated to any occupant of the office before 1941.

Franklin Roosevelt and Henry Wallace were the men who accepted the challenge to reform the Vice Presidency. Their experiment, unfortunately, could not be hailed as a great success. Seldom has a man served his leader with the selflessness of Henry Wallace, yet no Vice President managed so to bedevil a Chief Executive, albeit unintentionally. His four years in the No. 2 office will always be unique, because Henry Wallace was himself unique. In a lineup of forgettable Vice Presidents, he was one of a few who graced the office with intellect and energy. His successors have benefited from his mistakes, and they have strengthened the office at a pace swift enough to revive hopes that it may yet become the second most prestigious in our Government.

Who was this Vice President who dreamed of building TVA's around the world; who said that he had a great affection for grass; who hoped to find signs of the Second Coming in the barren deserts of Mongolia; who studied the aerodynamics of the boomerang; who had a sense of social justice years ahead of most of his contemporaries, yet who walked wide-eyed into the arms of the Communists?

He came from one of the most distinguished families in American agriculture—the Wallaces of Iowa. His grandfather, the first Henry Wallace, was a white-bearded ex-preacher clearly stamped as a member of the rural aristocracy. "Uncle Henry" was the founder and editor of *The Iowa Homestead* and later of *Wallaces' Farmer*, respected publications that shared tables with the Bible in farm homes across the Midwest. His son, Henry Cantwell Wallace, was Secretary of Agriculture under Harding and Coolidge.

The third generation was represented by Henry A. Wallace, who developed a scientific skepticism while still a boy. He rejected the theory of a corn expert that an ear with a "fine, strong middle" was the best because it looked the prettiest. His own experiments with corn proved otherwise, and the youth stumped the older generation with the question, "What's looks to a hog?"

The young scientist did not spare himself from experimentation. Determined to find a perfect diet, he partook of all manner of unsavory combinations of food, and he also fasted for a period. By the time he had completed his agricultural course at Iowa State, Wallace was the shy, introspective person he would remain throughout his public career.

Wallace developed a successful and profitable hybrid corn. He forecast an impending agricultural collapse after studying corn-hog ratio charts. In 1921 he succeeded his father as editor of *Wallaces' Farmer*, and he soon began to espouse strange theories that disturbed conventional people. He drew on mathematics, genetics, meteorology, comparative religion, and other subjects to illustrate the problems and the opportunities of the farmer. His father's death in 1924 left the third Henry to carry on the fight to win for the farmer a fair share of the booming prosperity of the 1920's. Failure of Republican Presidents to support agricultural legislation that Wallace deemed essential prompted him to forsake his father's party and turn to the Democrats.

Through his editorials and his lobbying in Washington, Wallace drew the attention of Rexford Guy Tugwell, a member of Franklin Roosevelt's 1932 pre-convention Brain Trust. Roosevelt invited Wallace to Hyde Park for a discussion of farm policy, and the Iowan apparently impressed the future President. Although Wallace had had only a minor role in shaping FDR's farm program, Roosevelt asked him to take the post of Secretary of Agriculture, once held by his father. Wallace accepted.

Farmers were desperate in 1933. Many preferred to burn their corn for fuel instead of selling it for the 10 cents a bushel which was all they could get. While children went hungry, demonstrators in Syracuse, New York, dumped milk into the streets. "The spectacle did us no credit as a civilized people," said Wallace. "I feel that all of us should earnestly examine our own minds and hearts, get at fundamentals, and try to cure the conditions that led to such bewildered haste and waste."

To stanch plummeting prices, Wallace turned reluctantly to scarcity economics. He prevailed on farmers to plow under 10 million acres of cotton and to slaughter 6 million pigs. The sacrifice of the pigs was not in vain; 1934 prices rose by 50 per cent. But the Chicago *Tribune* headlined Wallace as The Greatest Butcher in Christendom.

An annoyed Wallace remarked that it was "a marvelous tribute to the humanitarian instincts of the American people that they sympathize more with little pigs which are killed than with full-grown hogs. Some people may object to killing pigs at any age. Perhaps they think that farmers should run a sort of old-folks home for hogs. . . . But we have to think about farmers as well as hogs. And we must think about consumers and try to get a uniform supply of pork from year to year at a price which is fair to farmer and consumer alike."

All of the executive departments in Washington crackled with new ideas in those early New Deal days. Russell Lord, a biographer of Wallace, wrote that old-time Democratic party regulars discovered in dismay that the Capital was suddenly full of "eager-faced, immature technicians and academicians with lean bodies and no bellies, running around hatless, acting rather breathlessly mysterious and important, calling one another and the President by their first names." Wallace himself was a delight to cartoonists and pundits, a diffident man with an unruly thatch of hair, shaggy eyebrows, and a wistful faraway look in his eyes. A ghost writer for Wallace in those days recalled that the Secretary of Agriculture "gives me an eerie feeling that he really isn't listening when I talk with him. . . . He gives me a strong impression of considering himself a man of destiny, a person answering calls the rest of us don't hear."

If Wallace had devoted his life solely to helping the farmer, he would have been forgotten by now along with most of the other men who have served as Secretary of Agriculture. But he broadened his perspective and became an important, if curious, factor in American political life.

He subscribed in time to a form of "pantheism" and became convinced that science, nature, and religion are one. He regarded religion not only as a means of saving his soul from Hell, but also as a force capable of achieving the Kingdom of God on earth. He found "intellectual exercise" in Presbyterian sermons; he studied Darwin; at a Roman Catholic Mass, he felt an instinctive desire "to cross myself, and remain quietly kneeling after the conclusion of the mass, in silent adoration." He studied Judaism, Buddhism, Zoroastrianism, Mohammedanism, Christian Science, and Aristotelian logic. He became, finally, a member of a High Episcopalian parish, but still rebelled against what he called the "lukewarmness, the wishy-washy goody-goodiness, the infantile irrelevancy of the Church itself."

A newsman wrote that Wallace, "one of the most admirable and ridiculous figures of the New Deal, should have been born in the Middle Ages and set himself in the quiet of a cloister garden to commune with his soul and the Infinite. . . ."

Wallace, however, was not content merely to walk with God. He intended to practice his religion in his public life. He spoke of a struggle between the Common Man and the citadels of privilege, dating not merely from 1933, but from the time of the Old Testament. He asserted that "the Biblical record is heavily loaded on the side of the Progressive Independents." Furthermore, "The New Deal is Amos proclaiming the needs of the poor in the land of Israel. The New Deal is New England citizens dumping tea in Boston Harbor. . . . The New

Deal is Abraham Lincoln preaching freedom for the oppressed. . . ."

Thrust suddenly onto the national stage, Wallace saw his opportunity to evangelize among the masses. He poured hundreds of thousands of words into dictating machines and microphones. He traveled across the nation and around the world, seeking everywhere a Common Man, carrying the message of Franklin Roosevelt and the New Deal. He sailed on a tide of printed material—official documents, his speeches, and his books. In one year alone he traveled forty thousand miles, visited every state, spoke eighty-eight times, and wrote twenty articles and three books.

Even in those days of liberal revolution, Wallace outraced his contemporaries. He issued a call to which a younger generation would one day respond. While John Kennedy was still at prep school, Wallace wrote a book entitled *New Frontiers*, and he spoke of a land that could not be found on any map: "The land beyond the new frontier will be conquered by the continuous social inventions of men whose hearts are free from bitterness, prejudice, hatred, greed and fear; by men whose hearts are aflame with the extraordinary beauty of the scientific, artistic and spiritual wealth now before us, if only we reach out confidently, together."

In words that would be echoed on a bitterly cold inauguration day in 1961, Wallace wrote in 1934: "People may actually work harder than they did on the old frontier. . . . It is not a mushy, sentimental frontier, but one of hard realities, requiring individual and social discipline beyond that of the old frontiers."

He identified himself with the older generation among the Children of Israel who had not lived to see the Promised Land. Wallace said that it would be necessary "for the younger generation, hardened by travels in the wilderness, to come to maturity." He recognized the first outpouring of support for New Deal domestic reforms as an emotional response of men and women paralyzed by depression. He warned that they "must not only mean well in their hearts, but they must understand with their minds, the adjustments which must be made. . . ." The quarter century after 1934 saw economic recovery, war, reaction, cold war, and consolidation of New Deal gains under the Republicans. Finally came the thrust toward New Frontiers and a Great Society, toward an accelerated program aimed at achieving a balance of rights and responsibilities among the diverse members of our society. Wallace lived to see "the adjustments which must be made."

Wallace wrote in *New Frontiers*: "The ideals of the good life are relatively simple, but when it comes to working them out in practice the detailed decisions are endlessly perplexing." Wallace himself, the prophet of the New Frontier, was deemed—perhaps rightly so—as not capable of applying satisfactorily the principles he espoused—and so he would be denied the leadership of the Democratic party. Like Moses, he would not be permitted to enter the Promised Land.

If public service was a religion for Wallace, it was also a science. Science and technology, in his view, had made possible for the first time the elimination of want, ignorance, and squalor. He criticized scientists whom he felt had failed to develop a social point of view. He called on men and women in the laboratories to help regulate the output of goods in the age of abundance, so as to provide a generous distribution of that abundance to everyone. He said that technology made all persons in all nations interrelated and interdependent.

Before World War II, Wallace tried to rally public opinion against the false theories of the German Nazi regime. He warned that down through the centuries "one of the most popular political devices has been to blame economic and other troubles on some minority group." Referring to Hitler's policy on human sterilization, Wallace said that plant-breeding experiments had suggested that genetic improvement could not be achieved merely by sterilizing those individuals in whom weaknesses of the whole strain appeared. He contended that human defectives exist because the species contains within itself the elements that produce them. Scoffing at the allegedly superior characteristics to be found in pure "Aryans," Wallace pointed out that livestock breeding had shown: "The color of a cow's hair . . . has nothing to do with her ability to produce milk, and there is no reason to think that the color of a man's hair has anything to do with his ability to produce ideas."

And Wallace did not shirk from comparing Nazi racist doctrines with American attitudes toward Jews, Negroes, and poor whites.

Roosevelt's esteem for his Secretary of Agriculture grew as the latter spoke out forcefully on controversial subjects on which the President himself felt obliged to remain silent. But to others in Washington, Wallace was a maverick, a loner, and frankly incomprehensible. Gerald Johnson, an observer of the Washington scene, wrote that "a politician's friend is a man who gets him a better job, or who rounds up delegates for him in a convention, or who gives him shrewd advice. . . . Of this sort of friends Wallace has none, nor has he ever had any. . . .

"[He] has come to high office without the usual long and grueling training in the art of being all things to all men . . . he holds an office for which he has not fought and schemed, dickered and dealt, compromised and contrived through intense and wearying years."

In October, 1939, Wallace called for Roosevelt's re-election to a third term. No one knows when the President first decided to run again. But as he weighed other possibilities for the 1940 Democratic Presidential nomination, he concluded that the party might pass into the hands of conservatives or isolationists. Although he refused to announce his own candidacy, he turned his attention to recruiting a running mate to replace Garner, who had defected in opposition to a third term. In July, 1940, FDR asked National Chairman James A. Farley what he thought of Wallace as a Vice-Presidential candidate.

Farley said that Wallace would add no strength to the ticket and: "Beyond that I would not like to see him Vice President, even though I like him personally, because I think it would be a terrible thing to have him President . . . the people look on him as a wild-eyed fellow."

"You know, Jim," the President replied, "a man with paralysis can have a breakup any time. While my heart and lungs are good and the other organs [are] functioning along okay . . . nothing in this life is certain." He added: "It's essential that the man who runs with me should be able to carry on."

Despite third-term opposition within the party, FDR hoped for a unanimous "draft." However, other men, including Garner and Farley himself, had allowed their names to be placed in nomination. Chicago's Mayor Ed Kelly, host to the convention, attempted to stampede the delegates to the President, who was still pretending he didn't want the nomination. Kelly posted his superintendent of sewers in a dimly lit room below the floor of the convention, facing a microphone wired to the public-address system. Upstairs, after a carefully timed mention of the magic name Roosevelt, delegates heard a disembodied voice booming across the arena. It proclaimed that "We Want Roosevelt," "America Wants Roosevelt," "New Jersey Wants Roosevelt," and so on. Even delegates who favored FDR were disgusted by this clumsy attempt to bring about the President's renomination by acclamation. Robert Sherwood called it a "dreadful display of democracy at its tawdriest." But Roosevelt had his "draft," an overwhelming first-ballot nomination.

The party faithful were really upset by the next development. Harry Hopkins, the President's representative at the convention, passed the word that Roosevelt wanted Wallace for Vice President.

Roosevelt had turned to Wallace after the aging Secretary of State, Cordell Hull, had refused to accept second place on the ticket. Roosevelt, in Washington, summed up his case for Wallace in a telephone conversation with Secretary of Labor Frances Perkins, who was attending the convention:

"I think Wallace is good. I like him. He is the kind of man I like to have around. He is good to work with and he knows a lot, you can trust his information. He digs to the bottom of things and gets the facts. He is honest as the day is long. He thinks right. He has the general ideas we have. He is the kind of man who can do something in politics. He can help the people with their political thinking. Yes, I think it had better be Wallace."

FDR took a calculated risk in proferring Wallace to the delegates, but earlier he had made the mistake of allowing other candidates to believe that the race for Vice President would be wide open. (He was to err in much the same way four years later.) Secretary of the Interior Ickes noted in his diary: ". . . he should have sent word earlier to the principal candidates not to spend time and money and build up their hopes. . . . They would have understood this and proceeded accordingly."

Hopkins phoned Washington to tell FDR that the delegates were in revolt and might not go for Wallace.

"Well, damn it to hell," the President boomed, "they will go for Wallace or I won't run, and you can jolly well tell them so."

Roosevelt grew more angry by the minute as he listened to the radio and to the boos that greeted every mention of Wallace's name. He called for pen and paper, and began writing furiously. He handed a scribbled letter to Samuel Rosenman, a Presidential assistant, and told him to prepare it for release. Outside the President's office, Rosenman and General Edwin M. (Pa) Watson, the President's military aide, scanned the note. Roosevelt was announcing his refusal to accept the nomination; the letter was to be released in the event the convention failed to name Wallace.

Watson, badly shaken, wanted to tear up the letter: "I don't give a damn who's Vice-President and neither does the country. The only thing that's important to this country is that fellow in there. There isn't anyone in the United States who can lead this nation for the next four years as well as he can."

Rosenman, however, prepared the letter for release. The final version read in part:

"Until the Democratic Party through this Convention makes overwhelmingly clear its stand in favor of social progress and liberalism, and shakes off all the shackles of control fastened upon it by the forces of conservatism, reaction and appeasement, it will not continue its march of victory. . . .

"I wish to give the Democratic Party the opportunity to make its historic decision clearly and without equivocation. The party must go wholly one way or wholly the other. It cannot face in both directions at the same time.

"By declining the honor of the nomination for the Presidency, I can restore that opportunity to the Convention. I so do."

Back in Chicago, many of the Vice-Presidential aspirants were withdrawing from the race in deference to the President's wishes, but the contest still looked close. South Carolina's Senator James Byrnes hurried from delegation to delegation during the balloting, pleading for support of Wallace: "For God's sake, do you want a President or a Vice President?"

A fellow governor asked Leon Phillips of Oklahoma if he was supporting Wallace.

"Why, Henry's my second choice," he replied.

"Who's your first choice?" he was asked.

"Anyone—red, white, black, or yellow—that can get the nomination."

The balloting began, with only Speaker of the House William Bankhead formally opposing Wallace. A late surge put the Secretary of Agriculture over the top by a few votes. The mood of the convention was so ugly that Byrnes advised Wallace not to deliver his acceptance speech.

A delegate from Louisiana rushed up to George Allen and wailed indignantly: "No one wanted Wallace—absolutely no one. Name me just one man that did."

Allen replied, "Brother, that I can do—and that one man was Roosevelt."

Wallace's first campaign for elective office would be memorable. On the one hand, he excoriated the Republican party as the "party of appeasement." Those "who stand for business appeasement with Germany," he felt, were "the most dangerous of all fifth columns."

Yet in this same year, he published *The American Choice*, a curious document nearly free of polemics. As a judgment and prophecy, this book would be difficult to match. He presented a lengthy, no-nonsense dissertation on the conditions in the United States and the world during the first year of the war with Europe. Wallace correctly forecast that Stalin would be only an "*ad hoc* ally" of Hitler. Not content merely to assert that war was coming to America—he had been saying so for years—Wallace looked further ahead and wondered "whether we shall wake up sufficiently after this World War to conduct ourselves with a wisdom greater than that which we employed after World War I." With feeling against Germany running high—and with his own antipathy toward Hitler a matter of record—Wallace nonetheless advised his readers to "recall with compassion the conditions to which the German people were reduced in 1918, and ask ourselves how in the light of history the outcome could have been greatly different."

On a subject of domestic concern he wrote that soil despoliation "is not brought about by deliberate malice of social thugs. It is done with no thought of harm. We wound our country and threaten its future by thoughtless actions which are in part a response to needs, but more particularly the product of an inherited way of thinking—or not thinking—about the land."

Contemporaries of Wallace expressed mystification at how this fumbling speaker could win such enthusiastic support among rank-and-file voters. They obviously failed to consider the audience Wallace reached through his prolific writings, including his collected speeches. Many of these had been disappointing because of Wallace's poor delivery, but even in that strident voice, the words themselves conveyed an overpowering earnestness and sincerity.

In a period of uncertainty and anxiety, he spoke of the future with confidence. Privately, of course, he was beset by doubts, forever tottering along a narrow line between the concrete and the mystic, between sound analysis and intellectual flights of fancy. As long as the nation was swept up in a great crusade, it would march with Wallace without analyzing too closely his visions of a postwar utopia. But when the war ended, the people would become more concerned with the price of milk and less concerned with sharing a quart with every Hottentot. Only then would Wallace's grip on the public mind be lessened.

Controversy was the Iowan's lifetime companion. During the 1940 campaign the Democratic party's high command was shaken by the discovery of letters allegedly written by Henry Wallace to members of a tiny religious sect. Had these letters been published that fall, Republican Presidential candidate Wendell Willkie[1] might have won the election.

Many years before, Wallace had met Nicholas Konstantinovich Roerich, a short, bald, middle-aged man with a spade beard, who called himself the sole representative of the White Brotherhood of the East. Roerich had studied art and law in his native St. Petersburg. Archaeological expeditions had lured him to Kashmir, Turkestan, Tibet, Sikkim, and other strange lands. On one occasion he reportedly discovered an ancient Buddhist chronicle revealing that Christ had visited India as a young man. During his travels, he painted several thousand pictures. Many of these were placed in New York City's Roerich Museum, financed by admirers who thought he was a god.

[1] Willkie's running mate, Senator Charles McNary of Oregon, was, unlike Willkie, a champion of Federal power projects.

Wallace, after discussing the matter with Roerich, came to believe that somewhere on the lonely plains of Central Asia evidence might be found of the Second Coming of Christ. In 1935, while Secretary of Agriculture, Wallace placed Roerich in charge of an expedition to Mongolia. Roerich was supposed to be searching for drought-resistant grasses, but he was really hoping to find signs of the Second Coming. When Roerich made some controversial statements, the Mongolians concluded that he was some sort of a spy. At about the same time the United States Treasury Department charged Roerich with nonpayment of income taxes. Wallace became disenchanted with the mystic, and expelled him from government service. Roerich never returned to this country. Some of the Russian's loyal disciples became angry at what they regarded as a betrayal by Wallace, and one woman threatened to publish letters that she claimed Wallace had written to her, to Roerich, and to others.

During the 1940 campaign, newspaper publishers unfriendly to the Democrats obtained copies of the letters. Some were written in longhand, and others were typewritten on Department of Agriculture stationery. Signatures included "H. A. Wallace," "HAW," and "Galahad."

In one, the writer referred to the powers of an Oriental talisman: "Saturday night, after a very strenuous day, my eyes did not focus properly and I had to attend a Senatorial dinner. I remembered the lovely gift of musk and rose and a pinch of it cleared up my vision like magic."

Another example: "I have been thinking of you holding the casket—the sacred, most precious casket. And I have thought of the new country going forth, to meet the seven stars under the sign of the three stars. And I have thought of the admonition. 'Await the stones.' "

In 1933, in a letter to Franklin Roosevelt, Wallace had used language that would frighten any cigar-chomping ward politician. Warning against recognition of the Soviet Union, Wallace told FDR that "we must deal with the 'strong ones,' the 'turbulent ones,' the 'fervent ones,' and perhaps even with a temporary resurgence, with the 'flameless ones' who with one last dying gasp will strive to re-animate their dying giant 'Capitalism.'

"Mr. President, you can be the 'flaming one,' the one with

an ever upward-surging spirit to lead us into the time when the children of men can sing again. But I feel, Mr. President, that the perils concerning which I spoke to you last Wednesday must be successfully passed before we can enter safely into the time of the infinite unselfish expansion of the spirit."

Handwriting experts agreed that some of the Roerich letters had been written by Wallace, but the "damaging" ones were typewritten, and the experts could not agree on the signatures. The Democrats prepared to move the entire publicity staff of the national committee from Washington, D.C., to New York City to counter the charges.

"Why didn't *I* hear about this?" shrilled Harry Hopkins. "Why didn't I hear about this *sooner?* I've got my people in every newspaper office in the country."

A reporter dogged Wallace's campaign trail, seeking information on the letters. The candidate handed him a statement saying: "Your publisher . . . must know that the material in question is composed of malicous, spurious, fraudulent, and forged matter. He must know that it emanates from a source rejected as to credibility by courts of the land; that the same garbage has been hawked around for many years. . . ."

The storm passed, as the editors decided the documents were too hot to publish. The President shrugged off the incident. Eleanor Roosevelt wrote in her autobiography that Wallace "had simply been carried away by his intellectual curiosity. He was not realistic enough to appreciate how these letters would look to people who did not have the same kind of curiosity. . . . Mr. Wallace is perhaps too idealistic—and that makes him a bad politician." Roosevelt and Wallace were elected by a substantial margin.

The new Vice President said he welcomed the opportunity to get acquainted with the ninety-six senators, but he failed to win many friends on Capitol Hill. His first step was to remove Garner's private bar. He made himself comfortable in the tall-backed swivel chair on the Senate dais, and in fact often seemed to be dozing when the debate grew dull. But if critics hoped Wallace might die of boredom, they were disappointed. The Vice President was soon traveling all over the country, speaking before all kinds of groups about social problems and the threat of war.

Wallace urged a tough line against Japan. He warned Roosevelt that any sign of weakness or appeasement would be misunderstood by, and would give encouragement to, the Axis powers. He also spoke, early in 1941, of a second chance to make the world safe for democracy, and he called for the establishment of an international peace-keeping force after the war. In a magazine article written just before the Pearl Harbor attack—and while isolationists were still in full cry—Wallace talked about the peace that would follow the war:

"Thinking of the future peace . . . is not searching for an escape from the stern realities of the present . . . planning for the future peace must of necessity be a part of our all-out war program."

Wallace participated in meetings leading to the development of the atomic bomb. Nine days after Pearl Harbor, he discussed a "diabolical" new weapon with scientific and military leaders.

On May 8, 1942, before the Free World Association of New York City, Wallace delivered his most memorable speech. He called once more for the people to pay the necessary price for the freedoms they would attain on the day of ultimate triumph. Wallace, with sons in the army and navy, seemed overwhelmed by both grief and exaltation as he contemplated the unfolding drama of carnage and courage in which the United States had been involved for five months.

He began to speak a bit tremulously: "This is a fight between a slave world and a free world." Then his voice rang clear: "Just as the United States in 1862 could not remain half slave and half free, so in 1942 the world must make its decision for a complete victory one way or the other."

He reviewed man's march toward freedom, beginning with the American Revolution, a survey that included an assertion that the Russians and the Chinese were learning rapidly the meaning of liberty.

An almost parenthetical observation would bring more ridicule than anything he ever said: "Half in fun and half seriously, I said the other day to Madame Litvinov: 'The object of this war is to make sure that everybody in the world has the privilege of drinking a quart of milk a day.'"

A Quart of Milk for All the Hottentots, shrieked the opposition, which often displayed undue haste in projecting Wallace's abstractions into specifics.

But Wallace also made a more subtly controversial and important statement in that speech. With red-white-and-blue patriotism at its peak, he struck out against the prevailing mood: "Some have spoken of the 'American Century.' I say that the century on which we are entering—the century which will come out of this war—can be and must be the century of the common man."

Wallace sped toward his climax with an evangelistic fervor. He visioned a battle at the barricades against the monopolists, the exploiters, and the racists.

"No compromise with Satan is possible. We shall not rest until all the victims under the Nazi yoke are freed. We shall fight for a complete peace as well as a complete victory.

"The people's revolution is on the march, and the devil and all his angels cannot prevail against it. They cannot prevail, for on the side of the people is the Lord."

The Vice President was by now an international figure. He attracted huge crowds during a trip to Latin America in 1943, and was compared to Jesus Christ and Lincoln on the same day.

Wallace was capable of approaching a subject as a scientist. But in the case of the Soviet Union, he violated a basic precept of the scientific method. Having once decided that the Soviet regime was leading its people onward and upward toward democracy and liberty, he proceeded to gather only evidence to support this point of view. Those tendering evidence to the contrary were in danger of being labeled lackeys of fascism.

As noted previously, Wallace had opposed recognition of the Soviet Union. He wrote to Hull in 1933: "I was deeply shocked at the means which the Soviet government was using to collectivize the Russian farmers. . . . It was my kind of people who were being dispossessed, and I was appalled by the brutality of the Soviet methods."

In *New Frontiers,* he had written: ". . . I abhor the bitterness and violence which characterizes the Communistic approach to economic problems. . . ."

Somehow, at some point, Wallace reached his own private accommodation with Stalin & Co. Neither the butchery of the Old Bolsheviks nor the signing of the pact with Germany in

1939 prevented his *detente* with Moscow. Wallace was not a Communist, but he became a most useful tool of the Communists; some of the most worthy ideas ever advanced by an American public official were appropriated by them and cynically tailored to their own purposes.

It would be presumptuous to attempt to trace the tortuous paths of Wallace's mind that led him to the Kremlin gate. Possibly his error was in identifying himself too closely and too emotionally with the admittedly pitiable plight of the Russian people. The invasion of Russia by Hitler in 1941 drew the line clearly for Wallace. Once more it was Elijah *vs.* the prophets of Baal, Christ against Caesar, Roosevelt against the economic royalists.

In November, 1942, Wallace addressed 20,000 people at the Congress of American-Soviet Friendship in Madison Square Garden. Even assuming that it was necessary to lend a Vice President's prestige to the affair, he bubbled far beyond anything that needed to be said. Seeking to show that the two peoples would become good neighbors, he cited Tocqueville's comments on the similarities between Russians and Americans. But he omitted the Frenchman's reference to the Russian tradition of dictatorship and servitude.

He enthusiastically proclaimed that both countries were "striving for education, the productivity and the enduring happiness of the common man." Wallace assured his listeners that it was "because Stalin pushed educational democracy with all the power that he could command that Russia today is able to resist Germany."

Thereafter, Wallace seldom uttered a sensible word about Russia. As far as he was concerned, all the evidence was in, the lessons of history were clear, and the conclusions inescapable.

In other wartime speeches, Wallace filled the air with warnings. He said that World War III would be probable "if fascist interests motivated largely by anti-Russian bias get control of our government." He concluded: "If we define an American fascist as one who in case of conflict puts money and power ahead of human beings, then there are undoubtedly several million fascists in the United States." He complained about "midget Hitlers here who continually attack labor." He displayed only a shaky faith in American businessmen, warning: ". . . the people will smash their system unless they are willing to furnish such active leadership in wholehearted co-operation with labor and government as will prevent serious unemployment." In February, 1944, five months before a Democratic National Convention that would decide his political future, the Vice President charged that "American fascists at this very moment are desperately striving to control the delegates to the county conventions so that they may in turn control the delegates to the state and national conventions of both parties."

And so the man who might have led a charge across the New Frontier rode off instead into a red sunset.

On the eve of World War II, President Roosevelt decided to expand greatly the duties of the Vice President. The effects were far-reaching. The office underwent a profound change; and a sequence of events was set in motion which led to the political downfall of Henry Wallace.

On July 30, 1941, Roosevelt established the Economic Defense Board by executive order. Wallace was named chairman, and its members included seven Cabinet officers. Wallace was empowered to make final decisions whenever it was necessary to "expedite" work by the board. With employees numbering three thousand, and with duties related to imports, exports, and stock-piling of strategic materials, the heir of Alexander Throttlebottom suddenly became one of the most powerful men in the Capital. When bombs fell on Pearl Harbor, Wallace was at the zenith of his authority and prestige. He alone was invited by Roosevelt on December 7 to attend meetings with both the Cabinet and Congressional leaders. Now an executive in his own right, he was also the chief theoretician of the New Deal, a maker of policy, and a confidant of the President. But although he had been elected Vice President by the people, he served in his new capacity at the pleasure of the President. When he later became an open target for Congressional critics who distrusted him, his position was not secure.

After Pearl Harbor, Wallace's department was renamed the Board of Economic Warfare. BEW was soon on a collision course with the Reconstruction Finance Corporation under the administration of Secretary of Commerce Jesse Jones. Both organizations were engaged in the overseas procurement of strategic materials. The approach of Jones, a shrewd Texas banker, was marked by caution and frugality. Wallace spread his own men around the world in a whirlwind drive to snap up essential products as quickly as possible, and damn the expense. Wallace, while taking pride in the size of domestic agriculture surpluses, charged in March, 1942, that industry had not prepared for war by accumulating reserves. He advocated a planned economy and called the RFC's stock-piling program meager.

Dissatisfied at what he considered RFC procrastination, Wallace obtained from the President on April 13, 1942, an executive order permitting BEW to instruct the RFC to purchase anywhere in the world items ordered by BEW and at prices it set. Wallace was also given the right to advise the State Department on lend-lease agreements.

Jesse Jones was nettled by Wallace's insistence that "work clauses" be inserted in procurement and production contracts made by RFC subsidiaries with Latin-American countries. Wallace wanted to raise the standard of living of Amazon rubber workers to that of North American laborers. On one occasion he favored transporting 350,000 tons of food to 1,500,000 persons in the Amazon Basin on the theory that workers would produce more on a full stomach. Jones and others were convinced that the natives worked only to eat, and that if free food were distributed to all, they would promptly go to sleep under the nearest rubber tree. Wallace's critics were also aghast at the expense involved in feeding 1,500,000 persons, not to mention the transportation problem. Jones claimed that Wallace contemplated spending $400 million in an "Amazon Project" combining the rubber program with the more abundant life.

Secretary of State Cordell Hull joined Jones to complain about the executive order. The President told Wallace that he would not have issued the order had he known that the State and Commerce departments would oppose the transfer of authority. Wallace replied frankly that he had not sought approval of those departments because he knew that he would not get it.

President Roosevelt restored peace between Hull and Wallace by issuing still another executive order that assured Hull's full control over foreign policy, while leaving economic matters to BEW. But to Wallace, all issues had an ideological aspect. He gagged at the thought of doing business with Marshall Pétain's Vichy regime, which was clearly under the control of Fascists. Political considerations required, however, that the United States stay on good terms with Pétain. Wallace's associates moved slowly and ineffectively to implement State Department policy, and BEW has been held partly responsible for the rough reception given to the Allied invaders of French North Africa in 1942.

In January, 1943, Wallace again moved against the RFC. He issued an order allocating to BEW all power to buy, stockpile, and sell foreign critical materials. Jones, outraged, felt that the powers conferred on his agency by Congress could not be superseded by Wallace, and he refused to obey the order.

Congress viewed the Wallace maneuvers with increasing concern. Martin Dies, chairman of the House Committee on Un-American Activities, denounced certain BEW employees as pinkos, nudists, Communists, and world savers. Senator Kenneth McKellar proposed an amendment to an appropriation measure that would keep BEW expenses under the control of the RFC.

Wallace felt that the time had come for a showdown. His administrative assistant in BEW, Milo Perkins, was now pushing toward a more militant position. On May 21, 1943, Perkins learned that his son, a Marine flier, had been killed in a plane crash. Ten days later, he defended BEW policies before the House Appropriations Committee, the recent tragedy adding poignancy to his statement: "We are going ahead on the conviction that any economic program which will help shorten this war by a month, a week, or even a day is worth any reasonable price."

But it appeared that Congress was growing increasingly hostile to the Board of Economic Warfare. Perkins and Wallace drew up a blistering twenty-eight-page memorandum attacking Jesse Jones for his "obstructionist tactics . . . delay of the war effort . . . hamstring bureaucracy and backdoor complaining." Wallace hesitated for weeks before releasing the document, and finally did so on June 29, after what he said were further misrepresentations of BEW policy. The move was a clear appeal to public opinion over the heads of both the Administration and Congress.

In an equally long and bitter reply, Jones denounced Wallace's charges as "purposely misleading." He called the implication that he was impeding the war effort "maliciously false." Despite the seriousness of the charges, and the difficulty in determining the truth, Democrats reacted instinctively, the old guard defending Jones, and the liberals rallying behind Wallace.

The Vice President then issued a second statement, asserting that he did not intend to create the impression that Secretary of Commerce Jones's "personal motive was deliberately or intentionally to delay the war effort."

Jones called this latest reference to his alleged foot-dragging a "dastardly charge."

While Jimmy Byrnes and others worked behind the scenes to calm the combatants, Jones, Wallace, and Perkins continued a running battle that commanded as many headlines as the other war. Perkins charged that Jones had "failed dismally to build the government stock piles authorized and directed by the Congress." He added that Jones's "Rip Van Winkle approach to a commodity [quinine] that means life or death to our soldiers is simply incredible." He added that Wallace had done "what any red-blooded American would have done on discovering slimy things under a stone."

The President finally wrote a letter to Wallace and Jones declaring that the "acrimonious public debate" had made necessary a transfer of duties from both men. "In the midst of waging a war so critical to our national security and to the future of all civilization, there is not sufficient time to investigate and determine where the truth lies. . . ." FDR called for "a fresh start with new men unencumbered by interagency dissension and bitterness." The President abolished the Board of Economic Warfare and Wallace's job at the same time, removed Jesse Jones from his control of the RFC subsidiary corporations involved in international economic operations, and established an Office of Economic Warfare under Leo Crowley. Jones hailed the appointment of his friend Crowley as a personal victory. Vice President Wallace said simply: "In wartime no one should question the over-all wisdom of the Commander in Chief."

Despite the quarrel, the agencies did a tremendous job, the critically important commodities were obtained, and the war was won. The unfortunate experience did not discourage future Presidents from putting their Vice Presidents to work. But no other wartime dispute involved men of higher rank, or was waged with more publicity, or had such significance for the Democratic party. In earlier years, Roosevelt would not have lost control of such a situation.

William Allen White, in a letter to Wallace, wrote thoughtfully of the President's action:

"One of you men was wrong and one was right. It was the President's job to find out which and stand by him. I have upheld the President probably more often than any other Republican editor in the country. . . . But between you and me, twelve years is going to get him. I mean, get his keen sense of justice, get his quick reaction to evil. I know personally from experience that there is a certain zone which when a man has walked through it, he has got to be careful. Maybe Time was the scissors that Delilah used for shearing Samson! . . . I am afraid—deeply and morally afraid—because I love my country and want it to go right, that I can hear Delilah's scissors clicking. . . ."

While it was taken for granted that Roosevelt would run a fourth time, the outcome of the election was very much in doubt. Discontent over the war, disaffection in the South, and unhappiness over administration attempts to control farm prices, all raised danger signals for the Democrats. Before 1943 magazine articles almost invariably described Wallace as the heir apparent, the Democratic crown prince. But insiders around the White House were now convinced that Roosevelt would have to drop Wallace in 1944 in the cause of party unity.

Raymond Moley noted that this truth was not lost on the Wallace worshipers:

"The ideological boys had lost their Gandhi, now that Gandhi had lost his second garment. [Wallace] was the ideal and inspiration of every little world-planner in Washington. They launched their tiny skiffs in the torrent of his wordy discourse. They burbled their admiration of his cloudy philosophical exercises. They spoke in hushed tones of the master's mysticism, his delving into Asiatic religious lore. . . . After Roosevelt abolished the BEW . . . it was clear to them that they must forsake their high priest and follow the president."

Jesse Jones's autobiography contains the chapter "How

Henry Wallace Missed the Presidency," which reveals the importance he attached to the wartime feud. The bitterness a foe could feel toward Wallace is shown in language Jones used seven years after the events described above. He could still denounce the "smearing statements" and "vituperations" directed at himself; he called Wallace "arrogant" and lashed at his "uppity underlings," his "supersmart gang," his "socialist-minded uplifters," his "smarties," and his "long-haired, incompetent, meddlesome disciples."

The liberal publications made Wallace a hero and martyr. Many felt FDR had treated him shabbily, even betrayed him. Just a few days after being removed from his BEW post, Wallace praised the President in a speech at Detroit. He said that in any showdown, Roosevelt "always puts human rights first. There are powerful groups who hope to take advantage of the President's concentration on the war effort, to destroy everything he has accomplished on the domestic front for the past ten years." He said that sooner or later such men would be exposed.

The party professionals failed to realize that Wallace was building a loyal following among political amateurs and among labor and liberal groups. These forces were determined to keep him on the ticket in 1944. Many other men were equally determined that Wallace would be replaced.

But by whom?

★ ★ ★ ★ ★
★ ★ ★ ★ ★
★ ★

HARRY S. TRUMAN

"Why this awful fight over the Vice-Presidency? . . . [Are they] gambling . . . that he is going to die . . . ?"

The President became ill after returning from the Teheran conference in December, 1943, and he never fully regained his health.

He contracted influenza during a Christmas visit to Hyde Park. He also suffered from bronchitis, and a racking cough fatigued him by day and robbed him of needed sleep at night. Doctors listened to the continual coughing and worried about the strain on his heart. Always before, he had bounced back quickly from such seizures, but now, according to his doctor, he was "one day up and one day down."

We had been at war for two years, and the war had brought crushing burdens of work and strain to Franklin Roosevelt. His polio affliction also reduced his opportunities for exercise. The swims in the White House pool came less frequently. The steady gains in building up his muscular structure came to a halt. As Dr. Ross McIntyre saw it, "My problem, quite frankly, was to protect his reserves."

To lessen the load on the President's heart, McIntyre advised him to take off ten pounds through dieting. The President was so pleased with his "flat stomach" that he carried the diet beyond requirements. His face took on a hollow appearance, and his suits sagged. When a physical examination in the spring of 1944 turned up a moderate degree of arteriosclerosis and some changes in the cardiographic tracing, his doctors announced that FDR would take a two-week vacation. No one said where, of course, because wartime secrecy shrouded almost his every move.

Two weeks passed, and the press did not announce his return. Three weeks, a month. The rumor mill worked overtime, and would run on for years after his death: He was undergoing surgery at the Mayo Clinic. He was insane. He was suffering from *equine encephalomyelitis*, a disease heretofore found mainly in horses. He and Churchill had been poisoned at Teheran by a slow-working drug.

Oblivious to all this nonsense, the President lolled about at Bernard Baruch's South Carolina plantation, the Hobcaw Barony. He fished, dallied over his stamp collection, slept twelve hours a night, watched the azaleas bloom, and kept in touch with a world at war through air-mail delivery every couple of days.

The President returned to Washington in May. He looked better, and he said he felt better. But his doctors ordered him to cut his work day to four hours.

Taking note of the health gossip, National Chairman Robert Hannegan told a Jefferson Day dinner that the President was "fit and ready for the fight" despite "the malicious rumors to the contrary." The fight, of course, was the 1944 Presidential election. With the conventions almost at hand, Arthur Krock wrote that the Democratic Vice-Presidential nomination "would be held of greater importance than at any time in American history."

The incumbent Vice President, Henry Wallace, in speech after speech, was flailing away at Fascists, foreign and domestic. The country stirred uneasily, and so did some of the President's closest advisers.

Ed Flynn, the New York City Democratic boss, urged the President not to consider a fourth term. He also begged Eleanor Roosevelt to use her influence to keep him from running. But the President yielded to the pressures of other White House insiders who regarded his re-election as essential. When the President decided to run, Flynn concluded that "the obvious question was the nomination for the Vice-Presidency."

George Allen, secretary of the national committee, wrote later that top Democratic leaders "were determined that Roosevelt's successor would not be the boomerang-throwing mystic from the place where the tall corn grows."

And so began the most important and dramatic behind-the-scenes struggle for power ever fought within the framework of our convention system. One would expect that such a contest would be waged largely in secret. The war added the special circumstance that it was not in our interest to let Hitler know that Roosevelt was ill. The delegates could not be told in so many words that they should exercise greater care than usual in selecting a Vice-Presidential nominee. Yet the choice was made, and it was in many ways surprising, and in the light of history, in many ways successful.

And who would make this momentous choice? Certainly not the rank and file, because there is scarcely such a thing as a Vice-Presidential primary. The delegates? Technically they would nominate the Vice-Presidential candidate, although this convention is remembered today as one in which the delegates took an inordinate amount of "direction."

Would Roosevelt choose the nominee? His qualified endorsements, his procrastination, and his contradictory statements would reduce his influence and bring about the cliff-hanging climax. Who then, would choose the man to succeed Roosevelt? Several "bosses"—who presumed to speak for the diverse groups that composed the Democratic coalition—would make a compromise choice.

Foremost among the kingmakers was Robert E. Hannegan, of St. Louis, who slammed his way to the top in Democratic politics, burned himself out in the service of his party, and died at forty-six. He once told a reporter, "When I die, I would like to have one thing on my headstone—that I was the man who kept Henry Wallace from becoming President of the United States."

A professional athlete turned lawyer and politician, Hannegan was a cog in the St. Louis Democratic machine for a decade, his influence rising and falling with the shifting fortunes of factions within the party. In 1940, Hannegan came to one of those difficult decisions all politicians must face. He had to choose a favorite among three men running for the Democratic nomination for United States Senator. The embattled incumbent, Harry S. Truman, seemed to have little chance for victory as a result of the imprisonment of his political godfather, Tom Pendergast. His leading rival, Governor Lloyd Stark, was expected to roll up a 100,000 plurality in St. Louis, where the organization habitually opposed any candidate of the Kansas City-based Pendergast machine.

But St. Louis' candidate for Governor of Missouri, Lawrence McDaniel, was also in a tight nomination race. Truman supporters said that they would campaign for McDaniel statewide if St. Louis would swing to Truman. This offer was accepted. (The St. Louis and Kansas City organizations could deliver majorities at will.) It was a simple political deal that paid off for Truman and Hannegan beyond their wildest imaginations. Hannegan tipped St. Louis to Truman, who won renomination by fewer than 8,000 votes; he went on to defeat his Republican opponent in November.

In 1942, Senator Truman wanted Hannegan to be named Collector of Internal Revenue for the Eastern District of Missouri. The St. Louis *Globe-Democrat*, recalling some vote-fraud scandals, labeled Hannegan "the most discredited boss of a discredited political machine. . . ." Truman fired back that "Hannegan carried St. Louis three times for the President and for me. If he is not nominated, there will be no collector at St. Louis." Hannegan got the job, worked hard, and made a good record. Through Truman's influence he was named United States Commissioner of Internal Revenue in 1943 and then chairman of the Democratic National Committee in January, 1944.

A second power in the 1944 convention was Edward J. Flynn, a gentleman in politics who ran the most honest and efficient political machine in the country for a quarter of a century. Aloof and intellectual, he ruled New York City Democratic politics by remote control from his penthouse apartment overlooking the Hudson. An author, a student of history, an art collector, and an amateur horticulturist, he exercised leadership through a coterie of skilled lieutenants.

A former national chairman, Flynn was undeviatingly loyal to Franklin Roosevelt. "I'm for anything Roosevelt is for. I'm for whatever he wants."

Edwin W. Pauley, an oil millionaire, served as treasurer of the Democratic party during the war, and by 1944 was concerned about Roosevelt's health—or lack of it. George Allen, secretary of the national committee called Pauley the "Sir Galahad of the righteous band that set out to beat Wallace. . . ." Pauley headed the nationwide fund-raising drive for the 1944 election. In his trips across the country he campaigned against Wallace with the fervor of an evangelist.

Edward J. Kelly was another important factor in the 1944 decisions. When he became Mayor of Chicago in 1933 he gave up his all-night poker parties and burlesque shows and started attending the theater and reading best sellers. Kelly was a politician and a showman who guided the Windy City through both depression and war. He mixed ballyhoo, psychology, and patriotism with administrative efficiency to keep Chicagoland busy, prosperous, and united during World War II. A master organizer, Kelly stage-managed the 1940 and 1944 Democratic National Conventions. He was a craftsman at packing galleries and at hustling beefy party hacks to any spot in the city where a spontaneous demonstration was needed. In 1940 his "voice from the sewer" stampeded delegates to Roosevelt. But four years later he would almost meet his match in Sidney Hillman, who knew a little about political organization himself.

The Russian-born Hillman was tossed into a Czarist prison at seventeen for participating in a revolutionary parade. He later emigrated to the United States and became a powerful labor leader. One day he would alter the succession to the American Presidency by vetoing a leading candidate who was unable to "clear it with Sidney."

The first president of the Amalgamated Clothing Workers of America, Hillman led his union to prominence through thirty-five years of bitter, bloody battles with rival unions and employers. Hillman was the labor leader Roosevelt trusted most. In Washington during the early forties he served on the War Production Board, helping to convert peacetime production to preparations for defense. He was bedeviled by envious fellow unionists and by conservatives and journalists who feared that Hillman was in effect the prime minister of a labor government. Some persons also found cause for alarm in his Russian-Jewish origins.

The distraught Hillman suffered a heart attack in 1942 and retired from the Government. While in brief retirement he grew concerned by what he saw as a rising tide of reaction. In the light vote of 1942 the Republicans had narrowly missed capturing control of the House. Hillman, therefore, welcomed eagerly a proposal by CIO President Philip Murray for the formation of a Political Action Committee. The CIO-PAC, as organized by Hillman, worked generally with the Democratic party, and with a few progressive Republicans.

Armed with $700,000 from the CIO treasury, Hillman made labor a coherent, highly efficient political force. The PAC distributed pamphlets by the millions, pamphlets raising questions relating to peace and to postwar full employment that even New Dealers were neglecting. Hillman also showed his strength by defeating several conservative Congressmen in scattered primary elections. Within a few months the PAC had risen to a position of power within the party, power Hillman would not hesitate to use.

These five men—Hannegan, Flynn, Pauley, Kelly, and Hillman—became increasingly aware that President Roosevelt would listen to suggestions on the question of his fourth-term running mate. FDR, slipping physically and preoccupied with his wartime duties, was relaxing his grip on all matters political in the Democratic party. So the kingmakers began their search for a king, or in this case, a prince.

The field of contenders was scarcely smaller than the entire galaxy of major and minor satellites who had revolved around the presidential Sun King for a dozen years while managing somehow to remain in almost total eclipse themselves. Roosevelt had imposed his own image on the party, and had made little attempt, particularly during the war, to bring forward a successor. There was Wallace, of course, and no man could say for sure to what extent he had lost favor with the President. During much of the pre-convention period, Jimmy Byrnes was the most likely prospect. He had a long and distinguished public career—twenty-five years in Congress, Supreme Court justice, director of war mobilization, Secretary of State, and Governor of South Carolina.

Senator Byrnes was an unofficial member of the Roosevelt Brain Trust during early New Deal days. After a year on the Court, he gave up his lifetime tenure to take the mobilization post. He was an "assistant president" in charge of procurement, production, and distribution of civilian and military goods; his task was no less than the stabilization of the total wartime economy. In carrying out these duties, Byrnes had antagonized important labor leaders and his 1944 chances were jeopardized by two other factors: he came from the Deep South, and he had deserted the Catholic Church after marrying a Protestant girl. Nonetheless, his unquestioned ability stamped him as the candidate of a substantial group of party professionals and conservatives.

Alben W. Barkley was another possibility, as he almost always was. Barkley seemingly had all the qualifications Democrats look for in a Presidential or Vice-Presidential candidate. He was from a border state, was popular with all factions, and was a vigorous, partisan campaigner with a seldom-equaled sense of humor. No one could surpass his record of party service. Barkley's only trouble was his age. For as long as most living Democrats could remember, Barkley had been "too old."

He had first campaigned for public office by horseback in 1905. He had climbed as high as majority leader of the Senate by 1937, in which position he was pictured, by his own admission, "as a sort of rustic, amiable errand boy for the White House."

He complained that the nickname of "'bumbling Barkley' . . . stuck to me like the tar baby did to Br'er Rabbit." But if Barkley was loyal to the President, it was because the agrarian liberalism found in the New Deal was a part of Barkley's own heritage and ideals. He felt that his loyalty should be rewarded, and he was ready and willing to accept a place on the ticket in 1944.

If Barkley was too old, William O. Douglas had plenty of youth. Named to the Supreme Court when he was barely forty, the liberal Douglas was frequently mentioned for national office. Although he has never enjoyed great popularity with the public or the politicians, Douglas was a pragmatist and conversationalist who commanded FDR's attention. The appearance of his name in a mysterious letter written just before the convention would put him in strong contention.

Sam Rayburn, as a boy, dreamed of becoming Speaker of the House. He not only achieved this goal, but held that office twice as long as any other man. "The way to get along is to go along," he would say, and the gruff, stocky Rayburn got along by mastering the intricate rules of procedure and parliamentary strategy, by displaying undeviating party loyalty, and by biding his time. He was perhaps the greatest compromiser since Clay, and although he came from a Southern state, he pushed through the House more legislation concentrating power in the national government than any other man. Garner, too, had been Speaker and Vice President, and in 1944 Rayburn seemed in a position to duplicate that feat.

There were other candidates: Paul McNutt, Scott Lucas, John G. Winant . . . the list of favorite sons and dark horses runs on and on, and of course contains the name of Senator Harry S. Truman of Missouri.

Truman had none of Wallace's intellectualism, little of Rayburn's legislative skill, none of Byrnes's *savoir-faire*, none of Douglas' youth. On top of all this nothingness, Truman had been tagged for years as the "Gentleman from Pendergast," an ambassador as it were from Kansas City to the District of Columbia, the representative of one of the most corrupt of modern political machines. His strongest recommendation (laughable in view of his subsequent career) was that he had offended almost nobody.

A onetime farmer, soldier, and haberdasher, Truman found himself out of a job and $20,000 in debt at the age of thirty-eight. But he was well known and popular with farmers and veterans in the Kansas City area and in 1922, under circumstances that are not clear, he was elected County Judge (Commissioner) for eastern Jackson County, Missouri, with the support of the Pendergast brothers. Four years later he was elected Presiding Judge of Jackson County, which includes Kansas City. He supervised the spending of more than $60 million for roads and public buildings, without a hint of scandal, insisting that contracts be awarded to the lowest bidder, without favoritism to financial supporters of the Pendergasts. Tom's friends complained, but Pendergast stood up for Truman, while at the same time conceding that he was "the contrariest cuss in Missouri."

Truman plodded along, incorruptible, in a city filled with gambling dens, houses of prostitution, all night saloons, and other Pendergast enterprises. His campaigns for public office were almost always hard scraps, but the Pendergast supply of votes seemed inexhaustible. Truman always carried the cemeteries. He always did well in the vacant lot at 700 Main Street, where, according to the registration rolls, 112 persons lived.

In 1934, Pendergast had a hard time finding a candidate for United States Senator. Truman's record was excellent, he was politically "clean," and Pendergast persuaded him, somewhat against his will, to make the Senate race. In the Democratic primary, Truman trailed hopelessly in outstate returns, but surged to a narrow victory with a 93 per cent majority in Kansas City.

Truman's first six years in the Senate were without distinction, but he did work hard and conscientiously. He supported the New Deal all the way.

In 1937 the Democratic Governor of Missouri, elected with Pendergast support, rebelled against the Old Boss, and ordered a cleanup of Kansas City registration lists. Some 60,000 ghostly voters were given a decent burial. Judges and election clerks were indicted by the score, and the Pendergast machine was dealt a severe blow. Pendergast himself had neglected to report a $315,000 bribe on his income-tax return, and was packed off to prison. Truman said later: "Tom Pendergast never asked me to do a dishonest deed. He knew I wouldn't do it. When Tom Pendergast was down and out, a convicted man, people wanted me to denounce him. I refused. . . . I wouldn't kick a friend." With the fall of Pendergast, it appeared that Truman would be defeated in the 1940 Democratic primary, but the intervention of Robert Hannegan tipped the scales in his favor.

The year 1941 marked the turning point in Truman's Senate career. The country was preparing for war. National defense machinery was being expanded enormously, and huge contracts were being negotiated in haste. Truman's own experiences as a Jackson County Commissioner had taught him that "public contractors are not very good spenders of public money unless watched." The Senator drove 30,000 miles to inspect war camps and defense plants. He returned to Washington convinced of the need to set up a committee to investigate the national defense effort. He did not wish to see another dreary postwar inquiry whose sole purpose would be to fix the blame for money already lost, strayed, or stolen. He wished instead to check on each major war program as it evolved and to watch for bottlenecks, waste, and graft.

The Senate gave approval to his resolution for a Senate Special Committee to Investigate the National Defense Program, and Truman was tapped to be its chairman. Concerned with facts rather than headlines, the committee members toiled in bipartisan harmony throughout World War II. Seldom had a national Administration co-operated fully in permitting an investigation of itself. Truman's committee got results, and demonstrated a sense of fairness and responsibility. On a total appropriation of $925,000, the Senators saved the nation $15 million.

But the investigations had an even more phenomenal result. Harry Truman became a power in the Senate, and for the first time commanded respectful attention from his colleagues and from the public. Early in 1944, Washington newspapermen voted him the civilian next to Roosevelt who knew most about the war.

In December, 1943, Roosevelt jumped the gun on the Presidential year by declaring that "Dr. New Deal" had been replaced by "Dr. Win-the-War." Pundits inferred that domestic reform was on ice for the duration, that FDR's hat was in the ring for the fourth time, and that he would campaign on the issues of winning the war and winning the peace.

But Wallace, in January, asserted: "The New Deal is not dead. If it were dead the Democratic Party would be dead and well dead. . . . Roosevelt, God willing, will in the future give the New Deal a firmer foundation than it has ever had before."

Although Roosevelt was pleased with this spirited defense of the New Deal, groundwork for the ditching of the Vice President was already being laid. For more than a year before the convention, Treasurer Ed Pauley toured the country, raising funds and lining up opposition to Wallace. He got local leaders to tell Roosevelt that the Democrats would suffer seriously with Wallace on the ticket. In Washington Pa Watson, the President's military aide, worked in tandem with Pauley. He cleared the way for anti-Wallace Democrats to see Roosevelt, while barring the path of pro-Wallace men. Slowly, Roosevelt's enthusiasm for Wallace ebbed, to be replaced with a gnawing doubt. Pauley said later, "My own intensive activities in this regard were occasioned by my conviction that Henry Wallace was not a fit man to be President of the United States. . . ."

In January, party leaders met with Roosevelt at the White House to discuss the Vice Presidency. Pauley, Hannegan, Flynn, and Frank Walker, the outgoing national chairman, attended. All the leading contenders were discussed, and a rather shaky consensus was reached that Truman was the best bet. The President said he was favorably impressed with the Senator's qualifications, the first time he is known to have spoken approvingly of Truman in the context of a discussion of the Vice Presidency. But Roosevelt was far too shrewd to commit himself. Hannegan and possibly Pauley began to campaign for Truman at this point, though they didn't dare to claim that they had the President's support.

From January on, speculation about the Vice Presidency continued unabated in the press. Names popped in and out of syndicated columns like jack-in-the-boxes. Rayburn became the early favorite, with eighteen members of the national committee and twenty-five members of the House lining up in his corner. While making some Western speeches, Rayburn and Truman joshed each other about the Vice Presidency, endorsed each other, and began to realize that they were both candidates.

Five months before the convention, the six leading prospects were Wallace, Byrnes, Truman, Rayburn, Barkley, and Douglas. They were about evenly matched, but unforeseen events toppled one contender after another until only one little Indian was left standing on the second ballot at Chicago.

Early in 1944 the President asked for $10.5 billion in new revenue, a sum he thought necessary to prosecute the war. With great difficulty, Rayburn and Barkley pushed through a bill raising $2.3 billion. Barkley, especially, worked hard to get even the smaller amount approved. Back to the Senate came one of FDR's most scorching vetoes, with the statement, ". . . it is not a tax bill but a tax relief bill providing relief not for the needy but for the greedy."

Barkley, shaken, pondered his next move for twenty-four hours, then rose in the Senate to deliver a devastating attack on the President. He called Roosevelt's veto message "a calculated and deliberate assault upon the legislative integrity of every member of Congress." He complained that he had carried FDR's flag as majority leader for seven years with little help from the President. He noted that Roosevelt had criticized a tax concession to timberland operators and had cited his own experiences as a timber man.

"I do not know to what extent the President is engaged in the timber business," Barkley sneered. "I do know that he sells Christmas trees." This slur stunned Roosevelt, whose first successful business venture had been the sale of Christmas trees off inherited land. Barkley, who had never stood so tall in the Congress, successfully persuaded the Senate to override the veto. Then he resigned as Majority Leader.

The President sent a conciliatory letter to Barkley. The Majority Leader, mollified, allowed himself to be re-elected, and even wrote a gracious letter to the President that helped restore their friendship. But the savagery of the exchange destroyed any possibility that the two men might share the same ticket in 1944.

In the South, a restive anti-New Deal tide carried away another Vice-Presidential hopeful. The South had been grumbling about New Deal invasions of states' rights, about the abolition of the two-thirds rule, and about the administration efforts to pass a bill permitting all soldiers to vote—which the South saw as a move to bring the franchise to Negroes.

In April, the Supreme Court ruled that Texas Democrats could not deny the right of Negroes to participate in primary elections. When Texas Democrats met in state convention a month later, more than half the delegates were in open revolt against Roosevelt. Their ultimatums to the national party provoked a walkout by the loyalists, who elected their own national-convention delegates. Now began a running battle of charge and countercharge, carrying all the way to the credentials committee at Chicago, which seated both delegations and divided their votes.

The Texas-size brawl had dashed the aspirations of the state's favorite son, Sam Rayburn. Flynn, for one, scratched Rayburn off the narrowing list of prospects. The Speaker phoned Truman, said it was impossible for him to seek the nomination, and asked the Missouri Senator to support someone else. Rayburn, the early favorite, polled exactly two votes at Chicago.

On May 20, Roosevelt announced, "I have asked the Vice-President . . . to serve as a messenger for me in China. . . . Eastern Asia will play a very important part in the future history of the world. . . . The Vice-President, because of his present position, as well as his training in economics and agriculture, is unusually well fitted to bring both to me and to the people of the United States a most valuable first-hand report. . . . He left today and will report to me upon his return, which is expected about the middle of July."

Needless to say, this terse announcement received every possible interpretation. Outwardly, the mission was a sign of the President's continued confidence in Wallace. But what did FDR mean by the phrase "present position"?

The convention would open July 19, only three days after "the middle of July." The Vice President's absence during the delegate-hunting season would not hurt his cause much, in view of his alleged inability to win friends and influence people, and his political mentor and assistant, Harold Young, remained at home to head up the nomination fight.

The strangest episode in the search for a 1944 Vice-Presidential nominee involved Wendell Willkie. Until April, Willkie had been seeking a second Republican Presidential nomination, but he gave up after his defeat in the Wisconsin primary. In June, the Republicans nominated New York Governor Thomas E. Dewey.

Time passed, and Willkie failed to endorse the Republican ticket. He had a large following, and he wanted Dewey to concede some points to the internationalist, progressive Republican point of view. A flurry of speculation that he might run for Vice President with Roosevelt played into his hands. This step was not out of the question; as a contemporary example, Britain had a wartime coalition government. The possibility of enticing Willkie and his followers into the Democratic camp tantalized Roosevelt. He wanted the Willkie vote without having to pay too high a price. Willkie, alert to the President's political cunning, moved warily himself.

Roosevelt was also toying with a long-range scheme to realign the major parties. The President wanted to gather all the liberals together while driving the conservatives—including the South—into the opposite corner. Willkie could be the instrument by which this realignment could be effected.

In May, reports were heard that Willkie would be named Secretary of the Navy to make his name more acceptable to the convention. Willkie wrote to a columnist: "If I had a notion that I was the only one qualified to serve as Secretary of the Navy. . . . Or if I really thought that such action on my part could unify the people, I would, of course, accept. Not believing either of these things, I would, of course, not accept."

On July 5, Willkie and Samuel Rosenman met secretly for two hours in New York, and discussed the plan to realign the parties. Eight days later Roosevelt wrote to Willkie, inviting him to call at the White House, "but not on anything in relationship to the present campaign." Roosevelt wrote the letter only six days before the convention, at a time when he was leaving for a trip to the West Coast; clearly, there was no chance that they would meet before the convention.

About this time, George Norris, an opponent of Willkie from TVA days, heard that he might get the nomination. He telegrammed a protest to Roosevelt. The President's reply on July 17 contained one of those sentences that tests the mettle of historical detectives: "I don't think there is any possible danger of Willkie, though feelers were put out about a week ago." The story behind those "feelers" remains a mystery.

One would expect that as the hour of decision neared, Roosevelt would scratch one possibility after another, until a single name stood alone. But he never did. The President was either unable or unwilling to come to grips with the problem and has left behind a clutter of contradictory evidence. He customarily kept open alternative lines of action, but in this case he refused to settle on one alternative. He told many men that the convention would be open, and beyond that he gave each of several men reason to believe that he had Roosevelt's blessing. The President was older now, and tired, and ill. He really dreaded having to decide what to do about Henry Wallace. In early summer, with Wallace out of the country, and with Truman making no move toward the nomination, Roosevelt found himself being nudged in another direction.

An economic adviser, Louis B. Wehle, urged him to support Byrnes, but the President replied, "he's a backslid Catholic" and added that a monsignor had told him "among people of that faith there is no forgiveness for a backslider." He said that the party could not afford to buck the Catholic vote. But in April, while he was a guest of Bernard Baruch at the Hobcaw Barony, Roosevelt found himself under intense pressure from Baruch in behalf of Byrnes. By now he must have been aware that his highly competent "assistant President" wanted the job, and must have found it distasteful to reject Byrnes solely because of his mixed religious background.

Sidney Hillman, sniffing the political air and detecting a shift of "inside" sentiment toward Byrnes, called at the White House on June 9. He stressed that the CIO had endorsed Wallace and that he, Hillman, would give the Vice President full support. He reminded Roosevelt that Byrnes had opposed sit-down strikes and in the course of his wartime duties had clamped a lid on wages. Hillman said that Byrnes was considered unfriendly to organized labor and would jeopardize the Northern Negro vote.

But temporarily, at least, FDR seems to have resolved these conflicting arguments in Byrnes's favor. On June 13, Hannegan tried to persuade Byrnes to become the candidate for Vice President, saying that the President had told him he would rather have Byrnes than anyone else. The next day Roosevelt asked Byrnes to become permanent chairman of the convention, pointed out that Joseph Robinson had used the same position as a springboard to the nomination in 1928, and predicted, "History will repeat itself." Several days later Roosevelt again called on Byrnes to become a candidate. Byrnes, at sixty-five, facing probably his last opportunity to run for national office, and knowing full well that his candidacy would evoke a storm of reaction from labor and Negro spokesmen, found himself yielding to the temptation.

Yet, a few days later on June 22, the President told Governor Ellis Arnall of Georgia, a Southern liberal, that he desired that Wallace be renominated, and Arnall promised to deliver Georgia's delegates to the Vice President. Five days later, Roosevelt told two of his aides, "Of course, everybody knows I am for Henry Wallace." But then he began to talk about other possibilities, adding, "There is one we have got up our sleeve and that is Henry Kaiser. He is talking about great plans in employing five million people by building jitney airplanes for everybody. He would make a great appeal."

Curiouser and curiouser!

Most of the big city bosses—except Flynn—scarcely spoke the same language as Wallace, and did not trust him. But by early July, Roosevelt realized that the opposition to the Vice President ran deeper. Rosenman and Ickes, both good New Deal liberals, told the President that the politicians were right. Rosenman felt that Wallace's lack of tact had antagonized too many people, and that many of his progressive and well-meaning proposals had come out in the press sounding like schemes for unrealistic worldwide charity handouts.

Roosevelt exclaimed to Rosenman, "I am just not going to go through a convention like 1940 again. It will split the party wide open . . . it may kill our chances for election this fall, and if it does, it will prolong the war and knock into a cocked hat all the plans we've been making for the future."

On July 6, Flynn weighed in with the results of his own cross-country survey. He reported that Wallace would cost Roosevelt several large states, notwithstanding the support of Hillman's Political Action Committee in industrial areas. Already a Gallup Poll had been published showing Roosevelt leading Dewey by only 51-49 per cent. Flynn and Roosevelt combed the list of possible nominees to find the man who would cost Roosevelt the fewest votes. Flynn wrote later that Truman "just dropped into the slot." He was nobody's enemy, he came from a border state, he had made no "racial" remarks, his labor votes were sound, and his defense committee work was outstanding. The President asked Flynn to get a group of party leaders together at the White House on Tuesday, July 11, and to inject Truman's name into the conversation.

Now Roosevelt had some explaining to do. Wallace was on his way back to Seattle from the Orient. He would have to hear the bad news that he was out, but Roosevelt didn't have the heart to face his ex-protégé. Rosenman got the unhappy assignment, but Harold Young had alerted the Vice President that the "inside boys" at the White House had their knives out. Wallace met Rosenman and Ickes after his return to Washington, stalled them off, and obtained a luncheon appointment with the President on Tuesday, July 11, a fateful day.

That very morning, eight days before the convention, Roosevelt announced that he was a candidate again. "All that is within me cries out to go back to my home on the Hudson. . . ." he said, but as a good soldier he would serve again if nominated and elected. He implied that he would accept the nomination without strings, and would not again demand the nomination of Wallace—or anybody else. The political pundits concluded that the race was open—more or less—but that Wallace didn't have a chance. Yet no one knew for sure who was going to replace him.

Wallace arrived for lunch and attacked head on his critics' complaints that he couldn't be nominated or elected. First, he reported that Harold Young had nailed down 290 first-ballot votes, half the number needed for the nomination. Second, he showed Roosevelt a Gallup Poll (scheduled for release July 20), giving Wallace 65 per cent of the rank-and-file Democratic vote for Vice President. Barkley had 17 per cent, and no one else had more than 5 per cent (Truman had 2 per cent).

So the politically naïve Wallace was far out in front in both delegate and popular support.

"Well, I'll be damned!" said the President. Now he could hardly ask Wallace to get out of the race. The Vice President said that he wanted to try to win the nomination on his own. Poor Roosevelt! Undoubtedly one of our most astute politicians, he nonetheless dreaded saying No to a personal friend, especially one who had rendered long and loyal service to his Administration. The meeting that could have put an end to the Wallace candidacy ended on a farcical note, with Roosevelt agreeing to write a letter endorsing the renomination of the Vice President!

Seven men—Roosevelt, Flynn, Hannegan, Walker, Pauley, Kelly, and George Allen—dined at the White House that same night, July 11. Before the meeting, Flynn told Hannegan that "Truman was the man." Hannegan, who had been hearing a lot of talk about Byrnes, said he didn't believe it but that he would persuade Kelly and Allen to agree on Truman.

An air of conspiracy hung over the gathering. The President sat at the head of the table, reminiscing, of all things, about attempts that had been made on his life. The elders of the Democratic party shifted uneasily as Roosevelt recalled in detail the attempts that had been made to kill him through food poisoning. He described the attempt to assassinate him in Miami in 1933. The most chilling note, however, was the obvious fatigue and listlessness of the President. Allen wrote later that those present sensed that he would not live much longer.

After dinner, talk turned to arrangements for the convention and to the Vice Presidency. Each candidate for that office was appraised in terms of his political strength and his sympathy with the Administration's program. The President listened, mostly. Rayburn was dismissed because of the Texas split. Byrnes was considered carefully, with those present divided on the importance of the religious issue. Torn between personal and political considerations, the conferees conceded regretfully that Byrnes's long record on filibustering against antilynching bills, plus all his other debits, simply had to disqualify him.

Little time was spent discussing Wallace. There is no evidence that Roosevelt mentioned his agreement to write a letter endorsing the Vice President. Roosevelt brought up two other names—John G. Winant, ambassador to England, and Douglas. The President said that Douglas had a sort of Boy Scout quality, and that he also played an interesting game of poker. Neither of these names set off any sparks.

Barkley was discounted when the President recalled that the Kentucky Senator was older than he. The only name left was Truman. Roosevelt observed that the Senator was able and loyal, and a smart politician. Unlike his guests, Roosevelt was not thinking primarily of the possibility that the next Vice President would become President; but he did remember how the Senate's rejection of the Treaty of Versailles had crushed Woodrow Wilson's dream of peace. Soon another peace treaty would come before the Senate. The President wanted a Vice President who was known and trusted in the Senate, a man who could help save the peace treaty—and the peace.

The group discussed thoroughly Truman's relationship to the Pendergast machine. The President's son-in-law, John Boettiger, was listening in, and brought up an unpopular subject, Truman's age. This bothered Roosevelt, a bit sensitive perhaps to Thomas E. Dewey's charge that the nation was being run by tired, old men. Truman was sixty, and no major party convention had ever nominated a pair of men past sixty.

Hannegan and Pauley tried to change the subject, but the President sent for the Congressional Directory to check on Truman's age. Pauley grabbed the book and held it on his lap. The President, aware by now of the sentiment of the group, turned to Hannegan and said, "Bob, I think you and everyone else here want Truman."

What happened next is lost amid uncertain memories and contradictory statements of men who gloried in the role of kingmaker. The consensus is that the President indicated that Harry Truman was the best man for the Vice Presidency, but the conspirators who hung on Roosevelt's every word were afraid to attempt to force an irrevocable commitment from him. Somewhat abruptly, Pauley signaled that the conference was over, and the guests began to take their leave.

Hannegan knew of Roosevelt's propensity for changing his mind, and the stakes were high. The choice of Truman would seem to many to be so incredible (and delegates were after all not so tractable) that Hannegan decided he needed more than a verbal endorsement. As the others waited downstairs, he returned to the President's study, and left again with a trophy of rather dubious worth. On the back of an envelope, the President had scribbled, "Bob, I think Truman is the right man. FDR."

Right for what? Once again Roosevelt had stalled for time. The President agreed to follow up the note with a more specific endorsement in a couple of days. In the meantime, he could reflect on why he had so carelessly promised the Vice Presidency to three different persons; he could draw on his knowledge of the English language in an attempt to fulfill all his pledges at once; and he could seek some means of retaining the friendship of candidates who would have to lose.

He couldn't possibly wriggle free of his promise to write a letter endorsing Wallace, but perhaps he could get Byrnes to withdraw. Once again he could not bring himself to mention the subject to the man whom he saw almost every day. Before Walker left the White House that night, Roosevelt turned to him and said, "Frank, will you go over tomorrow, and tell Jimmy that it's Truman, and that I'm sorry it has to be that way."

The next morning Walker told Byrnes something of the

meeting the night before, especially that Flynn had repeated his opposition to Byrnes. Byrnes, who beyond any doubt now wanted the nomination desperately, phoned the President. "I would like to know if you have changed your opinion about my being a candidate."

Once again Roosevelt chose the easy way out: "You are the best-qualified man in the whole outfit and you must not get out of the race. If you stay in, you are sure to win."

The two men talked politics the next day, Thursday, July 13, in Roosevelt's office. The President said he was certain that Wallace would not be renominated, but knew that he would insist on running. Byrnes conceded that it was proper for Roosevelt to write a letter expressing a personal preference for Wallace without insisting on his nomination. But Byrnes then pinned Roosevelt down:

"I said that if he did that, of course he could not thereafter express a preference for anyone else. He said he would not do so, and because he had previously talked to me about being a candidate, he wanted me to know what he was going to do. He also said that . . . I could rely upon his promise that he would not express a preference for anyone."

Byrnes was not worried by Roosevelt's impending endorsement of Wallace who, in Byrnes's view, couldn't win in any case. Byrnes told FDR that if the field were left open, he would probably become a candidate. He even offered to resign his job as war mobilization director while seeking the nomination. The President must have winced, since Byrnes was indispensable in his present position. Now he wanted to resign to seek an office Roosevelt had already promised in two other directions, and his resignation would force the contest into the open, exposing the President's duplicity. The President persuaded Byrnes to stay on, pointing out that he himself would be away from the White House for a few weeks and would need Byrnes "to mind the store."

The weight of evidence indicates that on this same day, July 13, Roosevelt wrote the letter he had promised Hannegan on the night of the eleventh. The body of this letter, a thirty-seven-word literary masterpiece, almost extricated FDR from an untenable position. It should now be examined in the light of the pledge that Roosevelt had just made to Byrnes:

July 19

Dear Bob,

You have written me about Bill Douglas and Harry Truman. I should, of course, be very glad to run with either of them and believe that either one of them would bring real strength to the ticket.

Always sincerely,
Franklin Roosevelt

The letter was dated for the opening day of the convention, about the time it would have to be used.

Roosevelt begins, "You have written me. . . ." This is nonsense. There is no reason why Hannegan should have written about Douglas, in whom he had no interest.

He continues: ". . . about Bill Douglas and Harry Truman." Grace Tully, the President's secretary, has declared flatly that Douglas' name appeared first in the original version of this letter, dictated on the thirteenth. Some of the principals have denied that there was ever a version in which Douglas' name came first. But the testimony of Miss Tully, a competent witness without known bias toward any candidate, must be accepted.

What was the consequence of this sudden introduction of still another name—Douglas? With the mentioning of two names, the value of the letter to either was sharply reduced, and would create confusion in the minds of the very delegates who were supposed to be swayed by this testimonial. If the President were solidly committed to Truman, he might logically throw in a second name to avoid the appearance of dictating to the convention. *But*, would the second name be that of Douglas, a *real* possibility? The President knew that any name coupled with that of Truman would be the target of abuse by the bosses seeking to nail down the nomination for the Missourian. Douglas was a close friend of Roosevelt, and the appearance of his name shows that he was, in the President's mind, still a possibility, and that his was not just a dummy name used to fill out a letter of endorsement for Truman.

Roosevelt goes on: "I should, of course, be very glad to run with either of them. . . ." Thus, he does not say that he would "prefer" to run with either of them. Technically, he had kept his promise to Byrnes.

The President concludes: ". . . and believe that either one of them would bring real strength to the ticket." This was significant, since the worried Democrats were looking for the running mate who would cost Roosevelt the fewest votes. This phrase helped Truman.

But Roosevelt still had promises to keep. From a White House typewriter popped the following, which the President decided should be read before the entire convention by the permanent chairman:

My dear Senator Jackson: [1]

In the light of the probability that you will be chosen as permanent chairman of the convention, and because I know that many rumors accompany all conventions, I am wholly willing to give you my personal thought in regard to the selection of a candidate for Vice President. I do this at this time because I expect to be away from Washington for the next few days.

The easiest way of putting it is this: I have been associated with Henry Wallace during his past four years as Vice President, for eight years earlier while he was Secretary of Agriculture, and well before that. I like him and I respect him and he is my personal friend. For these reasons I personally would vote for his renomination if I were a delegate to the convention.

At the same time I do not wish to appear in any way as dictating to the convention. Obviously the convention must do the deciding. And it should—and I am sure it will—give great consideration to the pros and cons of its choice.

Very sincerely yours,
Franklin D. Roosevelt

The letter cites only the most incidental, personal considerations in support of Wallace. The author lists no special qualifications that the Vice President might bring to his job during a second term, and refrains from saying that his renomination would strengthen the ticket. The letter sounds generous until compared with the efforts Roosevelt made in Wallace's behalf four years earlier. The President's call for an open

[1] Senator Samuel Jackson of Indiana.

convention in the last paragraph would seem to be a signal that his endorsement of Wallace carried little conviction.

Hillman stopped by the White House that day, saw copies of both letters, and told Roosevelt that the PAC would support Wallace as long as he had a chance, but that if he failed, Hillman would not oppose Truman.

Wallace again had lunch with the President, who told him that Flynn and the others had been in on Tuesday with assertions that the Vice President's renomination would hurt the ticket. Wallace offered to withdraw but the President said that he would not think of accepting such an offer. Wallace, who kept notes at the time, asked the President if he would recommend any other name to the party leaders. Roosevelt replied simply, "No." As Wallace started to leave, Roosevelt called him back to whisper with obvious warmth, "While I cannot say it that way in public, I hope it will be the same old team."

On Thursday, July 13, the President left Washington for California, by way of Hyde Park and Chicago. The primary purpose of the trip was a war council among Roosevelt, General MacArthur, and Admirals Leahy and Nimitz. The President had also scheduled an inspection tour of Pacific Coast naval bases. The trip was secret, and mystery surrounded the President's whereabouts during the convention.

At noon on Friday, the fourteenth, Byrnes talked to Hannegan and Walker in Washington. They told Byrnes that, as matters stood, if any of the President's friends should ask them about his position, they would have to say that he favored Truman or Douglas. Byrnes repeated Roosevelt's statement to him on the previous day, and Hannegan said, "I don't understand it."

Neither did Byrnes, who did not like the way Hannegan was talking. He decided to phone the President at Hyde Park. With the precision that characterized the man, he took out his shorthand pad (he had once been a court stenographer) and wrote down several questions for the President. The conversation that followed, which he recorded verbatim, was a sorry battle of semantics between a weary, evasive President and a usually perspicacious assistant whose ambition had badly clouded his vision.

Byrnes began by leading the President over the same ground

that they had covered the day before: "I understood from you that you would write a letter to Henry Wallace. It was my understanding from your statement to me yesterday that you would not authorize any person to quote you as saying you preferred any candidate other than Wallace."

"I am not favoring anybody," Roosevelt replied. "I told them so. No, I am not favoring anyone."

"Bob Hannegan and Frank Walker stated today that . . . they would be obliged to say to their friends that from your statements they concluded you did not prefer Wallace but did prefer Truman first and Douglas second, and that either would be preferable to me because they would cost the ticket fewer votes than I would."

"Jimmy, that is all wrong. That is not what I told them. It is what they told me. . . . I was asking questions. I did not express myself. . . . They can state their own opinion but they cannot state mine. I have not given my opinion to anyone."

Byrnes continued to harass the President, seemingly determined to win the verbal battle if nothing else: "If they make the statement, notwithstanding your letter to Wallace, that you have expressed a preference for Truman and Douglas, it would make it very difficult for me."

"We have to be damned careful about language. They asked if I would object to Truman and Douglas and I said no. That is different from using the word 'prefer.' That is not expressing a preference because you know I told you I would have no preference." And Roosevelt must have spoken the following words in a plaintive tone: "After all, Jimmy, you are close to me personally, and Henry is close to me. I hardly know Truman. Douglas is a poker partner. He is good in a poker game and tells good stories."

Later Byrnes read the transcript of his conversation to Hannegan, who repeated, "I don't understand it." Byrnes wrote in his memoirs that he would not have entered the race had he known of the Douglas-Truman letter. Hannegan did not volunteer any information on that subject. Now that a fourth man had received a presidential blessing, the national chairman must have been close to despair.

Soon after getting reassurance from the President, Byrnes saw some more good news. Over a White House news ticker came a press-association story reporting that Senator Truman had just issued a statement saying that he would not be a candidate for Vice President. A happy Byrnes reached for the telephone and asked for Independence, Missouri.

In the last weeks before the convention, Harry Truman was vaguely aware that his name was under consideration, and once told newsmen, "If Bob Hannegan is running me for Vice President he is doing it without my knowledge and without my consent."

The Senator was a truly humble man who recognized his limitations and who believed sincerely that the next Vice President might be summoned to the Presidency during critical times. He honestly felt that he was not fully qualified to assume the highest office, and he did not wish to have his family embarrassed by the rehash of the Pendergast relationship that could be expected to come with a Vice-Presidential nomination.

On Friday, Truman was packing his bags for the trip to Chicago; although the convention was still five days off, he was assigned to the platform committee. The phone rang. It was Byrnes, at that time one of his closest friends in politics. Byrnes said he had seen the news item stating that Truman would not be a candidate. He said he had decided to run himself, and he asked Truman to place his name in nomination. Truman said he would be happy to do so. He later wrote that during this conversation Byrnes said he had the President's support, and that Byrnes had conveyed the impression that his nomination was all settled. Byrnes denies in his memoirs that he claimed Roosevelt's support, saying that as of that moment, it would not have been true.

Truman went to the convention and campaigned hard in Byrnes's behalf, only to learn eventually that he, not Byrnes, was the anointed one. Years later, sadly enough, the two men became bitter enemies, and Truman charged that Byrnes had not been truthful in this conversation.

As for Douglas, it is not known to what degree he was aware of all these maneuvers. He could not be expected to poll many votes as long as Wallace was a contender because both men drew their support from the progressive wing of the party. The Justice didn't want the nomination. Weeks before the convention, he went to his remote fishing cabin in the Wallowa Mountains in Oregon, and left behind with Senator Maloney of Connecticut strict instructions to keep his name off the floor of the convention.

At 6:30 P.M., Friday, July 14, the President and his party boarded a train at Hyde Park and began a leisurely trip westward.

The next day the special train arrived in Chicago for a service stop. Most passers-by had no reason to suspect that the President was aboard, though a few noticed a trainman exercising a black Scottie that looked familiar.

Hannegan went to the station to get what he hoped would be definitive instructions on the Vice Presidency. Some accounts say that Kelly accompanied him. As much as he wished to see Truman nominated, Hannegan wanted most of all to stop Wallace, and in order to do that he would have to push a candidate who was acceptable to the President and who was willing to run. Truman was not only insisting that he was not a candidate, but he was openly campaigning for Byrnes. Hannegan and Roosevelt—like Pendergast before them—knew just how stubborn Truman could be. Hannegan could not afford to put all his chips on his fellow Missourian, and the only logical alternative at this late date was Byrnes.

But what about the opposition to Byrnes from Hillman and Flynn? It is plausible that Hannegan and Roosevelt reasoned that in an open convention Byrnes could override this opposition; and if he couldn't, then Flynn and Hillman could take the blame. The President himself could thus avoid having to ask Byrnes to step out.

Kelly—possibly through Hannegan—conveyed to Roosevelt the information that notwithstanding Flynn's opinion, Chicago Negro leaders would accept Byrnes as Vice President. (Kelly's motives are not clear, but he apparently hoped to produce a deadlock, and then to slip Illinois Senator Scott Lucas into the nomination.)

The upshot of the Hannegan-Roosevelt huddle that day was a declaration from the President: "Well, you know Jimmy has been my choice from the very first. Go ahead and name him." But he said it would be necessary to consult Hillman, because of the importance of the labor vote and because of his previous criticism of Byrnes.

But Hannegan wasn't missing any bets. Suppose Byrnes' enemies succeeded in derailing his candidacy? Then Hannegan would have to pull the Douglas-Truman letter out of his pocket to head off Wallace. Even though Douglas' name had top billing in the letter, it would be almost impossible to nominate him, so Hannegan proposed to the President that the letter be retyped with Truman's name first. He was more likely to accept the nomination, and he would be more acceptable to the delegates (and to Hannegan). Roosevelt agreed to this action.

In Byrnes, Hannegan now had a strong candidate to run against Wallace, with Truman in reserve. But before Hannegan left the President's private compartment that day, Roosevelt uttered four little words that would haunt both men for the rest of their lives. The words were probably spoken casually, and received casually. The President reminded Hannegan to "Clear it with Sidney."

These words, coupled with the switch in the names of Truman and Douglas, altered the course of American history—perhaps even the history of the world.

"Clear it with Sidney" soon was misquoted as the more ominous: "Clear *everything* with Sidney." The latter combination, first used in a column by Arthur Krock in the New York *Times* on July 25, set off a panic by extremists who had always hated Hillman and who now thought they saw a Marxist-Zionist plot to take over America.

Even before these four words saw print, Westbrook Pegler was frenetic: "Hillman! In God's name! How came this non-toiling sedentary conspirator who never held American office or worked in the Democratic organization to give orders to the Democrats of the United States!" But Hillman, as the spokesman for one of the leading elements within the party, had a perfect right to be consulted on a subject of importance to the party.

Krock later wrote that "Clear it with Sidney" was the correct version of the quotation, and that it referred only to the Vice-Presidential nomination.

But all this was still in the future as Hannegan left the President's office on the train that Saturday. He stopped by the desk of Grace Tully, a presidential secretary: "Grace, the President wants you to retype this letter and to switch these names so it will read 'Harry Truman or Bill Douglas.' "

Miss Tully later wrote: "By that narrow margin and rather casual action did one man rather than another, perhaps one policy rather than another, eventually arrive at the head of the American government in April of 1945."

Mayor Kelly phoned Byrnes in Washington, and told him of the meeting at the depot: "The President has given us the green light to support you and he wants you in Chicago." Byrnes soon left Washington by train. About this time, Kelly told Barkley that it was "in the bag for Jimmy." Jonathan Daniels recalls that Byrnes arrived in Chicago on Sunday morning "in a marching, if not a strutting, self-confidence." He had "the conqueror's air."

Hillman and Truman met for breakfast Sunday morning. Truman's committee had been sharply critical of Hillman at times, but Hillman knew that the Missouri Senator was a friend of labor. The grim-faced leader of the CIO-PAC listened to Truman's pitch for Byrnes. Hillman replied curtly: "Labor's first choice is Wallace. If it can't be Wallace, we have a second choice, but it isn't Byrnes."

"Who then?"

"I'm looking at him," Hillman said.

Truman protested that he was not a candidate, and the conversation ended.

Hillman told a press conference later that day that the PAC had no second candidate, and was not in Chicago to trade with anybody, but to nominate Wallace. Hannegan, however, stole the day's biggest headlines by announcing at another press conference that Roosevelt had written a letter setting forth his views on the Vice Presidency. The reference was to the Wallace letter, and Hannegan refused to speculate on its contents, but said he supposed it would be read to the convention. He said nothing about the Truman-Douglas letter.

On Sunday night Byrnes dined with Hannegan and several other party leaders. Hannegan and Kelly were now prepared to endorse Byrnes publicly. Frank Walker chimed in with "You know my position; I'm for whoever the President wants;

now that he has told these fellows to nominate you, I'm for you." The group estimated that Byrnes could rely on about 700 delegate votes.

Then Hannegan turned to Kelly and said, "Ed, there is one thing we forgot. The President said, 'Clear it with Sidney.'" Byrnes declined to approach Hillman, and Hannegan volunteered to do so.

The national committee met in the Stevens Hotel late Monday afternoon. Ed Flynn, arriving late, got to the hotel just in time for the meeting. Hannegan spotted him, rushed him into a corner, and exclaimed: "It's all over. It's Byrnes." Flynn said that was impossible, that the President wanted Truman. Flynn demanded a meeting of party leaders to settle the matter once and for all.

Byrnes's candidacy collapsed at this meeting, held Monday night in a secret apartment Hannegan had obtained away from the center of the city. Walker, Kelly, Hillman, and Philip Murray were among those present. Flynn declared that he had pledged his vote to Truman, and would not go back on his pledge. To use Flynn's words, "I talked, I argued, I swore, and finally they said if the President would tell them again he was for Truman they would agree."

Roosevelt was still traveling West on the train when Flynn got him to the phone. He told the President that with Byrnes on the ticket, he would lose New York and probably the election. Hillman also talked to the President. Speaking for himself and for labor in general, he vetoed Byrnes. He contended that Byrnes's restrictions on wages had robbed union men and women of many of their gains under the New Deal. Flynn insisted that Roosevelt tell the party leaders that he favored Truman for Vice President. The President spoke in turn to Walker, Hannegan, and Kelly.

Hillman and Flynn had combined forces long enough to KO Byrnes. Soon they would square off on behalf of Wallace and Truman, respectively. Truman, learning of the latest shift in the wind, asked Byrnes Monday night for a release from his pledge of support, though he apparently had not yet reconciled himself to becoming a candidate.

Byrnes made one last pathetic effort to reach an understanding with Roosevelt. He phoned FDR in San Diego, but the President would not come to the telephone. The battle of semantics was over. Byrnes addressed a letter to the chairman of the South Carolina delegation, in which he said: "In deference to the wishes of the President, I ask that my name not be placed before the convention as a candidate for the Democratic nomination for Vice President." Daniels wrote later that Byrnes "seemed, as he sat afterwards in the White House box, a small tragic Irishman even to those who opposed him."

Byrnes left Chicago before the convention ended. But before doing so, he talked for a while with Barkley, who had agreed to place Roosevelt's name in nomination.

"You are going to nominate Roosevelt, aren't you?" Byrnes asked.

"Yes," Barkley answered.

"If I were you," Byrnes said, "I wouldn't say anything too complimentary about him."

Attention now focused on Wallace and Truman. Senator Jackson released the Wallace letter Monday evening, with pro- and anti-Wallace delegates giving predictable interpretations. On Tuesday, Hannegan began to tighten the screws on the reluctant Truman. He showed the Senator the note Roosevelt had scribbled on the envelope on the night of the eleventh.

"Bob, look here. I don't want to be Vice-President. I bet I can go down on the street and stop the first ten men I see and that they can't tell me the names of two of the last ten Vice-Presidents. . . ."

Legend has it that Truman did everything that week except crawl under the rug. Columnists told of the reluctant candidate wringing his hands in anguish and going through other emotional gyrations. Such a performance would not be in Truman's character, but unquestionably he and his wife yielded to mounting pressure only with great reluctance.

Hannegan was wringing his hands, too. Once he exclaimed to Walker, "It's all over; our candidate won't take it—we have no candidate." Hannegan still hesitated to show Truman the Truman-Douglas letter. He may have feared that if the Senator had seen the second name he would have had one more excuse to run away from the contest.

Tuesday night, Kelly and Hannegan began to pass the word to influential delegates that the President wanted Truman. That night, on the eve of the opening session, states began caucusing, and the "returns" were not encouraging to the bosses. Thanks to the CIO, Michigan was nearly unanimous for Wallace. The Vice President led in Pennsylvania, 2-1. Nebraska and Oregon favored him. Truman tried to prevent his own delegation from voting for *him*, but a motion to do so carried unanimously.

Wallace was tired after his Asian trip, but he yielded to pleas from his supporters, and flew to Chicago on Wednesday morning. He told a jammed press conference, "I am in this fight to the finish." Referring to the President's letter endorsing him, he said, "I told the President in justice to himself and to myself that there should not be anything in the nature of dictation to the convention. The letter did what I suggested."

Wallace could count on the support of a number of veteran New Dealers, the CIO, Negro leaders, and a scattering of professional politicians with strong union constituencies. The CIO carried the brunt of his battle. The union men turned out almost all the literature, placards, and banners. Hillman's troops did not hesitate to assume the challenge in this, their first chance to flex political muscles in the arena of a national convention. Later, it would be said that Wallace's campaign would have fared better had it been run in the usual manner by "civilians," rather than by the militant legions of the Political Action Committee. But without the CIO there would have been no Wallace campaign.

Wallace declined to attend any caucuses, saying that he didn't wish to influence delegates by personal contact, which Governor Arnall thought "seemed strange politics indeed to a Georgia politician accustomed to rather direct approaches to vote-getting."

At noon Wednesday, July 19, Hannegan rapped his gavel for order, and the convention was officially in session. Everyone was talking now about hints from Hannegan that he had received a letter from the President endorsing Truman. "The convention is in the hands of the enemy!" a Wallace leader exclaimed. Harold Ickes fired off a telegram to Roosevelt denouncing bossism and saying that the defeat of Wallace would be "your greatest political mistake in twelve years." Philip Murray addressed PAC delegates from twenty-eight states. Speaking softly and shaking his fist, Murray repeated: "Wallace . . . Wallace . . . Wallace. That's it. Just keep pounding." PAC claims of first ballot strength for the Vice President rose to 350, then 400.

Wallace, a delegate from Iowa, attended the evening session, and his appearance brought cheers from the galleries, mixed with some boos. By now Hannegan, Flynn, and New Jersey's boss, Frank Hague, were openly campaigning for Truman. The withdrawal of Byrnes was triggering a rush of anti-Wallace delegates to the Missouri candidate. But several more delegations were lining up for Wallace, and the contest still looked close as the hour of decision neared.

At noon Thursday, July 20, the Democrats went into session again. Senator Jackson of Indiana, the permanent chairman, in a shockingly partisan speech, asked, ". . . how many battleships would a Democratic defeat be worth to Hirohito?" and ". . . could Goebbels do better himself to bolster Axis morale than the word that the American people had upset this administration. . . . We must not allow the American ballot box to be made Hitler's secret weapon!"

Jackson swung hard at a Republican orator who had said that the American people wanted youth instead of decadence. "That last word 'decadence' is an indecent slander, if intended for the President. Roosevelt is in his full vigor and in the flower of his energy. He has more rugged vitality in him today than any two men the opposition has to offer."

At almost the same moment, the subject of these remarks was flat on his back on the floor of his private railroad car in San Diego.

It was morning in San Diego. The President, in the course of his travels, had stopped to review a landing exercise by the Fifth Marine Division. James Roosevelt, the President's oldest son, was stationed near San Diego, and on Thursday morning, before the exercise began, he visited his father on the train.

They reminisced about the family and about politics. The President indicated that he was resigned to the dumping of Wallace. Suddenly Roosevelt turned white, and his face took on an agonized look.

"Jimmy, I don't know if I can make it—I have horrible pains!" He struggled to get the words out.

Roosevelt was certain that he was suffering from some sort of acute digestive upset. Both men rejected the thought of calling a doctor, and they feared that cancellation of the President's appearance at the exercise would create concern. Roosevelt asked his son to "help me out of my berth and let me stretch out flat on the deck for a while—that may help." For ten minutes the President lay on the floor of the railroad car, his eyes closed, his face drawn, his body occasionally convulsed as waves of pain stabbed him. Then he opened his eyes, breathed deeply, and said, "Help me up now, Jimmy." Then he went out to review the exercise.

His only known reference to the incident was in a note to Eleanor the next day, saying: "I got the collywobbles. . . . Better today. . . ."

In Chicago, Senator Jackson completed his speech, then read to the convention the letter Roosevelt had addressed to him concerning Wallace.

Next came the nominations for the office of President. Barkley put up Roosevelt's name with appropriate gestures and adjectives. When he concluded with the magic words "Franklin Delano Roosevelt" the crowd whooped for thirty minutes.

The roll call for nominating speeches reached Iowa. A delegate from that state wished to second the nomination. Up to the rostrum came none other than Henry Wallace. Old-timers were astounded by this violation of convention tradition by a man who was himself a candidate for a nomination. But the unpredictable Vice President was there, ready to make the most courageous speech of his life.

The party leaders were stunned by the reception he received. Across the canyon-like expanses of the Chicago arena came wave after wave of thunderous applause. Much of the clamor rolled from the public galleries. Four years before he had been heavily booed in this same hall. But since 1940, Wallace had become, to many Americans, the symbol of the Common Man, the defender of the New Deal against the subtle conservative erosion from within the Democratic party itself, the courageous underdog pitted against the mysterious big-city leaders.

Wallace stood there, tousle-haired, his elbows resting on the rostrum, on the one hand the shy scientist, on the other hand an ambitious public man, seeking approval, wanting blood, drawing sustenance and courage from the ranting and cheering, the shining knight ready to battle the bosses.

Even today, the official transcript of his speech, including crowd reaction, crackles with excitement. He said, in part:

> The future belongs to those who go down the line unswervingly for the liberal principles of both political democracy and economic democracy regardless of race, color or religion. [Applause and cheers.] The poll tax must go. [Applause and cheers. Boos.] Equal educational opportunities must come. [Applause and cheers.] The future must bring equal wages for equal work regardless of sex or race. . . . [Applause and cheers.]
>
> The Democratic Party in convention assembled is about to demonstrate that it is not only a free party but a liberal party. [Applause.] The Democratic Party cannot long survive as a conservative party. The Republican Party has a monopoly on the conservative brains and the conservative dollars. [Applause and cheers.] Democrats who try to play the Republican game inside the Democratic Party must always find that it just can't work on a national scale. [Applause.]
>
> There is no question about the renomination of President Roosevelt by this Convention. The only question is whether the Convention and the party workers believe wholeheartedly in the liberal policies for which Roosevelt has always stood. [Applause.]

In the Presidential balloting, Roosevelt swamped Senator Harry Byrd of Virginia, 1,086 to 89.

During this busy week, party leaders in Chicago talked several times with the President by phone. One such call, probably late on Thursday afternoon, sealed the fate of Harry Truman. He had been summoned to Hannegan's suite in the Blackstone Hotel, where Hannegan, Walker, Flynn, Pauley, and Allen were waiting. Again came the pleas to become a candidate. Truman still resisted. Hannegan showed him the Truman-Douglas letter. Finally the National Chairman put in a long-distance call to the President. Roosevelt's strong voice boomed loudly through the receiver, which Hannegan held away from his ear. Others in the room could hear the President.

"Bob," Roosevelt said, "have you got that fellow lined up yet?"

"No," Hannegan replied. "He is the contrariest Missouri mule I've ever dealt with."

"Well, you tell him," the voice thundered, "if he wants to break up the Democratic party in the middle of a war, that's his responsibility."

A loud click signaled an end to the conversation.

Truman, stunned, sat for a minute or two and then got up and began walking around the room. The others watched, not saying a word. "Well, if that is the situation, I'll have to say yes, but why the hell didn't he tell me in the first place?"

Before the night session, Hannegan at long last released to the press the contents of the Truman-Douglas letter. Why the delay? First, it was dated the nineteenth, and Hannegan had to pursue the fiction that it was written then. Second, the Douglas boosters, such as they were, would now have little time to capitalize on the letter. Third, he had built the suspense to just the right pitch. When releasing the letter, Hannegan said he hoped Truman would win.

And Truman was now saying publicly, "I am a candidate and I will win."

Party leaders had considered pushing through Truman's nomination on Thursday night, after the President's long-distance acceptance speech. But this idea was abandoned when the bosses learned what was happening at the stadium. This was the night that both sides threw parliamentary procedure out the window, and used brute force.

Neale Roach, in charge of certain convention physical arrangements, phoned Pauley that the Wallace people had counterfeited tickets and had forced their way into the stadium. The galleries were filled with CIO minions, many of them high-school and college students, waving Wallace banners and parading about. The organist was blasting away with "Iowa—That's Where the Tall Corn Grows."

Pauley rushed to the stadium to find pandemonium. Delegates couldn't get to their seats. Although the capacity was 20,000, crowd estimates that night ranged as high as 40,000. Kelly claimed that the Wallace people did not force their way in, but that he let them in to give them their fling. The huge crowd sweltered through preliminary speeches, and then Jackson announced: "As the following address will come to you by radio, please hold your applause . . . until it is finished."

Silence fell across a semidarkened arena. The dazzling Klieg lights focused on an empty rostrum. The disembodied voice of Franklin Roosevelt rumbled through the speakers. The effect was eerie. He spoke from an unnamed naval base, ". . . in the performance of my duties under the Constitution. The war waits for no elections. Decisions must be made—plans must be laid—strategy must be carried out." He said: "I shall not campaign in the usual sense for the office. In these days of tragic sorrow, I do not consider it fitting. Besides, in these days of global warfare, I shall not be able to find the time. . . ."

When Roosevelt finished, the crowd applauded for three minutes. Then came a brief lull. Suddenly someone shouted, "We Want Wallace." The cry was echoed from all corners of the stadium. Parades began on the floor, and a dozen state placards were waved in the air. The organist played the Iowa Corn Song over and over. "Cornier and cornier," George Allen said. The New York *Times* reported that "an atmosphere of stampede was heavy in the air." Allen wrote that "it could have been Wallace if the vote had been taken [that] night. . . . It could have been a stampede."

To counter the CIO blitz, the bosses acted with desperation. Hannegan reportedly ordered the outer doors of the stadium thrown open, permitting still more hundreds of persons to pour in. This newest flood of humanity paralyzed the Wallace demonstration. Women fainted, losers in the gasping struggle to find oxygen. Pauley ordered Roach to get a fire ax and sever all wires leading to the amplifiers unless the organist stopped playing the Wallace theme song. Mayor Kelly proclaimed a fire hazard. Jackson recognized a friendly delegate who moved for a motion to recess. The ayes were smothered by a thunderclap of "No! No!" The ayes have it, Jackson ruled, and banged down the gavel for the last time that evening.

It had been a frightening exhibition of democracy in action.

Throughout the night the managers of the various candidates scrambled for votes. A week of rumors, demonstrations, tumult, and shouting had left the delegates wary and stubborn. A dozen favorite sons jumped into the contest, reasoning that anything could happen now. Delegates in the crucial states of Illinois and New York revolted against bossism. Flynn declined to press for a caucus vote. Ickes swung half the Illinois votes to Wallace, and Kelly snatched them back by pushing through a resolution supporting Lucas as a favorite son.

On Friday, Kelly and Hillman both tried again to pack the stadium. The CIO cadres were as well organized as a football cheering section. During the afternoon, 4 hours and 13 minutes were required for the delivery of 27 nominating and seconding speeches on behalf of 12 candidates. Thousands of persons stirred restlessly in their seats, alternately cheering and yawning. All waited for the voting that would end months of maneuvering and speculation.

By now, the nerve center of the Truman campaign had shifted to Private Room H at the stadium, accessible by a dark corridor underneath the speaker's stand. Delegates by the dozen were herded to this spot by their state leaders. Harry Truman, complete with Missouri grin, green suit, and outstretched hand, greeted them for three hours. Behind him, Kelly, Flynn, and the others hunched over telephones and tally sheets.

Upstairs, Truman had been placed in nomination by Missouri Senator Bennett Clark in a brief, undistinguished speech that evoked little enthusiasm. Then California yielded to Iowa, and Wallace's nomination by Judge Richard Mitchell set off a prolonged demonstration. Five persons—liberals all—seconded his nomination. The bitterness of their speeches bared the fears of the party's left wing that the forces of conservatism and bossism would that day undermine and perhaps end the progressive era dating from 1933. Excerpts:

"The Democratic Party seeks and honors great political leaders, but there is no place in the Democratic Party for political bosses. . . . [Wallace] is shy, he is too sincere to be a manipulator. He is too honest for double dealing. He has not, Mr. Chairman, been schooled in the devious ways of politics. . . ."

". . . The Democratic Party is not going to Munich to appease those who have fought its policies. . . . They say that he is a dreamer, a visionary, an idealist—as if these were hateful and damning words. I say to you now, where there is no vision, the people perish."

"The American people are through with political steamrollers; they are through with smoke-filled rooms, and they are through with dictator bosses. . . . We love him for the enemies he has made."

The roll call reached Illinois. Up popped Kelly with his ludicrous nomination of Scott Lucas. Everybody knew what he was up to, and Kelly was almost jeered out of his own stadium. His fumbling speech ranged from the sublime ("This man is a mine-run man. He is a country boy from the farm.") to the ridiculous (". . . every man and woman attending as a Delegate here will go away from this Convention feeling that it was a Democratic Convention, not controlled by any man or any set of men.").

"We want harmony at this convention," Kelly exclaimed.

"We want Wallace," the crowd roared.

"We want a ticket," Kelly said.

"We Want Wallace," thousands shouted.

Finally Kelly stopped, and an endless procession of his hired, spontaneous demonstrators streamed into the arena with signs proclaiming: BUSINESS WANTS LUCAS; LABOR WANTS LUCAS: EVERY SOLDIER, SAILOR AND MARINE WANTS LUCAS, and on and on. This phoniest of demonstrations continued amid much heckling and laughter until the placard-bearers shuffled shamefacedly out the door.

Other speeches were heard for other men, some already lost in history. Then quiet came to the stadium. Harry Truman joined his wife in a box seat. Wallace was asleep in his apartment. It was 4:52 P.M.

". . . the Clerk will call the roll of the states. . . ."

Alabama led off with 24 votes for its own Senator, John Bankhead.

Arizona and Arkansas gave Truman an early lead. California passed. Wallace came on fast with a breakthrough in a generally hostile South. He picked up nine of Florida's 18, and all of Georgia's 26, thanks to Arnall. In the Midwest, Wallace swept Iowa and Kansas, won 34 in Michigan and 24 in Minnesota.

Upsets do occur. Roosevelt had been told for months that Wallace couldn't possibly be renominated, even with his full support. Others were certain that the issue had been settled far in advance of the convention. But here was Wallace, leading his nearest competitor by more than 100 votes, with more than one third of the country heard from. In a total convention vote of 1,176, the winner would need 589. At this point, Wallace had 180½, Truman 76, and all the others 177.

Would the trend hold up? Missouri gave 32 to Truman. Many states scattered their votes. Frank Hague delivered 24 of 34 votes to Truman. Now Wallace led by only 201 to 156.

New York, with 96 votes, sharply divided between Wallace and Truman, couldn't even agree on what totals to announce. The state passed until the end of the roll. While New York huddled, Wallace opened up a big lead. Ohio split six ways, Wallace outpointing Truman 24½ to 19½. Oregon, 14 for Wallace. Next up, Pennsylvania, and a smashing victory for the Vice President, 46½ to 23½. The Senator gained in some smaller states, but Wallace swept Washington, West Virginia, and Wisconsin.

The end of the roll was reached. Then California, which had passed, gave Wallace 30, Truman 22. Wallace held his biggest lead, vis-à-vis Truman, 406½ to 244—a margin of 162½ votes. The gallery claque whooped at every Wallace gain.

New York was called again. Could Flynn keep the Empire State, a bastion of liberalism, away from Wallace? If not, a stampede to the Vice President might carry him over the required 589. The chairman of the delegation announced a majority for Truman, but the figures were challenged by a delegate. Jackson ordered that New York be polled. With some delegates having only ½ vote each, the poll dragged on for thirty-five minutes. The final count showed 69½ for Truman, 23 for Wallace. Flynn had held the line.

Puerto Rico gave six to Truman, and the first ballot was complete. But delegates could still switch their votes before the results were announced. Wallace was well ahead, but his momentum had been blunted by the big Truman vote in New York. The favorite sons sat tight, and the totals became official. Wallace had 429½, Truman 319½, Bankhead 98, Lucas 61, and Barkley 49½. Eleven other candidates trailed farther back. There would be another ballot.

The Wallace forces apparently relaxed, confident that their long lead would assure victory on the second ballot. The CIO, which could pack a stadium, seemed less adept at the intricate maneuvering on the convention floor. Meanwhile, the bosses realized that the decision might be near, and stepped up the pressure on favorite sons to withdraw in favor of Truman.

The second ballot was one of the most significant and confusing roll calls ever taken. Developments outraced the ability of the tally clerks to keep score. The lead changed hands seven times.

Slowly, surely, the favorite son votes began to shift toward the two leaders. Wallace showed gains over his first ballot totals, but Truman was gaining faster. Several nervous delegations, waiting to see which way to jump, asked permission to pass "while we take a poll." Illinois and Kentucky stayed with Lucas and Barkley. Hannegan and Flynn sat side by side at the front of the platform, staring out against the glare of the lights, searching for a trend.

Now came the first big break. Maryland Governor O'Conor announced his own withdrawal, and cast Maryland's 18 votes for Truman. The Senator led by two votes, but Michigan wiped that out with 35 for Wallace. Flynn tightened his grip on New York: Truman 74½, Wallace 18. Truman now led, 246 to 187.

Oklahoma cracked next. The state had supported its Governor, Robert Kerr, the popular keynote speaker, who had visions of being a compromise candidate. Pauley pointed his finger at Kerr, and gave the signal for Truman. The Governor paled slightly, then turned 22 more votes over to the Missouri Senator. A number of Southern delegates swung to Truman, who led 391 to 325½.

Wallace rallied. Washington, West Virginia, and Wisconsin again gave him 55. The clerk began to call seven states that had passed. California again divided 30-22 for Wallace. Truman had the narrowest possible lead, 431 to 430½.

All that had gone before seemed to count for nothing now, and the future of the nation turned on the preferences of a dwindling band of fence straddlers. Most of Indiana stayed with Paul McNutt, but Wallace got six votes and nudged ahead for the last time. Kansas gave him 16 more, and Wallace led by 20½. But Mississippi gave all 20 to Truman, who also won narrowly in Massachusetts and Montana.

Now all the delegations had been heard from. The second ballot was over, or was it? The count: Truman 477½, Wallace 473.

Senator Bankhead switched 22 Alabama votes to Truman, and South Carolina added a few. Truman had 501. Then the storm broke. Jackson recognized his fellow Hoosier, Frank McHale, who grabbed a mike to declare: "I desire to . . . withdraw [McNutt's] name from this race as Vice President and I ask at this time that our delegation be given an opportunity to be polled so that we may change our vote." Up jumped Kelly to announce that Illinois was caucusing to change its votes. Kelly had stayed with Lucas too long, and was running hard to catch a bandwagon. Indiana counted its votes quickly, and announced 22 more for Truman, two for Wallace. Hannegan yelled down to Kelly from the platform, "Come on in. It's all we need now."

And, in truth, the contest was all over but the shouting, and there was plenty of that. A dozen states were clamoring for recognition. New York gave 93 to Truman. Massachusetts threw all 34 to the Senator, whose total climbed to 587. Kansas removed all doubt by swinging 16 more to Truman.

The states continued to shift their votes in the wildest stampede in convention history. In all, there were 44 announced changes, some states being heard from three times. After considerable scratching of heads and pencils, the tally clerks decided that Truman had received 1,031 votes, while 105 remained with Wallace to the bitter end. The galleries were subdued now.

As Truman swept to victory, James Reston of the *Times* turned to Sidney Hillman. "What do you say to that?" Hillman replied, "We were for Wallace always, but *not against Truman.*"

Truman was halfway through a ham on white when he was grabbed by police and hauled to the platform. Amid the applause, he picked up a gavel and banged for order. "Give me a chance, will you please?" and the words would seem more appropriate nine months later. Then he spoke. "You don't know how much I appreciate this very great honor which has come to the great State of Missouri. There is also connected with it a very great responsibility, which I am perfectly willing to assume."

Harry left the platform, found his wife, and they fought their way to the exit with the help of Secret Service men and police. Grasping hands reached out at them, and others in the crowd stared at the smiling, bespectacled, unfamiliar face of the man from Missouri. The Senator and his wife got into a car.

Bess Truman, plain, plump, shy, and unsmiling, turned to him and exclaimed, "Are we going to have to go through this all the rest of our lives?"

Truman was silent.

Her next words were more muffled: "What would happen if he should die? You'd be President."

His answer, if any, was lost in the motor's roar. Apparently, Harry had forgotten to Clear It With Bess.

And Wallace told newsmen, "I feel freer now. I was not rehired. If I were a candidate I would have to follow a schedule and deal with issues from a partisan standpoint. This way, I can do more for liberalism."

Roosevelt later told Arnall: "I had no idea that Wallace would get as many delegates as he did. When my train stopped at Chicago during the convention I was told that under no circumstances could Wallace receive the nomination."

No one will ever be able to make a great deal of sense out of the President's behavior before this convention. Of course he was tired, and preoccupied with the war. But with good reason he has been acclaimed as one of our most astute political statesmen. In this case he had made the error of permitting sentiment to displace the merciless, cold calculation that must apply in the rendering of such a judgment. He allowed himself to be pulled too many ways by too many men. He was terribly afraid of hurting someone's feelings, yet his own procrastination opened the door to the humiliation of some of his closest associates.

In a contest such as this, the winner and the losers can be pointed out. But the reader, not the author, must assign the roles of hero and villain on the basis of his own political predilections. Summing up the case for the kingmakers, George Allen wrote: ". . . democracy's politicians can be as strong and pure as Knights of the Round Table. . . . I cherish Pauley's recollection of me as a 'faithful ally' in his anti-Wallace conspiracy. Bosses are held in ill repute in the United States—and with some justice—but this was a time when the bosses saved the country's bacon."

But George Norris wrote to Wallace, asking:

"Why this awful fight over the Vice-Presidency? . . . I am wondering if I am wrong about this. I am wondering if the gambling chances are that he is going to die before he serves out his next term if he is reelected. . . . Is that why the machine was so anxious to defeat you? . . . Cold-blooded politicians that handle the various political machines are not moved by any patriotic sentiment. These are the gamblers in the world of politics."

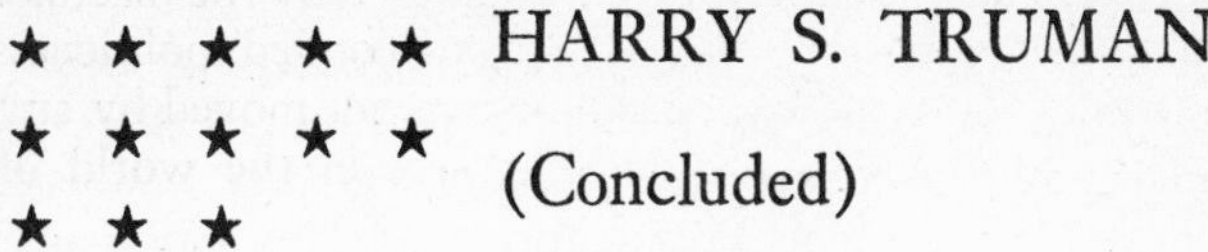

HARRY S. TRUMAN

(Concluded)

"God raises up leaders.

We do not know the process. . . ."

After Roosevelt returned from his Pacific trip, he and Truman conferred on campaign strategy, and then the Vice Presidential candidate was on his own—more or less. George Allen, secretary of the national committee, accompanied the nominee during most of his campaign, with the intention of guiding him past some of the political shoals heretofore unfamiliar to the Missourian. In the fall of 1944 Truman gained the valuable experience in the whistle-stop technique that he would use with great success four years later. In his campaign for the Vice Presidency, the Senator was most effective before small crowds—and most of the crowds were small.

On several occasions in recent years, the "out" party has found it inexpedient to concentrate its attack on a popular incumbent President running for re-election, and has therefore directed a great deal of criticism toward the President's running mate. In 1944, the Republicans did not pass up chances to hit at Roosevelt through Truman. First, of course, there was his association with Tom Pendergast, although this issue was a bit frayed by 1944 thanks to the incorruptible stance taken by the Senator's investigating committee. Potentially more serious was a copyrighted article in the Hearst press which claimed that Truman had been a member of the Ku Klux Klan. The candidate immediately instituted libel action against Hearst, but dropped the suit after the election was won. Many years before, an unsuccessful effort had been made to get Truman into the Klan.

The circumstances of Truman's nomination for Vice President were not overlooked by the Republicans. The GOP Vice-Presidential candidate, Governor John Bricker of Ohio, made it his business to lecture the opposition on the subject. Bricker sided with the conservative wing of his party, and had not followed the lead of his Presidential candidate, Governor Dewey, toward a more internationalist position in foreign affairs. Bricker picked up the "Clear it with Sidney" phrase. He denounced what he called the Democratic party's "vicious alliance with Sidney Hillman and the Political Action Committee." Bricker charged that Roosevelt and the New Deal were in the hands of the Communists. He complained: "Hillman brought to this country his Old World political concepts of power politics and class hatreds; and they have no part in our American political life." Bricker added gratuitously: "When people come here we have a right to insist that they accept our system of government."

After CIO-sponsored candidates lost badly in the September election in Maine, Chairman Hannegan asserted that Roosevelt had never uttered the words "Clear it with Sidney." But he could hardly deny the major role that the CIO was playing in the campaign, and the labor organization's support seemed to be a mixed blessing.

Roosevelt's physical condition continued to be discussed (mostly in private) during that fall. Several times before his nomination, Truman had indicated concern about the President's health, but he properly kept his thoughts to himself after the national convention.

FDR was re-elected in the closest of his four Presidential races. On January 20, 1945, Truman took the Vice Presidential oath at the somber wartime inaugural ceremony on the South Portico of the White House, and then settled inconspicuously into the chair above the Senate floor. His most important assignment from Roosevelt involved the retiring Vice President, Henry Wallace. After losing the 1944 nomination to Truman, Wallace had campaigned with great energy for the election of the Democratic ticket, and in payment for his "sacrifice," FDR offered Wallace a choice of any Cabinet post except

Secretary of State. Wallace decided he wanted to be Secretary of Commerce, and this meant booting out his old antagonist, Jesse Jones. If Jones was shocked at his peremptory dismissal, the Senate was in arms. The Commerce Department nomination of Wallace provoked the same party faction that Roosevelt had sought to placate by accepting Truman in 1944. Now Truman went to work to persuade the Senators to accept Wallace. But Wallace won approval only after the Senate had passed a bill stripping the office of much of its lending and spending power and after some fast parliamentary footwork by Truman and Majority Leader Barkley.

Roosevelt spent only a few weeks of his short fourth term in the Capital (his trip to Yalta required more than a month), and he held few Cabinet meetings. Truman attended these, and said later that he benefited very little from his participation. In a carry-over from the Garner days, Roosevelt conducted many of his discussions with individual Cabinet members in private. Aside from the Cabinet meetings, Truman conferred with the President only twice during his eighty-two days as Vice President. Several years after he succeeded Roosevelt, he remarked that he was the worst prepared man for the responsibilities of the Presidency since Andrew Johnson. The Vice President had not even been told of the existence of the atomic bomb.

The Senate had adjourned late in the afternoon of Thursday, April 12, 1945, and Harry Truman wandered over to Sam Rayburn's office for a drink and some political small talk. At 5:05 the President's press secretary called, and told Truman to come to the White House as quickly as possible. The Vice President supposed that Roosevelt had returned a few days early from his Warm Springs vacation and wanted to see him on some matter. He slipped out of the Capitol Building, eluded the Secret Service men, went to the White House, and was told that he had just become the thirty-third President of the United States.

A few minutes after Truman left his office, Sam Rayburn's telephone rang again. Congressman Lyndon Johnson, who had just stopped by, remembered that the Speaker didn't say anything; there was "just a kind of a gulp." When Rayburn told him the news, Johnson was left in a state of near shock at the passing of the man who had first encouraged him to run for Congress eight years before. Still in a daze, he wandered from the office and encountered a newspaper correspondent.

"He was just like a daddy to me always; he always talked to me just that way," Johnson blurted. "There are plenty of us left here to try to block and run interference, as he had taught us, but the man who carried the ball is gone—gone."

Truman took the oath at 7:08, and called on the Cabinet members to stay in office. He wrote later that his new job "was really something to think about," but he decided first to go home, "get as much rest as possible and face the music."

The next day, Truman met reporters, his blue eyes peering owllike from thick-lensed glasses. "Boys, if you ever pray, pray for me now. I don't know whether you've ever had a load of hay fall on you, but when they told me yesterday what had happened I felt like the moon, the stars and all the planets had fallen on me. I've got the most terribly responsible job a man ever had."

Reporters, who take almost any shock in stride, had trouble —along with everybody else—in picturing Harry Truman as Chief Executive. They found it awkward to address him as "Mr. President," and they skirted custom by prefacing their questions with "Sir," or with no form of address whatever. In time, however, both the reporters and Harry Truman would become accustomed to the fact that he was President.

However, the first weeks were most difficult, and Truman went too far in pleading his "unfitness" and "inadequacy" for the office. When some of these comments turned up in the newspapers, old friends cautioned the President. Senator Barkley spoke to him along these lines:

"Mr. President, I realize how you feel about this job you have inherited, and I respect you for your humility. But you have got the job, and you have the responsibility. You are President of the United States and I hope you will no longer deprecate your own personal situation or minimize your ability to carry on the task to which you have been called.

"God raises up leaders. We do not know the process, but, in the wisdom of Almighty God, you have been made President. You will have all the help that any of us can give you. Have confidence in yourself. If you do not, the people will lose confidence in you. However humble and contrite you feel, you have got to go forward and lead this nation out of war. Have trust in the God Who brought this about and He will enable you to do what you have to do."

With the possible exception of Fillmore, no accidental President ever faced so quickly the necessity of demonstrating his fitness to lead the nation. The Compromise of 1850 was being debated when Fillmore succeeded, but on no other previous occasion had Congress even been in session at the time of a President's death. Furthermore, Truman was the first person summoned to the Presidency by death since the development of modern mass communications; radio and newsreels brought him immediately to the attention of all. And most important, the war was speeding toward a climax, with peacetime problems already on the horizon.

Heeding the advice of Barkley and the others, Truman began to assert himself. If anything, he now seemed to render his decisions too abruptly, and he began to appear too sure of himself. He perpetuated this image long after it was necessary to reassure the public, and opened himself to criticism that he acted impulsively. But such was seldom the case. Historians looking back on Truman's eight years of war, cold war, and domestic turmoil have concluded that the little man from Missouri came up with the right answers more often than not, and that his decisions were not the result of impulse or whimsy.

He started out with unprecedented popular support. George Gallup found that 87 per cent of the public approved of the way he was handling the job. At first, policies were not his own, but Roosevelt's. In his first speech to Congress, he pledged to carry the war to its conclusion along the lines laid down by his predecessor. He affirmed that the San Francisco conference would convene on schedule on April 25 to draw a charter for the United Nations. The honeymoon lasted about five months; in September, 1945, Truman announced a bold, twenty-one-point peacetime domestic program. It went beyond the scope of the New Deal, and its No. 1 promoter seldom spent an unruffled day in office after its announcement.

Truman seemed ill prepared to fill the great void left on the world stage by the death of Roosevelt. In July, he met British Prime Minister Churchill and Soviet Premier Joseph Stalin at Potsdam. Churchill said years later that he found himself hostile to the man who had replaced his old friend Roosevelt. As for Stalin, Truman professed that he liked "Old Joe" and said that he was a prisoner of the Politboro. Even allowing for his wrong appraisal of the Soviet tyrant, one must concede that Truman became alert to the menace posed by world communism. Aid to Greece and Turkey, tough talk in Iran, and the establishment of the Marshall Plan and NATO were actions of an administration conscious of its new obligations. There are some indications that, had Roosevelt lived through his fourth term, well past his prime both physically and mentally, he might have put more faith than warranted in his wartime collaborators in Moscow.

Truman's determination to assert a hard line against the Soviet Union contributed to the political demise of the two men who had been his most serious competitors for the Vice Presidential nomination in 1944. In 1945, Truman had appointed his old friend, Jimmy Byrnes, Secretary of State, and he had inherited Henry Wallace, as Secretary of Commerce. He felt obligated to keep Wallace in the Administration because of his large and boisterous following. However, Byrnes and Wallace each felt that he should be sitting in the White House instead of Truman, and each undertook to prescribe United States foreign policy. Early in his administration, Truman had permitted his Cabinet officers an unusually large area of freedom in formulating departmental policies. Taking this cue, Byrnes frequently failed to consult Truman in foreign-policy matters. This got so bad that one day a reporter asked the President if he supported a certain position taken by the State Department. Truman bristled in anger.

In Truman's judgment, Byrnes's independence went beyond permissible limits at the conference of foreign ministers in Moscow in December, 1945. Without consulting the President, Byrnes proposed and won adoption for an atomic-energy-control declaration which in the President's view was favorable to the Soviet Union. Other positions taken by Byrnes with respect to the Middle East and Eastern Europe also met with Truman's disapproval. According to Truman, he read the "riot act" to his Secretary of State upon the latter's return to this country from Moscow, and ended with the complaint: "I'm tired babying the Soviets." Byrnes denied later that he had received such a lecture, but in any event the Administration thereafter assumed a stiffer posture toward Russia, and Truman took a firmer grip on his foreign policy.

Next, Henry Wallace wandered off the reservation. In September, 1946, in a Madison Square Garden speech, he sharply criticized what he called Byrnes's "Get Tough with Russia" policy. He called, instead, for a policy of accommodation with the Soviet Union. Byrnes, then in Paris attending another foreign ministers' meeting, complained to Truman about the speech, and offered to resign immediately. Truman denied that he had approved Wallace's speech in advance. Wallace said that he had. The uproar rendered Wallace a political liability to the Administration, and Truman asked for and obtained his resignation.

The President wrote to his mother and sister, "Well, I had to fire Henry today, and of course I hated to do it. . . . If Henry had stayed Sec. of Agri. in 1940 as he should have, there'd never have been all this controversy, and I would not be here, and wouldn't that be nice? [Press Secretary] Charlie Ross said I'd shown I'd rather be right than President, and I told him I'd rather be anything than President. . . . Well, now he's out, and the crackpots are having conniption fits. I'm glad they are. It convinces me I'm right."

Wallace was indeed out after holding high office in Democratic Administrations for thirteen and a half years. He was the last Roosevelt legacy in Truman's Cabinet, the last of the New Dealers, and his departure removed any doubts as to Truman's determination to be President in fact as well as in name.

Four months later, Byrnes followed Wallace into limbo. He never fully regained the confidence of the President after their early misunderstanding over control of foreign policy. Truman, who had tried so hard to make Byrnes Vice President, said years later, "He failed miserably as Secretary of State."

They kept in touch for about two years after Byrnes left Washington. Then, in 1949, at Washington and Lee University, Byrnes delivered an address that included criticism of Administration domestic policy. The President wrote to his former friend in terms reminiscent of Andrew Jackson's message to John C. Calhoun. "Since your Washington and Lee speech I know how Caesar felt when he said, '*Et tu Brute*.' "

Byrnes replied that his speech had contained no direct criticisms of the President, and added, "I hope you are not going to think of me as a Brutus because I am no Brutus. I hope you are not going to think of yourself as a Caesar, because you are no Caesar."

Byrnes and Wallace, both of whom wanted to be on the ticket in 1944, were rather irregular in their Democratic loyalties thereafter. Wallace voted for himself in 1948. Both voted for Eisenhower. Then Wallace returned to the Democratic column in 1964, but Byrnes supported both Nixon and Goldwater.

The Wallace campaign in 1948 was, of course, a fiasco. He formed his third party, the Progressive party, with himself as Presidential candidate, and with a pledge to seek the friendship of the Soviet Union. He was asked: Are the Communists running your campaign? Answered the candidate: "If they want to help us out in some of these problems, why God bless them, let them come along."

Wallace polled 1,157,140 votes, only 2.4 per cent of the total. He failed to win any electoral votes. The former Vice President later acknowledged errors in his assessment of the Communists. But his harsh, earnest voice was not heard again in the political arena.

After the Republicans won control of Congress in 1946, Truman's prestige dipped so low that many persons doubted that he could be nominated for President in 1948. Southern conservatives were already in revolt against his civil-rights program. And a liberal bloc, including James Roosevelt and several big city bosses, hoped to draft General Dwight Eisenhower. They persisted in this effort even though Eisenhower gave no evidence either that he was a Democrat or that he wanted the nomination. The Eisenhower bubble burst early in July, 1948, when the General unequivocally took himself out of the running for the Democratic nomination. Supreme Court Justice Douglas also refused to be considered. Only Harry Truman was left, and he was renominated at Philadelphia by nearly 4-1 over Senator Richard Russell of Georgia. The apathetic delegates who voted for him were generally resigned to a Democratic defeat in November, though they had preserved intact the twentieth-century tradition that a Vice President who succeeds to the Presidency by death is entitled to try for a term of his own. But Wallace was already attacking from the left, and the adoption by the Democrats of a strong civil-rights plank provoked a walkout by Southern delegates bent on forming still another "third" party.

Notwithstanding Truman's commitment to a progressive program that went beyond the New Deal, he did not enjoy solid support from the liberals, and he hoped to secure their allegiance by persuading Justice Douglas to accept the Vice-Presidential nomination. It seemed for a while that the two men who had shared the endorsement in Roosevelt's mysterious letter four years before might share the ticket in 1948. But once again, Douglas said No.

The delegates then settled the Vice Presidential question with their jubilant reception of a fighting keynote speech by Senator Barkley. He offered no apologies for the sixteen-year record of leadership by the Democratic party, but instead carried the fight to the Republicans. And when he finished his address, the delegates paraded and cheered for half an hour. Barkley had been more or less available for the Vice-Presidential nomination at nearly every convention from 1928 on. In 1948, Barkley allowed: "I am willing. . . . But it will have to come quick. I don't want it passed around so long it is like a cold biscuit."

Truman talked to Barkley on the phone, and congratulated him on his speech. Barkley said there was talk of his getting the Vice-Presidential nomination, and that he would be willing to accept. Truman, without a candidate for the post, gladly threw his support to Barkley, who was nominated by acclamation. The two men had been close friends for years, and Barkley had served Truman loyally as Senate Democratic leader. He was seventy, and Truman was sixty-four, and their 134 years added up to a new record as the oldest ticket ever offered to the voters by a major party. The honor that came to Barkley in Philadelphia in 1948 was overdue, and came four years too late to serve as a steppingstone to the White House.

At the 1948 convention, the old warhorse was not only the Vice-Presidential nominee, the keynote speaker, and the temporary chairman; he was also the chairman of the committee to notify the Vice-Presidential nominee of his victory. The latter task had always been perfunctory, but never more so than in Barkley's case.

The Republicans were already in the field. Governor Dewey had been nominated again for President, and he had chosen California's Governor Earl Warren for the Vice Presidency. In 1944, Warren had declined to accept the same nomination. But 1948 looked like a Republican year, and Warren said he would take second place after Dewey agreed to invest the office with more authority than it had held in the past. Dewey was an able administrator, but how he would have used Warren's abilities will, of course, never be known. Warren had always drawn a great deal of support from progressive voters. His nomination brought recognition to the booming Western section of the nation. But also of significance, for the first time in the entire history of the Republican party, the Middle West —the GOP heartland—was not represented on the national ticket. In the November general election the Republicans lost most of the Midwest—and the election.

While Truman carried the campaign to the whistle stops, Barkley belied his age by conducting the first national, full-blown "prop stop" campaign. Flying in a chartered plane, the *Bluegrass*, he visited 36 states in six weeks, traveled 150,000 miles, and spoke more than 250 times.

All the polls said that the Democrats would lose, but they won. For Truman, the victory climaxed the most fantastic rise from obscurity since the time of Chester Alan Arthur, and vindicated the judgment of the delegates who had supported him for Vice President in 1944.

Barkley's imperishable contribution to the Vice Presidency was the word "Veep," concocted by his grandson, who thought the title "Mr. Vice President" was a little high-toned. Barkley mentioned the term at a press conference, and "Veep" caught on, but only for Barkley. Richard Nixon declined to accept the title, saying that it was an honorary tribute to Barkley.

In a more serious vein, Congress passed a statute at Truman's request in 1949, designating the Vice President as a member of the National Security Council. The NSC is assigned by law with "the integration of domestic, foreign, and military policies relating to national security." As a member of the NSC, Barkley participated in the decision to intervene in Korea in 1950 and in the decision to recall General Douglas MacArthur in 1951 from his duties in the Far East. Vice President Wallace had served as chairman of the Board of Economic Warfare, but that had been an *ad hoc* assignment, from which he was removed by Roosevelt. Barkley's appointment to the NSC was protected by statute, and marked the most significant advance in the Vice Presidency up to that time.

Barkley continued to preside over the Senate, and with his unsurpassed sense of humor he watched for opportunities to enliven the proceedings. Once, Senator Kenneth McKellar of Tennessee complained that a colleague had yawned while he, McKellar, was making a speech. Barkley pondered the merits of the objection and then solemnly ruled: "The yawn of the Senator from Illinois will be stricken from the record."

The Vice President also undertook many semiofficial assignments, often as a representative of President Truman. Barkley was much in demand for a time at various festivals—Cherry Blossom festivals, Apple Blossom festivals, and such. Invariably, the Veep had a chance to crown a queen at these affairs, and he got much practice in what he called the "osculatory business."

Alben Barkley was our oldest Vice President, and he was the only one to marry while serving in that office. Barkley's first wife had died in 1947. Thereafter, newspaper columnists had him married off to several eligible Washington women. Barkley himself, already many times a grandfather, never expected to marry again until he met Mrs. Carleton Hadley, a St. Louis widow, in the summer of 1949, on a Potomac cruise given by Mr. and Mrs. Clark Clifford. From the time he greeted the thirty-seven-year-old stenographer at the top of the gangplank, Barkley pretty much monopolized Jane Hadley's time, both in Washington and in St. Louis. But a Vice President cannot engage in courtship without attracting a good deal of attention, and the nation followed his progress with growing enthusiasm throughout the summer and fall of 1949. Unlike any Vice President before him, Barkley wrote love letters while presiding over the Senate. He recalled later: "I think I would have tolerated anything, even the most outrageous sort of filibuster, to keep the Senators talking so I could get my love letters written." In October, the couple announced their engagement, and the news was important enough to cause the interruption of the Edgar Bergen show for a news bulletin.

There was some speculation about how Barkley had proposed to Mrs. Hadley. In this context, the Milwaukee *Journal* reprinted the famous words of Thomas R. Marshall that a Vice President "cannot speak; he cannot move; he suffers no pain; and yet he is perfectly conscious of everything that is going on about him." They were married in St. Louis on November 18. Barkley, who had received almost every honor short of the Presidency, wrote later: "I have been doubly blessed in life, having had the good fortune of being married to two lovely and wonderful women. No man could say more."

In 1952, for the first time in his life, Barkley sought the Democratic Presidential nomination.[1] Truman pledged his support. The Vice President went to Chicago confident that he could win, but leaders of organized labor intervened, saying that Barkley was "too old." And, in fact, he was. He was seventy-four, and his eyesight was failing. After this rebuff from labor he withdrew from the contest and delivered a farewell address to the convention. Governor Adlai Stevenson of Illinois won the nomination, and chose for the Vice Presidency, Senator John Sparkman of Alabama, a liberal, except on civil rights, who had opposed the Dixiecrat movement four years before.

Barkley left office in 1953, grew restive, and ran again—successfully—for the Senate in 1954. In the spring of 1956, he addressed a mock political convention at Washington and Lee University. He said, "I would rather be a servant in the house of the Lord than to sit in the seats of the mighty." These

[1] While Barkley was the Veep, in 1950, another attempt was made to assassinate a President. Two Puerto Rican nationalist fanatics attempted to kill Truman, who was then living at Blair House during the reconstruction of the White House. One of the men got as far as the front steps of Blair House. They exchanged gunfire with Secret Service men and policemen. In a hail of twenty-seven bullets, five persons fell. One Puerto Rican and one policeman died of their wounds. During the battle, the President looked out of an upper-story window to see what was going on.

words brought warm applause, which was still continuing when the former Vice President toppled backward onto the floor. A few minutes later he was dead.

★ ★ ★ ★ ★
★ ★ ★ ★ ★
★ ★ ★ ★

RICHARD M. NIXON

"I told him he would have to chart his own course. . . ."

In August, 1945, newspapers in California's Twelfth Congressional District printed a publicity handout that had come through the mail in the form of an advertisement. The "want ad" was promoted by 100 Republicans in the district who were seeking a "Congressman candidate with no previous political experience. . . . Any young man, resident of district, preferably a veteran, fair education, no political strings or obligations and possessed of a few ideas for betterment of country at large, may apply. . . ."

Lieutenant Commander Richard Nixon was in Baltimore that fall, waiting for his discharge from the Navy. An acquaintance asked him, on the phone, if he were a Republican and if he would like to run for Congress. Nixon was interested, went before the Committee of One Hundred, and won its approval. A former lawyer who had served in the South Pacific during World War II, the thirty-three-year-old Nixon seemed to be the intelligent and ambitious type of man who might go far.

From the time of his first campaign for Congress in 1946, Richard Nixon was embroiled in almost constant controversy. For eight years he served as Vice President, where many of his predecessors had found obscurity; Nixon's name was seldom out of the headlines. He became the first incumbent Vice President since Van Buren to win a Presidential nomination, and he missed the White House by a handful of votes. He was his party's principal campaigner, and served as a lightning rod for Democratic attacks on the Eisenhower administration. He presided over meetings of the Cabinet and the National Security Council during the President's illnesses. In the manner of Garner during early New Deal days, Nixon acted in a liaison role between the executive branch and the Congress. And he carried his country's message abroad, occasionally under the wildest of circumstances.

To many Americans he was a shining young knight driving the Communists and the crooks out of Washington. To the cartoonist Herblock, he was a heavy-jowled, unshaven demagogue climbing out of a sewer to attend a political rally. Nixon, who actually stood somewhere between these two extremes, seemed to be searching for his identity no less assiduously than the observers of the Washington scene who watched his career unfold.

In 1946, Democrats frowned at Nixon for the first time when his campaign leaflets proclaimed that he was fighting "the PAC, its Communist principles and its gigantic slush fund." He pinned the liberal label on his opponent and was carried into office on the conservative tide of the first postwar election.

For nearly two years, he was just one of many freshman Congressmen (the greenest in town, said one newspaper). Then, in the summer of 1948, Alger Hiss, a former high official in the State Department, appeared before the House Committee on Un-American Activities, of which Nixon was a member. He came voluntarily to deny allegations by Whittaker Chambers, a senior editor of *Time* magazine, that he and Hiss had been members of an underground Communist apparatus in Washington during the 1930's. Hiss impressed the committee favorably. He said that the name Whittaker Chambers meant nothing to him. He reviewed his own record of public service, including his participation in the Yalta and San Francisco conferences. He effectively projected the image of a man who had been the victim either of mistaken identity or of a vicious libel. But Nixon, on the basis of his own legal experience, thought that Hiss's performance was too smooth, too pat; the Congressman felt that Hiss had overstated his case.

However, the other members of the committee did not share this assessment, and they wanted to drop the matter. They had been taking a verbal pounding because of the nature of some of their past investigations. Now it appeared to the public that the Congressmen had allowed Chambers to use the committee room as a sounding board for the worst kind of a libel against a man whose integrity and loyalty had never been questioned. But Nixon argued that in view of the seriousness of the charges, the committee had an obligation to find out who was telling the truth. Nixon proposed that instead of trying to ascertain whether Hiss was a Communist, the committee should first merely try to find out if he had been truthful when he said that he had never known a man named Whittaker Chambers. Nixon drew up a long list of questions concerning fine points that a man might know about a close friend. The committee questioned Chambers in executive session, and he described Hiss's personal and family life with such detail that Nixon became convinced that the two must have known each other.

The committee investigators tracked down all available evidence that might establish the truth of Chambers' story. At a subsequent hearing, the committee lulled Hiss, a bird watcher, into admitting what Chambers had told Nixon in secret testimony—that Hiss had once spotted a rare prothonotary warbler in a swampy area by the Potomac. There were other connections, including a 1929 Ford with a "sassy little trunk on the back," which Chambers said Hiss had given to him. Nixon went to Chambers' Maryland farm to obtain additional data. The investigation was one of the most dramatic in the annals of Congress. Hiss equivocated on his previous position as more ties between the two men came to light. Nixon, time and time again, came up with the key questions and the key evidence that strengthened Chambers' case.

Chambers repeated his charges outside the committee room, and Hiss sued him for libel. Chambers then produced the famous—and misnamed—Pumpkin Papers, microfilmed copies of government documents which Chambers said Hiss had given him for relay to the Soviet Union. When Chambers handed over some incriminating documents that had been typed on a Woodstock typewriter owned by Hiss, the latter's case began to fall apart. He was eventually indicted and convicted of perjury.

The Hiss case brought to Nixon a well-deserved national reputation as a resourceful investigator, and as a relentless and articulate opponent of the Communist conspiracy. But Nixon wrote later that his triumph had not been total, that he had won the undying enmity of members of the "intellectual community" who had been trapped out on a limb in their defense of Alger Hiss.

Unlike some of the other prominent Communist fighters in Congress, Nixon was an internationalist, a supporter of collective security pacts, and foreign aid and reciprocal trade programs. In domestic issues, he generally supported the conservative position.

In 1950, Nixon ran for the United States Senate. He opposed Helen Gahagan Douglas, a Congresswoman and actress who had survived a rough Democratic primary in which "soft on Reds" charges had been bandied about. Nixon dusted off these charges for use in the fall campaign. Democrats were furious when they saw a Nixon leaflet printed on pink paper and purporting to show that Mrs. Douglas had voted the same way as Vito Marcantonio, the fellow-traveling New York Congressman, on 354 occasions. They rightly charged that such compilations of voting records can be arranged to prove almost anything. Nixon campaigned hard on the Communists-in-government issue, and was elected by 681,000 votes.

Shortly before he was nominated for President in 1952, General Eisenhower wrote down the names of five men who would be acceptable to him as a running mate. Nixon's name headed the list. Eisenhower, then sixty-one, wanted a young Vice President capable of carrying on should an emergency arise. He believed that Nixon's political philosophy squared generally with his own, and that the California Senator could most effectively exploit the public concern about foreign and domestic communism. And putting Nixon in the spotlight would take the play from the aggressive but ineffective Senator Joseph McCarthy of Wisconsin, then at the height of his own anti-Communist kick.

After Eisenhower was nominated, party leaders met to consider his recommendations, and they enthusiastically approved Nixon.

During the campaign, Eisenhower conducted his "great crusade" in somewhat lofty terms, while Nixon slugged it out with the opposition. The Vice Presidential candidate criticized Adlai Stevenson, the Democratic candidate, for submitting during the Hiss trial a deposition attesting to the good character of the defendant. Stevenson pointed out that he was not testifying as to Hiss's guilt or innocence, but was only fulfilling his duty in telling the court what he knew of Hiss as a person. When a news magazine reported: "Stevenson claims to have a plan for bringing the [Korean] war to a successful conclusion," Nixon demanded that Stevenson make his plan known immediately to the joint chiefs of staff.

Soon, Nixon found himself under a barrage so heavy that his own political career seemed at an end. On September 18, the New York *Post* headlined a SECRET NIXON FUND, and told of a " 'millionaire's club' devoted exclusively to the financial comfort of Senator Nixon. . . ." The fund in question was, in fact, not secret, and was financed by business and professional people. It was established to pay for political activities in which any officeholder must participate, and which Nixon, who was not wealthy, could not afford to pay for himself. The money—$18,235 in all—had been used for transportation, mailing and office expenses.

The *Post* story provoked a great hue and cry among the Democrats, who professed to see Nixon as a captive of special interests. There was an ominous silence from Eisenhower's campaign train. Then the Republican New York *Herald Tribune* printed an editorial calling for Nixon to offer to withdraw from the ticket. Eisenhower, who had pledged to clean up the "mess in Washington," implied that Nixon would have to come "clean as a hound's tooth." Governor Sherman Adams of New Hampshire, a member of Eisenhower's campaign staff, ordered an independent, nonpartisan audit of the fund, which was found to be legal and aboveboard. But mail and advice poured into the Eisenhower headquarters, and it ran no better than 50-50 in favor of the Vice Presidential candidate.

Eisenhower pondered what to do about Nixon, and gladly subscribed to the idea of letting the voters make the decision.

Nixon agreed to go on nationwide television to present his side of the story, and to ask the viewers to write to the national committee saying whether Nixon should stay or go. Nixon's radio and TV appearance cost the Republicans $75,000, and was the best investment they ever made. His telecast was delayed until Tuesday, September 23, five days after the original *Post* story. By the time Nixon went on the air, the Democrats had expended all of their ammunition, and the Senator had his chance just as suspense had been built to a peak. Sixty million persons tuned in to see what he would say and do. To add to the drama, Republicans had just turned up a "secret Stevenson fund," involving money paid by Illinois businessmen to Stevenson, who then used the money to supplement the salaries of low-paid Illinois state officials; the latter did not know the identity of their benefactors.

Nixon had spent two days outlining his remarks. Realizing that his own future and that of his family hung on the outcome of his address, he had driven himself to the emotional snapping point. Then, just before he went on the air, Governor Dewey phoned. He said that Eisenhower's top advisers had met and decided that Nixon should announce his resignation at the conclusion of his broadcast. He implied that the general shared this view. Dewey asked Nixon what he was going to do. Nixon exploded, telling Dewey that if he wanted to find out he had better listen to the broadcast. And he slammed down the receiver.

Face to face with the people, Nixon spoke "as a candidate for the Vice Presidency and as a man whose honesty and integrity has been questioned." The heart of his argument was that he had not profited personally from the expense fund, that none of the donors had received any favors, and that the fund had permitted him to serve the people better. Nixon described his automobile, the equity in his California and Washington homes, his life insurance, and his stocks; he listed all the money he owed to his bank, to his parents, and in mortgages. Using the best courtroom technique, he interspersed his defense with jabs at the opposition. In reference to Truman administration scandals, he said: "Pat doesn't have a mink coat. But she does have a respectable Republican cloth coat, and I always tell her that she would look good in anything."

Nixon reached the height (or depth) of drama by confessing that he had accepted one gift. "It was a little cocker spaniel dog . . . black and white, spotted, and our little girl Tricia . . . named it Checkers. And you know, the kids, like all kids, loved the dog, and I just want to say this, right now, that regardless of what they say about it, we are going to keep it."

Then the defendant became the prosecutor, and demanded that Stevenson explain his own secret fund. He noted that the Democratic Vice Presidential candidate, Senator Sparkman, carried his wife on the government payroll. He called on both to reveal their entire financial history. Nixon concluded by predicting that, as a fighter against the Communists, he would be the target of more smears; but he said that he would continue to fight against the "crooks and the Communists and those that defend them. . . ." He asked his listeners to let the national committee know whether he should stay or get off the ticket.

The response was thunderous. Motion Picture Producer Darryl Zanuck telephoned the studio to applaud "The most tremendous performance I've ever seen." At a political rally in Cleveland, Eisenhower watched Nixon on television while 16,000 persons listened over a public-address system. The general then spoke to his wildly pro-Nixon audience, declaring that he had just seen an example of courage, and that he would "rather have a courageous man at my side than a whole boxcar of pussyfooters." Some 300,000 messages bearing one million signatures were received at GOP headquarters in Washington, and the sentiment ran 350 to 1 in favor of Nixon. The letters contained donations of more than $60,000.

Next day came the lachrymose finale to this episode, with Nixon flying to meet Eisenhower in Wheeling, West Virginia. The general exclaimed, "You're my boy," then read to the press a letter of praise that presumably clinched matters, from "one who has known Richard longer than anyone else. His Mother."

As an aftermath, Stevenson, Sparkman and Eisenhower all published their income-tax returns for the previous ten years. Release of financial data has now become routine for candidates for national office.

Many sophisticated persons scoffed at Nixon's "soap-opera performance," but they were in the minority. By describing his personal financial problems, the candidate had found common cause with the average man, who also could afford nothing better than an inexpensive coat for his wife, and who also wondered how he could ever pay off the mortgage on his home. But while he had decisively turned the tables on the Democrats, the long-term impact was mixed. Earl Mazo, a Nixon biographer, wrote that persons who remembered that telecast most vividly thought it was horrible. Mazo suggests that that incident marked the origin of the feelings expressed so often in later years in the words, "I don't like Nixon, but I don't know why."

The landslide of November, 1952, placed the executive branch in the hands of the Republican party for the first time in twenty years. Nixon was sworn in as Vice President on January 20, 1953, 11 days past his fortieth birthday. Only Breckinridge had been younger. Eisenhower had promised Nixon that he would be invited to participate "in all the meetings where policy is developed." Doors and filing cabinets were opened for his benefit. The Vice President was permitted to see the most secret security information as well as intelligence reports submitted daily from around the world. From the Pentagon came regular briefings on military affairs. Nixon attended meetings of the Cabinet and the National Security Council and—in a break with the past—he presided over these bodies when the President was absent for any reason. Marshall had presided at Cabinet meetings when Wilson was in Paris, but did not attend at all when Wilson was sick. In eight years, Nixon presided at 19 meetings of the Cabinet and at 26 sessions of the NSC. In the privacy of the NSC meetings, he apparently adhered to the "eyeball to eyeball" philosophy of standing firm against Communist threats, urging a more militant foreign policy than Eisenhower ever enunciated in public. The Vice President also attended weekly meetings between the President and congressional leaders.

But the President was reluctant to assign specific executive duties to the Vice President "because if you happen to have a Vice-President that disagrees with you, then you have . . . an impossible situation." Nonetheless, by the time Nixon left office, the concept of the working Vice President had been firmly established, and only at some risk would future political conventions return to the habit of "balancing" national tickets with men of differing political philosophies. If the Vice Presidential nomination is no longer thought to be available as a booby prize for the defeated faction, then we may expect that a party will have one more reason to strive for a broad consensus within its ranks.

Nixon was named chairman of the President's Committee on Government Contracts, established in 1953 to receive and investigate complaints of racial discrimination in companies that had been awarded government contracts. Three years later he proclaimed: "We've abolished racial segregation in . . . Federal contracts and civilian employment." Allowing for the exaggeration, it is true that Nixon's committee, armed principally with a weapon called "Persuasion," obtained compliance in a number of cases.

The Vice President was also named chairman of the Cabinet Committee on Price Stability, which studied United States economic trends, and proposed means of preventing inflation.

As a political adviser, Nixon rendered important service to the administration. In his relatively short political career, he had learned more about politics than many of the older officials in the executive branch who had come from the ranks of business and finance. Nixon was regarded as a political broker, not only between Capitol Hill and the White House, but also between the conservative and moderate factions within the party. Richard Rovere called him a "double agent."

One page from Nixon's political primer for executive officers read as follows: "Get to know personally and promptly the key committeemen for your unit. Don't take with you, or send to represent you at the Capitol, aides prominently associated with the Truman Administration. If you get a formal, tough letter from a member of Congress (and try to prevent such a situation from arising) answer it verbally in a very friendly way."

Nixon labored in the Capitol cloakrooms in behalf of Eisenhower's legislative program, and warned the President in advance about any program he knew would not sit well in Congress. Nixon removed any doubt that the Throttlebottom era was gone. He said of his job, "I like it much better than service in the House or Senate. In the vice-presidency you have an opportunity to see the whole operation of the government and participate in its decisions."

Nixon, the preacher of party unity, couldn't control the intransigent radicalism of Joe McCarthy. The Wisconsin Senator had labeled the Roosevelt and Truman administrations as twenty years of treason, and after Eisenhower had been in office for a while, McCarthy was talking about twenty-one years of treason. McCarthy would occasionally listen to Nixon, thanks to the latter's record in the field of hunting Communists. But after he failed to curb McCarthy's attacks on the administration, Nixon spoke on radio and television against "unfair methods for fighting Communists" which "help destroy freedom itself." He said: "When you do it unfairly and with irresponsibility all that you do is to give ammunition to those who oppose any action against the Communists. . . . Men who have in the past done effective work . . . have, by reckless talk and questionable method, made themselves the issue rather than the cause they believe in." McCarthy, unheeding, stumbled down the path toward condemnation by the Senate.

Thanks to another tradition rooted in the Nixon years, future aspirants to the Vice Presidency will have to polish their international table manners. Wallace had traveled some, Garner had visited the Far East, and Barkley had eaten Thanksgiving turkey with the enlisted men in Korea. But in eight years, Nixon visited fifty-four countries. Some of his travels were designated as good-will tours, and some were semiofficial in nature; all brought valuable experience. Nixon's foreign travels required more exertion than any of his other duties. Jet-age travel plays hob with human metabolism, and a hopscotch tour through southeast Asia, for example, can bring an everchanging kaleidoscope of languages, foods, customs, and taboos. Before leaving on a trip, Nixon underwent intensive State Department briefings on our relations with each country on the agenda, and on problems confronting that country. (This cooperation with a Vice President was in marked contrast to the grumbling from Secretary of State Cordell Hull when Henry Wallace "meddled" in foreign affairs.) Nixon returned from his trips with ideas and suggestions. Back from Asia in 1953, he urged the welding of an anti-Communist alliance stretching from Turkey to Japan. On returning from Africa in 1957, he worked to improve the quality of the diplomatic personnel assigned to the difficult yet increasingly important posts in that continent. As a firsthand witness to the unfolding worldwide struggle with the Communists, Nixon spoke with authority in this country on foreign affairs.

Democrats never forgot Richard Nixon's tactics in the 1954 congressional campaign. Ike wasn't up for re-election, and the Vice President carried the main burden of the campaign. In his relentless attempt to save Republican majorities in both branches of Congress, Nixon flew 26,000 miles, visited 95 cities in 31 states, delivered 204 speeches, and met the press more than 100 times. Adlai Stevenson called it an "ill-will tour." Nixon concentrated on familiar themes—Korea, communism, and corruption. Theoretically, he should have been defending the administration, but he was always more effective on the attack, and attack he did.

His charges very nearly added up to an indictment of the entire Democratic party as the party of treason, and the Democrats themselves seemed eager to so interpret his position. Nixon said that the Communist party was "determined to conduct its program within the Democratic Party." He said that under the Eisenhower administration, Reds, fellow travelers, and security risks were being kicked out of the government by the thousands. In rebuttal, Democratic National Chairman Stephen Mitchell recalled the story of the police chief who claimed that he had seized thousands of murderers, kidnapers, and parking violators, when the records showed that he had one suspected murderer, one suspected kidnaper, and 2,000 parking violators. (Later, administration officials testified that nearly half of the persons dismissed as security risks had been hired since Eisenhower became President.) Nixon said that if the Democrats were returned to office, all the security risks would be rehired.

Stevenson complained that Nixon represented "McCarthyism in a white collar," and the Vice President referred to that statement as an attack on working people, a "snide and snobbish innuendo towards the millions of Americans who work for a living in our shops and factories." This sort of "debate" did little to clarify the issues of the campaign.

Only ten years before, Vice President Wallace had been tying the Fascist label to the elephant's tail. Would Vice Presidents in the future add the new and unlovable role of political hatchet man to their other new duties?

Eisenhower entered the campaign, and talked primarily about unemployment, the farm problem, and Administration accomplishments at home and abroad. He gave little attention to the Communist issue. Republicans disagreed as to the effectiveness of Nixon's tactics. Some feared they might antagonize the voter; others interpreted the screams from the Democrats as evidence that the Vice President had struck a weak spot in the enemy defenses. In the election the "out" party gained, as it almost always does, and the Democrats narrowly won control of both houses of Congress.

Nixon looked back on the 1954 campaign with some regret. He continued to hit hard thereafter, but his tactics never again stirred such animosity. Even Sam Rayburn, who had once said Nixon had been "cruel," and "I don't like cruel people," conceded later that Nixon had matured in his approach. The Vice President continued to be the target of considerable invective, but matters did not get so bad as in the days of Vice President Van Buren, who had presided over the Senate with a brace of pistols on his desk.

From the Republican viewpoint, at least, the stridency of Democratic criticism of Nixon could be partly explained as a reaction to persistent reports that Eisenhower would retire at the end of his first term. Eisenhower had considered saying in his inaugural address that he would serve only four years. Later, he named several men as possible successors, with Nixon's name first. As speculation continued with respect to the future of both Eisenhower and Nixon, an alarming and totally unexpected development threw the Republican leadership into confusion.

When Nixon first heard about Ike's illness, on a Saturday afternoon in September, 1955, he wasn't a bit concerned.

The Washington *Evening Star* reported that the President, who was vacationing in Colorado, had a slight case of indigestion. (In the same state, thirty-six years before, minus one day, Woodrow Wilson had delivered his last speech at Pueblo before suffering his "nervous breakdown.") Nixon recalled that Eisenhower had suffered digestive upsets before, and thought no more about the matter until Press Secretary James Hagerty phoned, and asked the Vice President if he were sitting down. Then he told Nixon that Eisenhower had been stricken by a heart attack.

Nixon wrote later that he was in a state of near shock for about ten minutes. Then he asked his close friend, Acting Attorney General William Rogers, to come to his home. (The Attorney General, Herbert Brownell, was vacationing in Spain.)

Reporters, meanwhile, had been told the truth about Eisenhower's illness, some thirteen hours after he had been stricken at the Denver home of his mother-in-law. The false report had averted commotion until the President could be removed to the hospital. Now, while Nixon and Rogers discussed the crisis, reporters milled around outside the Vice President's home. Pat told them that her husband was not there, and that she didn't know when he would return. They waited. Television cameras arrived, and floodlights were focused on the front of the house in anticipation of Nixon's arrival. Nixon desired neither to be interviewed nor photographed. He knew that a photograph of himself—either smiling or with a frown or a furrowed brow—would be subject to misinterpretation by the public. While the Vice President's older daughter drew the attention of the press by wandering onto the front lawn, Nixon and Rogers ducked out the back door. A few minutes later, safely lodged in the latter's home in Bethesda, Maryland, they were reviewing the newest predicament in which the Vice President found himself.

Eisenhower's attack was classified as "moderate." The President, recalling the secrecy surrounding Wilson's illness, ordered his doctors to "Tell the truth, the whole truth; don't try to conceal anything." And so the details began to pour forth. Eisenhower ordered the National Security Council and the Cabinet to meet on schedule under the chairmanship of the Vice President.

Nixon was the third of our Vice Presidents to be confronted with a problem of Presidential disability. Like Chester Arthur and Thomas Marshall, he faced an extremely delicate situation. For years, he had been the target of criticism based on his youth, his partisanship, and his alleged incapacity to undertake the duties of the Presidency. The Vice President's problem, as he saw it, was to provide leadership without appearing to lead.

From the time he first met reporters on Sunday afternoon, he was poised, calm, and quietly confident that the President would recover. Behind the scenes, Nixon was helping to make some major decisions. He believed the public would put more trust in a civilian heart specialist than in military doctors, and at the suggestion of Secretary of the Treasury George Humphrey, the services of Dr. Paul Dudley White were obtained.

In conferences with members of the Cabinet, Nixon supported the concept of "team" leadership and "business as usual." Furthermore, as Nixon put it later, "any semblance of a struggle for dominance on the team would be scrupulously avoided." All members of the Cabinet subscribed to these principles at a meeting called by Nixon on September 30, six days after the heart attack. Nixon presided from the Vice President's chair. He read the latest medical report on Ike's condition. Secretary of State John Foster Dulles urged that Presidential Assistant Sherman Adams be sent to Denver to establish the sole official source of information from the hospital room; otherwise, he said, other persons (unidentified) might presume to speak for the President on various subjects. The Cabinet endorsed the Denver assignment for Adams. (This decision had first been approved at a meeting of the National Security Council on the previous day, at which Nixon had also presided.)

After the Cabinet meeting, Nixon announced that "at the present time the policy decisions that have been made in the foreign and economic fields are sufficiently clear and well-defined that no changes are needed or contemplated in the near future."

During these early difficult days, the Government was carried along by inertia. Eisenhower delegated no authority to Nixon, and the Vice President, after consulting the Attorney General, declined to claim any. Fortunately, Congress was not in session, and the Russians were not causing any trouble.

In 1964, Nixon wrote that during the President's three illnesses, "although I did not take over the reins of government, I was the captain of the team that kept the Ship of State on course while the President was incapacitated." But if Nixon was the captain, Sherman Adams was the quarterback. The flinty New Englander, bearing the title Assistant to the President, had been the General's chief of staff since his inauguration. Even before Eisenhower fell ill, Adams exerted more influence on the executive branch of the Federal Government than anyone else. Members of the Cabinet (except Dulles) who wished to see the President stated their business to Adams. Policy proposals from the various departments were submitted in writing to Adams, who knew the President's mind, and who often made final decisions himself. "O.K., S.A." in the margin of a document usually meant clear sailing when it reached Eisenhower's desk. Adams was driven by a determination to protect Eisenhower. "We must not bother the President with this," he would say, firmly turning aside an administration official who had come to the White House on a question he considered to be of importance. Adams did much of the hiring and firing in the administration, and occasionally took the rap for an unpopular policy. It is not surprising that Eisenhower considered him indispensable. Quipsters wondered what would happen if Adams died and Eisenhower became President.

After the President fell ill, Adams intensified his activities along the lines described above. While Hagerty churned out an impressive amount of detail on the patient's treatment and recovery, Adams' own intensive efforts went largely unpublicized. Eisenhower was initialing papers four days after he was stricken, but his full recovery was not announced until 143 days after the attack. Political Scientist Louis Koenig wrote that during this period Adams was nothing less than Acting President of the United States.

And what of Richard Nixon, the man on whom authority should devolve? He had carried out his duties with discretion and good sense, but Marshall had done as much in 1919. Adams, like Mrs. Wilson before him, ran the government during the President's incapacity, regardless of what the Constitution might say. Nixon was busy enough, even busier than usual; but only the ceremonial duties (plus the NSC and Cabinet chores) devolved on the Vice President. He did sign several nonlegal papers of little significance. He visited the President in Denver on October 8, a full week after Adams arrived on the scene. Nixon then returned to Washington. In the spirit of team play, the "captain" had decided to let the quarterback call the signals.

On February 29, 1956, President Eisenhower announced that he would be a candidate for a second term. He had been assured by doctors that his recovery was complete, and that he could expect to continue an active life for many years. He felt that he had not fully achieved his goals of modernizing the Republican party and of placing the nation on the firm foundations of peace and prosperity. He was asked if Nixon would be his running mate again. The President was evasive, saying that he could not properly express an opinion until he had received the Presidential nomination. While this was, strictly speaking, correct political etiquette, his statement served only to stir speculation on the subject. For once, the importance of the Vice Presidential nomination was not lost on the public. Everyone felt that if Eisenhower were re-elected, his Vice President would have a better than average chance to succeed to the Presidency during the next four years. And the recent dramatic upgrading of the office meant that the next Vice President would be a formidable candidate for the 1960 Presidential nomination under any circumstances. Nixon, ironically, could have become the victim of his own success. Some people wondered if he were the man to serve in the office that, largely through his own willingness to take on assignments, had zoomed in responsibility.

On March 7, one week after announcing his candidacy, Eisenhower gave his famous reply to a question about Nixon: "I told him he would have to chart his own course and tell me what he would like to do."

More than two months before, on December 26, 1955, the President had conveyed this message to Nixon personally. He said that he was most disappointed that the Vice President's popularity had not risen higher. He suggested that Nixon's career might benefit if he entered the Cabinet. The President said that Nixon could hold any Cabinet job that he wanted except Attorney General and Secretary of State. The subject came up five or six times that winter during private meetings between the two men. The President pointed out that no Vice President since Van Buren had succeeded a living President. Nixon always gave the same answer, in these terms: "If you believe your own candidacy and your Administration would be better served with me off the ticket, you tell me what you want me to do and I'll do it. I want to do what is best for you." And Ike would always praise Nixon's work and say, "No, I think we've got to do what's best for you."

Nixon did not want a Cabinet job. To begin with, he believed that he was getting valuable executive experience right where he was. But more importantly, he knew that he could not accept another post without giving the impression that he had been "dumped." The Vice President knew that Eisenhower was getting advice from a variety of sources. Some Republicans wanted Nixon dumped, and others believed sincerely that he would profit from experience in the Cabinet. Most of the professionals, however, wanted the same ticket renominated.

In the course of his efforts to "chart his own course," Nixon considered retiring from public life. He was hurt by Eisenhower's failure to ask him outright to run again. The period after the President's heart attack had been one of continuing tension. After months of walking on eggs during Eisenhower's disability, Nixon did not welcome the prospect of becoming the storm center of another campaign. When he first heard Eisenhower's statement to the press on March 7 that the Vice President should chart his own course, Nixon decided that the time had come to make a frank announcement that he would not be a candidate. He would not force himself onto the ticket, and since the President would not ask him to run again, Nixon decided that the only means of breaking the impasse was to bow out. National Chairman Leonard Hall headed him off. Hall, a close political friend, said that Nixon's withdrawal would split the Republican party. He persuaded the Vice President to delay his decision, and within a week Nixon had reasons to change his mind. Messages poured in from friends pledging support and saying that Eisenhower was being ungrateful, especially considering Nixon's conduct during the President's illness.

Then, on March 13, Nixon received the whopping total of 22,936 write-in votes for Vice President in the New Hampshire primary. (Later, he got 30,000 write-ins in the Oregon primary.) Thereafter, the President edged closer to endorsing Nixon, telling the press: "I am very happy to have him as an associate in government. I would be happy to be on any political ticket in which I was a candidate with him. Now, if those words aren't plain, then it is merely because people can't understand the plain, unvarnished truth."

On April 27, a reporter asked the President if Nixon had reported back on charting his own course, and Ike replied: "He hasn't given me any authority to quote him, any answer that I would consider final and definite." Nixon saw that it was time to act. He came to the White House that afternoon, said that he had hesitated because he didn't wish to force himself on the ticket, and that he would be honored to run again. The President arranged a press conference to permit Nixon to announce his availability, and Hagerty followed up Nixon's statement by saying that the President was delighted. So, it seemed, were most Republicans.

And then, boom, once again the unexpected. On the night of June 7, the President was stricken with severe stomach cramps. His ailment was diagnosed as ileitis. Rushed to a hospital, he underwent an emergency operation to relieve an obstruction in the lower intestines. The operation was successful, but the President suffered greater pain over a longer period than in the case of his heart attack.

The upshot of Eisenhower's latest illness was a revival of the "health issue" and a rehashing of the Nixon candidacy by the pundits. Into these muddied waters leaped Harold Stassen with his "Dump Nixon" campaign. Stassen was the President's disarmament adviser, but his behavior was anything but disarming. He trotted to the White House in July armed with some polls he had ordered himself, and which purported to show that Nixon, if renominated for Vice President, would reduce Ike's vote by 6 per cent. His figures showed that the best bet for Vice President would be Governor Christian Herter of Massachusetts. Herter, a former Congressman and a future Secretary of State, was then almost unknown beyond the borders of the Bay State.

Stassen asked the President's permission to open a campaign for an "Ike and Chris" ticket. The President, never one to dictate under such circumstances, said that he would not object to Stassen's move. Stassen even obtained a month's leave of absence to promote this project. With characteristic solemnity and unabashed optimism, he announced his campaign for Herter. He created his hullabaloo just in time to steal valuable headlines from Eisenhower, who had left for Panama—six weeks after major surgery—to attend an important conference of hemisphere heads of state. Stassen's headline-grabbing in itself irritated some of the President's closest aides.

Stassen gave aid and comfort to the Democrats, sowed confusion in the Republican ranks, and forced Chairman Hall to declare again and again his conviction that the ticket would be Eisenhower and Nixon. The only Republican of any prominence to support Stassen was Governor Goodwin Knight of California. Stassen hadn't told Herter that he was going to run him for Vice President and Herter, embarrassed by the whole business, effectively took himself out of the picture by announcing that he would place Nixon's name in nomination at the convention.

Stassen, however, was convinced that Herter could be drafted, and urged the delegates to give serious consideration to their choice. Stassen opened "Ike and Chris" campaign headquarters in Washington, cranked out propaganda, and allowed himself to be interviewed on national television shows. Superficially, Nixon's position was similar to that of Henry Wallace in 1944. That year, an ailing President yielded to pressure and agreed to the dumping of a controversial Vice President. But Nixon, unlike Wallace, enjoyed massive support within the party organization. Even Republican leaders who were not for Nixon—and they were few—were not about to let Harold Stassen appear to be calling the shots at the convention.

At San Francisco, Stassen capitulated, and agreed to second Nixon's nomination. Nixon went from delegation to delegation, campaigning as if in the fight of his life. The 1952 ticket was renominated unanimously, but not without one moment of levity. During the roll call for Vice Presidential nominations, a Nebraska delegate, Terry Carpenter, announced that he wished to place the name of "Joe Smith" in nomination. Reporters, starving for news, jammed the aisles around the Nebraska delegation. Carpenter explained that "Joe Smith," who was fictitious, was a symbol of an open convention. Permanent Chairman Joseph Martin, not amused, ordered the sergeant-at-arms to escort Carpenter off the floor.

In the fall campaign, the Democrats openly discussed the President's health and the implications of Nixon's nomination. The Americans for Democratic Action declared in a twenty-eight page pamphlet that "the career and character of Richard Nixon pose a somber issue in the 1956 campaign." Adlai Stevenson, once again the Democratic Presidential nominee, warned that "every piece of scientific evidence that we have, every lesson of history and experience, indicates that a Republican victory . . . would mean that Richard M. Nixon would probably be president of this country within the next four years." Nixon's name drew the most boos at Democratic rallies, and Stevenson called the Vice President "this man of many masks."

But in 1956, the voters were introduced to the "New Nixon." Before the canvass began, Eisenhower and Nixon agreed that the Vice President's speeches ought to be on a higher level than in the past. Nixon, knowing that the country was giving more attention than usual to a Vice President's candidacy, declined to reply in kind to personal attacks directed at himself. He moved toward the center, and disappointed the McCarthyites by soft-pedaling the Communist issue. He said in September: ". . . the entire problem of communism, foreign and domestic, is too important for partisan criticism or political sniping." And he said that neither party had a monopoly on honesty, or on a desire to do what was best for the people. Jack Bell, an author and political writer for the Associated Press, noted that almost everything Nixon did was calculated well in advance and carried out with technical perfection. Bell wrote: "Always, under every circumstance, there was the feeling that Nixon was carrying out a preconceived plan—that a mental blueprint was being followed with exquisite technique. . . . Nixon was bold, shrewd, smooth, and effective—but it showed on him. He could have admiration and respect but not adulation."

In the last days before the election, the Hungarian revolution and the Suez crisis riveted the attention of the voters. The election itself was a landslide for Eisenhower, who won by a plurality of 9.5 million votes, 3 million more than in 1952.

President Eisenhower's third illness occurred late in 1957. On the afternoon of November 27, Mrs. Ann Whitman, the President's personal secretary, ran into Sherman Adams' office, almost in tears. "He tried to tell me something but he couldn't express himself. Something seemed to have happened to him all of a sudden." His personal physician, Dr. Howard Snyder, rushed to the White House. The President tried to say, "Go away from me," but the words wouldn't come. He reluctantly agreed to get some rest.

Dr. Snyder believed that he had suffered a stroke. A neurologist was called. Meanwhile Eisenhower got up, and said it was time for him to dress for a formal White House dinner for King Mohammed V of Morocco. When Adams and Dr. Snyder tried to convince him not to go, he became troubled. "If I cannot attend to my duties, I am simply going to give up this job. Now that is all there is to it." And he stalked out of the room.

Adams summoned Nixon to the White House and described in detail the events of the day. He spoke in his usual crisp, unemotional manner. But then Adams exclaimed: "This is a terribly, terribly difficult thing to handle. You may be President in the next twenty-four hours."

Eisenhower finally agreed to let the Vice President represent him at the state dinner. The guests and the press were told only that the President had suffered a chill. Specialists, meanwhile, had made their diagnosis: Eisenhower had suffered a stroke, an occlusion of a small branch of the middle cerebral artery on the left side, probably caused by a vascular spasm or a blood clot.

The next morning, Nixon and Attorney General William Rogers (who had succeeded Brownell) came to the White House to get a more definitive word on the President's condition. The doctors said that the President's stroke was mild and transitory, and had caused a speech impairment. His reading, writing, and reasoning powers were unaffected. On the basis of this information, the Attorney General concluded that the illness presented no legal problem, and that it would not be necessary to delegate any power to the Vice President.

The pre-1967 Constitution did not state who should make such a decision, but Rogers used good judgment in acting as he did. In Wilson's time doctors had doled out political advice along with their medicine. Now the nation's highest legal officer was assuming the responsibility.

But the doctors could not rule out the possibility that Eisenhower's stroke might be the first in a series. They wanted him to rest for sixty days, or at least observe only a very light work schedule. Rogers' optimistic decision may have been based on his awareness of Eisenhower's amazing ability to bounce back, and on the knowledge that he simply would not remain idle for long, even at the risk of dying in action.

When the public learned of the President's true condition, many calls were heard in favor of his retirement. It was said that he had served his country long and well, and now at last it was time to step down. Many persons believed that even if he recovered, he would face a lingering mental impairment. Some columnists favored a temporary delegation of powers to Nixon. The stroke had come at a bad time. The NATO heads of state were scheduled to meet in Paris in less than three weeks. The Soviet Union had just orbited its first sputnik. Signs of the 1958 recession were visible. A new legislative program, and State of the Union and budget messages would soon be due. The President had told reporters on March 7, 1956: "I have said unless I felt absolutely up to the performance of the duties of the President, the second I didn't, I would no longer be there in the job, or I wouldn't be available for the job."

At a press conference, Nixon said that the President was fully capable of making important decisions and that there was no thought of delegating any of his authority, but administration leaders did consider sending Nixon to represent Eisenhower at Paris. The NATO heads of state agreed to meet with the Vice President and Nixon prepared for what would have been the most important assignment ever given to a Vice President. But the fantastic Eisenhower luck held. The President was determined to go to Paris, and he did, astounding his doctors and the nation. Soon, he was fully recovered.

Once again, the delegation of authority to Nixon had failed to materialize, but Eisenhower decided that it was finally time to act on Presidential inability. In February, 1958, he called the Vice President and the Attorney General into his office, and said that he thought he had the problem licked. He handed each a letter, setting forth these procedures: If the President were unable to perform his duties, he would so inform the Vice President, who would become acting President. But if the President were unable to communicate with the Vice President, the latter "after such consultation as seems to him appropriate," would decide if a state of disability existed, and if so, he would take over. In either event, the President would determine when the disability had ended, and he would then resume his duties.

This agreement was made public in March, 1958. It applied only to Eisenhower and Nixon, and was no more than a stopgap arrangement in lieu of a constitutional amendment. House Speaker Rayburn called the memorandum illegal, since it would create an "Acting President" unknown to the Constitution. However, President Kennedy and Vice President Johnson agreed to an almost identical arrangement in 1961; after the assassination, Johnson followed the same course with House Speaker John McCormack, who, from November 22, 1963 until January 20, 1965, was next in line for the Presidency.[1]

Throughout his second term, several other dramatic events kept the Vice President very much in the public eye.

On April 27, 1958, Nixon and his wife left Washington for a three-week good-will tour of eight Latin American countries. A number of personal appearances were scheduled, plus discussions with national leaders on economic and other problems. On May 1, Nixon represented the United States at the inauguration of Argentine President Arturo Frondizi. Then in Lima, Peru, the Vice President encountered a hostile demonstration in front of his hotel, and he was barred from speaking at San Marcos University by a rock-throwing Communist mob. Nixon and his associates had to fight their way through another mob to get back into their hotel; Nixon reached the door by kicking aside a hulking agitator who had spat directly in his face.

While such incidents captured the biggest headlines, Nixon succeeded in getting his message to the public in seven of the countries he visited. He frequently received warm receptions from students, editors, labor leaders, and others when he pledged United States support to Latin efforts to overcome poverty and attain fiscal and administrative stability. He denounced the Communists as cowards who were loyal not to their own countries but to an international conspiracy.

On May 13, the Vice President and his party landed at an airport twelve miles from the Venezuelan capital, Caracas, and

[1] These informal arrangements are discussed further in Chapter 19, "Presidential Succession and Inability."

found a huge, sign-waving, cursing throng on hand. At the "welcoming" ceremony Nixon and Pat stood at attention while a band played the Venezuelan national anthem. Nixon felt what seemed to be rain, then discovered that dozens of the Communists and their allies were standing above him, at the railing of the airport observation deck, showering spit on himself and his wife. The Nixons remained at attention until the anthem had ended.

The motorcade into Caracas was terrifying. As the Venezuelan police escort melted away, twelve United States Secret Service men fought off a wild killer mob that had surrounded the enclosed automobiles. Pat Nixon was riding in the limousine behind the one occupied by the Vice President and the Venezuelan foreign minister. The spit flew so heavily that Nixon's driver turned on the windshield wipers. The rioters battered the cars with rocks, pipes, fists and feet. The glass splattered into the car, cutting Nixon's face, and striking the foreign minister in the eye. The mob began to rock the car, intending perhaps to overturn it and set it afire. A Secret Service agent drew his revolver, vowing that if they were all goners, he was going to take a few Communists along with him.

Slowly the cars began to push forward. They cut off from the prescribed route, and slipped away to the American Embassy. By declining to attend a wreath-laying ceremony, Nixon missed another mob waiting with a cache of homemade bombs. From his redoubt at the embassy, the Vice President canceled all appearances, and invited Venezuelan officials to call on him. He received the provisional President and the rest with deliberate coolness, and in their talks he emphasized the foolishness of trying to run a government in coalition with the Communists.

Meanwhile, President Eisenhower moved to protect the Vice President and his party, dispatching a United States Navy task force to a point thirty miles off the Venezuelan coast. On board, Marines and paratroopers stood ready to aid the Venezuelan authorities, but they were not needed. Some semblance of order was restored in the Capital, and on the next day the Nixons attended a lavish and lengthy luncheon across town. Finally the visitors were escorted back to the airport, down a route that had been cleared by tanks and tear gas. The

Nixons flew to Puerto Rico; the next day they landed in Washington, with President Eisenhower among 15,000 persons at the airport for a much different type of reception from the one in Caracas. Nixon was applauded widely for his courage, but the accolades were not unanimous. Walter Lippmann called the trip a fiasco, a diplomatic Pearl Harbor.

Nixon felt that his trip had long-range benefits because Latin America could no longer be taken for granted. He called for a realization that the Latins were a proud people, and longtime friends who did not wish to be treated in the same way as the developing countries of Asia and Africa. He recommended that United States government personnel endeavor to reach the opinion-makers in South America—the editors, labor leaders, teachers, and students; and he argued that the Communists could be eliminated as a threat only if a shoring up of economic institutions were accompanied by a strengthening of military and internal security forces.

Having jousted with Communist street rabble, Nixon had an opportunity in 1959 to take on the Red heavyweight, Soviet Premier Nikita Khrushchev. He flew into Moscow on July 23 to open the American National Exhibition at Sokolniki Park. Khrushchev, in a truculent mood, and with a "show me" attitude, joined Nixon at the exhibition on July 24. The Premier was invited to say a few words of greeting before cameras equipped with a new type of color television tape. Preening himself like the NBC peacock, Khrushchev went on a red-faced rampage before the color cameras. He denounced the captive nations resolution recently adopted by the United States Congress. He said that the Soviet Union was prepared to go to war to protect itself, and that his country would soon catch up with the United States economically. Nixon, as host, wished to avoid being rude; he tried to calm the Premier, who taunted him by saying that he, a coal miner, could outargue a lawyer on the relative merits of communism and capitalism. The color tape, shown later in many countries, showed the Premier to be both arrogant and effective. Nixon found himself on the defensive.

As they strolled past the exhibits, the two leaders continued their verbal sparring match, with Nixon jabbing away more forcefully. By the time they reached the kitchen of a model home, both were slugging hard. Now, in the splendor and efficiency of a model United States worker's home, Khrushchev was forced onto the defensive. The Soviet press had said that the model was about as typical of the United States as the Taj Mahal was of India. Khrushchev claimed that some Soviet workers could also enjoy such comforts, and that their homes were built to last. But he sounded less convincing now. He said that he resented the American attempt to make Soviet citizens dumbfounded and ashamed by such a display of prosperity. Nixon replied that the United States was not trying to overawe the Russians, that they would be interested in the display, just as Americans had been interested in a recent Soviet exhibit. The Vice President asserted: "To us, diversity, the right to choose, the fact that we have a thousand different builders, that's the spice of life. We don't want to have a decision made at the top by one government official saying that we will have one type of house. That's the difference. . . ."

Khrushchev still argued that it was better to have one model of washing machine than many. Nixon, not wishing to belabor his point, beamed back, "Isn't it better to be talking about the relative merits of our washing machines than the relative strength of our rockets?" Khrushchev agreed, but said that American generals insisted on boasting about rockets. He reminded Nixon that the Soviets had rockets, too.

The time was past for prattle about TV and washing machines. Nixon declared: "To me, you are strong and we are strong. In some ways, you are stronger than we are. In others, we are stronger. But to me it seems that in this day and age to argue who is the stronger completely misses the point. . . . No one should ever use his strength to put another in the position where he in effect has an ultimatum." He pressed on: "When we sit down at a conference table it cannot all be one way. One side cannot put an ultimatum to another. It is impossible."

Khrushchev accused Nixon of issuing ultimatums and threats, while in fact he was doing the same himself. He boasted of the superiority of Soviet weaponry. He chose to ignore Nixon's plea for negotiation as a means of settling disputes. Khrushchev mentioned the word "peace," both agreed that that was what they sought, and the foofaraw subsided. Khrushchev thanked the model housewife for the use of her model kitchen, and the two men departed.

That night Nixon officially opened the exhibition with a speech printed in full in *Pravda* and *Izvestia*, in which he explained the tenets of American democracy and the basis of American material progress.

On July 26, Nixon and Khrushchev discussed the full range of East-West problems during a five-and-a-half-hour "lunch" at the Premier's dacha outside Moscow. This time, in comparative privacy, Nixon could speak with less restraint, and he presented the American position on foreign bases, Germany, atomic testing, and other matters. But Khrushchev didn't modify his position on any subject.

During the next four days, Nixon toured Russia, often in the manner of an American stump speaker, and found friendly feelings toward the United States on the part of the average Soviet citizen. On August 1, he spoke on Soviet radio and television, a unique achievement for an American. He placed responsibility for the preservation of peace on Khrushchev, and said that the regime must cease its efforts to communize the world.

Nixon's trip was headlined around the world, and was considered a great personal triumph. When he spoke a year later of electing a President who could stand up to Khrushchev, the voters remembered the kitchen debate, the "Sokolniki Summit."

Late in 1959, Nixon had another opportunity to test his statesmanship, this time on the domestic labor scene. A paralyzing 116-day steel strike had been halted at least temporarily by a Taft-Hartley injunction, which was due to expire on January 26, 1960. Before leaving the country in early December, President Eisenhower asked Nixon and Secretary of Labor James Mitchell to intervene directly, but secretly, in the steel talks. Mitchell and Nixon met with spokesmen for the industry and the steelworkers' union, both at Nixon's home and at New York's Waldorf-Astoria Hotel. The Vice President convinced the industry leaders that union president David McDonald would accept nothing less than the compromise proposed by the administration. Nixon reminded the steel leaders that a crippling steel strike in an election year might force Congress to side with labor; compulsory arbitration, federal wage and price fixing, and even seizure of the plants might be the results.

The representatives of management, knowing that Nixon was speaking for the President, and that he might be the President himself in another year, accepted the administration's position at the end of December. "Vice President Nixon would make a good President," said McDonald. He hastened to add that John F. Kennedy, Hubert Humphrey, and others would make good Presidents, too. The settlement was criticized as inflationary, but it was the first steel settlement since World War II not accompanied by a price increase.

Since Andrew Jackson had procured the Presidential nomination for Martin Van Buren in 1836, only four Vice Presidents had been serious candidates for the Presidency, and none had come close to winning. Breckinridge accepted the nomination of the Southern wing of the Democratic party for the wide-open contest in 1860; he made a respectable showing, winning nearly one fourth of the electoral votes. Fairbanks tried in 1908, but had little chance for the Republican nomination against William Howard Taft. Garner's cause in 1940 became hopeless when Roosevelt stood for a third term. And Barkley's age ruled him out in 1952.

How then did Nixon romp home with the Republican nomination? First and foremost, he had succeeded—where others had failed—in making a silk purse out of a sow's ear. Although the ranks of the Vice Presidents have included several able men, Nixon was the first to possess the energy, ability, and the opportunity to make the most of his job. Furthermore, his political skills had been tested and sharpened in a series of stormy and publicity-filled personal crises.

In a very special way Nixon benefited as had no previous Vice President. Due to the uncertain status of Ike's health, the Republican leaders knew that Nixon could succeed to the Presidency at almost any time. No Republican wanted to oppose openly a man who might be dishing out Federal patronage "this time tomorrow." With Nixon standing at the threshold of the White House from 1955 on, opposition within the party was immobilized.

Nixon also jumped into the void left by Eisenhower's unwillingness to participate actively in the day-to-day leadership of the Republican party; by the end of his first term, the Vice President had logged more than 100,000 miles in political travels, and won in the process the gratitude of the candidates for whom he spoke. During these tours, Nixon wooed and won the support of those who finance Republican Presidential campaigns. Also, he planted himself squarely in the middle of that famous mainstream—both conservatives and progressives might grumble occasionally, but they supported him when the time came.

A final reason for Nixon's easy victory in 1960 lay in the shortage of serious competition. Eisenhower was concerned about the failure of the Republicans to develop more men able and willing to compete for the national leadership. The President envied the ability of Britain's Conservative party to come up with at least two or three top men when a Prime Minister retired. Under Britain's parliamentary system, competition for leadership is concentrated in the House of Commons, and from the mold of party discipline and the rough and tumble of political rivalry, the ablest men are propelled toward the top of the pyramid. But in the United States, prospective Presidents may pop up almost anywhere—or nowhere. Someone remarked that Eisenhower's original Cabinet consisted of nine millionaires and a plumber. Most had come from the world of business, and none of them won a wide political following. As for Congress, no GOP Presidential prospect appeared after the death of Senator Robert Taft in 1953.

Off-year elections often supply new names for the Presidential speculation, but 1958 saw an almost unprecedented Republican defeat. The election produced only one serious threat to Nixon's candidacy, in Nelson Rockefeller of New York. Rockefeller was elected Governor by a margin of 573,000 votes. The Gallup Poll showed him challenging Nixon in rank-and-file Republican Presidential preferences. But the Governor, who was willing, was tied down by his obligations to New York; furthermore, he was obliged to ask for an increase in New York state taxes, which did not help him nationally.

From a strategical standpoint, Rockefeller's position was difficult. Nixon was so closely identified with Eisenhower's policies that the New York Governor could hardly criticize him without seeming to be against the national Republican administration. Rockefeller did not shirk from speaking out when he frankly disagreed with Eisenhower or Nixon—as in the areas of national defense and civil rights—but when he did so, he drew the opposition of a broad portion of the professional party workers and officeholders. Furthermore, criticism by the liberal Rockefeller helped Nixon solidify his position with the conservatives, who thought that they had detected the Vice President moving toward the political center. When Nixon and Rockefeller reached an accommodation just before the convention, the conservatives protested, but Nixon had the nomination clinched by then. In December, 1959, after carefully considering his chances, Rockefeller announced that he would not seek the nomination.

But what position would Eisenhower take on the nomination? In 1956 he told Emmet John Hughes, one of his speech writers: ". . . the fact is, of course, I've watched Dick a long time, and he just hasn't grown. So I just haven't honestly been able to believe that he *is* presidential timber." A year later, the President said he favored Robert Anderson, the secretary of the treasury, but Anderson made no moves toward the nomination. On still another occasion the President named several possibilities, in addition to Nixon; in Hughes' words, Eisenhower did not regard the "eventual succession of Nixon as a blessing either inevitable or irresistible." In the spring of 1960, however, the President declared his support of Nixon.

The Vice President knew that his problem was not to win the nomination but to defeat Kennedy in the fall, and to achieve that end he was determined to unite the party. He went to New York three days before the convention to reach an agreement with Rockefeller on a fourteen-point statement of party principles. The accord assured the Governor's active support for the ticket and served as a basis for a party platform. Nixon flew to Chicago to mollify disgruntled conservatives and members of the platform committee who thought they had completed their labors. Senator Goldwater, the conservative spokesman, refused to become a rallying point for the dissidents. Nixon received the votes of 1,321 delegates, with only 10 from Louisiana being cast for Goldwater. A hex on Vice Presidents, dating from the time of Van Buren, had been broken at last.

Nixon began his hunt for a Vice-Presidential running mate before the convention. He ordered his pollster to test several names in combination with his own, pairing each against the Kennedy-Johnson ticket chosen by the Democrats. He also discussed the Vice-Presidential nomination with Eisenhower and his close political advisers. Nixon wanted a man who could assume the duties of the Presidency, who shared his own viewpoint on major international and domestic issues—and who could strengthen the ticket. Nixon narrowed the choice down to United Nations Ambassador Henry Cabot Lodge and Senator Thruston Morton of Kentucky, the national chairman. (Rockefeller refused to be considered.) Morton was popular with party leaders, and was an effective speaker. Lodge was better known, having often been seen on television while delivering sharp and effective rebuttals to the Soviet United Nations delegates. Nixon wanted to stress foreign policy in the campaign.

After his nomination, Nixon called thirty-two party leaders together to get their views on the Vice Presidency. Most agreed that Lodge was the man. The Ambassador was nominated unanimously.

In recent years, most Vice Presidential candidates have managed to get into hot water at least once during the campaign, and Lodge was no exception. While campaigning in Harlem, he was asked if the Republicans would appoint a Negro to the Cabinet. He was quoted as saying that the Republicans were pledged to do so. Nixon denied that he had made any such commitment, and the apparent dispute between the candidates created a furore. (Nixon wrote later that Lodge had in mind that he [Nixon] would appoint Ralph Bunche, a Negro, as Ambassador to the United Nations.) Lodge explained that he meant Nixon would appoint a "qualified Negro" to the Cabinet, but the semantic difference was lost on many. Many Negroes and Southern whites eyed the Republican candidates with skepticism after this exchange.

Another repercussion of the Lodge campaign was felt four years later. In the spring of 1964, Lodge received wide rank-and-file support for the Republican Presidential nomination. Lodge, then serving a Democratic administration as Ambassador to South Vietnam, said nothing. But supporters in this country did campaign for him in several Presidential primaries. Lodge won in New Hampshire and finished second in Oregon. In these primaries he defeated Senator Barry Goldwater, piling up 111,000 votes to 70,000 for Goldwater. An April Gallup Poll showed Lodge leading Goldwater among Republican voters, 42 per cent to 14 per cent. In the face of these developments, Goldwater and his supporters charged that Lodge had taken frequent midday naps during the 1960 campaign, and had generally failed to campaign effectively—allegations denied by the Lodge supporters.

The point of the Goldwater position seemed to be that there is a direct relationship between how hard a candidate campaigns and the number of votes he can win. But Lodge must have impressed a great many voters between those alleged naps in 1960. He had been away from politics since then, yet he was swamping Goldwater in the polls and primaries, even though Goldwater had spoken hundreds of times throughout the country after 1960. Lodge refused to seek the nomination in 1964, his opportunity passed, and the Republicans chose Goldwater.

The 1960 Presidential campaign was the century's closest. A shift of fewer than 12,000 votes in the right states would have given victory to Nixon. He lost by one tenth of one percentage point in the popular vote, and anybody who remembers that campaign has his own idea about what one thing Nixon should have done to change the result.

This discussion of the 1960 campaign will be limited to the mention of a couple of incidents relating to the fact that Nixon was the Vice President. After the conventions, Nixon, Kennedy, and Johnson returned to Washington for a special session of the Senate. Kennedy, from his seat near the back of the chamber, and Nixon, from the dais, waited impatiently to start the campaign. The Vice President could not safely slip away and risk missing a tie vote. Nixon did leave on weekends, but the real opening of his campaign was effectively delayed.

A facetious remark by Eisenhower in August haunted Nixon. The President was asked at a press conference: "What major decisions of your Administration has the Vice President participated in?" Ike replied, "If you give me a week, I might think of one." Nixon was pitching his campaign on an "experience" theme, and the remark, taken literally by many, did not help.

To the end of the 1960 campaign, Eisenhower believed that Nixon could have run a better race had he accepted a Cabinet appointment in 1956. He reportedly told intimates that the office of Secretary of Defense would have provided a better base for a Presidential bid.

Theodore H. White has written of Nixon as a poor boy who surged upward from his origins on the thrust of enormous internal drives, carrying with him an excessive desire to be liked, and when rebuffed, "a bitter, impulsive reflex of lash-backs." Scaling the political walls in competition with men of great wealth and family prestige, Nixon came to trust almost no one, while searching for the answers to the riddles of his own career in prolonged, brooding, moody periods of introspection. Emmet John Hughes wrote that in private Nixon was not given to partisan excesses, but was instead laconic and clinical, reflective and withdrawn, not confident but groping. White suggests a relationship between Nixon's "uncertain impulse" and the mottled culture of his native southern California, "where the synthetic and the genuine, the exquisitely beautiful and the grotesquely ugly, mingle without distinction. . . ."

Nixon, not by his own account but by those of others, was determined to be his own man, to break away from the fatherly image of Eisenhower, to "chart his own course" as Ike would say, but without having to weigh his obligations to Eisenhower along with what he felt were his obligations to himself. Nixon was stung by his near-repudiation by Eisenhower in 1952, by the President's repeated suggestions that he step down to the Cabinet in 1956, and by occasional slights. Nixon's book, *Six Crises*, contains much applause for Eisenhower, yet at times the writer seems almost to be apologizing for the President. Nixon mentions that Eisenhower never thanked him personally for the services he rendered to the administration during the period when Eisenhower was recovering from his heart attack. He offers the excuse that the General simply took it for granted that any subordinate would do his duty as the occasion required, and that no acknowledgment or expression of appreciation was necessary. (On several occasions, such as after his trips abroad, Nixon did receive verbal or written thanks from the President.)

Nixon finally won his release at the 1960 Republican convention. Ike congratulated him on his nomination, remarking that he was "at last free to speak freely and frankly. . . ." But Nixon never really broke away from Eisenhower. In the campaign, the candidate who wished to attack was obliged to defend the Administration. The high-school debating champion from Whittier won the televised debates on points and lost the Presidency by precincts. And it was probably Eisenhower's vigorous entry into the campaign in its last ten days that helped bring Nixon so close to victory.

Four years later, the wealthy, uncomplicated Goldwater would be crushed under history's greatest landslide, but he and his supporters would shrug the whole thing off as some sort of moral victory ("26,000,000 Americans Can't Be Wrong!"). Nixon, given to introspection, would for years after ponder those suspicious returns in Illinois, and try to figure out how he had managed to lose in Texas.

★ ★ ★ ★ ★ LYNDON B. JOHNSON

★ ★ ★ ★ ★

★ ★ ★ ★ ★ *"this grandson of a 'federate soldier. . . ."*

The last four Democratic Presidents—Roosevelt, Truman, Kennedy, and Johnson—were professional politicians with the professional's appreciation for the use of Presidential power. All, likewise, were aware of the frustrations of the Vice Presidency. Yet three of the four accepted Vice-Presidential nominations which came to them with little or no effort. The fourth, Kennedy, tried for the nomination in 1956, sustained his only political defeat, and benefited by the experience.

As noted before, few men mount serious campaigns for the Vice-Presidential nomination, on the assumption that the Presidential nominee will make the choice himself. But in 1956, friends of John F. Kennedy decided that they would at least let their fellow Democrats know that the Massachusetts Senator was interested. Adlai Stevenson seemed well in the lead for the Presidential nomination. Sargent Shriver, Kennedy's brother-in-law, went to see Stevenson, to get a line on Adlai's position on the Vice Presidency. Stevenson was noncommittal, but Shriver gained the impression that he might throw the contest open to the delegates. The Kennedy camp decided to prepare for a floor fight at the Chicago convention, just in case. It would have been unlike the Kennedys to make only a halfhearted effort to gain what seemed to be within reach. On the basis of Shriver's information, the Senator and his associates went all out for the nomination.

The Kennedy staff prepared a lengthy analysis, chock full of statistics, showing how a Catholic would help the ticket. This analysis was placed in the hands of Democratic leaders. (Kennedy later decided to emphasize his personal merits as a candidate, and asked backers not to stress his Catholicism.) His staff also prepared brief biographies of almost everyone who had even remotely been suggested for the Vice-Presidential nomination. This memorandum was also sent to Democrats around the country, on the theory that even if the nomination were not thrown open to the convention, Adlai would at least consult with some of these leaders before designating his choice. Each biographical sketch contained an appraisal of the prospect's strengths and weaknesses. Here is how the Kennedy staff assessed the Vice-Presidential qualifications of Senator Hubert Humphrey of Minnesota:

"Strongly pro-Stevenson; married; young and healthy; not a veteran; state adjacent to Stevenson's (11 electoral votes); 8 years' experience in Congress; good vote getter; nationally known; considered active ADA'er to Stevenson's left; 'right' on farm issue and Taft-Hartley; good speaker and personality; not wealthy."

Humphrey, alas, seemed to fall short in some respects. So did all of the others, except one. Not surprisingly, the memorandum carried this conclusion: "It would appear that the best of a good group is Senator Kennedy—young, but not as young as [Tennessee Governor Frank] Clement . . . now fully recovered from his spinal operation; holder of a brilliantly heroic combat record; married to a lovely wife . . . author of a highly praised best-seller; widely known and popular; a proven vote-getter against big odds . . . with a winning charm . . . independently wealthy. . . ." etc.

Some Democratic old-timers must have regarded this as an amateurish appeal. But the approach by Kennedy and his staff is significant in two respects. First, it suggested the dispassionate manner in which Kennedy would handle the selection of his own running mate four years later. Secondly, the analysis of the 1956 prospects points up the number of factors that must be taken into consideration in choosing a candidate. It is no longer possible merely to draw up a list of prospective Presidential or Vice-Presidential nominees, and then simplify the problem by leisurely lining out the names of all the Catholics, all who are divorced, everyone over sixty-five and under forty, the Southerners, all who are from small states, and all who are members of—or in sympathy with—the Americans for Democratic Action or the John Birch Society. Certainly all these factors, and others, will continue to be weighed by the kingmakers, but none, apparently, will serve to disqualify anyone automatically. The shattering of convention traditions during the last twenty-five years has opened the opportunity for national office to many men who once never dared to hope.

At the 1956 convention, the supporters of Senator Kennedy—mostly personal friends, and members of his family and staff—set up the rudiments of an organization. They turned out press releases, arranged for "spontaneous" applause during his appearances at the rostrum, etc. Stevenson, his own nomination assured, asked Kennedy to place his (Adlai's) name in nomination. The Senator feared that this was meant to be the consolation prize, that Stevenson had someone else in mind for the Vice Presidency. Somewhat discouraged, Kennedy delivered the nominating speech for Stevenson.

After Stevenson was chosen late Thursday evening, he made a dramatic appearance before the convention, and announced that he would let the delegates pick his running mate. He said that the people had a solemn obligation to consider who would become President if the incumbent should die in office. He had two reasons for focusing attention on the Vice-Presidential nomination. First, he wanted to contrast the Democratic method with the dull, perfunctory manner in which the Republicans were about to renominate Eisenhower and Nixon. Moreover, he wished to remind the voters that President Eisenhower had had two serious illnesses.

Stevenson's announcement set off a wild all-night scramble. Tennessee alone had three candidates. Governor Clement had keynoted the convention ("How long, O how long . . ."). Senator Albert Gore, a Southern moderate, was pledged the unanimous support of the delegation, although many Tennesseans preferred Clement or Estes Kefauver. The latter had been an unsuccessful candidate for the Presidency in 1952 and 1956. Now, he would try for the Vice-Presidential nomination without the support of his own state.

By Friday afternoon, Kefauver and Kennedy were well in the lead for the nomination, but both had handicaps. The

South was generally hostile to Kefauver, a supporter of civil rights; and the professionals regarded him as something of a maverick. Kennedy was a Catholic, too young (thirty-nine) to permit the Democrats to emphasize Nixon's alleged lack of maturity, an opponent of high-farm-price supports, and suspect to the liberals because he had declined to commit himself on the Senate's condemnation of Senator McCarthy.

The voting began, and Kefauver jumped ahead. With 686½ needed to win, the first ballot gave Kefauver 483½, Kennedy 304, Gore 178, New York Mayor Robert Wagner 162½, Humphrey 134½, and 106 scattered. Kennedy had drawn surprising strength from the South. The farm states were for Kefauver.

The second ballot was a great show for television viewers, and was reminiscent of the Truman-Wallace race in 1944. Kennedy gained steadily as the lesser candidates dropped out. Wagner withdrew and gave 96½ New York votes to the Massachusetts Senator. Senate Majority Leader Lyndon Johnson announced the shift of 56 Texas votes from Gore to Kennedy. Both Johnson and Rayburn, the permanent chairman, wanted to stop Kefauver.

At the end of the second roll call—before the switching—Kennedy led Kefauver, 618 to 551½. Kentucky swung 30 more votes to Kennedy, raising his total to 648, only 38½ short of victory. But then Gore gave up his thin hopes, and permitted the Tennessee delegation to shift to Kefauver. An emissary from Lyndon Johnson pleaded for Oklahoma's bloc of votes, but Governor Raymond Gary remembered that Kennedy had opposed high-farm-price supports, and he gave Oklahoma's votes to Kefauver. Rayburn, clutching his gavel, looked into the sea of waving standards, hoping to find someone ready to go for Kennedy. But he had no luck. The tide had turned. Minnesota swung from Humphrey to Kefauver, and Missouri followed. It was all over. The Tennessee Senator swept to victory, 755½ to 589 for Kennedy. Perhaps some of the delegates had felt a last-minute anti-Catholic twinge, or a brief upsurge of sympathy for the heretofore luckless Kefauver.

But all was not lost for Kennedy. Stevenson and Kefauver carried only seven states in November, and Kennedy escaped the stigma of that defeat, which might have been blamed on his religion if he had been on the ticket. Kennedy learned at the 1956 convention that it was possible for a Catholic to get the votes of Southerners; in fact, almost the entire South was in his column on the second ballot. Finally, Kennedy knew now what kind of organizing was needed to win a convention nomination; mistakes and oversights committed in 1956 were not repeated in 1960.

But was this the way to choose a candidate? It could hardly be said that the melee on the convention floor that afternoon was a reflection of the calm deliberation that Stevenson wanted given to the Vice-Presidential nomination. The canvass had lasted only eighteen hours, and during much of this time most delegates were at least trying to get some sleep. Stevenson was presented with a running mate with whom he had battled all spring in a series of unusually rough primaries. Four years later, the next Democratic Presidential nominee would also choose a rival as his running mate, with unforeseen and dramatic results.

The four years passed, amid growing optimism on the part of the Democrats that they could reclaim the White House. In 1960, the Republicans would no longer have the still-popular Eisenhower on their ticket. The Democrats, strengthened by their gains in the 1958 off-year elections, stressed the need for new initiatives in both foreign and domestic affairs. Not surprisingly, several Democrats sought the Presidency, and two of them, Senators John Kennedy and Hubert Humphrey, planned nationwide primary campaigns.

One who chose to avoid the strenuous primary route was Lyndon Johnson, who had no time to "press the flesh," as he called it. As Majority Leader, he could not leave the Senate which had been his home for twelve years, and which had briefly become a prison. He wanted the Presidential nomination in 1960, but his fate was to stay in Washington and push through Congress the legislative record on which the Presidential nominee would run that fall. While Senators Kennedy and Humphrey campaigned, Johnson fought the battle for a civil-rights bill, for public housing, for an increase in the minimum wage, for more medical help for the aged, all the bills that, if Lyndon could only get them passed, would be pointed to with pride by the next Democratic Presidential nominee.

Early in the summer, the Senate recessed. On July 5, Johnson announced that he, too, was a Presidential candidate. He said that the front runner, John Kennedy, was too young. America, he said, needed a President with a little gray in his hair. But Johnson was too late; the convention would open in just five days. The primaries were over, and Kennedy had swept seven of them. The delegates were chosen, and Johnson's strength was mostly in the South. But once committed to the struggle, Johnson fought to the bitter end, testing the mettle of Kennedy's convention organization.

On the day before the balloting, Johnson and Kennedy met in joint debate before the Texas delegation and some guests from Massachusetts. The Texas Senator spoke of his wide experience in government. He pointed to his prodigious efforts in the Senate, and noted that during a six-day nonstop debate on the 1960 civil-rights bill, he had answered 50 quorum calls. But he said that "some senators" (Kennedy) had missed all the quorum calls and 34 of 45 roll calls on the bill. Johnson was stung by charges heard at the convention that he was not liberal enough to be a Democratic Presidential candidate, and on the next day he again took out his irritation on Kennedy. At a caucus of the Washington state delegates, Johnson boasted that he had been a fighting liberal from the days of Roosevelt. Then he unleashed a thunderbolt: "I was never any Chamberlain umbrella policy man. I never thought Hitler was right." The reference was to Joseph P. Kennedy, his opponent's father, who was the ambassador to Great Britain before World War II. Joseph Kennedy was a friend of Prime Minister Neville Chamberlain, but never became involved in efforts to appease Hitler.

John Kennedy shrugged off these last-minute sallies. The nomination was within his reach, and he wasn't going to make anybody else angry now. On July 13, Kennedy was nominated with 806 votes to 409 for Johnson and 306 for everybody else. Kennedy had won the support of a bare majority of the delegates, and the November election promised as narrow a victory at best. He needed the Vice-Presidential candidate who could help the ticket most, and that man was Johnson.

Born and raised in the dry hill country of south-central Texas, Lyndon Johnson early gained an appreciation for the land. He also gained, through his mother, a respect for education, and through his father—a state legislator—an awareness of what government could do to improve the lot of the people who struggled to survive in that inhospitable environment.

In 1931, when he was twenty-three and a graduate of Southwest Texas State Teachers College, Johnson was appointed secretary to Texas Congressman Richard Kleberg, for whom he had campaigned. Arriving on Capitol Hill, from which he would not stray far either physically or spiritually for his four decades in public life, Johnson soon acquired an instinct for searching out and attaining power. He rallied to the support of Franklin Roosevelt's New Deal and served it after 1935 as Texas administrator of the National Youth Administration. In the meantime he had married Claudia Alta (Lady Bird) Taylor, whose financial and political astuteness proved of inestimable value to Johnson.

Running as an avowed supporter of FDR in a crowded field of New Deal critics, Johnson was elected to the U.S. House of Representatives in 1937. Having attracted the attention of the President and the friendship of House Speaker Sam Rayburn, Johnson quickly gained influence in the House, and the flow of federally supported projects to his district—in the areas of housing, flood control, and power—began. After narrowly losing one race for the U.S. Senate in 1941, Johnson served in the Navy. A second try for the Senate in 1948 brought him victory by eighty-seven votes and the nickname Landslide Lyndon.

In the clubby atmosphere of the upper house, Johnson advanced swiftly, through the application of political skills and as a result of the vagaries of political elections. Within a period of six years, he was successively the assistant minority leader, the minority leader, and, from 1955, the majority leader. He rose through the support of the Senate's inner club, mostly Southerners like Georgia's Richard Russell, who directed the chamber without holding the formal positions of leadership themselves. But once the majority leader, Johnson not only led but came to dominate the Senate as no man ever had.

Johnson's leadership in the Senate was based on his ability to build up a cadre of Johnson loyalists among his colleagues while at the same time maintaining the best possible terms with de facto or potential political opponents. The most formidable public personality during those years was, of course, President Eisenhower, whose great stature discouraged an effective frontal attack by the Democrats. Johnson, along with House Speaker Rayburn, developed a theme that would become a cliché—they would support the President when he was right and oppose him when he was wrong. Often this meant supporting him when the less disciplined Republicans did not. The national Democratic chairman, Paul Butler, was aghast at the display of bipartisanship. So too were the Senate Democratic liberals—a small, ineffective, almost foolish clique during the 1950's. Johnson disdained the liberals as too idealistic and too emotional to be competent politically, but among them he found in Hubert Humphrey of Minnesota an energetic young man capable of overcoming youthful excesses and becoming an effective, pragmatic Senator. Of their relationship, more will be discussed later.

A single example will suggest some elementary principles that were a part of the Johnson technique of leadership. In the early 1950's Wisconsin's Republican Senator Joseph McCarthy waxed ever stronger in his cynical crusade against imagined Communist infestation of the Federal government. Johnson refused to attack McCarthy while he enjoyed wide support among the American people. And he did not want it to appear that he was trying to silence a Republican Senator seeking evidence of softness toward communism during the Truman Presidency. But when in 1954 McCarthy chose to probe alleged Communist influence in the U.S. Army, Johnson saw to it that the hearings were televised, knowing that McCarthy would betray himself not only as a man without civility but also as an investigator without substantive evidence to support his charges. After two months of television exposure, McCarthy was discredited. Furthermore, he had in the meanwhile personally attacked several of his colleagues, and the full Senate prepared to consider a motion of censure. Johnson secured the appointment to the committee of Democrats who were respected conservatives and who had never quarreled with McCarthy. The committee recommended condemning McCarthy, and Johnson then swung all forty-five voting Democrats behind that position, which carried the full Senate overwhelmingly. McCarthy never recovered.

Haunted by his eighty-seven-vote victory in the 1948 election, Johnson concentrated on building up his base of support in Texas for six years. After a true landslide victory in 1954, he turned his attention to establishing his credentials as a national political leader. In 1956 he declined to sign a Southern Manifesto, supported by his colleagues from the former Confederate states, which opposed the Supreme Court decision ordering school desegregation. A year later he broke a long pattern of opposition to civil-rights legislation, securing passage of a watered-down bill that established a Civil Rights Commission and dealt rather ineffectively with Negro voting rights. He forged the compromise that prevented a Southern filibuster. The bill, though hardly all that liberals wanted, kept Johnson viable as a national candidate without destroying his Southern base.

After driving himself beyond all normal limits, Johnson was struck down by a heart attack in 1955, at the age of forty-six. Though he recovered, the blow seemingly foreclosed any route to national office for one already handicapped by his place of birth. But through his energy and perseverance his prospects revived, and despite his unsuccessful bid for the Presidential nomination in 1960 he seemed at that point to be the key to the fate of the Democratic nominee, John Kennedy.

The case for Johnson as the Democratic Vice-Presidential nominee in 1960 was a strong one. He represented the South, the largest element of the party not reconciled to Kennedy's candidacy. In the South—and to a lesser extent elsewhere—anti-Catholicism of the most virulent sort still festered. In these states, the traditional bedrock of the Democratic party, Kennedy was either unknown or distrusted. Johnson, although he claimed that he was as much a Westerner as a Southerner, was the man who could hold the South in line for the Democratic ticket, if anyone could. Moreover, during the pre-convention campaign, Kennedy had said that if he could not win the nomination himself, he thought Johnson was better qualified to be President than anyone else.

Johnson had evinced no enthusiasm for the second office, and most knowledgeable people questioned whether he would exchange his powerful Senate leadership for the Vice Presidency. Other men were willing, even eager, to go on the ticket with Kennedy, who in fact had planted Vice-Presidential hopes with several men as part of his successful strategy for winning the top spot.

Political associates of John Kennedy do not agree on whether the Presidential candidate really hoped that Johnson would take the Vice-Presidential nomination. The two men met privately in Johnson's suite on the morning after Kennedy won his victory. Some say that Kennedy's offer of the Vice Presidency at that time was pro forma, that Kennedy merely intended to acknowledge Johnson's standing in the Congress and the South's position in the party.

Arthur Schlesinger, Jr., says Kennedy later said, "I didn't offer the Vice-Presidency to him. I just held it out like this"—he pretended to hold a small object close to his body—"and he grabbed at it."

Serious or not, Kennedy reminded Johnson that for years the Majority Leader had been stressing the importance of unity both in the party and in the nation; now, if he were not on the ticket, the Democrats would not be united for the campaign, and they would lose. The two men did not settle the issue at their morning meeting. Johnson said he would consider the invitation. Both men agreed to discuss the question of the Vice Presidency with party leaders.

When some of the Southerners learned that Johnson was in line for Vice President, they said that he would be betraying his principles as well as the South if he ran with the liberal, Catholic Kennedy. Speaker Sam Rayburn, his oldest and closest political adviser, cautioned against it; Johnson belonged in the Senate, said Rayburn. But when someone observed that he would have far less power as Vice President, Johnson replied, "Power is where power goes."

While Johnson weighed his decision, Kennedy appealed to Sam Rayburn to prevail on Johnson to accept. Rayburn remembered that another friend from Texas, John Nance Garner, had left the Vice Presidency a very unhappy man. The seventy-eight-year-old Speaker replied to Kennedy as follows:

"Up until thirty minutes ago I was against it, and I have withheld a final decision until I could really find out what was in your heart. You know, Jack, I am a very old man and sometimes given to being a little selfish, I am sure. I am in the twilight of my life, walking down into the valley. My career is behind me, but Lyndon is only approaching the summit of his. I am afraid I was trying to keep him in the legislative end where he could help me. Now the way you explain it I can see that you need him more. You are looking at the whole."

Lady Bird also favored Johnson's accepting, in the belief that the Vice Presidency would be a less strenuous job. Johnson saw another reason for saying yes. The Vice Presidency, a national office, might free him at long last from his identification as a Texas politician—with all its implications as a wheeler-dealer and as a servant of the oil interests. He would keep alive the possibility of running again for President eight years hence as a truly national figure.

Kenneth O'Donnell, a close Kennedy associate who initially opposed Johnson as the Vice-Presidential nominee, has written that Kennedy offered another, somewhat Machiavellian reason for choosing Johnson: "Did it occur to you that if Lyndon becomes the Vice President, I'll have Mike Mansfield as the Senate leader, somebody I can trust and depend on?"

But on Thursday afternoon Kennedy was finding opposition to Johnson. While some men hailed the idea of a Kennedy-Johnson ticket as a master stroke, several labor and liberal spokesmen were stridently opposed. In retrospect, the opposition was not so great as it seemed, not seriously extending beyond the Michigan and District of Columbia delegations, but Kennedy had difficulty gauging its force. As a result, the inclusion of Johnson on the ticket was not assured until mid-afternoon. Philip Graham, a friend of both men, kept them in touch by phone; Kennedy was finally able to tell Graham to tell Lyndon that the nomination was settled, and that they should proceed with the public announcements.

Even now—in the late afternoon—Bobby Kennedy came to Johnson's suite to tell Johnson that the nomination was encountering strong opposition and that Johnson should withdraw as the Vice-Presidential candidate; Johnson was shocked, and this incident apparently forever strained relations between himself and Bobby, with serious consequences for the party in the future. Graham again got John Kennedy on the phone; the candidate remarked simply, "Oh, that's all right; Bobby's been out of touch and doesn't know what's been happening."

Pierre Salinger, Kennedy's press secretary, later scoffed at the notion that Bobby was really trying to get Johnson to withdraw, or that Bobby was somehow acting on his own in the face of John Kennedy's obvious commitment at that point to Johnson's nomination. Bobby's purpose, Salinger wrote later, was to ascertain whether Johnson was really ready to make a fight for the nomination if that became necessary.

John Kennedy revealed his choice for Vice President with a firm public endorsement:

"I have said many times that in these days of great challenge, Americans must have a Vice President capable of dealing with the grave problems confronting this nation and the free world. We need men of strength if we are to be strong and if we are to prevail and lead the world on the road to freedom. Lyndon Johnson has demonstrated on many occasions his brilliant qualifications for the leadership we require today."

That night, Johnson was placed in nomination for the Vice Presidency by Governor David Lawrence of Pennsylvania. House Majority Leader John McCormack moved that nominations be closed. The Ayes were loud, but so were the Noes. The chair ruled that the Ayes had it, and Johnson's nomination was gaveled through. Vice President Richard Nixon, watching the convention on television, was impressed by the way Kennedy had forced his liberal supporters to accept Johnson; Nixon realized that Kennedy would be a formidable opponent in the fall campaign.

Johnson returned to Washington after the convention, and found that many of his friends were unhappy. To them, he dictated a form letter in which he said: ". . . no man can go into a political convention and come out with everything he wants. For my own part, I feel strongly that no man ever fulfills an obligation by turning his back on a duty to which he is called. I neither sought nor solicited the vice-presidency, but when the invitation to join Senator Kennedy on the ticket came, I had the choice of turning tail and abandoning any opportunity for Texas and the South to have a voice in the carrying out of national policy or of repaying the confidence of the Democrats from all over the country who voted for me for President."

To win the election, Kennedy needed to sweep the East, capture two or three of the larger Midwestern states, and win more than half of the South. Winning the South was largely

Johnson's task. Nixon campaigned in the large cities of the "New South." Johnson traveled from courthouse square to courthouse square, telling the gallused, unshaven idlers, the curious, the suspicious, and the politicians that the Democrats were going to win, and that the locals had better get on the band wagon. The reputation of the Great Persuader was on the line, and he won the support of the men whose language he spoke.

It should be noted, however, that Johnson's task was to carry the South, not to delude it. In Richmond he said he had not come to Virginia to promise Virginians exemption from their obligation to abide by the school desegregation decision handed down by the Supreme Court.

Johnson's biggest assignment was Texas and its 24 electoral votes. Late in the campaign—in Dallas—Johnson received a rowdy reception from a gang of right-wingers who had jammed the lobby of a hotel where Johnson was scheduled to speak. As he entered with his wife clinging to his arm, the demonstrators jostled them, insulted them, spat at them, and barely stopped short of physically attacking them. Johnson's instinct told him that he and Lady Bird must walk through the lobby slowly and with dignity. All Texas saw the scene in the hotel through the eye of the television camera. William S. White, Johnson's biographer and himself a Texan, wrote that citizens of his state, whatever their shortcomings, will not tolerate the harassment of a lady, and that from that day on, Texas tilted away from Nixon and into the Democratic column. Kennedy won the Presidency with only 34 electoral votes to spare, and 24 of them were from Texas.

Johnson also campaigned in the North, where many persons were taking their first close look at the LBJ style. Their impressions must have been mixed. After receiving a warm welcome in Boston, Johnson told his Yankee hosts that they had made "this grandson of a 'federate soldier feel lahk mah-ty tall cotton, let me tell you." Kennedy carried his home state that year, winning 60 per cent of the vote. But who would have believed that Johnson would carry Massachusetts four years later by a fantastic 76 per cent.

Finally the long 1960 campaign ended, and the Democrats won. Lady Bird Johnson said: "We are going back to the ranch tomorrow and be just plain vegetables for a few days." And they did.

"I am going to try to be the kind of Vice President that I would want if I were President," Johnson said, and he faithfully observed the pledge.

Kennedy gave Johnson a suite in the Executive Office Building next door to the White House, and Johnson also retained his office space at the Capitol. It was at the Capitol that Johnson suffered a well-deserved rebuff early in 1961, just before he was sworn in as Vice President.[1] Senator Mike Mansfield, elected to succeed Johnson as Majority Leader, moved that Johnson be empowered to continue presiding over the caucuses of the Senate Democrats while Vice President. Johnson had no thought of merely presiding. He intended to continue to lead his ex-colleagues as well. Unexpectedly, several Senators spoke out sharply against Johnson, some not because they had chafed under his iron rule but because they perceived a violation of the separation of powers between the legislative and the executive branch. Mansfield's motion carried, 46–17, but Johnson was stung by the opposition. He gaveled one subsequent caucus to order, turned over the proceedings to Mansfield, and never reappeared at a Democratic caucus.

After the embarrassment of the caucus vote, he lost interest in legislative affairs and seldom thereafter bestirred himself to help push Kennedy's New Frontier legislation through the Congress. Had he tried, he could not have been nearly as effective as in his Senate days. Mansfield, for his part, held the leadership reins loosely, and as a result the President's program languished on Capitol Hill.

The Vice President attended meetings of the Cabinet, the National Security Council, and of the congressional leaders. He received reports regularly from the Joint Chiefs of Staff and the State Department.

Johnson drew other assignments from the President. He headed the President's Committee on Equal Employment Opportunity, with the duty to ferret out racial discrimination

[1] Johnson had run for re-election to the Senate in 1960, and won, while simultaneously running for Vice President.

among contractors doing business with the government. The task—similar to that given to Vice President Nixon—was not without peril to Johnson, for many of the contractors did business in the South, still Johnson's political base. Furthermore, the President's brother, now Attorney General, took a direct and intense interest in overcoming job discrimination. Once, Bobby, in Johnson's presence, sharply rebuked James Webb, administrator of the National Aeronautics and Space Administration, for assigning only two men out of forty thousand in his agency to the problem of discrimination. The unpleasant scene, with its implications that the Vice President had not moved fast enough to secure NASA's compliance, reflected badly on Johnson.

As chairman of the President's committee, Johnson spoke at Gettysburg, Pennsylvania, on the site of the battlefield, on Memorial Day, 1963. In this, one of his best speeches, he appraised the status of the struggle for equal rights. He conceded that the Negro had been patient long enough. But he said that the aggrieved must not hurl themselves against the barricades, but work with perseverance and through the law. He concluded:

"The Negro says, 'Now.' Others say, 'Never.' The voice of responsible Americans—the voice of those who died here and the great man who spoke here—their voices say, 'Together.' There is no other way.

"Until Justice is blind to color, until education is unaware of race, until opportunity is unconcerned with the color of men's skins, emancipation will be a proclamation but not a fact. To the extent that the proclamation of emancipation is not fulfilled in fact, to that extent we shall have fallen short of assuring freedom to the free."

But Johnson was scarcely involved in the major civil-rights crisis of the Kennedy years. While the President and Bobby quarterbacked the moves that forced the admission of James Meredith as the first black student at the University of Mississippi, Johnson was in Texas. Supposedly, Johnson was the administration's link to the South, but in this showdown his powers of persuasion as Vice President paled by comparison with the powers available to—and used by—the Attorney General. On this occasion and on others—the Cuban missile crisis of 1962, for example—no one could doubt that Bobby Kennedy, not Lyndon Johnson, was second in John Kennedy's administration.

In his advisory role as chairman of the Aeronautics and Space Council (not to be confused with the powerful NASA), Johnson added his voice to others who successfully urged Kennedy to commit the United States to a manned landing on the moon. In 1962, Johnson accompanied Astronaut John Glenn during the space hero's triumphant parade through New York. Some persons thought Johnson was seeking to share some of the limelight with the first American to orbit the earth. In fact, the next President generally remained benign and inconspicuous; seldom had he taken such a back seat to anyone.

Johnson also served as chairman of the Peace Corps National Advisory Council, where he kept an eye on one of the President's favorite projects.

In his years in the Senate, Johnson's attention had been drawn more often to domestic problems than to international affairs. But the Vice President gained valuable experience during a number of foreign assignments that took him to thirty-three countries. His first trip was to Senegal in April, 1961, for the first anniversary of that African nation's independence. He went to the people, shaking hands, patting children's heads, and smiling at old women. In May, in a major sweep past the Cold War front lines, he visited Vietnam, the Philippines, Hong Kong, Formosa, Thailand, India, and Pakistan. Johnson carried to these countries President Kennedy's assurances that the United States would not abandon Southeast Asia to the Communists. In Saigon he hailed President Ngo Dinh Diem as the Winston Churchill of South Asia—an early example of the hyperbole by Johnson and others that frustrated efforts by average Americans to put the Southeast Asian tragedy in perspective. Diem was already besieged by an indigenous guerrilla movement in which Communists were a principal factor. According to a secret Pentagon document published in 1971—one of the "Pentagon papers"—the Kennedy administration reached a decision on May 11, 1961, to prevent Communist domination of South Vietnam, and to support covert military actions to achieve that objective. On May 12, in Saigon, Vice President Johnson raised with President Diem the possibility of sending United States combat troops to that country. But at that time Diem was interested in troops only in the event of an open attack on his country. On his return from Southeast Asia, Johnson in a memorandum to Kennedy urged greater United States involvement in the affairs of the area: "I recommend that we move forward promptly with a major effort to help these countries defend themselves." In obvious reference to his meeting with Diem, Johnson added, "American combat troop involvement . . . is not desirable. Possibly Americans fail to appreciate fully the subtlety that recently-colonial peoples would not look with favor upon governments which invited or accepted the return this soon of Western troops."

The Vice President's personal conduct on this and other trips abroad drew much attention. To United States diplomatic personnel abroad, Johnson was often abrasive and demanding. For its part, the State Department complained about the informal folksiness of the Vice President. In return, Johnson did not conceal his opinion about men he regarded as stuffed shirts.

He said, "We cannot demonstrate the essence and spirit of the American political system unless we get out of our limousines abroad as we would at home. After all, what dignity are we trying to prove—that of the office of Vice President or that of the human race?"

In Karachi began the saga of the Pakistani camel driver. On the way into town from the airport, the motorcade was surrounded by cheering crowds. Johnson climbed out of the car, and as he howdy'd and pawed his way through the circle of faces and hands, he came upon a small man waiting to cross the street with a load of sacked straw. LBJ shook the man's hand, and told him through an interpreter that it sure would be nice if he could come visit him in Texas someday. The Vice President went on his way without giving the matter any further thought.

Soon after he returned to the United States, Johnson learned that the camel driver, Bashir Ahmed, had accepted his invitation and would be coming shortly. It sounded like a publicity stunt, and it could have become a fiasco. But it was neither. Johnson had to go through with the business, which proved to be his greatest diplomatic success as Vice President. Sure enough, the unlettered Pakistani laborer showed up, and he won the hearts of his hosts with his gentleness and his sincerity. He told women reporters that when they spoke, petals dropped from their lips. A city accustomed to bombast was moved by his poise and dignity, and by the poetic words he chose to describe the Capital's wonders. The smiling little man flew to Texas as Johnson's guest, and slept in the bed once occupied by his own President, Ayub Khan. He returned home bearing gifts, and the pro-United States reaction in Karachi was sensational.

One of Johnson's political rivals shrugged philosophically at the Vice President's luck: "When Johnson rides right by millions of Pakistanis and picks out Omar the Tentmaker blindfold, what's the use?"

There were other trips: to reassure Berliners after the Wall went up in August, 1961; to Rome for a forty-minute audience with Pope John, and then again to Rome for his funeral; to Benelux and Scandinavia, and elsewhere. In the lands of the poor, he was saddened, and he likened the underdeveloped nations of today to the lonely, arid land along the banks of the Pedernales where he had grown up, and where he had seen so much progress.

In the United States, Johnson spoke hundreds of times while Vice President, but he was determined never to be trapped into a public conflict with the administration. White House clearance was obtained on every speech; he ducked press conferences where attempts might be made to draw him into disagreements with Kennedy. The man who had run the show in the Senate had no doubt about who was No. 1 now.

They were never close. Each had his own friends, and his own style, and his own memories of past abrasions. Johnson could not have been content in the Vice Presidency, and he could not have failed to reveal his discontent. All too often, the familiar speculation was heard that the Vice President would be "dumped" when Kennedy was renominated. Both men were embarrassed by such talk, and the President denied all the rumors. Even before his inauguration, Kennedy had said, "Anybody in this administration who thinks he will promote himself with me by biting at Lyndon Johnson has a very large hole in his head."

Not all members of the President's staff heeded that admonition, and the Vice President sensed that some men close to Kennedy regarded him with contempt. Johnson brooded over real or imagined personal slights.

The dump-Johnson speculation revived in the fall of 1963 when his former protégé, Bobby Baker, was charged in a lawsuit with utilizing his job as secretary to the Senate Majority for personal financial gain. As more aspects of Baker's dealings began to surface, Johnson seemed wounded politically. But events in early November appeared to firm up his position. At a press conference, Kennedy said that he wanted Johnson on the ticket in 1964 and that he expected that he would be. At a meeting between Kennedy and his key political advisers —not including Johnson—to lay plans for the 1964 campaign, the renomination of the Vice President was taken for granted. In Florida on the last Saturday of his life, Kennedy told Senator George Smathers that the dumping of Johnson would give the impression that the Bobby Baker scandal was worse than it then seemed to the public, and that Kennedy would in effect be conceding that he had made a mistake in choosing Johnson in the first place.

Johnson was intimately involved in one of the political trouble spots facing the Democrats in 1964. In Texas, Johnson and Governor John Connally were allied against a faction headed by maverick liberal Senator Ralph Yarborough. Connally and Yarborough were both up for re-election in 1964, and each faction had planned to field a challenger against the rival leader in the Democratic primary. To lend support to a shaky truce among Lone Star Democrats, Kennedy and Johnson flew to Texas in late November 1963. They appeared together in several cities. Their last stop was Dallas.

Johnson, demonstrating self-discipline, had shown that he could make the best of a cruelly ill-suited office in the reasonable hope that he could establish himself as a national figure with a fair chance for the Presidential nomination in 1968. Whether this man of such prodigious energy could have held himself in check for eight full years will never be known, for he was Vice President for just more than a thousand days. With the swiftness of a bullet, John Kennedy's Presidency ended before Johnson's eyes, in the sunlight in Dallas, on the early afternoon of Friday, November 22, 1963.

Lyndon Johnson became the eighth President by chance, and he alone of his select group inherited an extensive legislative program from his predecessor. The first Johnson—Andrew—

tried to implement Lincoln's reconstruction policies, and failed. Truman helped establish a United Nations, first projected by Roosevelt. Several administrations changed hands and changed course almost simultaneously. But the millions who had supported Kennedy were now joined by more who wanted the New Frontier enacted as a memorial to a martyred President. To these pressures on Congress, Johnson added the massive power of his own leadership. His objectives from the outset were to calm a shaken nation, to effect a smooth transition from one administration to another, and to pass Kennedy's program—some fifty pieces of legislation—further seasoned with some of Johnson's own ideas, all in time to go to the voters in the Presidential election of 1964. He succeeded in these objectives, perhaps too well.

To reduce the impact of the transition, Johnson held personnel turnover to a minimum. From the moment he took the oath as President at Dallas, Johnson surrounded himself with Kennedy's staff members, advisers, and Cabinet officers. He said all had the duty to their country to stay at their posts and work for the new President. They all did, at first, even those as closely identified with Kennedy as his brother Bobby, the Attorney General; and Ted Sorenson, his alter ego and speech writer. Johnson handled the Attorney General with special delicacy, knowing that if he stayed at his post the others would too. Johnson had within his circle of intimates too few men competent enough to staff the President's office—there were some notable exceptions—or to form a shadow Cabinet ready to take over the executive departments at a moment's notice. Dean Rusk, reportedly due for dismissal as Secretary of State by Kennedy, stayed in his Cabinet post for five more years, advocating broad United States military involvement in Vietnam all the while.

In an evening address to Congress televised nationally on November 27, Johnson struck the theme, "Let us continue," echoing Kennedy's "Let us begin" appeal from his 1961 inaugural address. After naming bills he hoped to see passed to "honor President Kennedy's memory," Johnson added what proved a futile exhortation to Americans to end "the preaching of hate and evil and violence."

Congressional leaders later said that elements of Kennedy's legislative program would have passed without his death and the emotional outpouring that followed. In particular, they believed, the time had come at last for a civil-rights bill eliminating discrimination in the use of all public accommodations, and such a bill did pass after a two-month filibuster was broken in the Senate in the spring of 1964. But Johnson's contributions were to keep the pressure constantly on the Congress and—unlike his handling of another civil-rights bill in 1957—to refuse any compromise.

After the initial numbing shock of the assassination wore off throughout the country, Johnson in the spring of 1964 began to test on the public the concept of a "Great Society." This was to be his vision of what America could be, a vision apart from, but not incompatible with, Kennedy's vision. The introduction of the Great Society would establish in the public's mind that the transition was being completed. At graduation exercises at the University of Michigan, Johnson called on Americans to seize "the opportunity to move not only toward the rich society and the powerful society, but upward to the Great Society.

"The Great Society rests on abundance and liberty for all. It demands an end to poverty and racial injustice. . . .

"The Great Society is a place where every child can find knowledge to enrich his mind. . . . It is a place where leisure is a welcome chance to build and reflect. . . .

"But most of all, the Great Society is not a safe harbor, a resting place, a final objective, a finished work. It is a challenge constantly renewed, beckoning us toward a destiny where the meaning of our lives matches the marvelous products of our labor."

As the first major step in achieving the goals of the Great Society, Johnson declared a "War on Poverty"—a wide-ranging scheme that embraced community antipoverty projects, a work-study program for needy college students, loans to low-income farmers and businessmen, and a Job Corps to provide basic education and work opportunities for slum youths in fresh environments. The antipoverty efforts were put together hastily, and in time they showed it. But the war on poverty—which in its concept reflected Johnson's idealism at its best—helped him become the fourth consecutive President-by-chance to win a full four-year term.

A major part of the President's re-election formula was a

welcome and unexpected surprise. We now turn to one of the most aberrant episodes in recent American politics—the Goldwater crusade of 1964. It was the work of a militant minority in the Republican party. For all the sense it made, it might as well have been performed (to borrow from the long title of that year's hit play) by the inmates of the Asylum of Charenton under the direction of the Marquis de Sade.

"One of the reasons I chose Miller is that he drives Johnson nuts."

So spoke the 1964 Republican Presidential candidate, Barry Goldwater, in explaining why he picked the obscure New York Congressman to run for the second-highest office in the nation. Reporters waited in vain for more details on William Miller's qualifications.

Miller, fifty years old, a Roman Catholic and a graduate of the University of Notre Dame, served in Army intelligence in World War II, and had an incidental role in the Nürnberg war crimes trials in 1945. In 1950, the young lawyer ran for Congress from a Western New York district, and was re-elected every two years thereafter, through 1962. His winning margins ranged as high as 43,000, but by 1960 his support was on the decline. After barely winning in 1962, he announced that he would not seek re-election.

His record in the House was conservative, although he generally supported civil-rights measures. Like Goldwater, he couldn't point to any major legislation bearing his name. In New York, he declined to ally himself with the liberal state Republican organization and he endorsed Nixon for the 1960 Presidential nomination, a rebuff to Governor Rockefeller. During his last years in Congress, Miller began to lose touch with his district (and in 1963 answered only 49 per cent of the roll calls, second lowest percentage in the House), because of his increasing commitments to the national Republican organization. In 1960 he served as chairman of the congressional campaign committee, and helped the GOP score a net gain of 20 seats in the House. From 1961 until July 1964, he was chairman of the Republican National Committee. He was a tireless and successful organizer, fund-raiser, and campaigner who won the loyalty of thousands of party workers across the nation. For Miller, politics was both a business and a pleasure.

A national political chairman is traditionally a caustic critic of the opposition. Ordinarily, he is a professional, but not an officeholder, and therefore doesn't need to worry about his own popularity. Miller, an effective speaker and phrasemaker, often succeeded in stinging the Democrats. He once said that John Kennedy didn't know the difference "between a sense of history and a sense of histrionics."

This, then, was the background of the man the Republicans nominated for Vice President in 1964. Miller should have remained where he could best serve, as chairman of the national committee. His replacement by the doctrinaire and relatively inexperienced Dean Burch created an upheaval at GOP headquarters. In moving Miller from one job to another, the Republicans were losers on two counts. Miller added nothing to the ticket for the simple reason that his qualifications duplicated those that his Presidential candidate already had or should have had. Miller could command the loyalty and dedication of the party organization, but Goldwater already had this support, to which he owed his nomination. Miller could rally the most partisan (and usually most conservative) of the faithful, but if Goldwater couldn't count on that vote, his cause was hopeless to begin with.

Why, then, was Miller nominated? And why is his nomination still significant even though Goldwater was beaten in the election?

The Vice-Presidential nomination cannot be examined in isolation, but only in the context of the total Republican picture as of the summer of 1964. For twenty-five years the conservatives had been pleading for "a choice, not an echo." Three times they had sought to win the nomination for Senator Taft of Ohio, and on another occasion their candidate had been Governor Bricker of Ohio. But between 1940 and 1960 the Republican Presidential nomination always went to candidates described by the conservatives as "me-tooers."

But the conservatives became more insistent that the Republicans nominate one of their own, and their claims grew more exotic with the passing years. Early in 1964 it was said that 18 million Americans who usually stayed at home would troop to the polls if only they were given a "choice." One must acknowledge that the conservatives worked long and hard for the party during these years, and one can also sympathize with their frustration at their repeated defeats at national conventions. But the Old Guardsmen didn't realize that they could maintain what leverage they had at the conventions only so long as their thesis could not be disproved.

In 1964, the luckless conservatives finally had a chance to show what they could do, but only under the worst of possible circumstances. The 1964 election would be held in the anniversary month of the assassination of their opponent's predecessor. And that opponent—Lyndon Johnson—was preaching unity and continuity to a nation that wanted both. Worst of all, they had in Barry Goldwater no ordinary conservative. While capable of articulating broad principles, Goldwater frequently faltered in attempting to relate those principles to specific issues, and thereby left the impression of being more extreme than he was. He appeared to endorse the idea that NATO commanders in Europe should have the power to use tactical nuclear weapons in an emergency on their own initiative. He once suggested making Social Security voluntary, which would gut the system as young people opted out. For months Goldwater tried to clarify his position on these two issues alone, but his earlier ill-considered remarks had a devastating effect on his campaign.

The final circumstance that foredoomed the conservative cause in 1964 was one of the conservatives' own choosing. After Goldwater's nomination became certain the candidate and his managers faced important tactical decisions. Should they compromise with the moderates by accepting their platform planks? Or by accepting a well-known moderate as Vice-Presidential candidate?

The answers were No. First, the Goldwater people were pledged to offer America a choice, and the choice must be clear and unsullied by a moderate platform or a moderate Vice-Presidential candidate.

Second, the Presidential candidate and his associates simply were oblivious to the importance that compromise and consensus play in winning an election. In a letter to Goldwater after his defeat, Virginia State Chairman Robert Corber pointed out that the nomination of Miller and the selection of Burch as national chairman served to foster disunity and a feeling of exclusion within the party. He said that these choices were interpreted as an indication that one faction intended to exercise total domination over the party. Corber noted that in the past "McKinley took Roosevelt for his running mate; Roosevelt accepted Garner; Kennedy selected Johnson, and so forth. Such choices as these are wise when there has been spirited competition for the nomination."

But in this case the nomination of a moderate for the second spot would have been regarded as hypocrisy. The Goldwater men knew this. When a Presidential candidate is taken from the mainstream of his party, he can accept a man whose thinking may be slightly at variance with his own without invoking criticism. Thus (in addition to the instances cited above by Corber), Eisenhower ran with Nixon, considered, in 1952, slightly more conservative than himself; and in 1960, Nixon chose Lodge, somewhat more progressive than himself; and these combinations could not be called hypocrisy. But the nomination of Goldwater, from the right-wing fringe of the party, simultaneously eliminated all the men who in normal years might logically be considered as Vice-Presidential possibilities. For example, every prominent Republican Governor and every Republican congressional leader had played an active role in winning passage for the 1964 civil-rights law. Yet Goldwater had voted against the law as unconstitutional; although he was personally free of any racial bias, his campaign was geared for an appeal to all of those who opposed the law.

At the convention there was still talk of nominating Governor Scranton of Pennsylvania (who had sought the Presidential nomination) for Vice President, but the severity and incisiveness of his criticisms of Goldwater ruled him out. However, had the Goldwater people been able to read the handwriting on the wall—that they were going to be routed in November—the nomination of Scranton for Vice President would have been useful in a negative sort of way. With Scranton on the ticket, the conservatives could have dismissed any defeat with assertions that his nomination had confused the issue, had forced Goldwater to modify his principles, and so forth.

Party leaders outside Goldwater's small inner circle were not even consulted on the Vice-Presidential nomination. The insiders were in absolute control of the convention; they dictated the nomination of the two men who would represent their long-lost cause, they wrote the platform, and they chose the issues on which the campaign would be fought. And lest the Republican moderates make the mistake of thinking that they were still welcome, the Presidential candidate reminded them in his acceptance speech that "those who do not care for our cause, we don't expect to enter our ranks in any case." The Democratic victory in November was the greatest ever in both percentage and plurality of the popular vote. Those who had wanted a clear-cut choice had received a clear-cut answer. The Goldwater-Miller ticket was *in extremis* from the day it was born.

In passing, we should notice one other bit of reasoning involved in the nomination of Miller. Goldwater leaders apparently concluded that nominating a Catholic for Vice President would force the Democrats to do likewise. And the most prominent Catholic possibility was Attorney General Robert Kennedy, who was considered unpopular in the South because of his identification with the civil-rights movement. After Miller's nomination, one Republican strategist was quoted as saying: "Johnson has got to have a Catholic. Otherwise, we'll get a lot of the Catholics who vote on the religious issue. Johnson is going to be under a lot of pressure to take Bobby anyway, and if he does we can sing *Dixie* all the way home." Johnson did not choose a Catholic for Vice President. Then, in November, he received the votes of an overwhelming majority of U.S. Catholics.

Nothing that Bill Miller could have said or done during the fall campaign could have materially changed the result, and for that reason he probably should have said a lot less. He labeled Hubert Humphrey, the Democratic Vice-Presidential candidate, a left-wing radical. When he told his listeners how terrible it would be if Humphrey ever became President, he served only to remind them that he—Miller—could become President in the same way.

Miller swung wildly at times. The Democrats must have been surprised to hear him say that "never, never did we ever call the Democrats a war party. . . ." He complained about Johnson's war record, saying that "he was back home again before the shooting even started." (Lieutenant Commander Johnson received the Silver Star from General MacArthur. Once his plane came under Japanese fire, and returned to its base with one engine knocked out. In July, 1942, Roosevelt ordered Johnson and all other members of Congress—Democrats and Republicans—back to Washington.) Emmet John Hughes, a former speechwriter for both Eisenhower and Rockefeller, wrote that Miller had brought to the campaign "all the respect for good taste, public intelligence, and world opinion that one would expect in a snarling local brawl for the county sheriff's badge."

Actually, Miller did a fair job of developing the issues, such as they were. He campaigned extensively, delivering essentially the same speech over and over, polishing and rephrasing for maximum effect. He managed to raise concern in the minds of his listeners over alleged scandals in the Johnson administration. But he could not devote all his efforts to the attack. Ordinarily, the "out" party does not need to go onto the defense, but Miller felt obliged to reassure his audiences that Barry Goldwater would not plunge the nation into war, that he would not put an end to farm subsidies, that he would not abolish social security, and so on. Miller's audiences were usually small, and were composed almost entirely of persons who were already converted.

As a footnote, it should be mentioned that Miller was singularly unsuccessful in driving Lyndon Johnson nuts.

No Presidential candidate ever spent more time, effort, and money in selecting a Vice-Presidential nominee than Lyndon Johnson. Although he was able to retain absolutely the final decision in his own hands, Johnson sought out the opinion of every person, organization, and special interest that was entitled to be heard on the subject.

On the day that he announced his choice, the President told reporters: "I think in all my life that I have never taken any decision more seriously than picking Humphrey. I have had one thing in mind above all others, that is that when fellows like you come to write the history of this period they will say that we paid attention to the main thing.

"I picked Humphrey because, in my judgment, and after checking with leaders all over the country, I was convinced that he would be the best man to be President if anything happened to me."

Speculation about his choice had continued almost unabated from the time he had become President. He did not shut off the discussion until the night of his own nomination at Atlantic

City, when he announced his preference for the senior Senator from Minnesota. The President had by then drained every drop of suspense out of the Vice-Presidential talk.

Attorney General Robert Kennedy, brother of the slain President, wanted the nomination badly. So did Adlai Stevenson, twice a Presidential candidate. Peace Corps Director Sargent Shriver, Defense Secretary Robert McNamara, California Governor Edmund Brown, Minnesota Senator Eugene McCarthy, and many others were willing.

To obtain an accurate reading on just where the party stood on the nomination, the President undertook a searching interrogation. He studied polls, some of them ordered by himself at a cost of thousands of dollars. Through personal conversations, and by use of the telephone, he canvassed the views of Northerners, Southerners, Governors, Congressmen, and spokesmen for the farmers, the workers, and the businessmen. He returned to certain key persons periodically to obtain a fresh report on their views.

The polls turned up several interesting facts. Johnson found that by coupling the name of any possible running mate with his own he lost a few votes. Humphrey would hurt the President in the South, McCarthy was not well known, and so forth. But the polls also showed that all the Vice-Presidential possibilities detracted from his support in about the same measure, and in no case by enough to jeopardize his election; he was so far ahead of the Republicans that he was free to choose almost anybody.

Shriver's prospects were dashed when Kennedy loyalists let it be known that they would not accept a Kennedy in-law on the ticket as a substitute for the Attorney General.

In retrospect, Kennedy's desire for the Vice Presidency seems astounding. But he recognized that Johnson was making a real effort to carry forward his brother's program, and he felt that Johnson and he could work well together in furthering that program. And of course as Vice President, Kennedy would be Johnson's logical successor when the Texan retired. Although Kennedy enjoyed wide public support, he was strongly opposed by Southerners and businessmen, and he was not acceptable to Johnson. Aside from the abyss between their political styles and personalities, they had not fully put aside bad feelings dating from the 1960 convention. Johnson also felt that an older, more experienced man—Kennedy was thirty-eight—had a better claim to the Vice Presidency. Finally, the President wanted very much to win re-election without recourse to direct support from the Kennedy name.

The Attorney General knew it would be futile to bring any pressure on the President in his own behalf. At the same time, he would not intercede to discourage persons promoting his nomination. In New Hampshire, the Kennedy boom almost got out of hand, when supporters organized a write-in campaign. If Kennedy should draw more votes for Vice President than Johnson did for President, the embarrassment to Johnson could only strain relations between the two men. The Attorney General finally cautioned his New Hampshire supporters, and he trailed the President in the balloting while obtaining a substantial vote.

As the months passed, and the President did not announce his choice, Kennedy became more bold; in fact, the Attorney General and some of his associates began to prepare for the possibility that Johnson would throw the convention open as Stevenson had done in 1956. Johnson came to believe that the Kennedy forces planned to blitz the convention, perhaps even by calling on Mrs. Jacqueline Kennedy, the late President's widow, for help.

Johnson responded, first by rescheduling a film tribute to John Kennedy from the first day of the convention to the day after the Vice-Presidential nomination. This ploy would avert an emotional overflow that could be translated into votes for the Attorney General. Then, in late July, Johnson decided that he should no longer permit Kennedy to build up his hopes. He called the Attorney General into his office, and told him that he had a bright future in the Democratic party, and might someday lead the country. But he added ". . . this is not the year and the Vice-Presidency is not the route."

Kennedy said that he would be glad to help the President during the campaign in any way that he could. But he was now ready to leave the administration in which he had once stood second in influence only to his brother. Five weeks later the Attorney General resigned to run for the Senate from New York.

On the day after he talked to Kennedy, the President broke the news to the rest of the country in a circuitous manner that perhaps only he could have devised. Johnson told reporters: "With reference to the selection of the candidate for Vice President on the Democratic ticket, I have reached the conclusion that it would be inadvisable for me to recommend to the convention any member of my Cabinet or any of those who meet regularly with the Cabinet." He then listed the men so eliminated, tucking Kennedy's name in among those of Dean Rusk, Robert McNamara, Orville Freeman, and others, almost as if he hoped no one would give it particular attention. Some of the casualties of this pronouncement never knew that they were in the running until they learned that they had been eliminated.

This transparent artifice at least served to soften the blow to Kennedy, and gave Johnson a means of suggesting that his Cabinet members were too valuable to be spared even for the second highest office in the land.

Kennedy, publicly, joked about the maneuver. He sent a letter to his Cabinet colleagues apologizing for having taken "so many nice fellows over the side with me." Speaking to some Democratic congressional candidates, he said, "I am a little bit in awe of you when I think of my own position. You are not members of the Cabinet . . . and therefore you are eligible for Vice President."

As the convention approached, the President seemed preoccupied with the idea that maybe he really did need a Catholic on the ticket, provided that his name was not Kennedy. Both Texas Governor John Connally—recovering from the near-fatal wounds suffered at the time Kennedy was slain—and Lady Bird had a Catholic candidate of their own. He was none other than Eugene McCarthy, the aloof intellectual who was Humphrey's junior colleague from Minnesota. Although both Minnesota senators were quite liberal, Humphrey had by far the greater national reputation for being so, and Connally feared his lack of appeal in the South. Furthermore, from the viewpoint of the Southern conservatives, Humphrey was far more likely than McCarthy to use the Vice Presidency as a springboard to the White House itself, considering his already-strong base of support in the labor movement.

Those members of Johnson's staff who had previously served John Kennedy threw their support to Humphrey rather than McCarthy. McCarthy and the Kennedys had never liked each other, and McCarthy had made a brilliant, emotional nomination speech for Adlai Stevenson at the 1960 convention. On the other hand, Humphrey had won the respect of the Kennedy loyalists for his efforts in behalf of President Kennedy's legislative program, despite their previous differences.

McCarthy finally concluded, correctly, that Johnson was not going to choose him for Vice President, and that he was in fact being used by the President to build up suspense. He sent a telegram to Johnson taking himself out of consideration, and released its contents to the press. McCarthy, miffed at the way Johnson had handled the Vice Presidency, was not thereafter as close to Johnson as he had been. Looking back on the 1960's, one recognizes the degree to which the course of American history was affected by the personal feuds among the leaders of the Democratic party.

During the first eight months of 1964 hardly a week passed without a new name being tossed into the Democratic Vice-Presidential sweepstakes. But almost from the time that he had succeeded to the Presidency Lyndon Johnson had been edging toward the choice of his old friend and longtime Senate colleague, Hubert Humphrey.

★ ★ ★ ★ ★
★ ★ ★ ★ ★
★ ★ ★ ★ ★
★

HUBERT H. HUMPHREY

"... when the gap between

rhetoric and reality

becomes too wide."

In some respects Hubert Humphrey's career resembled those of Lyndon Johnson and Richard Nixon. All were born poor; all grew into manhood during the Depression years; all were propelled upward by a relentless determination to succeed in politics. Humphrey and Nixon spent years living down the errors of youthful political exuberance. All suffered heartbreaking political setbacks.

Humphrey represented the Midwestern Populist tradition. His father, a South Dakota druggist, introduced his son to the writings of Jefferson, Bryan, and other leaders. Hubert, who was born in Doland, South Dakota, later moved with his family to the larger town of Huron. To live on the Plains in those years was to know dust storms and grasshopper invasions, and to know above all the hardship that came with economic blight. Once, young Humphrey quit school to help keep his father's store going. Hubert was renowned throughout his life for his optimism, and that was about all he had to cling to in the 1930's. In 1935, during a visit to Washington, he wrote to his fiancée: "I set my aim at Congress. Don't laugh at me. Maybe it does sound rather egotistical and beyond reason, but, Muriel, I do know others have succeeded. . . ."

But he was not to succeed in South Dakota. Though a registered pharmacist, Humphrey had no wish to continue in that career, and he and his wife moved to Minneapolis where at the age of twenty-eight he earned a degree in political science from the University of Minnesota. A year later he added a Master's degree from Louisiana State University.

Humphrey taught briefly, and worked for several government agencies including the WPA, and—after being given a medical deferment during World War II—turned to elective politics. Defeated for mayor of Minneapolis in 1943, Humphrey won the office on his second try two years later. He made headway in determined fights against crime and patterns of anti-Jewish and anti-Negro discrimination. Minneapolis adopted the country's first municipal fair employment practices commission. Mayor Humphrey was re-elected in 1947. Meanwhile, he achieved a union of the Democratic and Farmer-Labor parties, which provided him a strong base of support throughout his national political career.

In 1948, Humphrey ran successfully for the Senate, and quickly signaled his arrival on the national scene. At a generally desultory Democratic National Convention that assumed President Truman's defeat for re-election, Humphrey led the fight for a substitute platform plank committing the party to the adoption of Truman's civil-rights program. Humphrey sent some of the Southerners storming out of the convention and out of the party, and almost overnight won both the admiration and hatred of millions of persons. In the Senate, Humphrey reinforced his initial impression of militant liberalism. He flailed away at its ruling graybeards and at its hoary traditions, and in return found himself estranged from his colleagues and barred from any position of influence.

In sixteen years in the Senate, Humphrey modified his technique, if not his principles. The young liberal came to recognize the need for conciliation and compromise, and the need to labor within the framework offered by Senate rules and traditions. Curiously his tutor was a man only three years his senior who had entered the Senate in the same year—Lyndon Johnson. Johnson, who moved swiftly into a position of leadership, was not even on speaking terms with some of the Northern liberals. But Johnson recognized Humphrey as a man apart from the usual ideologue. Furthermore, they were both ardent New Dealers. The Texan undertook to make friends with Humphrey—never a difficult task—and to instruct him on how to get along with the Senate leaders, most of them conservative Southerners. In the short run Johnson needed at least occasional liberal support to achieve his legislative objectives, and Humphrey became the bridge to the liberals; but in the long run Johnson may have anticipated some grand design in which Humphrey might play a part.

Humphrey was one of the most open and forthright persons in American politics, and his merits and shortcomings as a public man were always visible for anyone to see. In his favor one could speak of his great energy—that above all else—his generosity, his missionary zeal, his creative thinking and legislative innovations, and his ability to skim a technical document or pick another's brains and to make use of what he had learned. But Humphrey was impulsive, glib, disorganized, and he talked too much. He was an undisciplined writer and speaker, stringing clichés like popcorn. He spent his energies in too many directions. Worst of all he was emotional. He would often laugh or cry or jump up and down. Robert Sherrill, a critical biographer, wrote in 1968: "He is still the friendly fat kid on the block."

A sympathetic biographer, Winthrop Griffith, explained what politics was for Humphrey: "work, years of it; fun, barrels of it; words, billions of them; paper, tons of it; miles, millions of them; and people—listening, demanding, denouncing, cheering, flattering, fawning, working, and voting. . . ."

And of course there were issues, maybe only dozens of them, but what issues! Medicare was his idea, sixteen years before it passed. So was the Food for Peace program. He introduced a bill to create a Peace Corps before John Kennedy picked up the idea. He was an early supporter of federal aid to education and of a nuclear test-ban treaty. He brilliantly managed the successful fight for the Civil Rights Act of 1964.

Communism was also an issue in all these years. And there could never be any doubt where Humphrey stood, despite the repeated charges of some Republican leaders. Humphrey always favored a firm stand against military and philosophical expansion from the Communist world. In 1947 he helped found the Americans for Democratic Action, a liberal anti-Communist organization designed to counter liberal sentiment forming behind Henry Wallace. In 1948 he was a leader in the fight to rout Communist elements seeking to gain control of the Minnesota Democratic Farmer-Labor party.

In 1954, with the Cold War still a fact of international life and with Vice President Nixon dusting off his "soft on communism" charges, Humphrey faced a re-election campaign. In August of that year, to the surprise of many, he introduced "A Bill to Outlaw the Communist Party." Some of the Senator's liberal friends were astounded. Many questioned the bill's legality. Even FBI Director J. Edgar Hoover felt that outlawing the party would merely drive it underground. But the members of the Senate embraced the bill, which passed by a vote of 84–0.

If, like Lyndon Johnson, Humphrey found success in the Senate, he shared Johnson's disappointment in the pursuit of delegates at the national conventions. In 1956, Johnson and Humphrey trailed badly in the balloting, respectively, for President and Vice President. Both were losers for the top office in 1960, Humphrey in a particularly cruel fashion. He was accused of being a draft dodger during World War II; and before the West Virginia primary, columnist Joseph Alsop called the Minnesota Senator, who was running against John Kennedy, the candidate of the bigots. Humphrey, beaten in both Wisconsin and West Virginia, and heavily in debt, must have been convinced that his chance for national office had ended. But then, with the death of Kennedy, came the new circumstances of 1964.

By the time the 1964 convention opened, dozens of political, academic, and labor leaders had pleaded Humphrey's cause in conversations with the President. No one else had so much support. As delegates gathered at Atlantic City, Humphrey discouraged his supporters from boosting him in public for fear that Johnson might feel pressured and might choose someone else, to reassert his own power. Before knowing he was the President's choice, Humphrey and several other persons undertook the hopeless task of reconciling a credentials dispute between rival black and white delegations from Mississippi. The solution—two blacks were seated as delegates and were promised reform in the choice of delegates to future conventions—satisfied nobody, but the quarrel did not jeopardize Humphrey's selection as Vice President.

Meanwhile, in Washington, Johnson, at the summit of his political power, was striding around the White House—some fifteen laps in all, with reporters panting along in the eighty-nine degree heat—expounding on his views on the Vice Presidency and what responsibilities the Vice President should accept. Johnson saw to it that Humphrey was informed of his thinking on the subject. The next Vice President was not to deviate from the President in public, he must not lobby for special interests, he must clear public speeches with the White House, and although debate on policy was permitted within the administration he must support decisions of the President once they were made.

Johnson then summoned Humphrey to the White House (Senator Thomas Dodd of Connecticut was invited along for the ride, to preserve the "suspense") and there the Minnesota Senator learned that he was indeed the anointed one. After a quick flight to Atlantic City, Johnson shattered a precedent by going before the delegates to—in effect—place Humphrey's name in nomination. In a rambling speech, he recited the qualifications he believed that a Vice President should possess. Finally, amid impatient groans and laughter, he named Humphrey as his choice. Humphrey, who had not yet been voted on, or even placed in nomination, marched out to the rostrum to receive the cheers of the crowd. The scrambled chronology of the proceedings didn't seem to bother anybody. When a President has achieved absolute control over a party, and almost total consensus within a party, he can afford to ignore the rules.

For Humphrey, the fall campaign was almost an anticlimax. Although he fired off some retorts, he generally brushed aside the vilification from the opposition with characteristic good humor. He drew the fire of Barry Goldwater, who tried to make his fellow Senator's full name sound sinister; his attacks on "Hubert Horatio Humphrey" drew a few laughs and fewer votes.

Johnson sent Humphrey into the hostile South, and the Minnesota man even managed to soften the hearts of a delegation of Houston millionaires. In Little Rock, on the home territory of Arkansas' segregationist Governor Orval Faubus, Humphrey revealed the disarming manner by which he had learned to turn aside wrath.

"We Democrats are a tumultuous lot," he said, smiling. "It isn't any secret that Governor Faubus and I have had some differences in the past. Mr. Dooley once saw his friend, Hennessey, shining up a set of brass knucks and asked where he was going. 'To a Democratic unity meeting,' Hennessey replied. 'I always go prepared.' "

For the time being, at least, that same Hennessey wouldn't recognize the Democratic party, which was, indeed, united in 1964. The unity was in large measure attributable to the extended emotional hangover from the Kennedy assassination. Alone among the eight accidental Presidents, Johnson had benefited greatly by a public sentiment, even a demand, that he be returned to office to carry to completion the work begun by his predecessor.

But even in victory the Democrats missed an opportunity. Had the 1964 Presidential contest been between Goldwater and John Kennedy, it is likely that the latter would have guided the debate along ideological lines with the object of meeting the conservatives head-on and disposing of their arguments once and for all. But Johnson, eager to win big to remove the last doubts as to his legitimacy, largely ducked serious discussion and preferred to conjure up among the voters grim thoughts of the consequences of electing Goldwater. Johnson said that American soldiers ought not to be sent to die in Asian wars.

Nineteen sixty-five was Lyndon Johnson's last good year—the year in which America saw briefly what the Great Society might have been—before the rip tides of Vietnam and urban violence and youthful unrest tore at the American psyche and threatened to loosen the nation from its traditional moorings. Johnson and Humphrey were inaugurated in January, joining a newly elected and lopsided Democratic majority in Congress. The President's major bills were swiftly enacted into law—a federal Department of Housing and Urban Development, the Voting Rights Act strengthening the Negro's power in the South, massive federal aid to education, medicare, and a billion dollars for impoverished Appalachia.

The new Vice President stepped into posts Johnson had held under Kennedy—chairman of the space council and of the Peace Corps advisory council. He was also assigned to oversee the co-ordination of federal efforts in the area of civil rights. He attended Cabinet and National Security Council meetings.

And Humphrey quickly assumed the role that he knew he must fulfill above all others—cheerleader for the President and all of his works. Said the man who had inspired more legislation of lasting importance than anyone else since World War II, "If I have some ideas, I give them to Lyndon Johnson. There's no Humphrey program, just the Johnson program. There are no Humphrey people, just Johnson people. And I'm one of them."

If "inside" reports from the administration are to be accepted, Johnson showed few kindnesses toward his Vice President and in fact Humphrey occasionally suffered the same verbal abuse received by other subordinates of Johnson. Humphrey, eager to please, redoubled his oratorical efforts in Johnson's behalf. Friends and supporters, as well as critics, thought Humphrey was abasing himself and said so, publicly and to Humphrey personally. But they would probably have been willing, in a charitable manner, to write off Humphrey's conduct as just another chapter in a life of verbosity had not the war in Vietnam begun to split the Democratic party.

Looking back on the tragic and irrational events that marked American politics in the 1960's, it is now hard to believe that for some time after Johnson's election in 1964 those who dabble in political speculation had little more to talk about than a Humphrey-Kennedy contest for President in 1972. In 1965, conventional wisdom, so grievously and frequently wrong in the years to come, forecast that Johnson and Humphrey would be returned to office in 1968 and that Humphrey and Bobby Kennedy would then fight it out for the 1972 nomination, with election probably assured for the victor. Perfunctory attention was given to the future of the Republican party after Goldwater, but such interest mainly centered on the question of who would control the wreckage. Theodore H. White's *The Making of the President, 1964,* published in 1965, carries the phrase, "When Johnson's Presidency ends in 1972. . . ." A year later the New York *Times* headlined an article about Humphrey and Kennedy "Front Runners for '72." Considering that a President had recently been slain and considering also that the urban landscape was being pockmarked with riots and the Asian landscape with bomb craters, it seems incredible that the pundits were charting the courses of American leaders so far in advance. It was the obedience of normally perceptive political leaders to the dictates of conventional wisdom that blinded them to the evidence that Johnson's world was collapsing around him, that Humphrey's attachment to Johnson's policies in Southeast Asia was damaging him seriously, and that Kennedy's opportunity might come earlier than 1972. Until almost the end of 1967, Humphrey versus Kennedy in '72 was just about the only show in town.

The limited United States military commitment to protect the South Vietnamese against Communist subversion began to expand rapidly after Lyndon Johnson became President. In 1964, after North Vietnamese torpedo boats reportedly fired on two United States destroyers, Congress passed, with only two Senators dissenting, the Gulf of Tonkin Resolution. It authorized the President "to take all necessary measures to repel any armed attack against the forces of the United States and to prevent further aggression." Three years later, Undersecretary of State Nicholas deB. Katzenbach called the resolution "the functional equivalent of a declaration of war," to the incredulity of many Congressmen who had voted for it.

In 1965, Johnson sank both fists into the tar baby. In February he initiated the bombing of North Vietnam. In July he increased American troop strength in Vietnam from 75,000 to 125,000, a major step down the road to an eventual force exceeding half a million. Escalations of the war in Vietnam were generally accompanied by assurances that "We seek no wider war," and the escalations themselves were represented as relatively painless, surgical, measured responses to Communist aggression. We could have both guns and butter, the President would say. Any suggestion that the war would be an inconvenience to the American people, let alone in time an intolerable burden, was dismissed.

Imagine then the President's anger when he learned of a speech that Vice President Humphrey had scheduled for delivery to the national governors' conference on July 27 in Minneapolis, the day before Johnson was to announce the troop increase. In the text of his speech as released to the press, Humphrey said that the announcement would bring the grief and anguish of war into thousands of American homes. He defended the move in an emotional, patriotic appeal for support. Johnson, at a briefing of congressional leaders and Cabinet members, rebuked the absent Vice President for creating undue alarm. Humphrey, learning of the President's anger, deleted the offending words before delivering his speech.

In 1971, the New York *Times* and other newspapers published excerpts from top-secret Pentagon documents revealing how the Johnson administration had floundered deeper and deeper into the Asian quagmire. Ted van Dyck, an adviser to Humphrey in the mid-1960's, said that in 1964 and 1965 the Vice President had opposed full-scale bombing of Vietnam and a buildup of American ground combat troops. This opposition was voiced at high-level Vietnam debates within the administration early in 1965. Van Dyck said that after Johnson began to put those policies into effect Humphrey was "systematically excluded" and "just plain frozen out" of Vietnam policy talks for nearly a year.

Professor John P. Roche wrote in 1971 that Humphrey's private disagreements with Johnson in 1964 and 1965 concerned tactics, not overall strategy. Roche drafted Humphrey's speeches during the critical year of 1965. He said that Humphrey doubted the efficacy of the bombing, but that the Vice President favored a firm U.S. role in Vietnam in order to contain Asian communism.

Publicly, Humphrey hewed religiously to the Johnson line on Vietnam—indeed he became more Catholic than the Pope. Seldom achieving the heights of an American Legion oratorical contest and often probing the depths of fatuity, Humphrey acclaimed Johnson as the greatest of the peacemakers, a sort of international sheriff, big iron on his hip, ready to pacify anyone daring to test America's power or will.

He put it this way on April 18, 1966: "We are not in Vietnam because of geography or who is in charge of a government. We are there because America has given a pledge to future generations to preserve law and order."

And on the very next day, "I think there is a tremendous new opening here for realizing the dream of the great society in the great area of Asia. . . ."

Always an optimist, Humphrey returned from a visit to Vietnam in 1966 and told Johnson, "the tide of battle in Vietnam has turned in our favor."

During another visit to Saigon in 1967, Humphrey characterized American involvement in Vietnam as "our great adventure and a wonderful one it is."

In February, 1966, Bobby Kennedy, now a Senator from New York, broke with the Johnson administration on the war. Johnson had been calling for a negotiated settlement, and Kennedy asserted, "To admit them [the Communists] to a share of power and responsibility is at the heart of the hope for a negotiated settlement. . . . It will require enormous skill and political wisdom to find the point at which participation does not bring domination or internal conquest."

Humphrey led the rebuttal, first with his famous remark that putting the Vietcong in the Saigon government was like "putting foxes in the hen house." He later elaborated on this theme, asserting that the Vietcong "engage in assassination, murder, pillage, conquest, and I can't for the life of me see why the United States of America would want to propose that such an outfit be made part of any government." Kennedy interpreted this to mean that the Vietcong were being asked to come to the negotiating table to surrender.

Johnson was forever sending emissaries abroad to explain or promote United States foreign policy, and Humphrey did his share of traveling. In foreign capitals he ran into opponents of the war. Members of the British Parliament questioned him sharply; demonstrators booed the Vice President in several cities. In Paris, President Charles de Gaulle told him that the United States would never win in Vietnam, that increased American military pressure would only make Hanoi more stubborn. Humphrey sought to overcome concern in the NATO nations that the European alliance was suffering because of American preoccupation with Asia. Visiting Vietnam early in 1966, during the period when an operative cliché in American policy was to "win the hearts and minds of the people," Humphrey publicly launched a U.S.-sponsored program of social, economic, and political reforms at the rice-roots level. A year later he represented the United States at the inauguration of General Nguyen Van Thieu as President of South Vietnam.

In fighting for humanitarian causes throughout the years, Humphrey has acquired numberless friends who had hoped to see him attain the Presidency. He could not understand why they now chorused, in effect, "Say it ain't so, Hubert." But support of the war was, after all, consistent with Humphrey's lifelong anticommunism. And there was his sense of duty to Johnson, his friend and patron of two decades and now his commander-in-chief. Humphrey found beyond comprehension any suggestion that he strike back at the man whose joy at being President had turned into deepening travail.

After leaving the Vice-Presidency, Humphrey spoke of another problem, the isolation of high office:

"Not only physical isolation, but you're isolated by a kind of network. . . . Your political education is directed toward one purpose—supporting Administration decisions. . . . Every morning, you start with those reports. From Security, C.I.A., State, Defense. And they're all full of information that buttresses a decision that's already been made. All that secret data in support of the policy that's already been made."

As we have seen, Humphrey did at one time oppose the bombing and the introduction of American ground combat troops, but on the basis of his public pronouncements it must be assumed that he swung solidly behind those escalations once they were put into effect. In 1966 and 1967, again according to former aide Ted van Dyck, his doubts revived. While in Saigon, the Vice President was shocked by information concerning widespread corruption within the South Vietnamese government. He warned President Nguyen Van Thieu in 1967 that domestic support for the war was wearing thin and that a reduction of the U.S. military role must begin. On his return to the United States he expressed this view to President Johnson as well.

If Kennedy or McCarthy had been Vice President in the late 1960's, either would have faced a serious decision. McCarthy said in 1968 that if he were Vice President he would remain silent on the war. Kennedy might have followed Garner's example and split openly with the President, perhaps running for President even while Vice President, as Garner did in 1940.

Late in 1967, Senator McCarthy decided to take the issue of the war to the people. He would run against Lyndon Johnson in selected Presidential primary elections in 1968. Humphrey sought to dissuade McCarthy, without success. Polls showed

McCarthy with little support nationwide, and his threat was discounted, though by now Johnson was considered vulnerable against the Republican nominee.

On November 29, the day before McCarthy announced that he would oppose the President, Robert McNamara said that he would soon step down as Secretary of Defense. Privately, he had become disillusioned about United States bombing policies and further escalation. At that time, his resignation was considered a straw in the wind, but perhaps no more. In Washington, public official optimism still prevailed. The enemy was resolute and tough, but would be defeated. Americans must persevere. They must stand firmly behind Lyndon Johnson, the only President they had. North Vietnam—whose troops had long since joined the guerrilla movement—could win only if the "nervous Nellies" in the United States undermined support for the war.

And then the calendar turned to 1968, the year the whole world watched.

On the night of January 29–30, while South Vietnam celebrated Tet, their New Year festival, the enemy forces struck. They attacked thirty provincial capitals and a number of United States and South Vietnamese airfields and bases, stormed the suburbs of Saigon, and even broke into the American embassy. The city of Hue was devastated. The attackers paid a terrible price, with tens of thousands reported killed. Lyndon Johnson and his advisers had been expecting a winter offensive by the enemy (Hubert Humphrey was not among those who had been briefed), and the President said it had been a "complete failure."

But the American people, watching the carnage on television, could not reconcile the ferocity of the enemy attacks with the assurances by their government that the war was being won. Tet robbed Johnson of the trust of his people. The holiday offensive was a great psychological victory for North Vietnam, in a war in which the Americans were measuring progress by meaningless "body counts" and "pacified villages."

During March the President and his policies came under insurmountable pressure from two sides. McCarthy ran nearly even with Johnson in New Hampshire and captured most of the delegates. Bobby Kennedy ended months of procrastination and declared his candidacy for President. Though the control of the party machinery seemed to assure Johnson's renomination, polls showed that the President would lose to McCarthy in the Wisconsin primary. The intensity of opposition to an incumbent President within his own party was virtually without precedent.

Simultaneously with the deterioration of the President's political support, General William Westmoreland, the United States commander in Vietnam, asked for 206,000 more American troops. Clark Clifford, reputedly a hawk, had succeeded McNamara as Secretary of Defense on March 1. But a careful review of both the military and domestic political implications of Westmoreland's request convinced Clifford that he must oppose further escalation. Also, Dean Rusk was now recommending a bombing pause. Meanwhile, Johnson asked a group of elder statesmen, including former Secretary of State Dean Acheson and retired General Omar Bradley, to make an independent determination of the situation in Vietnam. The group predominantly concluded that the President must halt the escalation and move to the conference table.

Johnson had already decided to address the public on Vietnam. His speech eventually passed through at least twelve drafts, becoming more dovish as pressures closed in on the President. In its final version the President announced a partial cessation of the bombing of the North. He declared his readiness to negotiate a settlement of the war.

And he concluded by saying that he would not seek nor accept another nomination from his party as President.

Thus collapsed Johnson's political career and the American effort to "win" the war in Vietnam on the field alone, without resorting to the conference table. The failure of the President and his policies sprang finally from the public's unwillingness to accept his explanation of what constituted vital American interests in Vietnam or what constituted an appropriate price to pay in blood and wealth. Aside from that the President had succumbed to a "credibility gap"—few people believed what he was telling them about the war, and few understood what it was all about beyond the tediously repeated slogans.

Three British journalists—Lewis Chester, Godfrey Hodgson, and Bruce Page—wrote in their outstanding study of the 1968 campaign, "The danger, for a nation as for an individual, comes when the gap between rhetoric and reality becomes too wide. In an individual, such a gap . . . is known as psychosis. A nation that indulges in too much self-glorifying rhetoric while unable to win a small war or to prevent deterioration in its social fabric is unlikely to be able to heal its real distempers."

Johnson was stepping down. But the war, and the rhetoric, would go on and on. At the end of March, 1968, American battle deaths stood at twenty thousand. They would more than double during the next three years.

Johnson had informed Hubert Humphrey of his plans to bow out. The Vice President had subsequently flown to Mexico City, where he heard the President's address on the radio at the American embassy. On his return to the United States, amid a chorus of pleas to declare his candidacy, Humphrey responded with unaccustomed caution. He had already been burned badly in Presidential politics. He had no effective organization of his own. His late entry into the primaries could bring humiliation at the hands of McCarthy or Kennedy. And he did not think it seemly to leap into the race immediately. He had to tell political leaders, under pressure from Kennedy, to hold off, that they wouldn't be sorry. They weren't. Humphrey had emerged as more than just the administration candidate, waving aloft Lyndon Johnson's tattered flag. He had constituencies of his own, created over almost a quarter-century of public service—the Negroes, the elderly, the workers. And now he had added the Southern and business establishments, for his rivals were criss-crossing the country not only stirring sentiment against the war but also challenging accepted values on a wide range of social and economic questions.

Humphrey's personal appeal had survived more than three frustrating years as Vice President. Polls at times showed him more popular than Johnson or Kennedy. If at times he seemed foolish, he could also demonstrate restraint and prudence. During two operations on Lyndon Johnson in 1965 and 1966, the powers and duties of the Presidency rested briefly with Humphrey, and the public could reflect on Humphrey as a potential President, either abruptly or by election. Now as a prospective candidate for the nomination he could count on the implicit support of the President, and whatever muscle the President could bring to bear on the party while he still sat in the White House. If all went well, Humphrey would have it both ways.

While benefiting from such support, he would not suffer from outright hatred that many persons directed at the President.

Humphrey suffered from a euphoria gap, however. A year like 1968 was no time for the Happy Warrior of American politics. It was more than just Vietnam. On April 4, Humphrey, still not a candidate officially, spoke out against "doubt and despair" and "those who would sell America short." Within hours Dr. Martin Luther King was assassinated. Weeks earlier the President's National Advisory Commission on Civil Disorders—the Kerner commission—had warned that the United States "is moving toward two societies, one black, one white—separate and unequal." The report blamed "white racism" for the black American's frustration and hostility. In the wake of Dr. King's death black America's anger welled over again. Rioting, looting, and burning swept cities from coast to coast, and left 46 dead, 2,600 injured, and property damage totaling forty-five million dollars in 125 cities. Middle America, in turn, hardened its attitude toward radicalism and unrest, and Humphrey, despite his use of the phrase in reference to Vietnam, did not come across as a "law and order" candidate.

In these charged circumstances, Humphrey declared himself a candidate for President on April 27. "Here we are," he bubbled, "just as we ought to be, the people, here we are, in a spirit of dedication, here we are, the way politics ought to be in America, the politics of happiness, the politics of purpose, and the politics of joy. And that's the way it's going to be, all the way, from here on in!"

The speech was otherwise a familiar recital of Establishment liberalism's visions for a better world for mankind. But events were soon to drain away the joy in Humphrey's soul. The strain of so many years of political jousting, of so many battles won and lost, had already taken their toll on the fifty-seven-year-old candidate. He was tired now and so were his ideas.

Humphrey and his staff began to seek a means of putting daylight between the candidate and Lyndon Johnson on Vietnam without losing the President's endorsement. Averell Harriman, chief U.S. negotiator at the Paris peace talks, which had opened in May, advised Humphrey that his statements on Vietnam would be taken as those of the administration, and Humphrey accordingly limited his references to Vietnam during the pre-convention period. Unqualified praise for the American effort gave way to implications that things would be different in the future. "Hubert Humphrey as Vice-President is a member of the team," he said in June. "Hubert Humphrey as President is captain of a team—there's a lot of difference." Some advisers thought he should burn his bridges with Johnson by resigning as Vice President. Humphrey recognized that a major step in his disengagement from Johnson would occur with his nomination for the Presidency, and in pursuit of that goal he conducted a cautious campaign, focusing on expressions of hope for an early peace with reproaches to the other Democratic contenders; he told them, "you do yourself, your party, and your President and your country a disservice by constantly downgrading your President, your party, and your country." Within weeks of his declaration of candidacy Humphrey seemed close to the nomination. The Southern conservatives and the Northern labor leaders were delivering a harvest of delegates.

On June 5, Senator Kennedy was shot fatally after claiming victory in the California primary. The tragedy at once moved Humphrey closer to the nomination and further from the Presidency. The Vice President said, after the election was over, that he would have won the nomination in any event, but that a defeated Kennedy, a professional and a loyal Democrat, would have quickly rallied his disappointed supporters behind Humphrey against the Republican candidate. But Kennedy's death so poisoned the atmosphere in the Democratic party that the nomination was worth less to the winner.

The "politics of joy" died with Kennedy, and were to be revived for Humphrey only fitfully thereafter. When in August Humphrey suggested that he and Kennedy had held remarkably similar views on Vietnam, four of the late Senator's supporters publicly rebuked the Vice President. They pointed out that Kennedy had said the United States must accept the principle of participation by the Vietcong in any future South Vietnamese regime, which Humphrey had dismissed as "putting foxes in the hen house."

Aside from the question of a coalition government in Saigon, debate within the Democratic party focused on the continued bombing of North Vietnam—only partly suspended by Johnson in March. The bombing of the North, which had begun in 1965, may be remembered as one of mankind's most destructive and futile exercises. The bombing was supposed to boost Saigon's morale, break the will of the Hanoi regime, stop the flow of military supplies to the South, and extract substantive concessions at the conference table. None of these goals, with the exception of the first, was accomplished during Johnson's Presidency.

The "stop the bombing" issue was carried before the delegates to the Democratic National Convention in the form of a minority report from the platform committee. Humphrey had urged the President to stop all the bombing. But the Vice President, whose prospective nomination for President could still come undone should Lyndon Johnson withdraw his support, was in no position to endorse publicly the minority report, or to suggest any acceptable compromise. The Republican nominee, Richard Nixon, paid a courtesy call on Johnson, and on leaving the meeting said that the bombings must go on. Could Humphrey dare break with the President? He could not. The minority report was rejected. Opponents of the war were so embittered by the heavy hand being wielded behind the scenes by the President that they talked of putting Johnson's name in nomination themselves, with the additional thought that the move might sidetrack Humphrey's drive. Senator McCarthy's speech writer Richard Goodwin cracked, "Why take the dummy when you can get the ventriloquist himself?"

With McCarthy the only strong rival still in the field, Humphrey moved steadily toward what should have been the high point in his political career. But a pervasive ugliness was settling over the convention and over the city of Chicago. Thousands of demonstrators, mostly young, had poured into the city. They ran the gamut from conscientious and generally disciplined supporters of McCarthy to an extreme fringe of hippies and Yippies. Overreacting, Mayor Richard Daley and President Johnson's agents on the scene—the President dared not attend the convention himself—had turned the convention into an armed camp. Barbed wire looped around the hall. Policemen, FBI agents, and private security men were everywhere. Delegates were obliged to get their plastic passes electronically validated every time they entered the hall. Reporters and antiwar delegates were assaulted and arrested on the convention floor without justification. Downtown, the throngs of demonstrators, denied a permit to march on the convention hall, clashed repeatedly with policemen. National Guardsmen and regular Army troops stood ready to enter the fray if needed.

What happened in the streets of Chicago during convention week was described three months later in a special report to the National Commission on the Causes and Prevention of Violence. The panel placed the principal blame for the violence on what it called a "police riot." The report condemned "unrestrained and indiscriminate police violence . . . often inflicted upon persons who had broken no law, disobeyed no order, made no threat." Sixty-three reporters and photographers were among those assaulted by the police.

Hubert Humphrey watched the clubbing and listened to the screaming from his twenty-fifth-floor suite in the Conrad Hilton Hotel. Finally, his eyes and skin irritated by the tear gas seeping through the window, he retreated to the bathroom and took a shower.

McCarthy's headquarters, also situated in the Hilton, were the object of a police raid. Convinced that objects were being thrown at them from McCarthy's suite—there was no evidence that they were—the police stormed the suite and beat the defenseless occupants without mercy and in the absence of any resistance. Richard Goodwin's assertion that the Vice President and Senator McCarthy were on their way to the suite subdued the police somewhat. In fact, Humphrey never got there; he was asleep and an aide refused to waken him. McCarthy arrived, and his shock at the bloodshed virtually foreclosed any hope that he could support the election of Hubert Humphrey, at least at any early date in the campaign. A few days after the convention, Humphrey declared: "It's time to quit pretending that Daley has done anything wrong."

Humphrey's conduct at the convention can be explained, though not excused, on several grounds. He was "only" the Vice President of the United States, powerless to give any official orders to anybody. He was dependent for the greatest honor of his life on a President of towering wrath who could destroy him with a single expletive. He was apparently unable to appreciate how deeply a generation had been wounded by war, assassination, and other violence. And he was oriented toward an antique style of politics that he had known all his life and that in the steamy turbulence of Chicago in 1968 was prevailing for perhaps the last time in America.

Humphrey's nomination for President—he received two-thirds of the total convention vote—was anticlimactic. He was the second incumbent Vice President since 1836 to receive a Presidential nomination, and like Richard Nixon in 1960 he would be the second to lose.

From the gloom of Chicago, two hopeful portents emerged for the Democrats. First, the delegates approved a series of reforms that opened the delegate-selection process to wider public participation in the future with accompanying guarantees that minority points of view within a state or local caucus or convention would be reflected proportionally. Second, Humphrey chose a Vice-Presidential nominee of more than routine interest.

Nelson Rockefeller was, apparently, Humphrey's first choice for the Vice Presidency. Rumors dating from 1968 that Humphrey had looked with favor on the New York Republican Governor as a running mate were confirmed by Rockefeller in 1971. He said he had received inquiries from a Humphrey representative and from Humphrey himself. Rockefeller did not receive a firm offer of the nomination. He said in 1971 that he had not considered the approaches seriously. An unidentified aide of Humphrey said in 1971 that in considering Rockefeller, Humphrey was looking for "a dramatic way of uniting the country."

Although there was no shortage of possibilities within the Democratic party, two of its most prominent figures were unavailable. Senator Ted Kennedy had, for several reasons, taken his name out of consideration for the Presidential nomination that his brother had died seeking. He showed no desire to be projected into the Vice-Presidential picture either. Senator McCarthy, the choice of more than 600 delegates for the Presidential nomination, refused to be considered, primarily because he was not prepared to endorse Humphrey for President even after his nomination. Had McCarthy's peace plank been approved, reconciliation would have been possible.

The U.S. Constitution does not, as some people suppose, prohibit two persons from the same state from serving as President and Vice President at the same time. In the situation at hand, it would prohibit the ten Presidential electors from Minnesota, assuming the Democratic ticket carried the state, from voting for both Humphrey for President and McCarthy for Vice President. If such a ticket won the national election by an electoral margin of ten votes or less, the Vice-Presidential nominee might have to be sacrificed. Another deterrent to the formation of such a ticket is the assumption that many voters in the other states would not approve the idea of two nominees from the same state. Such an assumption has never been tested.

Among Democrats receptive to the nomination, the choice narrowed in Humphrey's mind to Senators Edmund S. Muskie of Maine and Fred Harris of Oklahoma. Harris, at thirty-seven, was presumed to be a candidate who would appeal to youth. He had won recognition as a hard-working moderate liberal during four years in the Senate. But when Humphrey was asked which man he would prefer to see take the President's place in an emergency, he chose Muskie. Humphrey later added, "I went for the quiet man. I know I talk too much, and I wanted someone who makes for a contrast in styles."

Stephen Marciszewski, Senator Muskie's father, fled Poland in 1903 to escape conscription in the Czar's army. In the United States, he married a Buffalo, New York, girl, and they settled in Rumford, Maine. Edmund, a quiet and happy boy, experienced but was not particularly troubled by instances of anti-Catholic and anti-Polish prejudice. After winning membership in Phi Beta Kappa at Bates College, he graduated from Cornell University Law School and began practice in Waterville, Maine.

After service on U.S. Navy destroyer escorts during World War II, Muskie returned to the law, but soon won election to the Maine House of Representatives, where he became the Democratic floor leader. Muskie moved to the fore in the relatively weak and leaderless Democratic party in Maine, and was awarded with a gubernatorial nomination in 1954. Traveling twenty thousand miles and coming across effectively both in person and on the new medium of television, Muskie upset the Republican incumbent by a good margin. As Governor, he focused primarily on improving Maine's economic plight, and he won passage for most of his program in a legislature dominated by Republicans.

In 1958, Muskie unseated another Republican incumbent to win election to the U.S. Senate, the first Maine Democrat ever to go to the Senate by popular vote. Senator Muskie quickly established his independence by refusing to support a move by Majority Leader Lyndon Johnson to uphold the filibuster rule. As a result, Muskie got none of his requested committee assignments. Frustrated, he set out to make the best of his Senate career; he impressed his colleagues by hard work, and moved almost by default into the field of air and water pollution. With the luck or instinct or good judgment of the successful politician, he took up the issue that would soon stir the nation. Muskie became recognized as one of the handful of environmental experts in Congress.

In 1968, Democrats naturally hoped that Muskie's demeanor and low-key humor would attract supporters of Senator McCarthy. Doubtless this proved true, though Muskie had an ambiguous record on Vietnam. At the Chicago convention he spoke for the majority plank rejecting a bombing halt as a unilateral gesture by the United States. Yet during the campaign it was learned that he had written to President Johnson in January, 1968, urging him to stop the bombing without conditions. Only after the inauguration of Richard Nixon did Muskie pass the new litmus test for the doves by calling for a fixed early date for the withdrawal of all U.S. troops in Vietnam.

Muskie proved an asset in the fall campaign in another way that Humphrey had perhaps anticipated. The Republican Vice-Presidential candidate, Spiro Agnew, had been nominated first, and his record in government did not seem to be one to inspire confidence. As the campaign progressed Agnew's several verbal bobbles reinforced such a judgment. Muskie, six feet four inches and Lincolnesque, with a face projecting craggy honesty, a man who recoiled from the familiar catchwords and who was slow to speak, instilled trust in the voters. Some observers argued that Muskie appeared strong only because the other national candidates were so unimpressive. One technique that won friends for Muskie was his response to antiwar hecklers; when they tried to disrupt his speeches, he invited them to take the microphone and say their piece.

Humphrey, meanwhile, suffered from the woes of the office Muskie wanted. Prospects had vanished that the Vice President could run with all the advantages that the administration could provide while avoiding direct identification with Johnson's policy in Vietnam. In fact, Humphrey got only mild support from Lyndon Johnson, and was tagged by Richard Nixon as the willing inheritor of tired and discredited policies. Nixon, no dove, refused to discuss Vietnam in detail, alleging he might thereby jeopardize the Paris peace talks.

Johnson, remaining aloof during the early fall, remarked that he wanted to be fair to both Humphrey and Nixon. Speculation began that he would not be too disappointed by a Nixon victory. That seemed likely, for in the wake of the Chicago debacle Humphrey tumbled fifteen percentage points behind Nixon in the Gallup Poll and was running only seven points ahead of the independent candidate for President, George Wallace of Alabama. The Democratic campaign began disastrously. Humphrey's scheduling was inept. His personal staff had never been first-rate, and the late convention—originally planned to coincide with Johnson's sixtieth birthday—had left little time to organize for the campaign. Humphrey was heckled at almost every public appearance, money was in short supply, and McCarthy was refusing his endorsement.

To have the remotest hope of winning, Humphrey must signal a new course in Vietnam. Two years later, he recalled his dilemma in an interview quoted in the New York *Times*: "I had a President who was absolutely paranoid about the war . . . you've got to remember he had two sons-in-law who were over there. Why, anybody who said the *sllli*ghtest thing to him about change in Vietnam, why, my Lord. . . ." (Still later, Humphrey conceded that paranoid was "not the right word.")

In September, 1968, Humphrey told Johnson that he had a task force working on Vietnam. "Why you wouldn't have believed it. I've never in my life seen a man act that way. And that was just a task force."

A few days after Humphrey talked publicly about reducing the number of troops in Vietnam, Johnson told an American Legion convention that any such talk was irresponsible.

On September 30, Humphrey finally moved beyond the Johnson position on Vietnam, hesitant though his step was.

Convinced that the stand he was taking was not only right but essential to his campaign, he declared in a nationwide telecast from Salt Lake City, "As President, I would be willing to stop the bombing of North Vietnam as an acceptable risk for peace. . . ." He said he would reserve the right to resume the bombing in the absence of some reciprocal action by the North Vietnamese forces. He promised to begin "de-Americanization" of the war. Symbolically, the Vice-Presidential seal and flag were missing from the lectern.

The hecklers fell silent, and indeed started pursuing Nixon. The telecast brought in $250,000 in contributions. Humphrey began to gain ground rapidly in the polls, making the steepest advance ever registered by a candidate in the last weeks of a Presidential campaign. Before long, Humphrey even had Lyndon Johnson's and Eugene McCarthy's endorsements.

The most traumatic Presidential election of the century ended in appropriate fashion. Lyndon Johnson told the nation on October 31 that he had halted the bombing of North Vietnam completely. The North Vietnamese had agreed to admit the South Vietnamese to the conference table. Was the agreement only a contrivance by the President—a final grab at the peace mantle and a boost for Humphrey? The diplomatic maneuvering involving the Soviet Union and other countries that preceded the apparent settlement precluded such a simple explanation. In any event the political benefit for the Democrats faded the next day when the South Vietnamese cabinet and legislative assembly refused to be bound by an agreement made secretly by their president, Nguyen Van Thieu. Thieu was obliged to renege on his commitment. The Vietnamese were not above speculating in political futures. Eleven South Vietnamese senators now endorsed Richard Nixon for President. On this inane note the U.S. political campaign ended.

The voting was nearly a replay of 1960. But Richard Nixon stepped in to pick up an extra state here and there—Illinois in the Midwest, New Jersey in the East—and he won. Hubert Humphrey joined the long list of Vice Presidents who had failed to move by election directly to the highest office. On leaving public life—temporarily, as it turned out—he was, at least, a household word many times over. His successor was not that, and said so himself.

★ ★ ★ ★ ★
★ ★ ★ ★ ★
★ ★ ★ ★ ★
★ ★

SPIRO AGNEW

"... *not exactly the exercise of raw power.*"

In 1968, the year of the unexpected, the return of Richard Nixon was a surprise second to none. After leaving the Vice Presidency, he had lost a race for Governor of California. He had then moved to New York, and joined a prestigious law firm. Nixon was universally regarded as finished in politics. But like the grandmother hiding behind the chinaberry tree on Tobacco Road, Nixon was not far away, constantly observing the ebb and flow of politics and the rise and fall of others' fortunes, occasionally in view and then often taken lightly or even ignored, biding his time. In 1964 he tossed out a few remarks to the effect that the Republicans could do better than nominate Goldwater for President; but Nixon was not a candidate when the convention met. However, he stumped vigorously for Goldwater while many Republicans sat on their hands. He campaigned again in 1966, when the Republicans gained almost fifty seats in the U.S. House of Representatives. Through his good works for the party, by his ability to position himself in the middle of the Republican ideological spectrum, and his ability to seize the right issue and mine it for all the votes it had, and through indefatigable energy, Nixon reemerged as the leading contender for the 1968 nomination. He was chosen on the first ballot at the Republican convention at Miami Beach.

The year 1968 marked the only time other than 1800 (Adams against Jefferson) that each major party nominated a man who had been Vice President of the United States. But by 1800, Adams had already served four years as President.

Nixon's choice for a running mate seemed incredible to the public, and to many professional politicians as well, but within his own careful definition of the kind of man he was looking for, his choice was plausible and indeed almost inevitable.

In the fall campaign Nixon would face a Democratic party that, while divided, was not beaten. George Wallace was also in the field, competing with Nixon for the vote of those dissatisfied with the way the country was headed. Wallace, courting antiblack and antiestablishment sentiment, would run strongly in the South and compete with Nixon and Humphrey for the Border states.

To win the election, Nixon had to prevent Wallace from winning any states outside the Deep South while carrying most of the West, Midwest, and Border states. Unlike the 1960 election, which was a two-way contest, Nixon could not safely move even to the moderate left for a running mate because he had to guard against the Wallace threat from the right.

Nixon's party, though nominally united, had given almost half of its convention votes to the liberal and conservative favorites, Governors Nelson Rockefeller of New York and Ronald Reagan of California. Nixon wished to straddle the ideological gap within the party and to avoid a Vice-Presidential running mate who would appear to shift the balance in either direction. Before the convention Nixon wrote to three hundred party leaders, soliciting their opinions on who would make the best running mate.

When he arrived at the convention Nixon found that his own nearly certain nomination could yet come unstuck. Some of the Southern delegates, more disposed to Reagan, both ideologically and personally, than to Nixon, were considering shifting from Nixon to Reagan, who had declared his candidacy on the first day of the convention. Senator Strom Thurmond of South Carolina, a Republican for only four years but already a kingmaker, was in Nixon's camp, and he repeatedly assured his Dixie colleagues that Nixon was safe on the issues and on the Vice Presidency. In June, as a price for his support, Thurmond had extracted a pledge from Nixon for a strong national defense establishment. At Miami, Thurmond informed Nixon that much of the South was ready to go for Reagan, and he secured further assurances from Nixon that as President he would give the South some latitude in coming to grips with school integration. Nixon also assured Thurmond that the Vice-Presidential nominee would be acceptable to all sections of the party.

Thurmond held the Southerners in line, and Nixon won the nomination. In the twelve hours or so after his victory, Nixon met with four groups of party leaders, two in the early morning hours, and two later in the morning after the candidate had slept for a few hours. The leaders chosen to attend the meetings were carefully divided between conservatives and liberals with the evident expectation that they would take turns shooting down potential Vice Presidents identified with the opposite faction. The conservatives rejected New York Mayor John Lindsay, Oregon Senator Mark Hatfield, and others. The liberals said that a running mate like Reagan would bring disaster to the ticket in the Northeast. Nixon particularly disparaged "glamour boys," candidates who might outshine himself and who might cost the ticket as many votes in one segment of the population as they added in another.

While the liberals and conservatives expended their verbal ammunition on each other, the names of Governors Spiro Agnew of Maryland and John Volpe of Massachusetts moved gradually to the fore, with Nixon channeling the conversation in their direction. He suggested it might be wise to choose a Governor, one who could galvanize the other Governors, mostly liberals, into working for the ticket. And the man they were seeking should know something about the cities. And perhaps his selection should be geared to the middle-class ethnic vote, to the laboring men and women shaken by racial violence and the pace of social change. Agnew and Volpe met the ethnic qualification, as would Edmund Muskie, the Democratic Vice-Presidential nominee. Neither Agnew nor Volpe had any public identification to speak of—for that matter they were not well known within the party, particularly Agnew, who had been Governor only eighteen months. In retrospect it appears that from the start Nixon was maneuvering his advisers toward an Agnew candidacy. He probably had tentatively settled on Agnew even before arriving in Miami Beach.

After his meetings with party leaders, Nixon had Texas Senator John Tower phone Thurmond and ask the South Carolinian whom he would prefer between Volpe and Agnew. Not surprisingly, Thurmond chose the Border-state man rather than the New Englander. Thurmond could believe that he had participated in the final decision. Nixon said later that the choice between Volpe and Agnew was "very, very close." One factor that might have been decisive: Volpe had lost control of his own delegation to Rockefeller in the Massachusetts primary. But Agnew, who had once favored Rockefeller for President, switched to Nixon and brought most of his delegation with him.

Spiro Agnew's father, Theodore Spiro Anagnostopoulos, came to the United States from Greece in 1897. Settling in Schenectady, New York, and knowing little English, he had difficulty getting a job until a friend took the immigrant into his barber shop. Anagnostopoulos next opened a restaurant, then moved to Baltimore and opened a larger one. He went to court to change his name legally. He married one of his patrons, a widow with one son. Their second son, Spiro Theodore Agnew, was born in 1918.

Agnew was tall and thin as a boy—he was six feet at the age of thirteen—and shy. He was an average student. The Depression struck a cruel blow to the Agnew family; the restaurant folded, and Spiro's father sold produce door to door. When the bad times eased he opened another restaurant and saved enough to send young Spiro to college. The latter entered Johns Hopkins and studied chemistry for three years, then dropped out. He went to work at the Maryland Casualty Company, where he met his future wife, and began night courses at the Baltimore Law School. During World War II Agnew served as a company commander in the Tenth Armored Division and saw action at Bastogne.

Returning to law school, he completed his studies in 1947, and was eager to embark on a career that would support his growing family, which eventually included four children. He was twenty-eight by now, and not for some years would he square away his professional life. The next few years were a blur of jobs—clerk in a law firm, a brief and unsuccessful attempt to practice law on his own, claims adjuster for an insurance company, a second tour of Army duty during the Korean War, assistant personnel director for a grocery chain, assistant to a leading Baltimore attorney, researcher for the court of appeals rules committee, and finally another go at law practice. He was named legal counsel for a local of the Amalgamated Meat Cutters and Butcher Workmen of North America.

The Agnews moved to Towson, Maryland, north of Baltimore. Agnew began to make the moves that carried him to a higher office than that achieved by any other resident of America's newest and largest subculture, suburbia. The Agnews touched all bases—membership in the country club, the Kiwanis, the Inter-Community Association, and the PTA.

In 1957, after doing some volunteer work for the Republican party, Agnew won the support of party leaders for appointment to the zoning board of appeals for Baltimore County—which does not include the city of Baltimore. Agnew took his job seriously. In the rapidly growing suburbs, millions of dollars were involved in the requests for zoning variances. He asked so many questions embarrassing to the Democrats on the board that they blocked his reappointment in 1961. That was a mistake. In the following year, Agnew ran on a reform ticket for County Executive of Baltimore County, a position roughly that of a suburban mayor. Profiting from a Democratic factional fight, as he would in 1966 and on the national scene in 1968, Agnew was elected. Despite the defeat of his urban renewal plans, Agnew made a progressive record in those matters near and dear to suburbanites everywhere—new schools, higher teacher salaries, improved sewage systems, and so forth.

Agnew next looked to the governorship. Few Republicans thought their party had a chance to win the office, so Agnew breezed to the nomination. In the Democratic party, candidates of stature so divided the vote that the nomination fell to an elderly eccentric and perennial candidate named George Mahoney. He won the primary by opposing open housing and by use of the slogan "Your Home is Your Castle—Protect It." Liberal Democrats deserted him by the tens of thousands. Agnew swept to an easy victory.

During the campaign Agnew said frankly that it would be necessary to raise taxes. The Legislature, Democratic-controlled, gave him the increase and general fiscal reform. Agnew also won passage for a strong water pollution act and a liberalized abortion act. He led the fight for a new state constitution, but the draft document was rejected by the voters.

In the broad field of race relations, Agnew's first year in office was notable. He supported repeal of the three-centuries'-old state law banning mixed marriages. The first state open housing law south of the Mason and Dixon line was enacted. The state public accommodations law was made to conform with Federal legislation. He appointed blacks to state offices and judicial posts.

Throughout the 1960's most Republican Governors were in the moderate-to-liberal camp. Nelson Rockefeller, the dominant figure among Republican Governors, usually could count on wide support among them when thoughts turned to Presidential politics. In early 1968 Agnew became a national leader of the draft Rockefeller campaign. He professed confidence that the New Yorker would get into the fight for the Presidential nomination. But Rockefeller's private inquiries and polls showed that he faced an uphill fight against Nixon. He called a press conference for March 21 to announce what he would do. The decision was negative, but an aide neglected to notify Agnew, who called his own press conference to watch Rockefeller on television. Agnew was acutely embarrassed when Rockefeller took himself out of the race. Six weeks later, after the turbulent events of late March and April, Rockefeller changed his mind and entered the race. But it was too late to retain Agnew's support.

Meanwhile, events conspired to drive Agnew into a more conservative stance. Bowie State College, at Bowie, Maryland, was a dilapidated school with a predominantly black enrollment. In late March students complaining about the school's physical plant and demanding courses in black history seized and occupied several campus buildings. A few days later they decided to complain directly to the Governor. More than two hundred students jammed into the state capitol building on April 4. When they refused to leave at five o'clock, Agnew ordered all of them arrested. He said they were breaking the law, and rejected claims that they were exercising their constitutional rights of free speech and assembly. Liberals criticized Agnew's handling of the students.

Then, within hours of the mass arrests, Dr. Martin Luther King was assassinated in Memphis, and relations between

Agnew and the blacks were ruptured beyond repair. Riots swept Baltimore and nearby Washington, D.C. Whole blocks went up in flames, and people were killed. Agnew called out the National Guard. The Governor, having felt that he had done much for the black community—and doubtless unable to shake the conviction that minority groups ought to advance nonviolently as his own had done—seems to have taken the outbursts as a personal slap in the face, though the violence was nationwide. Although responsible blacks worked to cool the ghettos, Agnew felt that many of these leaders, who had been among his supporters, had failed him. His reaction was pure Agnew.

He summoned some one hundred black moderate leaders to his Baltimore office. The television cameras were present. He read a prepared speech that he had written. He noted that his guests did not include the "Hanoi-visiting . . . caterwauling, riot-inciting, burn-America-down type of leader." But then Agnew asserted that the moderates had been under pressure from black militants with "a perverted concept of race loyalty."

The Governor drove home his main point: "And you ran. . . . You would not openly criticize any black spokesman regardless of the content of his remarks. . . . You were intimidated by veiled threats; you were stung by accusations that you were 'Mr. Charlie's boy,' by epithets like 'Uncle Tom.' " Agnew praised the moderate leadership of Dr. King, Roy Wilkins, and Whitney Young. He repudiated extremism right and left, black and white. He challenged his auditors to do likewise—many of them already had, of course.

Agnew was moving toward an eloquent, conciliatory conclusion, but more than half of the blacks had walked out on him. "Together we must work first to prevent polarization and second to reduce tension. I will need your vision and your voice. Now as never before your articulate, responsible leadership is needed. I am prepared to do whatever I can to aid the innocent victims of last week's rampage, to alleviate clear abuses and to enlarge opportunity within the inner city. . . . So let us begin to rebuild the image of Baltimore. Let us work together—not as black and white—but as responsible citizens of Maryland who uphold the law; as concerned citizens who are united in their dedication to eliminate prejudice and poverty and any conditions which create hopelessness and despair."

Blacks remembered only the harsh words Agnew had spoken. They criticized him sharply: "He talked to us like we were children" and "He's as sick as any bigot in America." The speech finished him with the blacks. Whites largely supported him. From that point on the Governor often spoke out against civil disobedience and "permissiveness." Later, Agnew's speech of April 11 would be compared with the way Calvin Coolidge handled the Boston police strike of 1919, which made Coolidge a national figure and elevated him to the Vice Presidency.

By coincidence Agnew had met with Richard Nixon late in March in New York. Doubtless Nixon saw much of himself in Agnew—a child of the Depression, struggling upward from humble beginnings, law student, veteran, devoted family man, hard worker, party loyalist, underdog candidate. Doubtless too he was impressed by Agnew's composure, reinforced by his meticulous grooming—the *Men's Hairstylist and Barber's Journal* put the Governor on its best-groomed list—and his ability to discuss superficially the problems of the states and cities. After their meeting of March 29 Agnew said he was not ready to endorse Nixon, but that he had a high regard for him. After dinner with Agnew in Annapolis in July, Nixon remarked to an aide, "That guy Agnew is really an impressive fellow. He's got guts. He's got a good attitude." Nixon did not know Agnew well before the 1968 convention and had not the time to probe his mind for whatever substance it contained.

On the opening day of the 1968 Republican convention, Agnew publicly endorsed Nixon for President. The latter had already asked the Maryland Governor to place his name in nomination. When Agnew's moment came, on the evening of August 7, no one supposed he would be back for an encore the very next night. His speech for Nixon was in the great tradition of nominating orations—stupefying. It was delivered in Agnew's flat, deadly monotone.

After Nixon's nomination that night, Agnew and his family began to look forward to a vacation. They were preparing to leave Miami when, shortly after noon the next day, Agnew's hotel phone rang. He took the call, from Nixon. A minute later, he turned to Judy, his wife, and said, "I'm it."

Nixon then announced his choice at a press conference. Expressions of shock and disbelief swept the room. "Spiro who?"

was the question asked everywhere. Nixon exited without taking any questions. Agnew came on. He conceded that his name was not a household word, but he hoped that it would be in the next few months. He defended his record in civil rights, and said that such rights could not be achieved without the preservation of order.

Seldom is a Presidential nominee's choice for a running mate seriously contested on the convention floor. Agnew's nomination was challenged, without any hope of success, simply because beneath the façade of unity and Nixon's bland leadership there was a wing of the party that reached out toward the poor and underprivileged with a compassion that they felt Agnew did not possess. Mayor John Lindsay was a logical rallying point for the dissidents but he had agreed to second Agnew's nomination—a decision he later regretted (though not because he wanted the Vice Presidency). Governor George Romney agreed to the use of his name against Agnew. The Maryland Governor received 1,119 votes to Romney's 186, with 28 votes scattered or not cast. Agnew, accepting the nomination, said, "I stand here with a deep sense of the improbability of this moment."

Just after the convention, Nixon spoke again about Agnew: "You look a man in the eye and you know he's got it. . . . This guy has got it. If he doesn't, Nixon has made a bum choice." One experienced Republican leader who observed Agnew closely felt that Nixon had simply been fooled. He believed that Nixon, with his "vacuum-cleaner mind," had probably extracted Agnew's few original ideas in their two or three pre-convention meetings "and thought there might be more in the pipeline. He couldn't have been more mistaken."

Whatever they thought Agnew had, Nixon and his advisers recognized that they were working with a relative political amateur. They recalled how Nixon's 1960 partner, Henry Cabot Lodge, had involved Nixon in the issue of putting a Negro in the Cabinet. So Agnew received a quick course in press relations. Mock press conferences were set up, with the "reporters" firing questions at the nominee, first easy ones, then toughies. With practice, Agnew trimmed five-minute answers to ninety seconds.

Agnew was soon put to the test. Talking to reporters (real ones) on September 10, he accused Hubert Humphrey of being "squishy soft . . . soft on inflation, soft on Communism and soft on law and order. . . ." A tall charge against the man who had introduced the Communist Control Act of 1954. The Democrats responded with a sort of jubilant indignation, likening Agnew to the late Senator Joseph McCarthy. Nixon, not about to yield the spotlight to his running mate, sent one of his own speech writers to the Agnew operation. Agnew ate humble pie: "Had I realized what an effect this phrase would have, I would have avoided it like the plague. If I'd known I'd be cast as the Joe McCarthy of 1968 I would have turned five somersaults. I said 'squishy soft' and I'm not proud of it."

Would Agnew become the Barry Goldwater of 1968, one blooper following another? He would. In the process, he got something less than a fair shake from the reporters. Although some of his remarks showed an insensitivity based on a lack of understanding of the issues and inexperience as a politician—reasons enough to question his qualifications as a national candidate—he was not the cruel person so often painted in the press. Asked why he wasn't carrying his campaign into more ghetto areas, he replied: "When you've seen one slum, you've seen them all." The statement is distressingly true. In the core of almost any major city one will see the blighted faces of the children, the drug pushers, the rubbish, the poverty. The question to be answered was whether the Republicans would address themselves to America's urban problems. It was not answered to the satisfaction of many, either during the campaign or afterward.

Ethnic references plagued Agnew. At a news conference on September 13, he replied to a question concerning minority groups, "When I look out at a crowd, I don't see there a Negro, there an Italian, there a Polack." And eight days later, seeing a reporter whom he knew dozing on his plane, he asked, "What's the matter with the fat Jap?" Gene Oishi of the Baltimore *Sun*, subject of the remark, discouraged newspapermen who wanted to make something of it. But the story got out, and Agnew was denounced anew by Congressman Spark Matsunaga, a Democrat from Hawaii. By chance in Hawaii just when the story broke, Agnew put aside his prepared speech to make an almost tearful apology to an audience of several hundred. He told of his father's immigrant origins, and of how his family had suffered from ethnic slurs when he was a child. He compared his remark to routine "locker-room humor." Plaintively, he asked what had happened to the "camaraderie that exists among men which allows them to insult one another in a friendly fashion?" At the next stop on his Hawaiian tour, Agnew invited reporters to his suite for drinks. Their discussion of the incident became heated. It appeared that some younger reporters were out to "get" Agnew.

Agnew's speeches were largely carbon copies of his chief's—firmness in Vietnam coupled with a willingness to negotiate seriously, and at home protection of civil liberties within a framework of order.

Democrats pondered how they could exploit the evident weakness of Agnew's candidacy. Nixon, of course, was their principal target, not Agnew. But with Humphrey far behind Nixon in the polls, the "one heartbeat away" issue seemed worth a try. In his speeches, Humphrey pointedly praised his own running mate. The Democrats ran anti-Agnew advertisements on television. One showed Agnew's face and the sound of a beating heart. Another read "Spiro Agnew for Vice-President" and was accompanied by the sound of laughter.

Nixon, anxious to kill time with his long lead, campaigned less vigorously than some candidates in the past. He saw to it that Agnew was kept under wraps—the latter's schedule could not be called a whirlwind tour. Indeed, Agnew was hustled in and out of airports and speaking halls. He enjoyed long rests in hotels between public appearances. On the Monday evening before the voting, Humphrey and Muskie chatted during their final telecast after a tumultuous trip together through the streets of Los Angeles. Nixon appeared on his last telecast alone. He said that were he back at Miami Beach, he would choose Agnew again. He said Agnew had been the target of "vicious attacks" but that he was "cool under pressure."

On November 5, Nixon and Agnew captured states having 302 electoral votes. One faithless elector in North Carolina subsequently deserted them. That left the Republicans with just 31 more than a bare majority. Unquestionably Agnew's candidacy hurt Nixon in some states, but crucially, from Nixon's viewpoint, the nomination of Agnew saved most of a narrow band of key states lying to the north of "Wallace country" and to the south of "Humphrey country." The states in question were Kentucky, Tennessee, North Carolina, Virginia, Maryland, and Delaware. Had Lindsay been the Vice-Presidential nominee, Nixon might have lost both Carolinas and Tennessee to Wallace without commensurate gains in the Northeast. Had Reagan been on the ticket, Nixon likely would have held these states but would have lost Illinois and Ohio. Governor James Rhodes of Ohio had told Nixon at Miami that with Reagan as the Vice-Presidential candidate the Republicans would suffer a landslide defeat in Ohio. Nixon and Agnew did lose Maryland —the final irony—but held the other Border states and most of the Midwest and West, plus South Carolina (thanks to Strom Thurmond) and Florida, enough to make it. Nixon, in the final analysis, had picked Agnew not for any positive virtues at all, but because Agnew as a political cipher would cost the fewest votes in those states that would be most crucial in a photo-finish election. It was a gutsy move on Nixon's part, but it paid off, though barely.

A third Vice-Presidential candidate was in the field in 1968, the nominee of George Wallace's American Independent Party. The former Governor of Alabama wished to avoid his party being stamped as regional, but he had difficulty finding someone outside the South who essentially shared his opposition to school integration. Wallace would have avoided running with anyone if he could, in the belief that any other name would only dilute the magic of his own, but some state laws required that a party name both a Presidential and a Vice-Presidential nominee.

On October 3, Wallace introduced his choice, retired Air Force General Curtis LeMay, at a Pittsburgh press conference. During World War II, LeMay had made a science of bombing. He helped plan the atomic bomb attacks on Hiroshima and Nagasaki. After the war, in 1948, he directed the Berlin airlift, which saved the isolated German city from Communist pressure. He was then successively commander of the Strategic Air Command and Air Force chief of staff. The cardinal principle of his military philosophy was that an enemy of the United States could best be subdued by the merciless application of strategic bombing. During the Vietnamese war, he advocated bombing North Vietnam "back to the Stone Age." LeMay, while convinced that Communists were behind the civil-rights movement, was not a segregationist, and had encouraged the elimination of racial discrimination in the Air Force.

In his account of the 1968 campaign, Theodore H. White develops the theme that selecting LeMay for Vice President was a major blunder by Wallace. Wallace's support came from antiestablishment people who felt that the government, even including the Pentagon, had let the people down, that "they" had no appreciation for the feelings of the average guy who paid his taxes, carried a rifle in wartime, and who was buffeted daily by the social upheaval on every hand. In short, Wallace's was a G.I. constituency. The introduction of a retired general, and an unpopular disciplinarian at that, undercut the image of the quintessential underdog, ex-Air Force Sergeant George C. Wallace.

Meeting the press on that morning in Pittsburgh, and resembling somewhat a glowering Raymond Burr, LeMay needed just seven minutes to damage the Wallace campaign.

"We seem to have a phobia about nuclear weapons. The smart thing to do when you're in a war—hopefully you prevent it; stay out of it if you can—but when you get in it get in it with both feet and get it over with as soon as you can. Use the force that's necessary. Maybe use a little more to make sure it's enough to stop the fighting as soon as possible. So this means efficiency in the operation of the military establishment. I think there are many times when it would be most efficient to use nuclear weapons. However, the public opinion in this country and throughout the world throw up their hands in horror when you mention nuclear weapons, just because of the propaganda that's been fed to them."

LeMay said he didn't believe the world would end if the United States exploded a nuclear weapon, and pointed out that at Bikini atoll, the nuclear test site, "The fish are all back in the lagoons; the coconut trees are growing coconuts; the guava bushes have fruit on them; the birds are back." The rats, he said, were fatter than before.

Wallace broke in to emphasize that LeMay wanted to use nuclear weapons only as a last resort, that he preferred not to do so. The running mates took turns trying to clarify LeMay's views, and the latter finally observed, "I'll be damned lucky if I don't appear as a drooling idiot. . . ."

Americans do have an aversion to nuclear weapons, as Barry

Goldwater learned in 1964. When LeMay's candidacy was unveiled, Wallace stood at 21 per cent in the Gallup Poll—only 12 points below parity in a three-way contest. In the next month, he declined. Democratic workingmen returned to Humphrey. Southerners wanting a "change," and concluding Wallace couldn't win, shifted to Nixon. And it reasonably may be inferred that the selection of LeMay cost Wallace votes.

Nixon and Agnew were inaugurated on January 20, 1969. The new President's subdued and dignified inaugural address contained words that would haunt him. He said, "To lower our voices would be a simple thing." He continued: "In these difficult years, America has suffered from a fever of words; from inflated rhetoric that promises more than it can deliver; from angry rhetoric that fans discontents into hatreds; from bombastic rhetoric that postures instead of persuading.

"We cannot learn from one another until we stop shouting at one another—until we speak quietly enough so that our words can be heard as well as our voices."

Before their inauguration Nixon said he had special duties in mind for his Vice President, but he didn't spell them out. He said that Agnew would have office space in the White House and would share the President's staff rather than have one of his own. That was interpreted either as a means for the President to keep a sharp eye on Agnew, or—by Agnew himself—as a means of being "interjected into the mainstream." In any event, Agnew was given office space in the Executive Office Building, near the White House, and a staff of his own. Among the duties assigned to him, most notable was that of chairman of the White House Office of Intergovernmental Relations, created by Nixon by executive order. The Vice President thus became the administration's liaison man with the nation's Governors and mayors.

For the first time since Henry Wallace, the presiding officer of the Senate had not served in the Senate himself. Agnew demonstrated interest in mastering Senate rules as well as the body's informal folkways. But he violated protocol by lobbying on the Senate floor in behalf of the tax surcharge extension supported by the administration. "Do we have your vote?" he asked Senator Len Jordan of Idaho, a Republican. The Senator replied, "You did have until now." Thus was established Jordan's rule: When the Vice President lobbies on the Senate floor for a bill, vote the other way.

On August 6, 1969, the Senate voted on amendments to the military authorization bill. Several amendments would have killed the administration's antiballistic missile (ABM) program. The high tide of opposition to the ABM, considered by its opponents as unreliable, was reached in a 50–50 vote. Agnew cast the fifty-first vote against the amendment, though it would have died on a tie vote anyway.

In Agnew's first nine months as Vice President, few of his speeches made headlines. His public addresses dealt with the environment, the problems of minorities, and the space program. There was virtually no hint of the thunderbolts to come. Words fascinated Agnew. In a relatively civilized age, when taking after one's opponents with rock or club is socially unacceptable—in Agnew's circles, at least—he discovered that he could pound away orally at those in public life with whom he disagreed and that the news media would hasten to report the blows of his verbal sticks and stones. The Vice President was soon to win knee-slapping approval from his Middle American audiences who didn't always know what he was talking about, but loved it.

For all of his off-the-cuff mistakes in 1968, Agnew had mastered the delivery of the set speech. Always composed and neat, displaying in turn tight-lipped indignation, self-deprecating humor, and earnest advocacy of administration programs, he generally held his audiences in tight control, eliciting the emotions and responses that the occasion required. In six years of Maryland politics he had learned to exploit the evening newscast's brief film clip. He once told columnist Stewart Alsop, "If you want to get a point across, you say it in exciting language and then bland out everything else." A classic example of this technique was demonstrated in New Orleans on the night of October 19, 1969.

Most of that speech comprised a candid and detailed defense of the administration's measured withdrawal of U.S. troops from Vietnam; a carefully considered analysis of current draft law and projected reform; and a report on the status of the strategic arms race. Presentations of this nature, while they would not get headlines, would if delivered often enough firm up public support for the policies under discussion.

But so far as Agnew was concerned—and Nixon as well?—the time to rely solely or even primarily on reasoned discourse was past. Opposition to the war was reviving. Many hundreds of thousands of persons participated in nationwide ceremonies on Vietnam moratorium day, October 15; another major demonstration was scheduled in Washington, D.C., on November 15. A recession was in the making. Liberals were dissatisfied with Nixon's efforts in the field of civil rights. The news media had picked up these currents of unrest. It was time for the administration to tangle with the opposition, and it would begin by attempting to define who the dissidents were, what motivated them, and what should be done about them. Agnew's opening shot at New Orleans went like this:

"A spirit of national masochism prevails, encouraged by an effete corps of impudent snobs who characterize themselves as intellectuals."

Richard Nixon's relationship with his two hundred million constituents would never be the same after Agnew's famous sentence of October 19. Astute observers realized immediately that the course of debate in the country would veer onto a new path, and that Agnew would employ language that the President couldn't use.

Political leaders and writers pondered Agnew's sentence word for word. At the very least the "snobs" must include members of the academic community, always a center of opposition to the war in Vietnam. Did he have anyone else in mind? Use of "corps" suggested that a conspiracy was afoot to discredit the administration. Was the Democratic leadership a part of such a conspiracy, perhaps with help from some other source? And did he use "effete" in its dictionary meaning of "no longer fertile . . . worn out with age" to suggest that the liberal establishment had run out of ideas for coping with the nation's ills? Or did he anticipate that many people would equate "effete" with "effeminate"?

William F. Buckley, Jr., the Conservative theoretician and word-smith, didn't like the sentence at all. "Snob," he said, doesn't need an adjective. And "effete corps" doesn't hang together at all. Finally, prominent persons opposing the war not only "characterize themselves as intellectuals," they *are* intellectuals. Buckley asserted, "Agnew is not skilled in polemics and therefore should not engage in them without help."

The big question was the extent to which Nixon approved what the Vice President had said. Many Republican leaders protested privately to the White House that Agnew could damage the administration, but the shape of public opinion was not yet clear. On October 30, Nixon said publicly that the Vice President "has done a great job for this Administration."

That same night, at a GOP fund-raising dinner in Harrisburg, Pa., Agnew fired another salvo, surely some of the most vehement rhetoric heard from a President or a Vice President in a century. He began, "A little over a week ago, I took a rather unusual step for a Vice President . . . I said something." He proceeded to say a lot more. Agnew laid down a withering fire of contemptuous adjectives and nouns: "arrogant, reckless . . . idiotic . . . small cadres of professional protestors . . . glib, activist element . . . sick and rancid . . . vultures . . . merchants of hate . . . parasites of passion . . . ideological eunuchs. . . ." So far as one can determine from the text of this vague and rambling speech, Agnew tied all that verbiage to those who had demonstrated peacefully, even reverently, by the hundreds of thousands on October 15, or to those who more generally but with restraint were questioning the values of American society. Only rarely in the speech did he appear to focus on that lunatic fringe that advocates and practices violence. Indeed, Agnew's most outrageous prescription was clearly not to be applied to the violent ones, but was aimed at silencing "the decadent thinking of a few." He said, "We can . . . afford to separate them from our society—with no more regret than we should feel over discarding rotten apples from a barrel." But Agnew was not content to separate a few. If in the course of the debate that would follow "we polarize the American people, I say it is time for a positive polarization."

One could ponder endlessly Agnew's nightmare rhetoric at Harrisburg. He deplored the idea "that elected officials should decide crucial questions by counting the number of bodies cavorting in the streets"—this during a war in which phony body counts were being used as the basis for deciding that North Vietnam was losing the war. And in criticizing dissenters, Agnew used loosely an ugly word: he said it was "the self-righteous who are guilty of history's worst atrocities. . . . Evil cloaked in emotional causes is well disguised and often undiscovered until it is too late." Those words could be more appropriately applied to an event that had occurred in 1968 and that was brought to the public's attention two weeks after Agnew spoke—the massacre of more than one hundred South Vietnamese civilians at My Lai by soldiers in a U.S. infantry unit.

A serious complaint to be lodged against Agnew, particularly after he discovered his powerful appeal in some quarters, is that he rarely moved beyond a sweeping characterization of a problem. He bypassed opportunities to argue seriously the merits of some proposition, even after his forays against dissenters had gained him wide attention wherever he went. He was not alone in this failing, however. These years, from about the time of John Kennedy's death, featured an excess of hyperbole that would have gone begging in the public marketplace in more stable times. It came from all quarters—not only from Vice Presidents—and on all sides of all issues: the war, race, the economy. Voices of reason were smothered by the shouts of quacks and troublemakers peddling panaceas and recruiting constituencies with the help of the media. Both Nixon and Agnew properly made that point. Agnew had struck a deep vein of discontent in America. Millions were fed up—"up to here," as Nixon put it—with crime, pornography, ridicule of patriotism, burning cities, and with the spreading use of drugs and casual sex among the young. But although Agnew and to a lesser extent Nixon were capable of arousing the indignation of these people, they did not seem to be welding great numbers of them to a conservative, or Republican, alliance. The simplistic rhetoric attacking "the kids" and defending U.S. policy in Vietnam brought in recruits for what Nixon was to call "the silent majority," but such gains were transitory. Once the verbal tidal waves had washed over the average American and had receded, he had difficulty articulating in his own mind or to anyone else just why we were staying in Vietnam indefinitely. Quite often such a person eventually abandoned his support for administration policy.

President Nixon's most serious bid to rally public opinion behind U.S. policy in Vietnam was the aforementioned appeal to "the great silent majority of my fellow Americans." It came on November 3, 1969, four days after Agnew's speech at Harrisburg. The administration was making every effort to gain at least its share of media coverage in the period between the massive antiwar demonstrations of October 15 and November 15. The President told the country that in co-operation with the South Vietnamese he had adopted a plan to withdraw all U.S. ground combat troops on a fixed timetable. But he did not reveal the timetable. He also warned, "If a vocal minority, however fervent its cause, prevails over reason and the will of the majority, this nation has no future as a free society." In refusing to set publicly an early date for the total withdrawal of U.S. troops, he explained that the course he had chosen "is the right way." A year later polls showed that most Americans desired their Congressmen to vote for a bill setting an early date for complete withdrawal. Forced to choose between a policy that was "right" and one that had majority support, Nixon stayed on the former course.

When the polls turned against Nixon's policy, the administration abandoned the "silent majority" slogan. What concerns us here is the extraordinary efforts made, by Vice President Agnew in particular, to maintain majority support behind the President. In two remarkable speeches, on November 13 at Des Moines and on November 20 at Montgomery, Alabama, Agnew indicted the news media for a lack of objectivity. Now the people would learn the names of some of the "snobs" he had been savaging for a month.

The Des Moines speech criticizing television network news coverage was Agnew's most effective speech to date. First, it was scheduled to fall at or about the time of the evening news throughout most of the country, and all three networks carried it live. Second, the speech was well written and documented, and it was generally free of the inanities and slanders that marred so much of his oratory. One could, and many did, take strong exception to some of what Agnew said, but as an articulate, blunt presentation of a point of view, the speech succeeded.

Agnew charged that a "small and unelected elite" who "to a man . . . live and work in the geographical and intellectual confines of Washington, D.C., or New York City" selected the news clips that tens of millions of persons watched every night. What Americans saw on television, Agnew said, were people who were generally hostile to the administration and to establishment values, who espoused extreme views, and who often practiced violence. He said that the television producers and commentators "can make or break—by their coverage and commentary—a Moratorium on the war." How true! When, two days after Agnew spoke, more than a quarter of a million persons, perhaps the largest throng ever assembled in one place in the United States, demonstrated peacefully in Washington against the war, the networks virtually ignored the event.

Of the persons who rushed to defend the network newscasts against Agnew, no one sought to justify television's penchant for portraying violence. William H. White suggests that the expansion of newscasts from fifteen to thirty minutes in 1963 was a major event. News now became a half-hour drama with exciting sequences developed to keep the viewer in his chair. Because of the pursuit of ratings, people were depictd at their points of confrontation. Take, for example, a labor dispute that divides the public along ethnic lines. When a largely Jewish teachers' union strikes a school system enrolling mostly black children, television renders no service by nightly splicing together quotations by the noisiest spokesmen on each side, giving almost the impression they are shouting in each other's face. Particularly is such coverage gratuitous when no progress is made in the negotiations for days or even weeks at a time.

Nor could anyone, least of all the antiwarriors, dispute Agnew's assertion that extremists often crowd the moderates aside on the television screen. Television consistently conveyed the impression that largely peaceful and broad-based demonstrations against the war were dominated by a handful of fanatics waving Vietcong flags. Regrettably, the Johnson and Nixon administrations exploited the impression of antiwar radicalism as a means of discrediting all opponents of the war.

Agnew's speech at Des Moines had its roots in Nixon's "silent majority" speech ten days earlier. After the President left the air that night, the network commentators chewed over what he had said. The thrust of their remarks and of special studio guests tended to introduce points of view different from those of the President, not because the networks opposed Nixon's withdrawal plan in Vietnam but because they felt that other points of view should be put on the record. Strong exceptions to the President's policies were being taken by leading politicians in both parties. Networks seek to avoid obligations to grant equal time for opposing points of view on subsequent evenings in prime time. On November 3, 1969, they much preferred to use the vacant portion of Mr. Nixon's hour to suggest the alternatives in policy that he might have embraced and the cases to be made in their favor. Agnew charged that the President's words "were subjected to instant analysis and querulous criticism." But the administration had released the text of the speech before the telecast and had briefed newsmen on its contents.

Fred W. Friendly, former president of CBS news, recalled a similar situation five years earlier. After the Tonkin Gulf incident, President Johnson had gone on television to urge congressional approval of a resolution giving him a virtual blank check in Vietnam. The major buildup of U.S. forces dated from that time. Friendly rejected pleas of his Washington bureau to discuss Johnson's speech after he left the air. Friendly conceded in retrospect that CBS reporters should have pointed out—certainly without taking sides—that if U.S. bombers were sent against the North, bases would have to be built to accommodate the bombers, troops would have to be sent over to guard the bases, and hundreds of thousands of troops would follow once the first troops were drawn into combat.

In any event, a Gallup Poll taken after President Nixon's address showed that 77 per cent of the American people approved of his speech. Over the months his support would decline. The poll suggested that Nixon's audience was not turned against him because of anything said immediately after he left the air.

Though Agnew didn't mention them, he doubtless had in mind the impact his Des Moines speech would have on the individual television stations throughout the country. These stations, through loose affiliation, form the three major networks. Each station's license is subject to periodic review by the Federal government. The stations feel the pressure of the "silent majority" at the grass-roots level, and are often owned and staffed by men more conservative than those "elite" cloistered in New York and Washington. A station manager sensing or getting pressure from both government and the local population is likely to do just what many did do—complain to the network executives along the lines enunciated by Agnew.

At Des Moines and on later occasions Agnew emphasized that he opposed censorship in any form. He once observed, "This office isn't exactly the exercise of raw power." Yet on November 13 he also said that "perhaps it is time that the networks were made more responsive to the views of the nation. . . ." Again, the vague prescription. He thus suggested once more, in the heyday of the silent majority, that individuals and institutions should swim with the tide of national sentiment.

The Nixon administration did bring pressures on the network news operations. It sought through court order to obtain film shot but not used on the air. It seized a film interview given to CBS in confidence. White House aides asked newscasters to amplify remarks made on the air in news broadcasts and documentaries, and asked stations if they planned to editorialize after a Presidential speech and what they planned to say. Members of Congress and of the armed forces requested responses to extended queries and challenges to the accuracy of news items and documentaries.

"Hunger in America," a CBS documentary praised by Agnew in his Des Moines speech, came under his fire a year later. He said it was not true that a baby shown on screen had died of hunger, as CBS reported. Defense of the program against attacks by government critics cost CBS perhaps one hundred thousand dollars. Lost in the welter of arguments was the program's main thesis, not disproved, that many persons in the United States die of hunger.

The debate, in 1971, over another CBS documentary, "The Selling of the Pentagon," followed a similar course. CBS alleged that the Pentagon spent from 30- to 190-million dollars in one year promoting itself and anticommunism in general, and the Vietnamese war in particular, often in violation of the law. Agnew and other supporters of the defense establishment focused on allegedly deceptive splicing of remarks by persons appearing on the program in an effort to discredit the program as a whole.

Television documentaries are expensive to produce; the endless reruns of "I Love Lucy" are cheap. Harassed by the government, threatened by disaffiliation by local station owners, the network news departments understandably may be tempted to retreat from the responsibility that they have endeavored to discharge in the past. The voices of debate and dissent may yet disappear from the tube. When the Vice President said that he and the government were against censorship, he missed, or ignored, the crucial point.

Clark Mollenhoff, a Presidential assistant, said that Agnew's Des Moines speech reflected administration views and was in fact developed at the White House.

On November 20, 1969, in Montgomery, Agnew turned to the printed media. He said that the Washington Post Company operated the Washington *Post*, a television station, a radio station, and *Newsweek*, "all grinding out the same editorial line." Another way of putting it—which Mr. Agnew wouldn't—is that someone in Washington, D.C., who found such a "line" repugnant could choose from two other newspapers, three other major television stations, many other radio stations, and half a dozen other magazines and national newspapers similar to *Newsweek* in coverage.

The complaint against *Newsweek* presumably grew out of that periodical's distinguished reporting from Vietnam that repeatedly called into question the administration's official optimism on the war. Surely Agnew could not fault *Newsweek* for its columnists. Raymond Moley, a founder of the magazine and a contributing editor until his retirement in 1968—and a longtime friend and adviser to Richard Nixon—was an articulate representative of the conservative viewpoint. Milton Friedman was one of Barry Goldwater's and Richard Nixon's principal economic advisers. Kenneth Crawford (until his retirement in 1970) and Stewart Alsop (until his conversion in 1971) defended U.S. policy in Asia.

The Vice President also went after the New York *Times* with the preposterous assertion that the death of a publication like the New York *Mirror*, a sheet devoted largely to horse racing and similar diversions, somehow caused the *Times* to decline in quality. In giving examples of poor news judgment by the *Times*, Agnew made a weak and inaccurate case that was quickly dismissed.

Had Agnew wished to establish any credibility as a serious press critic, he could have cited any of several monopoly or near monopoly situations across the country in which the dominant newspapers were conservative, and mediocre as well. No one seriously believes that horseplayers are concerned about improving the breed, and no one of any competence believed that the Nixon administration was primarily concerned about upgrading the quality of news coverage. Politicians have long complained about the press. In 1952 Adlai Stevenson spoke of a "one-party press in a two-party country." Lyndon Johnson regarded an unfavorable news item as the act of an unfriendly publisher or a plant by a political antagonist. Barry Goldwater was angered by press coverage in 1964.

Richard Nixon's own rambling denunciation of the press after his defeat for Governor in 1962 stands as a low point in relations between public figures and the media. In charging thinly veiled bias, Nixon had said, "I believe if a reporter believes that one man ought to win rather than the other . . . he ought to say so." Agnew echoed that thought in 1970, proposing that government personnel interrogate network commentators on their political philosophies.

All persons have biases. Honest and competent newsmen—and that's most of them—subordinate their feelings in preparing their copy. Nixon and Agnew complained on the one hand that reporters should be unmasked, but argued on the other hand that their hostility was already clear.

Eric Sevareid replied eloquently to the Vice President: "Mr. Agnew wants to know where we stand. We stand—or rather sit—right here, in the full glare. At a disadvantage as against politicians; we can't cast one vote in committee, an opposite vote on the floor; can't say one thing in the North, an opposite thing in the South. . . .

"We can't use invective and epithets, can't even dream of impugning the patriotism of leading citizens, can't reduce every complicated issue to yes or no, black or white. . . ."

The advantages to be gained by Richard Nixon in taking on the press seemed to be outweighed by the risks. In the elections of 1960 and 1968 newspaper endorsements ran heavily in his favor. Might not Agnew's continuing barrage reduce that support in the future? As for threats, real and implied, directed at the television networks, prospects for swift political gains by the Nixon administration were slim. Finally, criticism of the press could invite changes in the relationship between the President and the reporters during news conferences. Nixon benefitted from those exchanges. He gave rehearsed and carefully organized answers to the questions, which he could reasonably anticipate. Reporters conceded that they were only props for a Presidential "performance." Nixon almost never said anything really new to them, and the audience to which he spoke was the nation at large, watching on television. Reporters treated the President with great deference; by way of explanation, they pointed out that the President is head of state as well as head of government, unlike the British Prime Minister, and is not to be addressed in a challenging or accusatory manner, nor were questions to be so precise in formulation as to pin the President to the wall.

But by the spring of 1971 questions were becoming sharper. Reporters began to follow up each other's questions on the same subject when the President waffled. In June, 1971, a reporter bluntly corrected a misrepresentation by the President. Displeased with the news conference format, suspicious of an administration "credibility gap" in Vietnam, and reacting to the abuse from the Vice President and others, members of the press were asserting themselves. Nixon was in danger of losing a safe forum for reaching the public.

The refusal of the American people to believe any longer what Lyndon Johnson was telling them about Vietnam had forced his retirement. Successive administrations would not square with the people concerning the struggle in Southeast Asia: The boys would be home by Christmas. The Communist supply lines had been cut. The South Vietnamese government, almost a model of democracy, must be preserved at any cost in American blood. American bombs almost never killed civilians. The enormous body counts of enemy dead proved that the North's manpower was low.

In fact, much of what the American people heard officially was an amalgam of breast-beating, self-deluding fantasies, half-truths, and lies. With energy and resourcefulness, the press tried to report what was really happening in Asia. In this context one can best explain Agnew's offensive against the media. If the competence and honesty of the press could be questioned so relentlessly that the people might discount its coverage of the war, the administration could gain enough time to withdraw from Vietnam on the slow and secret timetable that it felt was necessary.

Early in 1971 the South Vietnamese began to prepare for an invasion of Laos with U.S. air support. Before the offensive began the U.S. command in Saigon imposed a news embargo. The results of the offensive were at best mixed. Some supply trails were cut, but some South Vietnamese units were routed. President Nixon criticized news coverage of the invasion as distorted and incomplete. John Chancellor of NBC news replied:

"Various people in the Administration, including the President and the Vice President, have been making nasty cracks about the TV coverage of the campaign in southern Laos. They say we've not been telling the whole story, and that's true. We haven't been able to tell the whole story because we haven't been allowed to. Some of the people who have been complaining that the whole story hasn't been told are the people who tried to keep it from being told."

It remained for Eric Sevareid to put down the Vice President most forcefully: ". . . the central point about the free press is not that it be accurate, though it must try to be; not that it even be fair, though it must try to be that; but that it be *free*. And that means, in the first instance, freedom from any and all attempts by the power of government to coerce it or intimidate it or police it in any way."

Trips to Asia had become de rigueur for Vice Presidents, and Spiro Agnew traveled to that continent twice in 1970. He began the year in South Vietnam, one of eleven countries on a three-week itinerary. His objective was to explain the Nixon doctrine, which placed on other nations more of the responsibility for their own defense. At the same time he reassured foreign heads of state that the United States would meet its obligations. Even abroad the Vice President jabbed at unnamed antiwar critics in the United States. In August he hit many of the same Asian stops, and added Cambodia, under a new anti-Communist government. He stirred a new debate by saying that the United States would do all it could to help that government, a commitment unlike any made publicly by the Nixon administration.

The major storm over Cambodia had occurred between Agnew's Asian trips. On April 30 the President announced he was sending U.S. troops into Cambodia, along with South Vietnamese forces, to destroy enemy supplies and troop concentrations so that U. S. troops in South Vietnam could withdraw with greater safety. Critics charged that the Cambodian offensive, which lasted two months, widened the war. Dozens of college campuses erupted in demonstrations, some violent. At Kent State University, in Ohio, four students were killed and ten were wounded by National Guard troops during an antiwar protest.

Once again Agnew led the administration's verbal attack on its opponents. He conceded that the Guard at Kent State had overreacted and was responsible in some degree for the shootings. But most of his criticisms were directed elsewhere. As many colleges were forced to shut down because of the disruptions, or voted to do so, Agnew blamed the disorders on permissive administrators too ready to surrender to "nonnegotiable demands" by students. With calm and reason needed on both sides, the war of words escalated rapidly. Agnew deplored a column by Pete Hamill in the New York *Post*, which read in part: "When you call campus dissenters 'bums,' as Nixon did . . . you should not be surprised when they are shot . . . by National Guardsmen. Nixon is as responsible for the Kent State slaughter as he and the rest of his bloodless gang of corporation men were . . . for the pillage and murder that is taking place in the name of democracy in Cambodia. . . ."

Middle America's negative reaction to campus disorders provided the last show of strength for the silent majority. Domestic turmoil replaced the war as the major issue in the 1970 Congressional election, a tailor-made opportunity for the rhetoric of Spiro Agnew.

The choice of Agnew to lead the Republican fall campaign came as no surprise. Nixon, when Vice President, had assumed the same burden during off-year elections. In fact, as Agnew warmed to his task, Senator Eugene McCarthy called him Nixon's Nixon. The Gallup Poll found Agnew to be the country's third most popular figure, behind the President and the Reverend Billy Graham. No Vice President had ever placed so high. In his appearances throughout the country in the fall of 1970, Agnew raised $3.5 million for the party and its candidates. He was assured wide news coverage everywhere. Yet GOP candidates needing liberal votes to win discouraged his visits. Agnew, having committed himself to "positive polarization," proceeded to carry out that policy in 1970. He signaled his latest "tough line" by charging that leading Democratic antiwar critics had "developed a psychological addiction to an American defeat." He also asserted that a proposal by Senators George McGovern and Mark Hatfield (the latter a Republican) that Congress set a fixed early date for the end of U.S. combat in Vietnam was "a blueprint for the first defeat in the history of the United States."

These, then, were Agnew's themes—support the President on the war, and crack down on campus dissidents. He was swiftly set back on both fronts. A September Gallup Poll showed that Americans favored the Hatfield-McGovern proposal by a wide margin. And then the President's Commission on Campus Unrest, headed by William Scranton, a Republican, issued its findings, saying that "only the President can offer the compassionate, reconciling moral leadership that can bring the country together again." Distorting the commission's findings, Agnew said that "To lay the responsibility for ending student disruption at the doorstep of the President—in office twenty months—is 'scapegoating' of the most irresponsible sort." He called the report "more pablum for the permissivists," although it condemned without reservation violence by students and said that such students must be held criminally responsible.

Agnew labeled most Democratic Senators up for re-election "radical liberals." That phrase attempted to tie into one package the bomb-throwers and those well within the traditional political spectrum. The radical liberals, it developed, opposed the President on defense, foreign affairs, and law and order. Their ranks included one Republican, Senator Charles Goodell of New York, called by Agnew the Christine Jorgensen of the Republican party, a reference to the subject of a sex-change operation. Goodell lost to an independent Conservative candidate, James Buckley.

Given the tragedies of continuing war and domestic violence, the 1970 campaign ideally would have been a thoughtful discussion of the issues, insofar as that was possible. But Agnew chose to perform some of his most daring verbal acrobatics. He had discovered alliteration. If the voters remembered nothing about the issues or the candidates, they would remember Agnew's political dirty dozen: the pusillanimous pussyfooters, the vicars of vacillation, the nattering nabobs of negativism, and the hopeless, hysterical hypochondriacs of history—to name a few.

In the last days of the campaign President Nixon joined the

fray, and a campaign that had seemed silly now seemed reprehensible. The President called on the silent majority to answer the radicals and those shouting obscenities by voting Republican. The word "vote," he said, was more powerful than any other four-letter word. Democrats were equated with crime and violence. Seldom, if ever, had a President offered such a simple choice to the American people. At rally after rally, he would point to a handful of jeering dissidents and would say that they didn't represent the youth of America. What he didn't say was that the troublemakers had been ushered into the rallies to serve as foils for the President.

Never had a President and a Vice President teamed up to work the low road in a Congressional campaign. Nixon and Agnew abased their offices and showed contempt for the intelligence of the American people. They were the incumbents. They had a record to defend. It was, in many respects, a respectable one. In foreign affairs, the administration was helping to hold the line against war in the Middle East, was relaxing tensions with Communist China, and was making slow headway in strategic arms talks. Nixon and Agnew chose instead to tar their opponents with the brush of violence, obscenity, and crime. It didn't work. The Democrats benefited from the economic slump, and the so-called radical liberals had taken firm stands for law and order. Defending twenty-five of the thirty-five Senate seats, the Democrats won twenty-three, a net loss of only two. The Democrats gained eleven governorships and nine seats in the U.S. House of Representatives.

The Vice President professed to believe that the Republicans had done well. When several Republican Governors accused him of favoring polarization, he suggested that an election was "an attempt to divide the voters of the country between two or three candidates. . . ."

A poll of GOP state chairmen and national committeemen by the *Christian Science Monitor* showed that by 54–32 they wished that the Vice President would tone down his rhetoric. But the irrepressible Vice President was not long out of the news.

Early in 1971 he denounced Congressman William Anderson, a Democrat from Tennessee. He said that Anderson had praised as heroes the radical Catholic priests, Daniel and Patrick Berrigan. The latter had been indicted in an alleged conspiracy to blow up government heating systems in Washington, D.C., and to kidnap Henry Kissinger, President Nixon's national security adviser. Agnew asserted that Anderson had called for demonstrations in behalf of the Berrigan brothers. Anderson had not called the Berrigans heroes, nor had he called for demonstrations in their behalf. Agnew also erred in saying that both Berrigans had been indicted. The Vice President charged that Anderson was engaging in "emotional, self-serving claptrap" and "popping off for political advantage." Anderson represented a hawkish, Protestant district in Tennessee. Agnew, if anyone, might well refrain from accusing others of speaking for political advantage.

Then, in April, came an Agnew "first"—an apparent split with Nixon on policy. He questioned the thaw in U.S.-Communist Chinese relations being encouraged by the President. Speaking privately with nine reporters, the Vice President said that China had scored a propaganda victory when it played host to the U.S. table tennis team. Agnew had previously opposed the "ping pong diplomacy" at a meeting of the National Security Council, saying that it tended to undermine the pro-American Nationalist Chinese regime in Taipei. Expressing a reservation at the NSC meeting before final policy was formulated was one thing. Continuing to oppose the policy at an "off-the-record" meeting with reporters was something else.

In July, 1971, the President announced that he would visit Peking in the near future. Agnew was abroad, having been dispatched on a curious month-long, ten-nation tour that involved little diplomacy and much golfing. The Vice President evidently had not participated in discussions leading to Nixon's announcement.

The rift with the President revived periodic speculation that Nixon would dump Agnew from the 1972 ticket. One party professional said, "he simply has to be replaced. . . . He's too controversial; the image is too bad in places where we need votes. . . . Even if they try to give him a new image, and even if he manages to stick to it the changes won't be believable." But conservatives admired Agnew not only for what he said but also for his courage in saying it. "I can tell you that Agnew is more popular than Dick Nixon across the country, especially with Republicans," Barry Goldwater said. "There will be an open revolution if the President tries to get rid of him."

Nixon couldn't dump his Vice President as easily as a President could in the era before Vice-Presidential names became household words. Nixon had built up Agnew to the point that he couldn't be eased out of office without considerable political risk to the President. But by 1971 the President appeared to be opening other options for 1972. Nixon had not carried Texas in two Presidential races, and the Lone Star state's electoral bloc seemed more crucial than ever after Republican strength in the Midwest slipped in 1970. He named former Governor John Connally, a Democrat, as his Secretary of the Treasury, and former Texas Congressman George Bush, a Republican, as U.S. Ambassador to the United Nations. Nixon had briefly considered Bush for Vice President in 1968.

Spiro Agnew was not a complex man, nor was he a simple man in the unkind sense of that word. He was a direct man, and he was intelligent, but he was inexperienced, and after he acquired experience he was slow to shake the habit of aiming crude, personal abuse at men with whom he disagreed. Agnew's message was as direct as the man himself. Americans were forgetting the traditional values: patriotism was out of fashion. Symbols of authority—parents, government officials, educators—no longer commanded respect; in fact, some of them encouraged disrespect for authority and order. It was fair enough for a Vice President to address such problems, but his decision to do so in a partisan way led to his advocacy of polarization, a concept alien to democratic government. He once said, "I provide the safety valve for the frustrations of a large section of public opinion, because I am saying what they feel in their stomachs." But a national leader is not charged primarily with the responsibility for articulating the anxieties of some bloc within the total population; he might better try to suggest means of reconciling differences within the country short of civil strife.

Walter Lippmann wrote that Agnew had violated "an unwritten code of good manners." The code provides that political opponents will not regard one another as enemies. One proceeds in debate from the assumption that on both sides of public questions will be found men of reason and good will. Lippmann believed that Agnew meant to say "that the men he opposed were outside the American community, were exiles, were rotten apples, were lost souls to be rejected by the nation." Lippmann said that Agnew was "not American" when he "violates the boundary between partisanship and enmity, between tough campaigning and fighting words."

Surely the most disturbing attempt by Agnew to define his role came during a television interview. He said, "it is necessary for . . . the American people . . . to have a strong spokesman. When a fire takes place, a man doesn't run into the room and whisper, 'Would somebody please get the water'; he yells, 'Fire!' and I am yelling 'Fire,' because I think 'Fire' needs to be called here." In his denunciations of others for their public statements, Agnew represented himself as an authority on free speech. Anyone who has listened to discussions of the limits on free speech knows that the most frequently cited example of the need for verbal restraint is that of the "fire-in-a-crowded-theater."

If one shouts "Fire" in a crowded theater the bodies will pile up at the exits, trampled in the ensuing stampede—and Agnew was not advocating that. By analogy, in the American "theater" —or "room," to use the Vice President's word—were two hundred million people alarmed by crime and drugs, and frustrated by injustice, by a variety of daily tensions, and by a dubious battle ten thousand miles away. One hoped that the roomful of Americans would not stampede, that they would exit from within their walls of frustration in response to a calmer appeal to their better nature. The Vice President could yet join in such an appeal. But he will likely be remembered as he said he wished to be remembered, as the man who shouted "Fire!"

THE VICE PRESIDENT'S JOB

". . . it's a kind iv a disgrace.

It's like writin' anonymous letters."

The hours may not be as good as they once were, but the salary has risen sharply. Spiro T. Agnew received $62,500 a year, plus $10,000 for expenses (though all of this was taxable). John Adams did not fare so well. The House of Representatives, after voting $25,000 for George Washington, disagreed on the means of paying the Vice President. One member proposed payment on a *per diem* basis: a few dollars for every day he actually showed up to preside over the Senate. But even Congressmen who had little use for the Vice Presidency felt that this was shabby treatment for the nation's second highest officer. Representative John Page of Virginia observed that "as we have got him, we must maintain him." The House approved a salary of $5,000, which was increased thereafter from time to time.

However, the Vice President's obligations have increased more rapidly. Lyndon Johnson, who could afford to take the loss, spent about $100,000 a year as Vice President, mostly for official entertainment. The maintenance of the Johnson home, The Elms, a Norman house in northwest Washington, required a large sum. The Government has never provided an official residence for the Vice President. In years gone by, many of them lived in hotels. A hotel is not a suitable place to entertain dignitaries from other countries; now that Vice Presidents are world travelers, they may be obliged to repay hospitality they have received abroad. Spiro Agnew and his wife revived the custom of living in a hotel; they did not care to entertain often, and declined many dinner invitations themselves. Agnew said that he did not want a permanent Washington residence.

In 1957, President Eisenhower suggested that the attention of Congress "be directed to the acquisition and maintenance of an official residence for the Vice President." But nothing happened. The best solution would be for some wealthy Capital dowager to will or donate a home. In the absence of such a windfall, Congress may yet decide to purchase some suitable house. Little consideration has been given to building a new home.

Job security? Only seven Vice Presidents have been elected twice. The Constitution does not limit a Vice President to two terms, but no one has ever tried for more. Few ex-Vice Presidents have even remained in public life.

In 1951, Congress provided another form of security for the Vice President by authorizing the Secret Service to protect him. Secret Servicemen saved Nixon from possible death in Caracas in 1958. When rifle shots were heard at Dallas in November 1963, Agent Rufus Youngblood sat on Johnson, who was riding in the second car behind Kennedy in the motorcade.

Prestige? Clearly the office has attained a stature worthy of the ambitions of any American boy. Our only loss is in the passing of the Vice-President joke, a hardy perennial in vaudeville days. Herewith, a sentimental bow to Mr. Dooley's unmatched observation that "Th' Prisidincy is th' highest office in th' gift iv th' people. Th' Vice-Prisidincy is th' next highest an' th' lowest. It isn't a crime exactly. Ye can't be sint to jail f'r it, but it's a kind iv a disgrace. It's like writin' anonymous letters."

All these factors considered, it is likely that the competition for Vice-Presidential nominations will become more keen in future years. Most campaigns for the second office will continue to be conducted under cover, since in most cases the Presidential candidate will make the choice, and he will not likely react favorably to efforts to bring public pressure to bear in behalf of a particular candidate.

However, a change in our Presidential nominating system could force Vice-Presidential hopefuls to compete openly for the second office. If critics succeed in abolishing the national convention in favor of a nationwide Presidential primary, a Vice-Presidential primary may be conducted simultaneously. If so, the Vice-Presidential nomination would always fall into the hands of a man who had chosen not to compete for the Presidency itself. The simultaneous primary might result in a step backward to the nineteenth-century practice whereby the Vice Presidency generally went to second raters who would never be considered for the Presidency. As an alternative plan the parties might choose only their Presidential candidate in a national primary, then convene for the purposes of framing a platform and nominating a Vice-Presidential candidate.

But in the judgment of the author, the parties should continue to choose both candidates by convention. The parties on the whole have been doing a better job of choosing their nominees. National primaries might not succeed as well, and the prohibitive expense of such contests would accelerate the present trend toward wealthy candidates. The principal complaint about conventions focuses on the delegates, who have not been representative of the party as a whole. For its 1972 convention the Democrats adopted rules to insure wider public participation in delegate selection and to insure that delegates reflected the composition of party membership.

In the absence of the adoption of the national Presidential primary, it is likely that Vice-Presidential nominees will continue to be chosen much as in the past. The Presidential nominee should always be held responsible for the choice of his running mate. The prestige of the Presidential nominee will never be higher than in the hours just after his own nomination. If he cannot impose his will on the party at this point, he will not likely serve as a successful party leader in the four years to come. And if he cannot come up with the right choice for the Vice Presidency, then he should not be entrusted with four years of decision-making in the White House. This is not to say that the Presidential candidate should rely solely on his own judgment. Like Lyndon Johnson in 1964, he should canvass sentiment within the party, weighing all factors for and against each possibility.

In some cases, of course, the Presidential nominee will not be certain of his own victory until the convention meets and votes, and he will not have time to conduct a meticulous study. But he is almost certain to be aware of the qualifications of the leading contenders and of the role his Vice President would play in his administration so it should be relatively simple after some consultation with party leaders to designate the ablest man. Such firm action by future Presidential nominees would deny to us the excitement provided by the 1944 and 1956 Democratic conventions, but Vice-Presidential candidates should not be the product of the Presidential nominees' refusal to face their obligations.

Five months before he finally chose Humphrey, President Johnson was interviewed on television, and rejected the idea of throwing the Vice Presidency open to the convention. He explained that ". . . the Vice President is very close to the President. They have to agree on the same platform, and they have to run on the same ticket, and in order to be prepared for what might happen, the President must have great confidence in the Vice President, and make known to him his thoughts, his views, and all of his secrets, so that he can have the background for taking over if it becomes necessary, so the President's recommendation should not be treated lightly."

While both men chosen on the national ticket should share the same political philosophy, no one can object to a team balanced in other respects. Parties striving to obtain a broad internal consensus should not hesitate to pair a Westerner and an Easterner, a Senator and a Governor, an older man and a younger man, providing the nominees are otherwise qualified.

In future years it is likely that young, relatively unknown men will seek Vice-Presidential nominations, even on tickets they expect may lose, in order to obtain national exposure. Franklin Roosevelt first campaigned nationally as the Democratic Vice-Presidential candidate in 1920. Both John Kennedy in 1956 and William Scranton in 1964 would have gained valuable experience as Vice-Presidential candidates, though it would not have been without risks since their parties lost badly.

Once nominated, the Vice-Presidential candidate attempts to stay out of trouble and to carry his own state. In recent years the No. 2 men have not been markedly successful in either respect. From 1932 through 1968, the 20 Vice-Presidential nominees won their own states on only 11 occasions. Not since 1952 have both Vice-Presidential nominees carried their own states. This should tend to confirm the general belief that few voters are swayed from the Presidential choice they would otherwise make because of the appearance on a ticket of a particular Vice-Presidential candidate, even a favorite son. Lyndon Johnson in 1960 was among the few running mates to make a clear contribution to his party's success. More often, Presidential candidates have learned what Johnson discovered in 1964—that the coupling of any Vice-Presidential possibility with the top man on the ticket tends to deduct votes from the Presidential candidate.

As better men have been put up for the second office, they seem to have been embroiled in controversy more often than one would expect. Both Henry Wallace and Richard Nixon, in particular, were the centers of storms that brought anxiety to the Presidential candidates with whom they ran. It is likely that running mates will continue to find themselves the targets of opposition spokesmen who prefer to avoid too heavy an assault on the head of the ticket.

Today, a Vice-Presidential campaign entourage resembles that of the Presidential nominee, though on a smaller scale. Reporters are fewer in number, and their accommodations less satisfactory. The crowds are smaller and less enthusiastic. Newsmen must be prepared to hear the same speech over and over, with minor variations. Since the television networks are not likely to carry significant clips from what the No. 2 man said in Dubuque, the same speech remains fresh in Kalamazoo.

One disquieting trend in Vice-Presidential campaigning has been noticed from time to time in recent years. While some Presidential candidates have tended to take the "high road," to remain above the battle, their running mates have shown an inclination to take the "low road" in campaign tactics. If a campaign is to be filled with nothing but slurring attacks and lofty generalities, no effective dialogue between the parties is possible. Although voters are almost always disappointed by the length, tedium, and irrelevancy of political campaigns, they have found that meaningful discussion of the issues is most likely to occur in years when the election is expected to be close. The dialogue in 1960 among four unusually articulate candidates was above average. The debates in that year between the two Presidential nominees helped sharpen the issues for millions of voters. Face-to-face confrontation on television will always be fraught with peril for the participants, and until a satisfactory format for these exchanges is found, it would seem that the Vice-Presidential candidates could be paired off in national debates on an experimental basis. An exchange between Hubert Humphrey and William Miller would have proven more entertaining than most television fare. And if TV debates between the running mates become a tradition, a Presidential nominee will take greater pains to see that he is paired at the convention with a like-minded man, lest the opposition point up and exploit their differences while the nation watches.

From time to time, voters have objected to the constitutional "package deal" which prohibits them from splitting their ticket for the two national offices. The objection to a split vote is by now apparent, and one need only conjure up some wild combinations that might have been the result of ticket-splitting. What about Franklin Roosevelt-John Bricker in 1944? Or John Kennedy-Henry Cabot Lodge (both from Massachusetts) in 1960? It is unlikely that such an electoral "reform" will again be offered seriously.

Even so, it is not impossible that we might have a President and a Vice President from different parties at the same time. The Constitution provides that if the Electoral College fails to elect any Presidential candidate, the House of Representatives will elect a President from among the men receiving the three highest totals in the Electoral College. In the same situation, the Senate would choose a Vice President from between the top two men in the Electoral College voting. In the three-way Presidential race in 1960 (in which Senator Harry Byrd of Virginia received 15 electoral votes) a shift of a few votes would have prevented the Electoral College from making a choice for either office, and this situation might have come about. One can conceive of maverick Southern Congressmen attempting to swing the Presidential race to Nixon while the Senate was electing Lyndon Johnson. After the 1960 Congressional elections, Democrats controlled 29 of the 50 state delegations in the House, but five of these delegations were from the Deep South. The close Truman-Dewey election, held during the year of the Dixiecrat revolt, could also have ended in confusion. For this as well as other reasons we should hesitate to write too many explicit Vice-Presidential executive assignments into the Constitution.

Any discussion of the Vice President's duties—present and projected—must begin with his obligations in the Senate chamber.

Again, the Constitution prescribes in Article I, Section III: "The Vice President of the United States shall be President of the Senate, but shall have no Vote, unless they be equally divided." The first oblique reference in the Constitution to the President does not appear until the end of the next paragraph, giving the Vice President an ironic precedence not duplicated in any other way.

Since the Constitution calls for the election of a President pro tempore to preside when the Vice President is absent, it has never been essential for the latter to be tied to his job on Capitol Hill to the exclusion of any assignments that may come from the President. Nixon estimated that 90 per cent of his work was executive in nature, and that he spent an average of only 30 to 60 minutes a day in presiding. Two factors have kept our more energetic Vice Presidents from vacating the Capitol premises altogether in recent years. First, of course, their sense of duty, no matter how mundane that duty may seem, and secondly, the ever-present possibility of a tie vote and the consequent loss of some measure supported by the administration.

The President pro tem may be a far more influential person on Capitol Hill than the Vice President. He is usually the member of the majority party with longest service. Carl Hayden, a Senator forty-two years, held the office at age 91. The President pro tem is likely to have important committee work, so he in turn may hand the gavel to some junior member. Senator Ted Kennedy of Massachusetts, the youngest member of the Senate, was presiding on November 22, 1963, when he learned that his brother had been shot.

Parliamentary purists have long objected to the constitutional role assigned to the Vice President. He is not a member of the body over which he presides, nor is he chosen by that body. He may not even be a member of the party that controls the Senate. (Nixon presided for six of his eight years over a Senate Democratic majority.) And if the Vice President be considered a member of the executive branch, then his presence at the Capitol also violates the separation-of-powers principle.

On key issues, Senate voting is usually scheduled at some specified time, and both the majority and minority leaders of the Senate will generally keep an informal head count on an upcoming vote. These tallies usually alert the Vice President to the possibility of a tie, and in the absence of any such likelihood he can go about his business elsewhere in the city. But out-of-town and foreign assignments should not ordinarily be taken while the Senate is in session.

Even when party strength is almost equally divided, ties seldom occur. During Nixon's first six years, neither party had more than a three-man majority in the Senate. Yet in all of his eight years, Nixon was called on to break only eight ties. In all, Vice Presidents have voted about 200 times since 1789, an average of not much more than once a year. On the question of breaking ties, some parliamentary authorities raise an objection, saying that if a motion does not receive a majority it should be considered lost, and not resuscitated by the Vice President's affirmative action. And should the Vice President—who has attended no committee meetings, who has not participated in the preparation of the bill under discussion, and who has not participated in the debate—be allowed to cast the decisive vote?

If the Vice President's assigned duties have provoked controversy, so have his extracurricular activities on Capitol Hill. Most Vice Presidents—particularly those with previous legislative experience—have lobbied in behalf of legislation favored by the administration. Two of them within memory—Dawes and Garner—worked against measures favored by the administration. The Senate has generally been hostile to outside interference in its deliberations, though not so much so if the Vice President happens to be a former member of the "club." It was no coincidence that every Democratic Vice-Presidential candidate from 1944 to 1968 was a member of the Senate at the time of his nomination. Each (with the probable exception of Kefauver) was nominated with the idea that he would serve in a liaison role with Congress, and each Vice President from Truman to Humphrey proved effective in that respect.

Truman, in his memoirs, gave perhaps the best short assessment of what the Vice President can do: "The opportunities afforded by the vice-presidency, particularly the Presidency of the Senate, do not come—they are there to be seized. . . . The Vice-President's influence on legislation depends on his personality and his ability, and especially the respect which he commands from the senators. Here is one instance in which it is the man who makes the office, not the office the man."

Vice-Presidential lobbying may be considered still another violation of the principle of separation of powers. But the main objection to the Vice President's presence at the Capitol has nothing to do either with parliamentary subtleties or with political theory. Rather, it is that he should be gaining important administrative experience. Clark Clifford, who was special assistant to President Truman, thought that the Vice President would receive the best preparation for the Presidency "if he were the day-to-day working assistant to the President."

By statute the Vice President is a member of the National Security Council. He is also chairman of the National Aeronautics and Space Council. By executive order, he supervises the work of the Office of Intergovernmental Relations. Presidents may create other assignments for their Vice Presidents by issuing executive orders. But when talk turns to transferring Presidential powers directly from the President to the Vice President, the caution light must be flashed.

The Constitution places the "executive Power" in "a President," and it is apparent that the Vice President can be invested with some of the executive power only if the President surrenders some of his. In two centuries, the evolving Presidency has become the most powerful public office ever to be found in a free society. The President brings stability and strength to our Government, and symbolizes the unity of the nation. During the Vietnamese war, many members of Congress concluded that the President's freedom of action was too great. It was felt that Congress must participate more fully in deliberations on foreign policy and in observing its execution. There was no suggestion that the Vice President should have a greater role in foreign policy.

Former Vice President Wallace warned the Harvard Law School Forum in 1956: "There should be no legislation nor any constitutional amendment giving the office of the Vice President more power. It is vital that the power of the Chief Executive should not be diminished in any way by law. So far as the law is concerned, one man should run the executive branch of the Government, not two."

Nonetheless, admiration for the highest office has been tempered by the recognition that some means ought to be found to lighten the President's burden. In 1950, the McCormack Act authorized the President, subject to certain limitations, to delegate functions vested in him by law to the head of any department or agency in the executive branch. The Vice President seemed a logical prospect to inherit some administrative and ceremonial duties.

In 1956, in testimony before a Senate subcommittee headed by John Kennedy, former President Hoover proposed the creation by statute of an administrative Vice President. The subcommittee did not support this idea, but did say in its report that no further law was needed to enable the President to delegate administrative functions which may be a burden on him. The subcommittee added: "Congress should not take the lead in diluting the President's responsibilities or functions . . . unless such legislative authority is actually sought from the Congress by the President."

All this would seem to leave the Vice President in the same lonesome limbo that he has always occupied, completely at the mercy of the President insofar as executive duties are concerned. He may still be ignored altogether. Or he may be permitted to gain "experience" by handling such routine Presidential chores as proclaiming Mother's Day or National Pickle Week, or by receiving visiting delegations of Boy Scouts. Or we may go on as in the last twenty-five years, with the President picking the spots in which the Vice President is to serve.

As a final possibility, we might write into the Constitution a rather general provision such as: "The Vice President shall serve the President in such administrative capacity as the latter may deem appropriate." A flexible statement of this type would be superior to an attempt to cite in detail new Vice-Presidential responsibilities. The provision would serve as a prod to the Presidential candidate to choose the best available running mate, and as a lever for persuading qualified men to accept the nomination. The adoption of the Twenty-fifth Amendment to the Constitution in 1967 assures that any vacancy in the office of Vice President will be filled quickly. The amendment removes one barrier to the idea of spelling out more duties for the Vice President through statute or constitutional amendment. Any such duties would have been left undone during the fourteen months following John Kennedy's death.

With an adequate staff at his command and a sufficient salary, with the trust of the President, and with a rent-free mansion large enough to permit the necessary entertaining, an incoming Vice President could feel confident that he would be able to render four years of useful service to his country. We would still have no absolute guarantee that only the ablest available men would be chosen for the Vice Presidency, but of course no such assurance can be made for the Presidential office either.

Before long, an incumbent Vice President is going to be elected directly to the Presidency, smashing the hex dating from Van Buren's day. From now on the Vice President is quite likely to be the one person in the administration, after the President, who is most familiar with all the major problems facing the nation. A Governor from one state, a Cabinet member specializing in one area—and to a lesser extent, a Senator—will lack the broad perspective available to the Vice President. In a democracy it may not be appropriate to think of a crown prince or a line of succession, but it is likely that the Vice President will come to be regarded as the logical heir to the incumbent President. We would expect that Presidential nominations of the "in party" will frequently go to an incumbent Vice President in those years when the President is not seeking re-election.

The Vice President's chances in the November election would then hinge on voter approval or disapproval of the administration of which he had been a part for the previous four or eight years. If a Presidential nomination is to pass to the Vice President, then we may expect to see the President's party in Congress continue to work closely with the new administration led by the man who was heretofore second in command. With the Vice President advancing to the Presidency by election, we may also expect to see greater continuity in the executive branch, with experienced Cabinet members and members of the White House secretariat staying on to serve the new President with whom they had already been associated.

An unbroken sequence of such smooth, peaceful Presidential transitions presupposes that the minority party is standing idly by. Such will not be the case, of course, and the voters do reserve the right to throw the rascals out from time to time. Herein lies the principal problem for the aspiring politician who wants to follow the Vice-Presidential route to the White House. If he is to serve his eight-year apprenticeship in the Vice Presidency, then win the two terms of his own to which he is eligible, his party must win four consecutive elections, on top of any they may have won before our man entered the picture. On only four occasions has a party remained in power for sixteen or more consecutive years. A senator or governor can postpone his Presidential try if the stars portend defeat for his party in a given year, but a Vice President completing eight years in that office must either move up or drop by the wayside.

Moreover, this strategy requires an early start. He cannot wait until he is sixty before seeking the Vice Presidency, for after eight years—if he is successful—he will be almost seventy, too old to be President according to one of our lingering prejudices. In fact he cannot wait much past the age of fifty. The rising young statesman who made such a big hit at one convention at the age of forty-eight may find that four short years later he is already almost too old to settle for the lesser nomination. In *The Making of the President 1960*, Theodore White wrote—in reference to Hubert Humphrey, incidentally—". . . he was at that age of life, and the stars of politics so fixed, when he must reach for the Presidency this season . . . or not at all." An assassin's bullet gave Humphrey one more chance to break into the line of succession. In the future the second office will be sought most eagerly by relatively young men—many in their forties—who are prepared to travel the slow but possibly surest road to the White House.

PRESIDENTIAL SUCCESSION AND INABILITY

"God looks after fools, drunkards, and the United States."

What would happen if both the President and the Vice President should die during the same four-year period? The Constitution says: "Congress may by Law provide . . . what Officer shall then act as President . . ."

A member of the first Congress, Representative Aedanus Burke of South Carolina, saw no reason to lose any sleep over such a contingency. Delving into the laws of probability, he calculated that only once every 840 years would both the President and the Vice President die during the same term. Prophets of gloom and doom must concede that there is some basis for his optimism. Eight Presidents and seven Vice Presidents have died in office, and one Vice President resigned, yet no two of these vacancies occurred during the same term. The Twenty-fifth Amendment (1967) provides that a vacancy in the office of Vice President be filled quickly.

Nevertheless, Representative Burke might decide to recompute his odds if he came back to Earth today and beheld our H-bomb, our airplanes, and other advances in our civilization that permit us to liquidate large numbers of persons simultaneously. He might also consider how careless we are at times. In the motorcade at Dallas, for example, Kennedy and Johnson were both within the assassin's range at the same moment. Meanwhile, six members of the Cabinet were flying in the same airplane across the Pacific.

Both of the 1940 Republican candidates—Wendell Willkie and Charles McNary—died within the four-year period to which they sought election. In 1865, a plot to kill the President, the Vice President, and the Secretary of State came close to succeeding in all particulars.

Perhaps the grimmest mishap involving a cluster of national leaders occurred in 1844. The Vice Presidency was vacant, Tyler having succeeded Harrison. In February, President Tyler and a number of other dignitaries went aboard the warship *Princeton* for a Potomac cruise. Highlight of the excursion was to be the test firing of a famous new gun, the Peacemaker. In the morning, the weapon was fired successfully, to the delight of the passengers. Late in the afternoon, the President and his guests were below decks, still at the luncheon table. Word came that the gun would be fired again, and the celebrities began to drift upstairs. Secretary of State Abel P. Upshur called on the President to join him on deck, but Tyler paused to listen to a quartet of entertainers humming a familiar Virginia melody. "No, by George, Upshur," said the President, "I must stay and hear that song." And so he did, but the song was never finished. A shattering explosion from above brought Tyler scrambling up to the deck. The gun had misfired, and the President contemplated the results, thirty to forty persons sprawled about in grotesque heaps. Twelve persons were dead or dying, including the Secretary of State and the Secretary of the Navy. Tyler himself had been spared death or injury by mere chance.

The first line of Presidential succession was established in 1792 by Congress, which ranked the Senate President pro tempore and the Speaker of the House, in that order, below the Vice President. (These officials would not become President, but would succeed only to the powers and duties of the office; the Constitution is clear in this case.) This arrangement reflected the desire of Washington and Hamilton to guard against the possible succession of Thomas Jefferson, the Secretary of State.

The inadequacy of this sequence was bared during the crisis of 1881. President Garfield was shot on July 2 and died on September 19. The new Senate had convened briefly in the spring to consider Garfield's appointments, but had recessed without electing a President pro tem. The new House had not met, and had no Speaker. The Vice President, Chester Arthur, was considered by many to be unfit for the Presidency, and demands were heard for his resignation. But then who would have become President? We were able to limp through that difficult period thanks to Arthur's statesmanship.

Early in the next administration, Vice President Hendricks died in office, stirring new interest in the successsion question. In January, 1886, President Cleveland signed a statute by which Congress gave up its claims to the succession. The Secretary of State was placed first in line behind the Vice President, and he was followed by the other Cabinet members in the order in which their departments had been established.

So matters stood, until 1945, when Harry Truman succeeded Franklin Roosevelt. Truman opposed having the Secretary of State next in line for the Presidency. With the Vice Presidency then vacant, Truman said this meant in effect that he had the power to choose his own successor. (He also said that the line of succession should pass through elected, not appointed, officials.) His reasoning did not seem too strong, since almost every Presidential candidate designates his potential successor when he selects his running mate at the national convention. In either case, the President's power to name his successor is not absolute, since the convention can reject a Vice-Presidential aspirant it deems unworthy of the nomination, and the Senate can do likewise with a President's nominee for Secretary of State.

At any rate, Truman called in June, 1945, for a new statute putting the Speaker of the House and the Senate president pro tem ahead of the Cabinet members in the order of succession.

One of Truman's purposes in proposing the change was a desire to honor his old friend, House Speaker Sam Rayburn. Ironically, by the time Congress approved Truman's proposal, both houses had passed into control of the Republicans. They, not the Democrats, voted overwhelmingly in favor of the new succession statute in 1947, with the result that the House Republican leader and Speaker, Joseph Martin of Massachusetts, became next in line to Truman, who was still without a Vice President. Martin was an outspoken opponent of Truman's Fair Deal.

The assassination of President Kennedy stirred a wide demand among political scientists and columnists for a return to the 1886 succession law. The accession of Lyndon Johnson to the Presidency left Speaker John McCormack of Massachusetts (age seventy-one) and Senate President pro tem Carl Hayden of Arizona (age eighty-six) next in line. The possibility that Hayden might succeed was remote, since the elevation of the Speaker of the House to acting President would have required the House to elect a new Speaker, who would then take precedence over Hayden. As for McCormack, he had held positions of leadership among House Democrats for more than twenty years before being elected Speaker in 1962, but he was not regarded as conspicuously qualified to be President.

McCormack, saddened by the death of the President and concerned by the discussion of his own status, lost his temper at a press conference several days after the assassination. An aggressive woman reporter asked him if he might resign as Speaker. "I was elected Speaker and I'm staying Speaker," McCormack snapped. "I'm amazed, just amazed, that you can ask that. Are there no limits to decency?" He stalked out of the room.

In another interview, McCormack said that he favored the succession law as it stood, but that he "would not interpose the slightest obstacle," should Congress discuss a change. He also conceded that his age was a "legitimate" subject for discussion under the circumstances. But throughout 1964, in the absence of any call from the White House for a new succession statute, McCormack's colleagues chose not to hurt his feelings by pushing for a change. Besides, the Democrats did not want to revive memories of President Johnson's 1955 heart attack before the 1964 election.

With the inauguration of a new Vice President in 1965, McCormack was no longer sitting on the bubble, and Congress could proceed to re-examine the 1947 succession statute. An objective appraisal would show a preponderance of logic in favor of moving the Cabinet Secretaries ahead of the Congressional leaders in the line of succession.

The members of the Cabinet are the personal choices of the President and the initiators of his policies. They are almost always in the prime of life whereas the Speaker and the President pro tem are often old men. Moreover, for a total of some forty years, the House of Representatives has been in the hands of the party in opposition to the President. If Truman had died or become disabled in 1947 or 1948, the succession of Joe Martin could have provoked an abrupt and disorderly shift of leadership and direction at a time of serious foreign and domestic difficulties.

While it is true that the Secretary of State may be an authority only in the area of foreign affairs, it is precisely in this field that we need fear the consequences of death or disability. There is no question of domestic upheaval at a time of tragedy. The nation usually unites instantly behind a new leader. And our friends and enemies overseas will know what to expect—and will act accordingly—when a deceased or disabled President is succeeded by a Secretary of State both willing and able to continue the foreign policies then in effect.

Historically the Secretaries of State have surpassed the Speakers of the House in stature, as measured by their frequency of mention for the Presidency. Six Secretaries of State were elected President, five others received Presidential nominations, and seven others were strong contenders for Presidential nominations. Only one Speaker, James K. Polk, later became President, and only two others—Clay and Blaine, who were also Secretaries of State—won Presidential nominations. Even Sam Rayburn, perhaps the greatest Speaker of them all, did not clearly surpass in ability most of the able Secretaries of State who served during his years as Speaker.

The Cabinet members and the Congressional leaders will continue to be chosen—as they should be—for their ability to fulfill the responsibilities of their own offices, and without undue concern for the possibility that they might be called on to act as President. The chance that the succession might pass to any of them was reduced, as noted above and described below, by the adoption of the Twenty-fifth Amendment. Senator Kenneth Keating of New York proposed in December, 1963, that the Constitution be amended to provide for both an administrative Vice President and a legislative Vice President, with the former being available to take assignments from the President while the latter presided over the Senate. The succession would pass from one Vice President to the other. Someone else once suggested electing three Vice Presidents! But we have seen that all too often the nomination of our one Vice President has been dictated by whim. Cluttering up the scene with two or three Vice Presidents would serve only to downgrade the office that has been built up with such effort.

Filling the office of Vice President was one of the problems taken up by the Senate Judiciary Committee's Subcommittee on Constitutional Amendments after the assassination of President Kennedy. The deliberations of this subcommittee, under the chairmanship of Senator Birch Bayh of Indiana, were to lead eventually to the adoption of the Twenty-fifth Amendment. The proposal of Senator Keating for the creation of a second Vice President failed to win committee approval. Nor did the committee endorse a special election to fill a vacancy in the Vice Presidency. Such an election, occurring in the middle of a Presidential term, not only would be expensive but could result in the election of a Vice President who was not a member of the President's party.

Richard Nixon, testifying before the Bayh committee in 1964 when he was a private citizen, proposed that the Electoral College chosen at the previous national election be reconvened to approve a nominee for Vice President submitted to it by the President. He favored action by the Electoral College because it would contain a majority for the President's party; Congress, on the other hand, often does not. Senator Bayh, who later led a fight to abolish the Electoral College altogether in favor of the direct election of the President by popular vote, opposed giving any new duty to the electors. Nixon's proposal was not accepted by the subcommittee.

The relevant section of the new amendment, as approved by Bayh, the Senate, and three-fourths of the states, reads as follows:

"Section 2. Whenever there is a vacancy in the office of the Vice President, the President shall nominate a Vice President who shall take the office upon confirmation by a majority vote of both houses of Congress."

Thus, when a vacancy occurs, the President will nominate a Vice President in the manner that he now nominates a man for membership in his Cabinet, except that the nominee for Vice President must gain the approval of both houses, not just the Senate. If Congress rejects the President's first choice, he will nominate another man. In the past, in the vast majority of instances, the Senate has approved nominees for various offices submitted to it by the President. But considering the importance of the office of Vice President, one cannot preclude the possibility that a President's nominee could encounter difficulty in Congress, particularly if the Senate or House is not controlled by the President's party.

In the summer of 1965 the Bayh amendment was approved by the House and Senate and submitted to the states. Two years later, on the ratification of three-fourths, or thirty-eight, of the states, it became a part of the Constitution. Section 1 reads as follows:

"Section 1. In case of the removal of the President from office or of his death or resignation, the Vice President shall become President."

This language supersedes the ambiguous wording of Article II, Section 1, that vexed politicians and scholars from the time of William Henry Harrison's death. The new amendment conforms to the interpretation of Article II made by John Tyler after Harrison died.

Sections 1 and 2 of the new amendment, quoted above, presented little difficulty during the deliberations of Congress. But sections 3 and 4, which deal with Presidential disability, were approved in their final form only after extensive debate in Senator Bayh's subcommittee and in both houses of Congress; the wording was changed several times.

In 1964, Professor Clinton Rossiter described the problem of Presidential disability as "a situation that has no easy solution, perhaps no solution at all, except patience, prayer and improvisation." Also in 1964, Richard Nixon called the clause in Article II on Presidential disability "this one great defect in an otherwise remarkable document."

No attempt is made in the Constitution to define inability.[1] Is a President disabled if his airplane or space vehicle loses radio contact with the ground? if he shows signs of mental aberration? Doctors once told an editor of *The Saturday Evening Post* that it was amazing, by the law of averages, that no President had developed overt mental derangement.

How would a definition of inability be written to cover the following borderline situation? Roscoe Drummond studied the

[1] The words disability and inability both appear in Article II, Section 1. Only the latter appears in the Twenty-fifth Amendment. The words are used interchangeably here.

vast collection of notes, minutes, position papers, and personal exchanges among the participants at the Yalta Conference in 1945. Drummond concluded that without a doubt Roosevelt had not done his homework; he had failed to master the essential briefing papers, and was left at the mercy of the hard-bargaining negotiators with whom he met. Drummond reported that FDR's top advisers were unable to hold the President's attention while trying to convey the information he needed to know. He seemed unable to concentrate on the matters before the conference for any length of time. Admiral Ernest King believed that the President had shrunk from facing controversial issues because he could not stand the physical strain. Was this an instance of Presidential disability?

Modern efforts to come to grips with the problem date from the period of President Eisenhower's illnesses. In 1957, the President outlined for congressional leaders a proposed amendment dealing with Presidential inability. Sam Rayburn replied, "We have been getting along all right for 168 years without any trouble, and on top of that, Mr. President, you know what's going to happen? When you send this up to Congress the whole country is going to say: 'Uh huh, the President is in bad shape, this is just his way of putting Nixon in there.' "

Eisenhower laughed at this remark, but hopes for an amendment died with the laughter. Such attitudes as Rayburn's killed every attempt down through the years to write an amendment on disability. During the Eisenhower years, the Democrats were having no part of any arrangement that might make Richard Nixon acting President. (The New York *Post* managed to rise above principle in November, 1957, when Eisenhower suffered his stroke. The liberal *Post* called for Nixon to take over the President's duties, contending that the Vice President was better than no President at all, one of the few compliments that paper ever paid to Richard Nixon.)

Even Rayburn had second thoughts after Ike's stroke, and he supported a bill establishing a congressional commission to ascertain when a state of disability existed. Attorney General William Rogers rejected this proposal, saying that the congressional commission plan would infringe on the rights of the executive branch. He called instead for an amendment. The bill died.

With the prospect of action by Congress cut off, Eisenhower

drew up his disability agreement with Nixon,[2] which became a pattern for the similar arrangements between Kennedy and Johnson, between Johnson and McCormack, and between Johnson and Humphrey. But would Harry Truman have signed a similar pact with Speaker Joe Martin in 1948? Or Franklin Roosevelt with Garner in 1940? Such informal agreements rested solely on the mutual trust between the President and whoever was next in line for his office. Furthermore, the pacts provided that the Vice President (or Speaker) would consult with appropriate persons in the event that the President was unable to communicate his inability. But what if he were *unwilling* to communicate? In 1919, Vice President Marshall did not have access to enough information to make a sound judgment on the status of Wilson's health. On the other hand, Presidents Eisenhower and Johnson agreed to the publication of details of their illnesses and treatments. We have no guarantee that a future President or his doctors or his wife would provide a Vice President with satisfactory information. The adoption of the Twenty-fifth Amendment strengthens the hand of the Vice President and places greater pressure on the President and his associates to divulge the details surrounding an alleged case of disability.

With respect to the informal agreements of the period from Eisenhower to Johnson, we should be relieved that they were never put seriously to the test. Would the courts have upheld the legality of a bill signed into law by an acting President performing executive duties while armed only with a personal written agreement between himself and an ailing President? Without doubt the amendment is an improvement over those *ad hoc* arrangements.

The last two sections of the Twenty-fifth Amendment read as follows:

"Section 3. Whenever the President transmits to the President pro tempore of the Senate and the Speaker of the House of Representatives his written declaration that he is unable to discharge the powers and duties of his office, and until he transmits to them a written declaration to the contrary, such powers and duties shall be discharged by the Vice President as Acting President.

"Section 4. Whenever the Vice President and a majority of

[2] See pages 273–274.

either the principal officers of the executive departments or of such other body as Congress may by law provide, transmit to the President pro tempore of the Senate and the Speaker of the House of Representatives their written declaration that the President is unable to discharge the powers and duties of his office, the Vice President shall immediately assume the powers and duties of the office as Acting President.

"Thereafter, when the President transmits to the President pro tempore of the Senate and the Speaker of the House of Representatives his written declaration that no inability exists, he shall resume the powers and duties of his office unless the Vice President and a majority of either the principal officers of the executive department or of such other body as Congress may by law provide, transmit within four days to the President pro tempore of the Senate and the Speaker of the House of Representatives their written declaration that the President is unable to discharge the powers and duties of his office. Thereupon Congress shall decide the issue, assembling within forty-eight hours for that purpose if not in session. If the Congress within twenty-one days after receipt of the latter written declaration, or, if Congress is not in session, within twenty-one days after Congress is required to assemble, determines by two-thirds vote of both Houses that the President is unable to discharge the powers and duties of his office, the Vice President shall continue to discharge the same as Acting President; otherwise, the President shall resume the powers and duties of his office."

In another improvement over Article II, the amendment clarifies the status of a Vice President who takes over in case of Presidential disability. He succeeds only to the powers and duties of the office, not to the office itself. An ailing President may now safely relinquish his duties, secure in the knowledge that he can resume his duties upon the conclusion of his disability.

Senator Bayh's book *One Heartbeat Away* recounts from the inside the fight for the adoption of the Twenty-fifth Amendment. Differences of opinion within the Senate on some of the provisions of Section 4 proved almost impossible to resolve. There was the problem of who should determine if the President is disabled when he is either unwilling or unable to do so himself. Clearly, disability is not a matter just for the President's physicians to decide. Although the diagnoses of medical specialists should be given great consideration, the final decision must at least be shared by men able to weigh the President's condition in relation to the current national and international scene.

Should the responsibility have been placed exclusively in the hands of the Vice President? History has shown that Vice Presidents have been reluctant to act for fear of being labeled usurpers. Arthur and Marshall found themselves in especially difficult positions. The framers of the amendment nonetheless recognized that the Vice President has a role to play—but not an exclusive one. If the Vice President had sole responsibility for declaring the President disabled, his assertion likely would not command as much confidence from the public as one shared by other persons.

Senator Bayh and his colleagues assigned a share of the responsibility to the Cabinet. In the amendment the Cabinet is referred to as "the principal officers of the executive departments."

The members of the President's Cabinet have a vested interest in the maintenance of the status quo. If a Vice President took over as acting President, he presumably would be entitled to replace the old Cabinet with men of his own choosing. Also, if the Vice President happened to be a member of the opposite wing of the President's party, the Cabinet might fear that his accession would result in an abrupt and unwise shift in policy. Furthermore, the members of the Cabinet may sincerely feel that they understand the President's policies so well that they can safely carry them out over a reasonable length of time, until the President recovers from his alleged disability. Senator Bayh and his colleagues also recognized that an ailing President might dismiss those members of the Cabinet who had judged him disabled and replace them with men who would declare him competent to carry on. President Wilson's ouster of Secretary of State Lansing provides an ominous precedent. But the Congress finally concluded that no language could be formulated to deal adequately with that threat.

Allowing for all these objections that may be raised against a role for the Cabinet, it must be conceded that the heads of the executive departments are in a good position to make a judgment on the need for a temporary transfer of power. The Cabinet is a small body capable of acting expeditiously in time of crisis. The names and faces of the principal Cabinet members are familiar to most citizens, and they generally enjoy high prestige, assuming that the administration as a whole is popular. The Cabinet is in a good position to appraise any developing crisis that may be beyond the President's capacity to handle.

With these arguments to be made both for and against participation of the Cabinet in a decision on Presidential disability, the framers of the amendment hedged. They added the phrase "or of such other body as Congress may by law provide" to protect against changed circumstances in the future when participation by the Cabinet might be unsuitable for any reason. The "other body" could be a commission created especially for the occasion.

The courts were not assigned a role in the judgment of Presidential disability because the judiciary could become involved through litigation growing out of the provisions of the amendment.

Congress did not leave itself out of the picture. When a President disputes the assertion by his Vice President and the majority of his Cabinet (or of the "other body") that he is disabled, then "Congress shall decide the issue. . . ." (It should be noted in passing that such a dispute would likely arise only if the President was mentally ill.) Does the participation of Congress cause another breakdown in the separation of powers? Yes, but Congress already had the power under rare circumstances to elect the President and to remove him from office.

But could the Congress be expected to act with sufficient speed to resolve the crisis in the executive branch? The original House version of the amendment provided that the judgment by two-thirds vote that the President was disabled must be made by the Congress within ten days. The Senate, with its strong tradition of unlimited debate, would not accept such a time restriction. Facing the prospect that at the last minute the amendment might fail to receive congressional approval, the Senate reluctantly accepted a twenty-one-day limitation on their deliberations prior to voting the President disabled or not. Ten days would have afforded the Congress precious little time to collect and weigh medical evidence on the President's condition.

The Twenty-fifth Amendment rivals the Fourteenth in length, and surpasses all other amendments in wordage. Some members of Congress who opposed the amendment argued that the Constitution is largely a statement of broad principles, and that such a detailed procedure could better be handled by statute rather than by amendment. The critics said that if the arrangement proved unworkable in practice, a statute could be more easily replaced. Senator Bayh replied that the Constitution deals in great detail with the election of the President and that therefore detail is acceptable in an amendment dealing with disability. As to whether the Twenty-fifth Amendment will work in practice, only time will tell.

One at least may hazard a guess that the amendment will serve us better than continued reliance on the anonymous epigram "God looks after fools, drunkards, and the United States."

With the ratification of a carefully prepared if not perfect constitutional amendment, with the reliance on the good sense and patriotism of our leaders, we can at least face any future national misfortune free of the anxiety and despair that gripped Chester A. Arthur, Thomas R. Marshall, and others in years gone by.

More than a century ago a young Congressman, James A. Garfield, had a faith in the future unclouded by a dark vision of what that future held for himself. The words that he spoke when he learned of Lincoln's death must always ring true:

"God reigns, and the Government at Washington still lives!"

BIBLIOGRAPHY

The author has consulted more than 450 books and read perhaps 1,300 newspaper and magazine articles in gathering material for this book. Inasmuch as the book is intended only as a historical survey, I have not conducted any interviewing or turned to any manuscript sources. The following bibliography is necessarily limited. Particularly in the case of periodicals, I have listed only a few of the more significant sources.

Chapter 12 is based on material assembled for my unpublished Master of Arts thesis, *The Democratic Party's Nomination for Vice President, 1944,* prepared under the supervision of Dr. George Waller, chairman of the Department of History, Butler University, and his associates, to whom I am greatly indebted. Published accounts of the events leading to Truman's nomination differ widely. In the thesis, comprising more than 30,000 words, I was able to present various points of view and detailed evidence in support of my own conclusions. Much of this material has necessarily been eliminated from the account given in Chapter 12.

Individual articles in reference works have not been cited below, but I have turned frequently to the *Encyclopedia Americana,* the *Dictionary of American Biography,* and *Current Biography.* I also wish to acknowledge the assistance of the members of the staff of the New York Public Library, and of the libraries of Columbia and New York universities.

General References

BAIN, RICHARD C., *Convention Decisions and Voting Records.* Washington: The Brookings Institution, 1960.

BAYH, BIRCH, *One Heartbeat Away: Presidential Disability and Succession.* Indianapolis: The Bobbs-Merrill Company, 1968.

BELL, JACK, *The Splendid Misery.* New York: Doubleday & Company, 1960.

BINKLEY, WILFRED E., *American Political Parties: Their Natural History* (Third Ed.). New York: Alfred A. Knopf, 1958.

CORWIN, EDWARD S., and KOENIG, LOUIS W., *The Presidency Today.* New York: New York University Press, 1956.

DAVID, PAUL T., GOLDMAN, RALPH M., and BAIN, RICHARD C., *The Politics of National Party Conventions* (Rev.). New York: Vintage Books, 1964.

DONOVAN, ROBERT J., *The Assassins.* New York: Harper & Brothers Publishers, 1952, 1953, 1954, 1955.

FEERICK, JOHN, *From Failing Hands: The Story of Presidential Succession.* New York: Fordham University Press, 1965.

GRAFF, HENRY F., "A Heartbeat Away," *American Heritage,* Vol. XV, No. 5 (August, 1964).

HANSEN, RICHARD H., *The Year We Had No President.* Lincoln, Neb.: University of Nebraska Press, 1962.

HATCH, LOUIS C., and SHOUP, EARL L., *A History of the Vice-Presidency of the United States.* New York: The American Historical Society, Inc., 1934.

KENT, FRANK R., *The Democratic Party.* New York: The Century Company, 1928.

LEVIN, PETER R., *Seven by Chance: The Accidental Presidents.* New York: Farrar, Straus and Company, 1948.

LORANT, STEFAN, *The Presidency.* New York: The Macmillan Company, 1951.

MARX, RUDOLPH, M.D., *The Health of the Presidents.* New York: G. P. Putnam's Sons, 1960.

MOOS, MALCOM, *The Republicans: A History of Their Party.* New York: Random House, 1956.

PEIRCE, NEAL R., *The People's President: The Electoral College in American History and the Direct-Vote Alternative.* New York: Simon and Schuster, 1968.

Presidential Succession and Inability: A Statement on National Policy by the Research and Policy Committee of the Committee for Economic Development. New York, 1965.

POMPER, GERALD, *Nominating the President.* Evanston, Ill.: Northwestern University Press, 1963.

ROSEBOOM, EUGENE H., *A History of Presidential Elections*. New York: The Macmillan Company, 1957.

ROSSITER, CLINTON, *The American Presidency* (Second Ed.). New York: Harcourt, Brace & World, Inc., 1960.

SILVA, RUTH C., *Presidential Succession*. Ann Arbor, Mich.: University of Michigan Press, 1951.

TOMPKINS, DOROTHY C., *The Office of Vice President: A Selected Bibliography*. Berkeley, Calif.: University of California, 1957.

WAUGH, EDGAR W., *Second Consul*. Indianapolis: The Bobbs-Merrill Company, Inc., 1956.

WILLIAMS, IRVING G., *The American Vice-Presidency: New Look*. Garden City, N.Y.: Doubleday & Company, Inc., 1954.

WILLIAMS, IRVING G., *The Rise of the Vice-Presidency*. Washington: Public Affairs Press, 1956.

WOLD, KARL, *Mr. President—How Is Your Health?* St. Paul and Minneapolis: Bruce Publishing Company, 1948.

Additional References for Chapter 1

JOHN ADAMS—THOMAS JEFFERSON—AARON BURR

BOWERS, CLAUDE G., *Jefferson and Hamilton*. Boston: Houghton Mifflin Company, 1925.

BOWERS, CLAUDE G., *Jefferson in Power*. Boston: Houghton Mifflin Company, 1936.

DAUER, MANNING J., *The Adams Federalists*. Baltimore: The Johns Hopkins Press, 1953.

MILLER, JOHN C., *Alexander Hamilton: Portrait in Paradox*. New York: Harper & Brothers, Publishers, 1959.

MILLER, JOHN C., *The Federalist Era: 1789-1801*. New York: Harper & Brothers Publishers, 1960.

MITCHELL, BROADUS, *Alexander Hamilton: The National Adventure, 1788-1804*. New York: The Macmillan Company, 1962.

SCHACHNER, NATHAN, *Alexander Hamilton*. New York: D. Appleton-Century Company, Inc., 1946.

SCHACHNER, NATHAN, *Thomas Jefferson: A Biography*. Vol. II. New York: Appleton-Century-Crofts, Inc., 1951.

WANDELL, SAMUEL H., and MINNIGERODE, MEADE, *Aaron Burr*. Vol. I. New York: G. P. Putnam's Sons, 1925.

Additional References for Chapter 2

JOHN C. CALHOUN—MARTIN VAN BUREN

BASSETT, JOHN S., *The Life Of Andrew Jackson*. Two Volumes. New York: The Macmillan Company, 1911.

BENTON, THOMAS HART, *Thirty Years' View.* Two Volumes. New York: D. Appleton and Company, 1854.

COIT, MARGARET L., *John C. Calhoun.* Boston: Houghton Mifflin Company, 1950.

JAMES, MARQUIS, *Andrew Jackson: Portrait of a President.* Indianapolis: The Bobbs-Merrill Company, 1937.

JOHNSON, GERALD W., *America's Silver Age: The Statecraft of Clay-Webster-Calhoun.* New York: Harper & Brothers Publishers, 1939.

KOENIG, LOUIS W., *The Invisible Presidency.* New York: Rinehart & Company, Inc., 1960.

LYNCH, DENIS TILDEN, *An Epoch and a Man: Martin Van Buren and His Times.* New York: Horace Liveright, 1929.

MEIGS, WILLIAM M., *The Life of John Caldwell Calhoun.* Two Volumes. New York: The Neale Publishing Company, 1917.

MEYER, LELAND W., *The Life and Times of Colonel Richard M. Johnson of Kentucky.* New York: Columbia University Press, 1932.

SCHLESINGER, ARTHUR M., JR., *The Age of Jackson.* Boston: Little, Brown and Company, 1945.

SHEPARD, EDWARD M., *Martin Van Buren.* Boston: Houghton, Mifflin and Company, 1888.

STYRON, ARTHUR, *The Cast-Iron Man: John C. Calhoun and American Democracy.* New York: Longmans, Green and Co., 1935.

TURNER, FREDERICK JACKSON, *The United States 1830-1850.* New York: Henry Holt and Company, 1935.

VAN BUREN, MARTIN, *The Autobiography of Martin Van Buren.* Washington: The American Historical Association, 1920.

VAN DEUSEN, GLYNDON G., *The Jacksonian Era.* New York: Harper & Brothers Publishers, 1959.

WILTSE, CHARLES M., *John C. Calhoun: Nullifier, 1829-1839.* Indianapolis: The Bobbs-Merrill Company, Inc., 1949.

Additional References for Chapter 3

JOHN TYLER

ADAMS, JOHN QUINCY, *The Diary of John Quincy Adams.* (ed. by Allan Nevins.) New York: Longmans, Green & Co., 1928.

BROWN, EVERETT S., and SILVA, RUTH C., "Presidential Succession and Inability," *Journal of Politics,* XI (February, 1949).

CHITWOOD, OLIVER PERRY, *John Tyler: Champion of the Old South.* New York: Appleton-Century-Crofts, 1939.

CLEAVES, FREEMAN, *Old Tippecanoe: William Henry Harrison and His Time.* New York: Charles Scribner's Sons, 1939.

LAMBERT, OSCAR D., *Presidential Politics in the United States, 1841-1844*. Durham, N.C.: Duke University Press, 1936.

MORGAN, ROBERT J., *A Whig Embattled: The Presidency Under John Tyler*. Lincoln, Neb.: University of Nebraska Press, 1954.

PAUL, JAMES C. N., *Rift in the Democracy*. Philadelphia: University of Pennsylvania Press, 1951.

POAGE, GEORGE RAWLINGS, *Henry Clay and the Whig Party*. Chapel Hill: The University of North Carolina Press, 1936.

SEAGER, ROBERT, II, *And Tyler Too: A Biography of John & Julia Gardiner Tyler*. New York: McGraw-Hill Book Company, Inc., 1963.

VAN DEUSEN, GLYNDON G., *The Life of Henry Clay*. Boston: Little, Brown and Company, 1937.

(See also the books by Schlesinger and Van Deusen listed for Chapter 2.)

Additional References for Chapter 4

MILLARD FILLMORE

DYER, BRAINERD, *Zachary Taylor*. Baton Rouge: Louisiana State University Press, 1946.

GRIFFIS, WILLIAM E., *Millard Fillmore*. Ithaca, NY.: Andrus & Church, 1915.

HAMILTON, HOLMAN, *Zachary Taylor: Soldier in the White House*. Indianapolis: The Bobbs-Merrill Company, Inc., 1951.

NEVINS, ALLAN, *Ordeal of the Union*. Two Volumes. New York: Charles Scribner's Sons, 1947.

RAYBACK, ROBERT J., *Millard Fillmore*. Buffalo, N.Y.: Henry Stewart, Incorporated, 1959.

(See also the books by Coit and Johnson listed for Chapter 2, and the books by Poage and Van Deusen listed for Chapter 3.)

Additional References for Chapter 5

ANDREW JOHNSON

BISHOP, JIM, *The Day Lincoln Was Shot*. New York: Harper & Brothers Publishers, 1955.

GLONEK, JAMES F., "Lincoln, Johnson, and the Baltimore Ticket," *The Abraham Lincoln Quarterly*, Vol. VI, No. 5 (March, 1951).

HAMLIN, CHARLES E., *The Life and Times of Hannibal Hamlin*. Cambridge, Mass.: Published by Subscription, 1899.

LOMASK, MILTON, *Andrew Johnson: President on Trial.* New York: Farrar, Straus and Cudahy, 1960.

LOTH, DAVID, *Public Plunder: A History of Graft in America.* New York: Carrick & Evans, Inc., 1938.

MILTON, GEORGE FORT, *The Age of Hate.* New York: Coward-McCann, Inc., 1930.

OBERHOLTZER, ELLIS P., *A History of the United States Since the Civil War.* Vol. II. New York: The Macmillan Company, 1922.

RANDALL, J. G., and DONALD, DAVID, *The Civil War and Reconstruction.* Boston: D. C. Heath and Company, 1961.

ROSS, EARLE D., *The Liberal Republican Movement.* New York: Henry Holt and Company, 1919.

SANDBURG, CARL, *Abraham Lincoln: The War Years.* Four Volumes. New York: Harcourt Brace & Company, 1939.

SMITH, WILLARD H., *Schuyler Colfax: The Changing Fortunes of a Political Idol.* Indianapolis: Indiana Historical Bureau, 1952.

STRYKER, LLOYD P., *Andrew Johnson: A Study in Courage.* New York: The Macmillan Company, 1929.

WINSTON, ROBERT W., *Andrew Johnson: Plebian and Patriot.* New York: Henry Holt and Company, 1928.

Additional References for Chapter 6

CHESTER ALAN ARTHUR

CALDWELL, ROBERT G., *James A. Garfield: Party Chieftain.* New York: Dodd, Mead & Company, 1931.

CHIDSEY, DONALD B., *The Gentleman From New York: A Life of Roscoe Conkling.* New Haven: Yale University Press, 1935.

GOSNELL, HAROLD F., *Boss Platt and His New York Machine.* Chicago: University of Chicago Press, 1924.

HOWE, GEORGE F., *Chester A. Arthur: A Quarter-Century of Machine Politics.* New York: Dodd, Mead & Company, 1934.

JOSEPHSON, MATTHEW, *The Politicos, 1865-1896.* New York: Harcourt, Brace and Company, 1938.

MUZZEY, DAVID S., *James G. Blaine.* New York: Dodd, Mead & Company, 1934.

OBERHOLTZER, ELLIS P., *A History of the United States Since the Civil War.* Vol. IV. New York: The Macmillan Company, 1931.

ROBERTSON, ARCHIE, "Murder Most Foul," *American Heritage,* Vol. XV, No. 5 (August, 1964).

SMITH, THEODORE C., *The Life and Letters of James Abram Garfield.* Two Volumes. New Haven: Yale University Press, 1925.

STODDARD, HENRY L., *As I Knew Them: Presidents and Politics*

From Grant to Coolidge. New York: Harper & Brothers Publishers, 1927.

Additional References for Chapter 7

THEODORE ROOSEVELT

BISHOP, JOSEPH B., *Theodore Roosevelt and His Time.* Two Volumes. New York: Charles Scribner's Sons, 1920.

DUNN, ARTHUR W., *From Harrison to Harding.* Two Volumes. New York: G. P. Putnam's Sons, 1922.

HARBAUGH, WILLIAM HENRY, *Power and Responsibility: The Life and Times of Theodore Roosevelt.* New York: Farrar, Straus and Cudahy, 1961.

LEECH, MARGARET, *In the Days of McKinley.* New York: Harper & Brothers Publishers, 1959.

MORGAN, H. WAYNE, *William McKinley and His America.* Syracuse, N.Y.: Syracuse University Press, 1963.

OBERHOLTZER, ELLIS P., *A History of the United States Since the Civil War.* Vol. V. New York: The Macmillan Company, 1937.

PRINGLE, HENRY F., *Theodore Roosevelt: A Biography.* New York: Harcourt, Brace and Company, 1931.

ROOSEVELT, THEODORE, *An Autobiography.* New York: The Macmillan Company, 1913.

SCHRIFTGIESSER, KARL, *The Gentleman From Massachusetts: Henry Cabot Lodge.* Boston: Little, Brown and Company, 1944.

Selections From the Correspondence of Theodore Roosevelt and Henry Cabot Lodge. Vol. I. New York: Charles Scribner's Sons, 1925.

(See also the book by Caldwell listed for Chapter 6.)

Additional References for Chapter 8

THOMAS R. MARSHALL

ALLEN, FREDERICK LEWIS, *Only Yesterday.* New York: Harper & Brothers Publishers, 1931.

BAILEY, THOMAS A., *Woodrow Wilson and the Great Betrayal.* New York: The Macmillan Company, 1945.

BLUM, JOHN M., *Joe Tumulty and the Wilson Era.* Boston: Houghton Mifflin Company, 1951.

BLUM, JOHN M., *Woodrow Wilson and the Politics of Morality.* Boston: Little, Brown and Company, 1956.

DANIELS, JOSEPHUS, *The Wilson Era: Years of War and After, 1917-1923*. Chapel Hill, N.C.: The University of North Carolina Press, 1946.

GRAYSON, CARY T., *Woodrow Wilson: An Intimate Memoir*. New York: Holt, Rinehart and Winston, Inc., 1960.

HOUSTON, DAVID F., *Eight Years With Wilson's Cabinet, 1913-1920*. Vol. II. Garden City, N.Y.: Doubleday, Page & Company, 1926.

MARSHALL, THOMAS R., *Recollections of Thomas R. Marshall, Vice-President and Hoosier Philosopher*. Indianapolis: The Bobbs-Merrill Company, 1925.

SMITH, GENE, *When the Cheering Stopped: The Last Years of Woodrow Wilson*. New York: William Morrow and Company, 1964.

SULLIVAN, MARK, *Our Times: Over Here, 1914-1918*. New York: Charles Scribner's Sons, 1933.

THOMAS, CHARLES M., *Thomas Riley Marshall: Hoosier Statesman*. Oxford, Ohio: The Mississippi Valley Press, 1939.

TUMULTY, JOSEPH P., *Woodrow Wilson As I Know Him*. Garden City, N.Y.: Doubleday, Page & Company, 1921.

WALWORTH, ARTHUR, *Woodrow Wilson II: World Prophet*. New York: Longmans, Green & Co., 1958.

WHITE, WILLIAM ALLEN, *Woodrow Wilson*. Boston: Houghton Mifflin Company, 1924.

WILSON, EDITH BOLLING, *My Memoir*. Indianapolis: The Bobbs-Merrill Company, 1938, 1939.

Additional References for Chapter 9

CALVIN COOLIDGE

COOLIDGE, CALVIN, *The Autobiography of Calvin Coolidge*. New York: Cosmopolitan Book Corporation, 1929.

DAUGHERTY, HARRY M., and DIXON, THOMAS, *The Inside Story of the Harding Tragedy*. New York: The Churchill Company, 1932.

DAWES, CHARLES G., *Notes as Vice President, 1928-1929*. Boston: Little, Brown and Company, 1935.

FAULKNER, HAROLD U., *From Versailles to New Deal*. New Haven: Yale University Press, 1950.

FUESS, CLAUDE M., *Calvin Coolidge*. Boston: Little, Brown and Company, 1940.

HOOVER, HERBERT, *Memoirs: The Cabinet and the Presidency, (1920-1933)*. New York: The Macmillan Company, 1952.

LEACH, PAUL R., *That Man Dawes*. Chicago: The Reilly & Lee Co., 1930.

SULLIVAN, MARK, *Our Times: The Twenties*. New York: Charles Scribner's Sons, 1935.

TIMMONS, BASCOM N., *Portrait of an American: Charles G. Dawes*. New York: Henry Holt and Company, 1953.

WHITE, WILLIAM ALLEN, *A Puritan in Babylon: The Story of Calvin Coolidge*. New York: The Macmillan Company, 1938.

(See also the book by Stoddard listed for Chapter 6, and the book by Allen listed for Chapter 8.)

Additional References for Chapter 10

JOHN NANCE GARNER

BARKLEY, ALBEN W., *That Reminds Me*. Garden City, N.Y.: Doubleday & Company, Inc., 1954.

BURNS, JAMES M., *Roosevelt: The Lion and the Fox*. New York: Harcourt, Brace and Company, 1956.

FARLEY, JAMES A., *Behind the Ballots*. New York: Harcourt, Brace and Company, 1938.

FARLEY, JAMES A., *Jim Farley's Story: The Roosevelt Years*. New York: McGraw-Hill Book Company, Inc., 1948.

ICKES, HAROLD L., *The Secret Diary of Harold L. Ickes*. Three Volumes. New York: Simon and Schuster, 1953, 1954.

MOLEY, RAYMOND, *27 Masters of Politics*. New York: Funk & Wagnalls Company, 1949.

PERKINS, FRANCES, *The Roosevelt I Knew*. New York: The Viking Press, 1946.

TIMMONS, BASCOM N., *Garner of Texas: A Personal History*. New York: Harper & Brothers Publishers, 1948.

Additional References for Chapter 11

HENRY A. WALLACE

ALLEN, GEORGE E., *Presidents Who Have Known Me*. New York: Simon and Schuster, 1950.

BYRNES, JAMES F., *All in One Lifetime*. New York: Harper & Brothers Publishers, 1958.

CREEL, GEORGE, "Wallace Rides Again," *Colliers*, Vol. 113, No. 25 (June 17, 1944).

HERRING, HUBERT, "Henry III of Iowa," *Harper's Magazine*, Vol. 186 (February, 1943).

HULL, CORDELL, *The Memoirs of Cordell Hull*. Two Volumes. New York: The Macmillan Company, 1948.

JACKSON, GARDNER, "Henry Wallace: A Divided Mind," *Atlantic*, Vol. 182, No. 2 (August, 1948).

JONES, JESSE H., with ANGLY, EDWARD, *Fifty Billion Dollars*. New York: The Macmillan Company, 1951.

KINGDON, FRANK, *An Uncommon Man, Henry Wallace and 60 Million Jobs*. New York: The Readers Press, 1945.

LEUCHTENBURG, WILLIAM E., *Franklin D. Roosevelt and the New Deal, 1932-1940*. New York: Harper & Row, Publishers, 1963.

LORD, RUSSELL, *The Wallaces of Iowa*. Boston: Houghton Mifflin Company, 1947.

MACDONALD, DWIGHT, *Henry Wallace: The Man and the Myth*. New York: The Vanguard Press, 1947, 1948.

MADISON, CHARLES A., *Critics & Crusaders: A Century of American Protest*. (Second Ed.) New York: Frederick Ungar Publishing Co., 1959.

New York *Journal-American*, March 10, 1948.

New York *Times*, June 1-July 31, 1943; December 16, 1947.

Newsweek, March 22, 1948.

PHILLIPS, CABELL, "At 75, Henry Wallace Cultivates His Garden," *The New York Times Magazine*, October 6, 1963.

RAUCH, BASIL, *Roosevelt from Munich to Pearl Harbor*. New York: Creative Age Press, 1950.

ROOSEVELT, ELEANOR, *This I Remember*. New York: Harper & Brothers Publishers, 1949.

ROOSEVELT, FRANKLIN D., *The Public Papers and Addresses of Franklin D. Roosevelt*. Vols. 10 and 12. (ed. by Samuel Rosenman.) New York: Harper & Brothers Publishers, 1950.

ROSENMAN, SAMUEL I., *Working With Roosevelt*. New York: Harper & Brothers Publishers, 1952.

SCHLESINGER, ARTHUR M., JR., *The Coming of the New Deal*. Boston: Houghton Mifflin Company, 1958.

SHERWOOD, ROBERT E., *Roosevelt and Hopkins*. New York: Harper & Brothers Publishers, 1948.

TIMMONS, BASCOM N., *Jesse H. Jones*. New York: Henry Holt and Company, 1956.

TUGWELL, REXFORD G., *The Democratic Roosevelt*. Garden City, N.Y.: Doubleday & Company, Inc., 1957.

TULLY, GRACE, *FDR: My Boss*. New York: Charles Scribner's Sons, 1949.

WALLACE, HENRY A., *The American Choice*. New York: Reynal & Hitchcock, 1940.

WALLACE, HENRY A., *The Century of the Common Man.* New York: Reynal & Hitchcock, 1943.

WALLACE, HENRY A., *Democracy Reborn.* New York: Reynal & Hitchcock, 1944.

WALLACE, HENRY A., "Foundations of the Peace," *Atlantic Monthly*, Vol. 169, No. 1 (January, 1942).

WALLACE, HENRY A., *New Frontiers.* New York: Reynal & Hitchcock, 1934.

WALLACE, HENRY A., *Statesmanship and Religion.* New York: Round Table Press, Inc., 1934.

(See also the books by Farley (*Roosevelt Years*), Moley, and Perkins listed for Chapter 10.)

Additional References for Chapters 12 and 13

HARRY S. TRUMAN

ARNALL, ELLIS G., *What the People Want.* Philadelphia: J. B. Lippincott Company, 1947, 1948.

BARKLEY, JANE R., *I Married the Veep.* New York: The Vanguard Press, 1958.

BARNES, JOSEPH, *Willkie.* New York: Simon and Schuster, 1952.

CREEL, GEORGE, "Hannegan—in Again!" *Colliers*, Vol. 113, No. 13 (March 25, 1944).

DANIELS, JONATHAN, *The Man of Independence.* Philadelphia: J. B. Lippincott Company, 1950.

DAYTON, ELDOROUS L., *Give 'em Hell Harry.* New York: The Devin-Adair Company, 1956.

FLYNN, EDWARD J., *You're the Boss.* New York: The Viking Press, 1947.

GAER, JOSEPH, *The First Round: The Story of the CIO Political Action Committee.* New York: Duell, Sloan and Pearce, 1944.

JARMON, RUFUS, "Truman's Political Quarterback," *The Saturday Evening Post*, Vol. 218, No. 35 (March 2, 1946).

JOHNSON, DONALD B., *The Republican Party and Wendell Willkie.* Urbana, Ill.: University of Illinois Press, 1960.

JOSEPHSON, MATTHEW, *Sidney Hillman: Statesman of American Labor.* Garden City, N.Y.: Doubleday & Co., 1952.

MCCUNE, WESLEY, and BEAL, JOHN R., "The Job That Made Truman President," *Harper's Magazine*, Vol. 190, No. 1,141 (June, 1945).

MCINTIRE, ROSS T., *White House Physician.* New York: G. P. Putnam's Sons, 1946.

MCNAUGHTON, FRANK, and HEHMEYER, WALTER, *Harry Truman:*

President. New York: McGraw-Hill Book Company, Inc., 1948.

McNaughton, Frank, and Hehmeyer, Walter, *This Man Truman.* New York: McGraw-Hill Book Company, Inc., 1945.

Milligan, Maurice M., *Missouri Waltz.* New York: Charles Scribner's Sons, 1948.

Nation, 1944.

New Republic, 1944.

New York *Journal-American*, July 20, 1944.

New York *Herald Tribune*, July, 1944.

New York *Times*, August 1, 1943-April 30, 1945.

Newsweek, July, 1943-April, 1945.

Official Report of the Proceedings of the Democratic National Convention (1944). Published by the Democratic National Committee, 1944.

Powell, Gene, *Tom's Boy Harry.* Jefferson City, Mo.: Hawthorn Publishing Company, 1948.

Riddle, Donald H., *The Truman Committee: A Study in Congressional Responsibility.* New Brunswick, N.J.: Rutgers University Press, 1964.

Rodell, Fred, "Bill Douglas, American," *American Mercury*, Vol. LXI, No. 264 (December, 1945).

Roosevelt, Franklin D., *F.D.R.: His Personal Letters, 1928-1945.* Two Volumes. (ed. by Elliott Roosevelt.) New York: Duell, Sloan and Pearce, 1950.

Roosevelt, Franklin D., *The Public Papers and Addresses of Franklin D. Roosevelt.* Vol. 13. (ed. by Samuel Rosenman.) New York: Harper & Brothers Publishers, 1950.

Roosevelt, James, and Shalett, Sidney, *Affectionately, F.D.R.* New York: Harcourt, Brace & Company, 1959.

Rovere, Richard H., "Nothing Much to It," *The New Yorker*, Vol. 21, No. 30 (September 8, 1945).

Rubin, Victor, "You've Gotta be a Boss," *Collier's*, Vol. 116, No. 8 (August 25, 1945).

Salter, J. T. (ed.), *Public Men In and Out of Office.* Chapel Hill, N.C.: The University of North Carolina Press, 1946.

Smith, A. Merriman, *Thank You Mr. President.* New York: Harper & Brothers Publishers, 1946.

Time, July 1943-April 1945.

Truman, Harry S., *Year of Decisions.* Garden City, N.Y.: Doubleday & Company, Inc., 1955.

Van Devander, Charles W., *The Big Bosses.* Howell, Soskin, Publishers, 1944.

Wallace, Henry A., "How a Vice-President is Picked—Inside Look at U.S. Politics," *U.S. News & World Report*, Vol. 40, No. 14 (April 6, 1956).

WEHLE, LOUIS B., *Hidden Threads in History: Wilson Through Roosevelt.* New York: The Macmillan Company, 1953.

(See also the books by Barkley and Moley listed for Chapter 10, and the books by Allen, Byrnes, Lord, Rosenman, and Tully listed for Chapter 11.)

Additional References for Chapter 14

RICHARD M. NIXON

ADAMS, SHERMAN, *Firsthand Report.* New York: Harper & Brothers Publishers, 1961.

DE TOLEDANO, RALPH, *Nixon.* New York: Henry Holt and Company, 1956, 1960.

DONOVAN, ROBERT J., *Eisenhower: The Inside Story.* New York: Harper & Brothers Publishers, 1956.

EISENHOWER, DWIGHT D., *Mandate for Change: 1953-1956.* Garden City, N.Y.: Doubleday & Company, Inc., 1963.

GOLDMAN, ERIC F., *The Crucial Decade: America, 1945-1955.* New York: Alfred A. Knopf, 1956.

HUGHES, EMMET JOHN, *The Ordeal of Power: A Political Memoir of the Eisenhower Years.* New York: Atheneum Publishers, 1963.

MAZO, EARL, *Richard Nixon.* New York: Harper & Brothers Publishers, 1959.

NIXON, RICHARD M., "The Second Office," *The 1964 World Book Year Book.* Chicago: Field Enterprises Educational Corporation, Publishers, 1964.

NIXON, RICHARD M., *Six Crises.* Garden City, N.Y.: Doubleday & Company, Inc., 1962.

ROVERE, RICHARD H., "Nixon: Most Likely to Succeed," *Harper's,* Vol. 211, No. 1,264 (September, 1955).

WHITE, THEODORE H., *The Making of the President 1960.* New York: Atheneum Publishers, 1961.

(See also the book by Koenig listed for Chapter 2.)

Additional References for Chapter 15

LYNDON B. JOHNSON

BAKER, LEONARD, *The Johnson Eclipse: A President's Vice Presidency.* New York: The Macmillan Company, 1966.

BURNS, JAMES M., *John Kennedy: A Political Profile.* New York: Harcourt, Brace & Company, 1960.

DOROUGH, C. DOUGLAS, *Mr. Sam.* New York: Random House, 1962.
EVANS, ROWLAND, and NOVAK, ROBERT, *Lyndon B. Johnson: The Exercise of Power.* New York: The New American Library, 1966.
FULLER, HELEN, *Year of Trial: Kennedy's Crucial Decisions.* New York: Harcourt, Brace & World, Inc., 1962.
GOLDMAN, ERIC F., *The Tragedy of Lyndon Johnson.* New York: Alfred A. Knopf, Inc., 1969.
MOONEY, BOOTH, *The Lyndon Johnson Story* (Rev.). New York: Farrar, Straus and Company, 1964.
PERRY, JAMES M., *Barry Goldwater: A New Look at a Presidential Candidate.* Silver Spring, Md.: The National Observer, 1964.
SCHLESINGER, ARTHUR M., JR., *A Thousand Days: John F. Kennedy in the White House.* Boston: Houghton Mifflin Company, 1965.
WHITE, THEODORE H., *The Making of the President 1964.* New York: Atheneum Publishers, 1965.
WHITE, WILLIAM S., *The Professional: Lyndon B. Johnson.* Boston: Houghton Mifflin Company, 1964.

Additional References for Chapter 16
HUBERT H. HUMPHREY

GRIFFITH, WINTHROP, *Humphrey: A Candid Biography.* New York: William Morrow & Company, 1965.
POMPER, GERALD, "The Nomination of Hubert Humphrey for Vice-President," *The Journal of Politics,* XXVIII (August, 1966).
SHERRILL, ROBERT, and ERNST, HARRY W., *The Drugstore Liberal.* New York: Grossman Publishers, 1968.
VANDEN HEUVEL, WILLIAM, and GWIRTZMAN, MILTON, *On His Own: Robert F. Kennedy, 1964-1968.* New York: Doubleday & Company, Inc., 1970.
WHITE, THEODORE H., *The Making of the President 1968.* New York: Atheneum Publishers, 1969.

Additional References for Chapter 17
SPIRO AGNEW

AGNEW, SPIRO, *Collected Speeches of Spiro Agnew.* New York: Audubon Films, 1971.
CHESTER, LEWIS, HODGSON, GODFREY, and PAGE, BRUCE, *An Ameri-*

can Melodrama: The Presidential Campaign of 1968. New York: The Viking Press, 1969.

LUCAS, JIM G., *Agnew: Profile in Conflict*. New York: Award Books, 1970.

MARSH, ROBERT, *Agnew, the Unexamined Man: A Political Profile*. New York: M. Evans and Company, Inc., 1971.

SCHLESINGER, ARTHUR M., JR., "The Amazing Success Story of 'Spiro Who?'" *The New York Times Magazine*, July 26, 1970.

WITCOVER, JULES, *The Resurrection of Richard Nixon*. New York: G. P. Putnam's Sons, 1970.

Additional References for Chapters 18 and 19

THE VICE PRESIDENT'S JOB

PRESIDENTIAL SUCCESSION AND INABILITY

These chapters are largely summary, and many of the sources cited above have contributed to the conclusions drawn by the author. The periodical literature on the Vice Presidency, and dealing with the problems of Presidential succession and inability, is extensive. Writers whose articles have proved helpful to the author include Robert Bendiner, James M. Burns, Kenneth Crawford, Roscoe Drummond, Sidney Hyman, Arthur Krock, Walter Lippmann, Raymond Moley, Richard B. Morris, James Reston, Clinton Rossiter, Ruth C. Silva, and Lucius Wilmerding, Jr.

INDEX

Acheson, Dean, 329
Adams, John
in election of 1800, 341
feud between Hamilton and, 9, 10
opinion of Vice Presidency expressed by, 5, 9
as President, 11–12, 23
as Vice President, 6, 10
Adams, John Quincy, 42
chosen President, 24
quarrel of, with Calhoun, 25
Adams, Sherman
Denver assignment of, during Eisenhower's first illness, 265
Nixon summoned by, during Eisenhower's third illness, 272
role of, under Eisenhower, 265–266
"Secret Nixon Fund," audit by, 256
Agnew, Spiro
assessment of, 370–371
background of, 343–347
coins phrase, "radical liberals," 367
compared with Joseph McCarthy, 349
differs with Nixon on foreign policy, 369
justification of controversial speeches, 354–355
leader of 1970 Republican campaign, 366–368
in 1968 campaign, 337, 348–351
Nixon's choice of, as Vice-Presidential nominee, 242–243
opposes "permissiveness," 347
and race relations, 345–347
reaction of, to Kent State tragedy, 366
salary and domestic life of, 372
speculation about being "dropped" from 1972 Republican ticket, 369–370
speech of October 19, 1969, New Orleans, 355
speech of October 30, 1969, Harrisburg, 356–357
speech of November 13, 1969, Des Moines, 356–358
speech of November 20, 1969, Montgomery, 362–365
travels to South Vietnam and Cambodia, 365, 366
as Vice President, 353–354
Allen, George
Pauley characterized by, 199–200
quoted on "bosses," 237
quoted on 1944 Democratic National Convention, 231
Truman companion during Vice-Presidential campaign, 239
Wallace opposed by, 183, 197–198
at White House dinner prior to 1944 Democratic National Convention, 212
amendment, constitutional
Twelfth, 20
Twenty-second, 160
Twenty-fifth, sponsored by Senator Birch Bayh, 4, 46–47, 382, 384, 388–396
American Choice, The, 183
Americans for Democratic Action, 288
anti-Nixon pamphlet by, 270–271
Ames, Oakes, Credit Mobilier testimony by, 85–86
anti-poverty program, LBJ's, 300
Arnall, Ellis, 210, 226, 233, 237
Arthur, Chester A.
administration of, 107–108
background of, 91–92
death of, 109
dismissal of, from N.Y. Custom House job, 92
elected Vice President, 95
Guiteau approach to, 101, 102
New York Custom House official, 90, 91

Arthur, Chester A. (*continued*)
nominated for Vice President, 93–94
as President, 105, 386, 394, 396
reaction of, to Garfield's shooting, 100, 102, 103, 104, 125
relationship of, with Conkling, 105
Articles of Confederation, 7
Ashley, James M.
Andrew Johnson account of implication in Lincoln assassination by, 78–80
Atzerodt, George, part played by, in Lincoln's assassination, 66, 72–73, 79
Aukland, Lord, 36

Bailey, Thomas A., quoted on Wilson and the League, 142
balancing the ticket, 3, 20
desirability of, 315
folly of, 48, 259
nominees chosen for the purpose of, 50, 125
Bankhead, John, a contender for 1944 Vice-Presidential nomination, 233, 234, 236
Bankhead, William, a contender for 1940 Vice-Presidential nomination, 183
Barkley, Alben W.
appointed to National Security Council, 249
contender for 1944 Vice-Presidential nomination, 206, 234, 235
death of, 251
efforts of, in behalf of Wallace's appointment as Secretary of Commerce, 241
elected Senate majority leader, 170
FDR criticized in Senate by, 206–207
FDR's name placed in nomination for fourth term by, 225, 228
potential Vice-Presidential nominee in 1944, 206, 213
Presidential nomination sought by, 250, 279
qualifications of, for Presidency or Vice Presidency, 202
return of, to Senate after serving as Vice President, 250
Truman advised by, 242–243
as "Veep," 248–249
Vice-Presidential nominee in 1948, 247
Baruch, Bernard, 210
Bayh, Birch
author of *One Heartbeat Away*, 393–394
sponsor of Twenty-fifth amendment, 46–47, 382, 384, 388–396
Bell, Jack, Nixon's second Vice-Presidential campaign described by, 271
Benton, Thomas Hart
quoted on politics, 35
quoted on Van Buren, 36
Senate floor quarrel, with Foote, 59
as Senator, 25, 31
Berrigan, Daniel and Patrick, 368–369
Bill of Rights, 7
Blaine, James G. (the "Plumed Knight")
appointed Secretary of State, 95
Conkling derided by, 90, 95
contender for 1880 Presidential nomination, 89, 92
Garfield eulogy by, 109–110
Guiteau approach to, 101
implicated in Crédit Mobilier, 86, 89–90
Presidential nomination sought by, in 1884, 108, 109
"regent" prior to Garfield's death, 103
retirement of, 108
Board of Economic Warfare, *see* Economic Warfare, Board of
Booth, John Wilkes
behavior of, prior to Lincoln's assassination, 66–67, 79
missing pages from diary of, 79
others accused of conspiring with, 79–80
Borah, William E., opposition of, to League of Nations, 140
bosses, George Allen quoted on, 237
Botts, John Minor, charges preferred by, against Tyler, 49–50
Bradley, Omar, 329
Brain Trust, FDR's
Byrnes an unofficial member of, 201
Tugwell a member of, 176

Breckinridge, John C.
Confederate activities of, 64
Presidential candidate in 1856, 279
youngest Vice President, 63
Bricker, John
campaign charges made by, as 1944 Vice-Presidential candidate, 240
contender for Presidential nomination, 308
Bridges, Styles, 169
Brown, B. Gratz ("Boozy"), Vice-Presidential nominee (1872), 84, 121
Brown, Edmund, possible Vice-Presidential nominee in 1964, 313
Brownell, Herbert, Attorney General, 264, 272
Bryan, Charles, 1924 Vice-Presidential nominee, 164
Bryan, William Jennings
League of Nations compromise urged by, 141
Presidential nominee (1900), 119
Vice President Marshall advised by, 128
Buchanan, James
Ashley belief in poisoning of, 80
elected President in 1856, 64
Buckley, James, elected Senator in 1970, 367
Buckley, William F., quoted disapproving Agnew speech, 355–356
Bull Moose party, 64, 123
Burch, Dean, chairman of Republican National Committee, 308–309
Burke, Aedanus, ideas of, on Presidential succession, 384
Burr, Aaron
bankruptcy of, 15
characterization of, by Senator Mitchell of New York, 19
death of, 20
duel of, with Hamilton, 17
elected Vice President, 14
farewell address of, to Senate, 19
feud of, with Hamilton, 13, 15–16
murder indictment against, 17
nominated for governor of New York, 14
nominated for Vice President (1800), 12
revolt of, against Federal Government, 30
rivalry of, with Jefferson, 13–14
tried for treason, 19
as Vice President, 12, 14, 18
Bush, George, 370
Butler, Benjamin F., accusations against Andrew Johnson by, 80, 81
Butler, Nicholas Murray, 113
Byrd, Harry, 377
Byrnes, James
conversation of, with Truman concerning 1944 Vice-Presidential nomination, 220
Hillman opposition to, 210, 221–222
peacemaker in BEW-RFC battle, 193
potential fourth-term running mate for FDR, 201–202, 203, 206, 210, 213, 214–215, 218–221, 223, 224
relationship of, with Ed Flynn, 199, 215, 221
Secretary of State under Truman, 244
supporter of Wallace as FDR third-term running mate, 182–183
withdrawal of, as Vice-Presidential contender (1944), 224–225

Cabinet
and discussion of Twenty-fifth Amendment, 394–395
Jackson's, split over Eaton affair, 26–29, 33–34
question of a Negro in the, 282
Cabinet Committee on Price Stability, 260
Cabinet meetings
Coolidge attended, as Vice President, 148–149
Dawes's attitude toward, 156, 171
during Garfield's incapacity, 136
Garner attended, 168, 169, 171–172
Humphrey attended, as Vice President, 322
Lansing called, during Wilson's disability, 136
LBJ attended, as Vice President, 299

Cabinet meetings (*continued*)
  Marshall presided over, when Wilson was in Paris, 259
  Nixon attended, as Vice President, 259
  Nixon presided over, during Eisenhower illness, 264–265
  Truman attended, as Vice President, 241
Calhoun, John C.
  author of *South Carolina Exposition, The*, 30
  champion of the War of 1812, 25
  comparison of, with Jackson, 25
  death of, 59
  debate between Webster and, on nature of the Union, 39
  disagreement of, with Jackson over Eaton affair, 27–29
  elected Senator after resignation as Vice President, 39
  foe of Van Buren, 36
  nullification doctrine upheld by, 30, 35, 39
  quarrel of, with John Quincy Adams, 25
  resignation of, as Vice President, 39
  role of, in Missouri Compromise debate, 24
  role of, in Compromise of 1833, 40
  role of, in Compromise of 1850, 58
  Secretary of State, 49
  Secretary of War, 25, 32
  split with Jackson over Florida invasion, 32, 35
  states rights champion, 31–32
  as Vice President, 24–26, 38
Catholic vote
  FDR's concern for, in fourth-term campaign, 210
  received by LBJ in 1964, 311
Chambers, Whittaker, 253–254
Chancellor, John, quoted on censorship, 365
Chase, Salmon P., estimate of Fillmore message by, 61
Chase, Samuel, impeachment of, 18–19
CIO, role of in 1944 Presidential campaign, 231, 234, 240
  See also Political Action Committee
Civil Rights Act
  of 1866, 75
  of 1957, 294
  of 1964, 55, 306, 319
Civil Service Commission, establishment of, 107
civil-service reform, 55, 90, 99, 107
Clark, Champ, contender for 1912 Presidential nomination, 38
Clay, Henry
  Compromise of 1850 proposed by, 58–62
  death of, 62
  foe of Van Buren, 35–36
  leading Whig, 43
  national bank bill supported by, 47–48
  opposition of, to Jackson, 36
  Presidential aspirations of, 47, 51, 54, 56
  Presidential candidate (1831), 37
  relationship of, to Tyler, 44, 47–49
  resignation of, from Senate, 49
  resolution proposed by, to limit Presidential veto power, 49
  return of, to Senate, 58
  Secretary of State, 25
  Senator, 24, 25, 48
"clear it with Sidney," 200, 222, 240
Clement, Frank, potential Vice-Presidential nominee (1956), 287, 288
Cleveland, Grover, 122
Clifford, Clark
  opposed escalation of Vietnam War as Secretary of Defense, 329
  quoted on Vice Presidency, 380
Clinton, George
  death of, in office, 21
  Vice President under Jefferson and Madison, 21, 161
Colby, Bainbridge, 143
Colfax, Schuyler ("Smiler")
  involvement of, in Crédit Mobilier scandal, 85–86
  Presidential ambition of, 85
  questionable campaign funds of, 86–87
  ruling by, on charges against Andrew Johnson, 78
  Vice President, 85

Colfax, Schuyler (*continued*)
Vice-Presidential candidate, 83, 121
Committee on Equal Employment Opportunity, 299–300
Communists
demonstrations by, during Nixon's Latin-American tour, 274–276
Hiss connection with, 253, 254
McCarthy opposition to, 255, 261
New Deal alliance with, charged, 240
Nixon opposition to, 258, 261–263, 271
Wallace attitude toward, 189, 246
Compromise of 1833, 40
Compromise of 1850
debate on, 55, 58–62, 243
passage of measures known as, 142
Confederation, Articles of, 7
Congress
Southern representative barred from, in 1865, 75
and Twenty-fifth Amendment, 395
Conkling, Roscoe ("Lord Roscoe")
Arthur's relations with, 93–94, 100
attempt by, to re-enter Senate, 98–100
campaign manager for U. S. Grant, 90, 92, 93
conflict between Garfield and, over patronage, 94–98
death of, 109
description of, by H. Stoddard, 90
end of political career of, 103–104, 105
Republican party boss in New York, 90, 91, 93
resignation of, from Senate, 98
Senator, 94
word of Garfield shooting received by, 100
Connally, John, 304
named Secretary of the Treasury, 370
favors McCarthy for Vice Presidency, 1964, 315
Conover, Sanford, accomplice in plot to discredit Andrew Johnson, 79–80
Constitution, the
fiftieth anniversary of the adoption of, 41
flaw in, 11
Tyler's interpretation of, in the matter of Presidential succession, 18, 45, 46
Constitutional Convention
intent of, regarding Presidential succession, 46
question of Presidential disability raised in, 104
Coolidge, Calvin
anecdotes concerning, 149
attitude of, toward foreign affairs, 154
attitude of, toward prohibition, 154
background of, 146–147
Boston police strike ended by, 147
Cabinet meetings attended by, as Vice President, 148–149
characterization of, by A. P. Dennis, 154
does not choose to run, 159–160
economy preached by, 154, 157
elected President, 154, 156
elected Vice President, 163
Governor of Massachusetts, 146–147
Lippmann's opinion of, 149, 152
Marshall telegram to, 148
nominated for President, 153
nominated for Vice President, 146–148
oil reserve scandal handled by, 153
popularity of, 154
President, 151–154, 156–160
relationship of, with Dawes, 156–159
Stone named Attorney General by, 158
Vice President, 148, 149
Corber, Robert, opposed nomination of Miller, 309–310
Cornell, Alonzo, New York Custom House official, 91–92
court-packing bill, FDR's, 169
See also Supreme Court bill
Cox, James M., Presidential nominee (1920), 143, 163

Crawford, William
attempt to elect President, 36
letter written by, concerning Florida invasion by Jackson, 32
Crédit Mobilier scandal, 85–86
Curtis, Benjamin, 83
Curtis, Charles, Vice President under Hoover, 161
Custom House, New York, investigation of, 91–92, 94, 96
Czolgosz, Leon, McKinley assassinated by, 119–120

Daley, Richard, 333, 334
Dallas, George M.
Texas city named after, 53
Texas statehood favored by, 53
Vice President under Polk, 53–54
Daniels, Jonathan, description of Byrnes by, 223 225
Daniels, Josephus, 133
Daugherty, Harry
resignation of, requested by Coolidge, 152
scandal involving, 150, 152
Davis, Henry Gassaway, 1904 Presidential nominee, 124
Davis, Jefferson
hanging suggested for, 73, 76
letter supposedly written to, by Andrew Johnson, 79
Davis, John W., 1924 Presidential nominee, 164
Dawes, Charles Gates ("Hell and Maria")
appraisal of, 155
attitude of, toward Cabinet meetings, 156, 171
conduct of, in military spending investigation, 155
"Filibuster rule" attacked by, 157–158
first director of the budget, 156
nickname of, 156
Nobel Peace Prize awarded to, 156
nominated for Vice President, 155
opposition of, to Ku Klux Klan, 156
speech by, at 1925 inaugural, 157
Vice President, 155, 157–159
"Dawes Plan" for German reparation payments, 156
Dayton, William L., 1856 Vice-Presidential nominee, 65
death in office
Presidential, 6, 48, 50, 161, 384
Vice-Presidential, 21, 22, 63, 112, 122, 384
debates, great legislative, 30, 55, 57, 58, 61
Defense Program, National, Special Committee to Investigate Contracts under the, 205
Democratic National Convention
first, 37
1912, 125
1920, 163
1924, 163, 166
1928, 164
1932, 166
1940, 180–183, 200
1944, 190, 199, 200, 220, 223–238, 270
1948, 247–249, 318
1956, 288–290
1960, 290–291
1964, 312–313, 314, 315, 316, 320
1968, 333–336, 337
1972, 374
Democratic party
CIO-PAC influence with, 201
fragmentation of, 24
Garner quoted on, 171
pro-slavery, 67
split in, over slavery issue, 64
Democrats
Congressional majority held by, in FDR's second term, 169
New Deal, 168
of the South, 14–15
Texas, revolt of, against FDR, 207
two-thirds rule and (in 1924), 38
Tyler ignored by, in 1844, 51
Union supporters among, in 1864, 69
Denby, Edwin
involvement of, in oil-reserve scandal, 152
resignation of, as Secretary of the Navy, 152
Dennis, A. P., characterization of Coolidge by, 154
Department of Justice, investigation of, after Harding's death, 152
Depew, Chauncey M., 118

Dercum, Francis, decision by, on Woodrow Wilson disability, 133
Dewey, Thomas E.
  first nomination as Presidential candidate, 208
  Nixon resignation as Vice-Presidential candidate suggested by, 257
  second nomination as Presidential candidate, 248
  "tired old men" charge by, 213
Dickinson, Daniel, contender for 1864 Vice-Presidential nomination, 69
Dickinson, John, question of Presidential disability first raised by, 104
disability, Presidential, 104, 142, 391
  See also inability, Presidential
disability agreements between individual Presidents and Vice Presidents, 273–274, 391–392
Douglas, Helen Gahagan, Nixon campaign against, 255
Douglas, Stephen A.
  efforts of, in behalf of Compromise of 1850, 61
  political activity of, 63
Douglas, William O.
  contender for 1944 Vice-Presidential nomination, 202, 206, 213, 218, 220
  FDR letter concerning, as fourth-term running mate, 216, 219, 223, 229, 230
  refusal of, to consider 1948 Vice-Presidential nomination, 246
Dulles, John Foster, 265
Dunne, Finley Peter, advice by, to TR, 123

Eaton, John
  biography of Jackson by, 27
  resignation of, as Secretary of War, 33–34
  uproar caused by marriage of, 26–29
Economic Defense Board, 190
Economic Warfare, Board of
  abolished by FDR, 193
  clash of, with RFC, 190–192
  Wallace removed from, 249
Economic Warfare, Office of, established, 193
Eisenhower, Dwight D.
  amendment outlined by, concerning Presidential inability, 391
  attitude of, toward his own disability, 272, 273
  attitude of, toward Nixon, 255, 256–257, 258, 263, 267–269, 281, 283–284
  Byrnes voted for, 246
  Democratic Presidential nomination refused by, 246
  disability agreement between Nixon and, 273–274
  illnesses of, in office, 263–266, 269, 271–273, 279, 391, 392
  Nixon's opinion of, 284
  President, 259, 263
  Presidential campaign, first, 255–256, 258
  second-term candidacy of, 267, 271
  Wallace voted for, 246
Eisenhower-Nixon pact, 273–274, 391–392
Electoral College
  in deadlocked election, 24
  first, 9
  functioning of, 317
  reconvening of proposed, in filling Vice-Presidential vacancy, 329
  Van Buren's election, 40
electors, Presidential
  constitutional amendment concerning, 20
  performance of, 9–12
English, William H., 1880 Vice-Presidential candidate, 122
Essary, J. Fred, 137
Evans, Rowland, quoted on possible successor to LBJ, 6
executive power, transfer of, from President to Vice President, 380
expenses, Presidential and Vice-Presidential, 372

Fair Deal
  HST's domestic program, 243
  opposition to, 326
Fairbanks, Charles W.
  Presidential nomination sought by, 279

Fairbanks, Charles W. (*continued*)
 Vice President under TR, 123
Fall, Albert B.
 conference of, with Wilson during President's illness, 138
 imprisonment of, 153
 remark by, concerning Mrs. Wilson's "stewardship," 134
 resignation of, as Secretary of the Interior, 150
Farley, James A.
 characterization of Henry Wallace by, 180
 contender for 1940 Presidential nomination, 180
Federalists, 10, 11, 13–15, 17, 18, 22
"Filibuster rule" attacked and defended, 157–158
Fillmore, Millard
 background of, 56
 competition between Seward and, 57
 Fugitive Slave Act supported by, 62
 position of, on Compromise of 1850, 58–60, 61–62, 142
 Presidential candidate (1856), 63, 64
 Vice President, 57
 Vice-Presidential candidate, 56–57
financial data, release of, by candidates for national office, 258
Flynn, Ed
 attitude of, toward Wallace as FDR fourth-term running mate, 211
 FDR fourth term opposed by, 197
 New York City boss, 197
 relationship of, with Byrnes, 199, 215, 221
 supporter of Truman for 1944 Vice-Presidential nominee, 224, 229, 232, 235
 at White House dinner prior to 1944 Democratic National Convention, 212
Foote, Henry, quarrel of, with Benton in Senate, 59
foreign travels, Presidential and Vice-Presidential, 12, 130, 131, 168, 208, 261, 274–278, 301–303, 325–326, 365–366
Forsyth, John, Calhoun rebuked by, 38
Free Soil party, 64
Freeman, Orville, 315
Frelinghuysen, Theodore, 1844 Vice-Presidential nominee, 54
Frémont, John C., 1856 Presidential nominee, 65
Friendly, Fred W., quoted opposing censorship, 360
Fugitive Slave Act, 62
fugitive slave law, 59, 60, 61

Garfield, James A.
 Blaine's eulogy of, 109
 Cabinet appointments made by, 95
 conflict of, with Conkling over patronage, 94–98
 death of, 103, 105, 125, 385
 disability of, in office, 102–105, 385
 elected President, 95
 Guiteau approach to, 101
 implicated in Crédit Mobilier, 86
 Presidential nominee (1880), 90, 92–94
 quoted on Lincoln's death, 396
 shooting of, by Guiteau, 102
Garner, John Nance
 background of, 164
 Cabinet meetings attended by, 168, 169, 171–172
 contender for 1932 Presidential nomination, 166, 279
 co-operation of, with Hoover, 165
 Ickes opinion of, 168, 169, 172
 irritated by term "New Deal," 168
 legislative philosophy of, 165
 opposition of, to third term, 172, 180
 record of, in Congress, 165
 relationship of, with FDR, 168, 170, 172
 retirement of, 173, 295
 Speaker of the House, 165–166, 203
 Vice President, 167–168, 169–171, 203, 328, 379
George, Walter, "Filibuster rule" defended by, 157–158
Gerry, Elbridge, death of, while Vice President, 22
"gerrymander," 22

Godkin, E. L., quoted on Arthur as Vice President, 94
Goldwater, Barry
  Byrnes supported, 246
  contender for 1960 Presidential nomination, 281
  Humphrey derided by, 321
  Presidential candidate (1964), 283, 285, 307–312
Goodell, Charles, 376
Gore, Albert, contender for 1956 Vice-Presidential nomination, 288
Government Contracts, President's Committee on, 260
Graham, Philip, link between JFK and LBJ at 1960 convention, 296
Granger, Francis, 40
Grant, Ulysses S.
  attempted political comeback of, 89–90, 92
  conspiracy to kill, 79
  Guiteau approach to, 101, 102
  President, 6
  third-term bid by, 103
Grayson, Admiral Cary
  medical bulletins on Woodrow Wilson issued by, 132–133
  refusal of, to certify Wilson as disabled, 135
  report by, at Cabinet meeting, 136
  third-term nomination for Wilson objected to by, 143
Great Society, LBJ's concept of, 306, 322
Greeley, Horace
  attitude of, toward Grant, 84
  quoted on Andrew Johnson, 70
  quoted on secession, 68
Guiteau, Charles J.
  background of, 100–101, 109
  execution of, 106
  Garfield's assassination planned and carried out by, 101–102
  trial and sentencing of, 105–106

Hagerty, Jim, reports on Eisenhower's illness released by, 263–264, 266
Hague, Frank, Truman supporter in 1944, 227, 234
Hale, Robert S., protest against B. F. Loan speech by, 78
Half Breeds, 89, 92
  "stepladder investigation" by, 99
Hall, Leonard
  Eisenhower-Nixon 1956 ticket endorsed by, 270
  Nixon second-term Vice-Presidential candidacy influenced by, 268
Hamill, Pete, 366
Hamilton, Alexander
  Constitutional flaw spotted by, 11
  death of, 17, 18
  duel of, with Burr, 17
  feud between, and Burr, 13, 15–16
  feuding between John Adams and, 9–10, 11
Hamlin, Hannibal
  Vice President in 1860, 67
  Vice-Presidential nomination denied in 1864, 67, 69
Hancock, Winfield S., Presidential nominee (1880), 95, 101
Hanna, Mark
  death of, 121
  McKinley favored by, 114
  opposition of, to TR, 113–117, 119, 121
Hannegan, Robert
  Byrnes, alternate choice of, for 1944 Vice-Presidential nomination, 221–224
  city boss, St. Louis, 198
  "clear it with Sidney" phrase repudiated by, 240
  Collector of Internal Revenue, 199
  FDR fourth term approved by, 197
  opposition of, to Wallace, 198, 221, 222, 223
  sponsorship of Truman for 1944 Vice-Presidential nomination, 212, 214, 215, 218, 219, 221–227, 229–230, 235, 236
  sponsorship of Truman for Senator, 198–199, 204
Harding, Warren G.
  betrayal of, by appointees, 150
  Coolidge invited to Cabinet meetings by, 148, 149
  death of, 149, 150
  elected President, 148
  Presidential nominee (1920), 145, 148

Harris, Fred, 336
Harrison, William Henry ("Tippecanoe"), believed poisoned, 80
  death of, 45, 46, 104, 385, 390
  inauguration of, as President, 44
  one-term pledge by, 44, 47
  Presidential nominee (1840), 43
Hatfield, Mark, 342, 367
Hay, John, 114
Hayden, Carl, position of, in line of succession, 378, 387
Hayes, Rutherford B.
  civil service advocate, 90, 91
  comment of, on death of Garfield, 103
  New York Custom House investigation ordered by, 91
  President, 88, 93, 96
Hayne, Robert, famous debate of, with Webster, 30
Hendricks, Thomas A.
  death of, in office, 122
  Vice-Presidential candidate in 1876 and 1884, 87–88, 122
Herter, Christian, promoted as 1956 Vice-Presidential candidate, 270
Hill, Isaac, quoted on toast proposed at 1830 Jefferson Day dinner, 31
Hillman, Sidney
  attitude of, toward Truman as 1944 Vice-Presidential nominee, 218, 223, 224, 236
  Byrnes opposed by, as FDR 1944 running mate, 210, 221, 223
  denounced by Bricker, 240
  FDR's attitude toward, 200
  Pegler quoted on, 222
  power possessed by, 201, 222, 232
  Wallace supported by, for FDR's fourth-term running mate, 210, 211, 218, 223, 226, 236
Hiss, Alger
  character reference for, by Adlai Stevenson, 256
  charges against, by Whittaker Chambers, 253
  convicted of perjury, 255
  Nixon's part in case against, 253–254
Hobart, Garret A.
  death of, in office, 112, 122
  Vice President from 1897 to 1899, 122
Hoover, Herbert
  administrative Vice Presidency suggested by, 381
  landslide election of, 164
  League of Nations compromise advised by, 141
  Presidential nominee (1928), 161
  renomination of, 161
  Secretary of Commerce, 152
Hoover, J. Edgar, 320
Hopkins, Harvey, 181, 186
House, Colonel Edward M., 140
House of Representatives, election deadlock decided in, 24
Houston, David, 137
Hughes, Emmet John
  description of Nixon by, 284
  quoted on Eisenhower opinion of Nixon, 281
  quoted on Miller, 1964 Vice-Presidential candidate, 312
Hull, Cordell
  complaint against Wallace by, 191
  Vice-Presidential nomination refused by, 181
Humphrey, George, Dr. Paul Dudley White recommended by, 265
Humphrey, Hubert
  background of, 317–318
  and civil rights, 318, 319
  and communism, 319
  comparison of, with Nixon, 317
  contender for 1956 and 1960 convention nominations, 289, 320
  Goldwater derision of, 321
  in 1968 campaign, 338–339
  Presidential qualifications of, 330
  roles assigned to, in LBJ administration, 322–323
  seeks nomination in 1968, 330–335
  technique of selection as LBJ running mate, 320–321
  Presidential possibility for (Theodore White's view), 323–324
  Vice-Presidential nominee, 321–322
  Vice-Presidential qualifications assessed, 287, 320–321
  and Vietnam War, 324–327, 332

Ickes, Harold
attitude of, toward Wallace, 211, 226, 232
comments on Garner by, 168, 169, 172
illnesses, Presidential, *see* disability, Presidential; inability, Presidential
impeachment
of Samuel Chase, 18–19
of Andrew Johnson, 59, 79, 81–82
Tyler threatened with, 50
inability, Presidential
amendment concerning, outlined by Eisenhower, 391
difficulty of defining, 390–396
Eisenhower decision concerning, 273
FDR at Yalta an example of, 390–391
Clinton Rossiter quoted on, 390
Vice President's position during, 46–47
See also amendment, Twenty-fifth; disability, Presidential
inaugural speech
Harrison's, 44
Andrew Johnson's, 70–71
Lincoln's second, 71
Nixon's, 353
Tyler's, 45
inauguration day folklore, 63

Jackson, Andrew
attitude of, toward the Missouri Compromise, 24
biography of, by Eaton, 27
comparison of, with Calhoun, 25
conspiracy to discredit, 35–36
disagreement with Calhoun over nullification act, 30–32
Eaton affair, in first term of, 27–29, 34
Florida invasion by, 32
military exploits of, 25
President, first term, 26–38
President, second term, 38–40
second-term ambitions, 33
Senator, 25
Tyler dispute with, 43
Van Buren Presidential nomination endorsed by, 52, 279
Jackson, Samuel
FDR letter to, re fourth-term running mate, 217
permanent chairman, 1944 Democratic National Convention, 231, 234
speech by, at 1944 convention, 227, 228
Jefferson, Thomas
Chase impeachment brought about by, 18–19
opinion of Vice Presidency expressed by, 5
President, first term, 14–19
President, second term, 21
Presidential nominee, 11, 12, 341
rivalry of, with Burr, 12–14
third term declined by, 21
Vice President, 6, 11–12, 23
job security, Vice-Presidential, 373
Johnson, Andrew
accused of complicity in Lincoln's assassination, 67, 77–80, 102
attitude of, toward Confederates, 73–77
description of, 68
impeachment of, 50, 79, 81–82
inaugural speech by, 70–71
Military Governor of Tennessee, 68
plot to kill, 79
President, 73, 74, 83
re-elected to Senate, 83
Senator, 68
third-party support of, 64
Vice President, 67, 70, 107
Johnson, Hiram
defeated in 1924 California primary by Coolidge, 153
opposition of, to League of Nations, 140
Vice-Presidential nomination refused by, 145
Johnson, Lady Bird (Mrs. Lyndon B.)
as asset to LBJ, 292
in 1960 incident in Dallas, 298
quoted after 1960 campaign, 298–299
view of LBJ's accepting 1960 nomination, 296
Johnson, Lyndon B.
attitude of, toward Vice Presidency, 294, 297, 299

Johnson, Lyndon B. (*continued*)
  background and congressional career of, 291–294
  and Bobby Baker; speculation about being "dumped" in 1964, 304
  in campaign of 1964, 307, 311–312
  Catholic vote received by, 311
  chosen as 1960 nominee for Vice President, 294–297
  eligibility of, under two-term amendment, 160
  Great Society, concept of, 306, 322
  opposition of, to Kefauver, 289
  political philosophy of, 165
  President, 305
  Presidential ambitions of, 304, 320
  Presidential succession agreement with, 274
  reaction of, to FDR's death, 3, 241
  relationship with HHH, 311–312, 318, 323–326
  relationship with JFK, 294–297, 303–304
  relationship with RFK, 296, 300–301, 313–315, 326
  role in discrediting Joseph McCarthy, 293
  role in passing 1957 Civil Rights Act, 294
  Senator, 292
  technique of, in selecting a running mate, 311, 312–316, 320–323
  Vice President, 299–301, 303–304
  Vice-Presidential nominee, 7, 290–291, 297–299
  and Vietnam War, 325–330
  War on Poverty, 306
  war record of, 311–312
  Washington home of, 372
Johnson, Richard M., Vice President (1837), 40–41
Jones, Jesse
  dismissed as Secretary of Commerce, 241
  removed from RFC by FDR, 193
  Wallace antagonism to, as RFC administrator, 190–193
Julian, George, quoted on policy toward Rebels, 74

Kaiser, Henry, potential FDR fourth-term running mate, 210
Keating, Kenneth, constitutional amendment proposed by, 388–389
Kefauver, Estes
  Presidential candidate (1952), 288
  Vice-Presidential nominee (1956), 288–289
Kelly, Edward J., role of, at 1944 Democratic National Convention, 180, 200, 212, 221, 223, 224, 230–233, 236
Kennedy, John F.
  age of, on becoming President, 6
  birthday phone call to Garner by, 173
  choice of LBJ as running mate by, 291, 294–297
  death of, 160–161, 173, 304, 386
  Miller's characterization of, 308
  President, 299–301, 303–304
  Presidential nominee, 291, 297, 320
  Presidential succession agreement by, 274
  relationship with LBJ, 294–297, 303–304
  Vice-Presidential nomination sought by, 288–290, 375
Kennedy, Joseph P., reference to, by LBJ, 291
Kennedy, Robert F.
  death of, 332
  in 1968 campaign, 328, 330
  potential LBJ running mate, 311, 313–315
  relationship with LBJ, 296, 300–301, 313–315, 326
  resignation of, as Attorney General, 314
  speculation about role in 1972, 323–324
  and Vietnam War, 326, 327
Kennedy, Ted, 325, 378
Kern, John, 1908 Vice-Presidential candidate, 124
Kerr, Robert, contender for 1944

Kerr, Robert (*continued*)
Vice-Presidential nomination, 235
Khrushchev, Nikita, 46
Nixon encounter with, 276–278
King, Martin Luther, Jr., death of, 331, 345
King, William
advocate of two-thirds rule, 37
death of, after one month as Vice President, 63
Kissinger, Henry, 369
Know-Nothing party, 63, 64
Korea, intervention in, 249
Krock, Arthur, quoted on 1944 Vice-Presidential nomination, 197, 222
Ku Klux Klan
Dawes opposed to, 156
Truman falsely claimed to be a member of, 239

Landon, Alfred M., 1936 Presidential candidate, 169
Lansing, Robert
behavior of, during Wilson's illness, 135–136
regency of Edith Wilson challenged by, 134
resignation of, as Secretary of State, 136
Lawrence, David, 297
League of Nations, 131, 133, 134, 139–142
Leahy, Admiral, FDR war council with, 218
Lee, Robert E., 72, 77
LeMay, Curtis, as Independent candidate for Vice President, 1964, 351–353
Lenroot, Senator Irvine H., contender for 1920 Vice-Presidential nomination, 146
Lewis, John L.
Garner quoted on, 170
opinion of Garner by, 173
Lincoln, Abraham
assassination of, 67, 73
conspiracy to kill, 79
elected President, 64, 67, 70
Johnson accused of complicity in death of, 67, 77–80, 102
the politician, 69
second inaugural address by, 71
Lindsay, John V., 342
seconds Agnew's nomination, 1968, 348
Lippmann, Walter
Nixon Latin-American tour criticized by, 276
quoted, disapproving Agnew's rhetoric, 370–371
quoted on Coolidge, 149, 152
Livingston, Edward, 34
Loan, Benjamin F., accusation against Andrew Johnson by, 77–78
lobbying, Vice-Presidential, 320
Lodge, Henry Cabot, 1960 Vice-Presidential nominee, 282, 310, 348
Lodge, Henry Cabot, Sr.
attitude of, toward League of Nations, 131, 140–142
opinion of, concerning Coolidge, 148
permanent chairman, 1920 Republican National Convention, 146
regency of Edith Wilson protested by, 134
Logan, John A., 1896 Vice-Presidential nominee, 122
Long, Huey, rebuked by Garner, 167
Longworth, Alice Roosevelt, quoted on Coolidge, 154
Lord, Russell, quoted on New Deal, 176–177
Lowden, Governor Frank, potential nominee, 145
Lucas, Scott, contender for 1944 Vice-Presidential nomination, 203, 221, 233, 236

MacArthur, General Douglas
FDR war conference with, 218
LBJ received Silver Star from, 311–312
recall of, from Far East, 249
McCarthy, Eugene
antiwar candidate, 1968, 327–329, 330, 338
at Chicago convention, 333–336
contender for 1964 Vice-Presidential nomination, 313, 315–316
McCarthy, Joseph, 255, 261

McCarthy, Joseph (*continued*)
compared to Agnew, 349
LBJ's role in discrediting, 293
McClamant, Wallace, speech by, nominating Coolidge, 146
McClellan, General, 1864 Presidential candidate, 107
McCormack, John, in line of Presidential succession, 274, 297, 387
McCormack Act, 381
McCormick, Medill, 146
McDaniel, Lawrence, nomination deal with, 199
McDonald, David, influence of, as union president, 278–279
McGovern, George, 367
McIntyre, Dr. Ross, FDR's health guarded by, 196
McKellar, Kenneth
BEW expense control proposal by, 192
complaint by, in Senate, 249
McKinley, William
assassination of, 111, 119–120
attitude of, toward TR as running mate, 114–116
President, 111, 119
Presidential nominee, 118
McNamara, Robert
contender for 1964 Vice-Presidential nominee, 313, 315
resigns as Secretary of Defense, 328–329
McNary, Charles
death of, 385
Wilkie's running mate, 184
McNutt, Paul, contender for 1944 Vice-Presidential nomination, 203
Madison, James, 21, 22
Mansfield, Mike, 296, 299
Marshall, Chief Justice John, 18
Marshall, Thomas R.
background of, 126
behavior of, during Wilson's illness, 137–138, 392, 394, 396
controversial observations by, 127–128
death of foster child of, 139
foreign guests entertained by, 139, 143
New York *Times* comments on, 128, 129
quoted on Vice Presidency, 59, 128, 148, 250
Vice President, 125–130, 137–138, 139, 143
Martin, Joseph
permanent chairman, 1956 Republican National convention, 270
position of, in line of Presidential succession (1947–48), 386, 388, 392
Martineau, Harriet, quoted on Calhoun, 39
Maynard, Judge Horace, Andy Johnson praised by, 69
Mazo, Earl, comment of, on Nixon's "Checkers" speech, 259
Merritt, E. A.
New York Custom House collector, 92
shifted to diplomatic post, 96
military spending, post-World War I investigation of, 155
Miller, William E.
background of, 307–308
comments of, on Humphrey, 311
Goldwater running mate, 307–312
Kennedy characterized by, 308
LBJ's war record assailed by, 311–312
Missouri Compromise, 24
Mitchell, James, asked to intervene in steel strike, 278
Mitchell, Judge Richard, 232
Mitchell, Samuel, quoted on Burr, 19
Moley, Raymond, quoted on Wallace, 194
Monroe, James, 13, 22, 24, 25
Morton, Levi P.
Garfield-Conkling disagreement over, 95
Governor of New York, 122
Vice-Presidential nomination suggested for, 93
Vice-Presidential nominee, 122
Morton, Thruston, considered as Nixon running mate, 282
Murray, Philip
Political Action Committee proposed by, 201
Wallace supporter in 1944, 224, 226
Muskie, Edmund S.
background of, 336–337
Vice-Presidential candidate, 1968, 338

National Aeronautics and Space Council, 9, 301, 380
National convention vs. National primaries, 113–114
National Defense Program, Special Committee to Investigate Contracts under the, 205
National Republicans, 35, 37
National Security Council
  Humphrey attended meetings of, as Vice President, 322
  LBJ attended meetings of, as Vice President, 299
  Nixon attended meetings of, as Vice President, 259, 264
  Vice President a member of, 8, 248, 380
"National Union" party, 69, 77
Nesbitt, George F., 87
New Deal, 176
  basic laws of, overturned, 169
  Communist alliance charged against, 240
  Garner's attitude toward, 167, 168, 172
  states rights vs., 207
  Truman supported, 204
  Wallace's attitude toward, 178, 190, 205, 228
New Freedom, 123, 127
New Frontier
  a memorial to JFK, 305
  urged by LBJ, 299
New Frontiers, 178
  quote from, 188
New Nationalism, 13
New York *Post*, urges Nixon to assume Presidential duties, 1957, 391
Newsweek, target of Agnew, 1969, 362
Nixon, Richard
  addresses "silent majority," 358–360
  Byrnes supported, 246
  campaign tactics of, 262–263, 271
  characterizations of, 253
  comparison of, with Humphrey, 317
  conduct of, during Eisenhower illnesses, 263–266, 272, 273, 279, 391
  Congressman, 252–253
  Eisenhower attitude toward, 255, 256–257, 258, 263, 267–269, 281, 283–284
  foreign travel, 274–276, 278–279
  Hiss investigation instigated by, 253–255
  intervention of, in 1959 steel strike, 278–279
  Khrushchev debate with, 276–278
  Latin-American good-will tour, 274–276
  in 1970 campaign
  opinion of Eisenhower, 284
  opposition of, to Communists, 253, 261
  Presidential race by, 6, 281–282, 283–285, 297–298
  proposes that Electoral College review Vice-Presidential nominations, 389
  secret fund uproar involving, 256–259
  Senator, 255
  Six Crises by, 284
  Stassen campaign to "dump," 269
  supports Agnew's rhetoric, 356
  "Veep" title refused by, 248
  Vice President, 252, 259–283, 379
  Vice-Presidential nominee, 255–256
  and Vietnam war, 358–360
nominating system, possible change in, 374
nominations, manner of making prior to 1824, 36
Norris, George
  Dawes ribbed by, 159
  letter from, to Wallace, 238
  Willkie opposed by, 209
Novak, Robert, quoted on possible successor to LBJ, 6
Nullification, doctrine of, 30, 31, 33, 39

O'Donnell, Kenneth, quoted on LBJ, 296

Parker, Alton B., 1904 Presidential nominee, 119
patronage disputes
  between Conkling and Garfield, 94, 96–97, 99
  in Fillmore regime, 57, 62
  between Platt and TR, 112

Pauley, Edwin W., role of, in 1944 Presidential campaign, 199, 200, 201, 205, 206, 212, 214, 229, 230, 231, 235, 237
Peace Corps National Advisory Council, 301
  Humphrey as chairman, 322
  LBJ as chairman, 301
Pegler, Westbrook, quoted on Hillman, 222
Pendergast, Tom, Truman association with, 199, 203–204, 213, 221, 239
Pendleton, George H., 1864 Vice-Presidential candidate, 107
Pendleton Act, 107
Perkins, Frances
  FDR conversation with, on Wallace, 181
  quoted on Cabinet meetings, 172
Perkins, Milo, BEW policies defended by, 192
Petain, Marshal, 192
Pickering, Timothy, quoted on Southern Democrats, 14–15
Pierce, Franklin, President, 63
Pinckney, Thomas, 1796 Vice-Presidential candidate, 11
Platt, Thomas Collier
  forgotten, 103
  New York political boss, 112
  opinion of Blaine by, 108
  resignation of, from Senate, 98
  Senator, 95, 112
  "stepladder" investigation of, 99–100
  TR Vice-Presidential race urged by, 112, 113, 115, 117
Plumer, William, quoted on Burr, 17–18
Political Action Committee (PAC)
  activities of, 211, 223, 226, 240
  formation of, 73
  Nixon fighting, 253
pollitical parties, beginning of, 11, 20
politicians, professional, as Presidents, 286
Polk, James K.
  President, 328
  Presidential nominee, 51
Pomerene, Atlee, 153
powers, Presidential, 8
President, acting, 42, 45, 46, 266, 274, 391, 393–394
President pro tempore, 378
Presidential campaign, 1960, 283–285, 290–291, 294–299
Presidents, accidental, 6, 51, 60, 62, 74, 121, 160, 304
Price Stability, Cabinet Committee on, 260
Progressive party, 64, 246

Quay, Matthew, TR's Vice-Presidential candidacy aided by, 115, 116, 117

racial discrimination, 260, 294, 299–300, 318–319, 331, 345–347
Radicals, post-Civil War attitudes of, 74, 75–77, 81–82, 83
Randolph, John
  attacks on John Quincy Adams by, 25
  quoted on Calhoun, 39
  Van Buren described by, 26
Rayburn, Sam
  ability of, 388
  appraisal of, by Nixon, 263
  attitude of, toward disability amendment, 391
  opinion of, on LBJ's Vice-Presidential candidacy, 292, 294, 295–296
  opposition of, to Kefauver, 289
  potential Vice-Presidential nominee, 203, 206, 207–208, 213
  Speaker of the House, 202–203
  Truman desire to honor, 386
  word of FDR's death received at office of, 241
Reagan, Ronald
  possible candidate for Vice President, 1968, 341–342
reconstruction, post-Civil War, 55, 75
Reconstruction Finance Corporation (RFC), 190–193
Reid, Whitelaw, 122
Republican party, 24, 65, 67
Republican National Conventions, 82, 89, 113–114, 123, 145, 308–311, 340–343
Republicans, 11, 12–13, 21–22, 82, 127, 246
Roberts, Owen J., 153
Robertson, William H., New York Custom House appointee, 96–98, 105,

Robinson, Joseph T.
death of, 170
opposition of, to Dawes's speech, 157
Vice-Presidential nominee, 164, 210
Rockefeller, Nelson
and Agnew in 1968 campaign, 345
functions of political parties, according to, 292
potential Presidential nominee, 280–281
rebuffed by Miller in 1964, 307
refusal of, to run as Vice President, 7, 282
Roerich, Nicholas Konstantinovich, 185
Rogers, William
congressional commission on Presidential disability opposed by, 391
Nixon counselor during Eisenhower disability, 263, 272–273
Romney, George, Presidential contender, 1968, 348
Roosevelt, Eleanor
comment by, on Wallace, 186
urged to prevent FDR fourth-term candidacy, 197
Roosevelt, Franklin D.
Barkley criticism of, in Senate, 206–207
"court packing" bill proposed by, 169
death of, 3, 241
first term, 168
fourth term, 160, 197, 229, 231
health of, 196–197, 201, 213, 240
Presidential power exercised by, 4
relationship between Garner and, 168, 170, 172–173
second term, 169
Senatorial purge undertaken by, 171
stricken with polio, 163
Texas Democrats revolt against, 207
third term, 160, 172, 180–182
vacillation of, in choice of fourth-term running mate, 198–238
Vice-Presidential candidate, 163, 286, 375
at Yalta, 241, 390–391
Roosevelt, James, 227–228
Eisenhower favored by, 246
Roosevelt, Theodore
Assistant Secretary of the Navy, 111
Bull Moose revolt led by, 64, 123
Governor of New York, 111–113
President, 111, 120–121, 153
shot during 1912 campaign, 124
Vice President, 119
Vice-Presidential candidate, 116–118
Root, Elihu, 114
Rosenman, Samuel, 182
attitude of, toward Wallace, 211
meeting of, with Willkie, 209
Ross, Edmund G., 82
Rossiter, Clinton, quoted on Presidential inability, 390
Rovere, Richard, Nixon characterized by, 260
Rusk, Dean
eliminated as Vice-Presidential possibility, 1964, 315
Secretary of State, 305
Russell, Richard, contender for 1948 Presidential nomination, 246
Russia
Nixon tour of, 278
Wallace's attitude toward, 189

salaries, Vice-Presidential, 312
Salinger, Pierre, quoted on LBJ's nomination as Vice President, 296–297
Scott, General Winfield, 1852 Presidential nominee, 62
Scranton, William, contender for 1964 Presidential and Vice-Presidential nominations, 310, 375
secession, 40, 68
second-term precedent, resolution concerning, 160
Secretaries of State as potential Presidents, 388
Senate, relationship of, with Vice Presidents, 379–380
Senators, popular election of, 95
Sevareid, Eric, quoted opposing Agnew's charges, 363, 365
Sewall, Arthur, 1896 Vice-Presidential nominee, 122

Seward, William H.
  antagonism between Fillmore and, 61–62
  Compromise of 1850 opposed by, 59
  plans to kill, 72, 79
  Secretary of State, 69
Sherman, James, death of, prior to election, 123–124
Sherman, John
  Presidential ambitions (1888), 114
  Presidential dark horse (1880), 90
  Secretary of the Treasury, 94
Shriver, Sargent
  interest of, in 1964 Vice-Presidential nomination, 313
  Kennedy supporter for 1956 Vice-Presidential nomination, 286
"Sidney, clear it with," 200, 222, 240
Six Crises (Nixon), 102
slavery, controversy over, 58–62, 67
Smathers, George, quoted on "dumping" LBJ, 304
Smith, Alfred E., contender for 1920 Presidential nomination, 163
Sorensen, Theodore, joins Johnson administration, 305
South Carolina Exposition, The, 30
Soviet Union
  Truman's attitude toward, 244
  Wallace's attitude toward, 188–189
    See also Russia
Sparkman, John
  Nixon criticism of, 258
  Vice-Presidential nominee (1952) 250
Special Committee to Investigate Contracts under the National Defense Program, 205
spoils system, 35, 103
Stalin, Joseph
  Truman's meeting with, 244
  Wallace's admiration of, 188, 189
Stalwarts, 89, 93–96, 100–102, 103
Stanton, Edwin
  dismissal of, by Andrew Johnson, 81
  resignation of, 82
  Secretary of War, 66
Stassen, Harold, campaign by, to "dump" Nixon, 269
states rights, 31, 44, 49, 207
Stevens, Thaddeus, 70, 75, 81
Stevenson, Adlai
  comments of, on Nixon, 262, 271
  Presidential nominee (1952 and 1956), 123, 250, 286, 288, 289
  Vice-Presidential nomination desired by (1964), 313
Stevenson, Adlai E., 1892 and 1900 Vice-Presidential candidate, 122
Stoddard, Henry
  description of Conkling by, 90
  quoted on death of Conkling, 109
  quoted on Garfield, 92
Stone, Harlan Fiske, Attorney General, 152, 158
strike
  sit-down, FDR and Garner quarrel over, 170
  steel, halted by Taft-Hartley injunction, 100
succession, Presidential, 384–396
  intent of Constitutional Convention concerning, 46
  TR's idea of, 120
  Truman's idea of, 386
  Tyler's view of, 45–46
Sumner, Charles, 71
Supreme Court bill, FDR's, 171
    See also court-packing bill

Taft, Robert A.
  appraisal of, 111
  contender for Presidential nomination, 202, 308
Taft, William Howard
  League of Nations Compromise advised by, 141
  Presidential nominee (1908 and 1912), 123, 279
Taft-Hartley injunction, 278
Taggart, Tom, 126
tariff problems in 1824 and 1828, 30, 39, 47
Taylor, Zachary ("Old Rough and Ready")
  believed to have been poisoned, 80
  California statehood urged by, 58
  death of, 60–61, 142, 335

Taylor, Zachary (*continued*)
President, 57
Presidential nominee (1848), 56
Tenure of Office Act, 81, 82
Thieu, Nguyen Van, President of South Vietnam, 326, 339
third parties, 64, 84, 246
third term, *see* Roosevelt, Franklin D.
Thistlethwaite, Mark, 138
Throttlebottom, Alexander, 4, 161, 190
Thurman, Allen G., 1888 Vice-Presidential nominee, 122
Thurmond, Strom, advises Nixon, 341–343
ticket splitting, 317
Tilden, Samuel J., 1876 Presidential nominee, 87
Tompkins, Daniel D., Vice President, 22–23
Tonkin Gulf Resolution, 324, 360
Truman, Harry S.
attitude appraisal of, as President, 243
assassination of, attempted, 250
assessment of Vice Presidency by, 380
attitude of, toward being President, 245
attitude of, toward Soviets, 244
attitude of, toward Vice-Presidential candidacy 209, 220, 223
background of, 203
Barkley's advice to, 242–243
end of friendship with Byrnes, 245–246
Klan membership attributed to, 239
opinion of, on Presidential succession, 326
opinion of, on Vice Presidency, 5
President, 3, 4, 241–242, 286
relationship of, with Pendergast, 199, 203–204, 213, 221
Senator, 198–199, 204
Vice President, 3, 174, 240
Vice-Presidential nomination of, 108–238
Wallace "fired" by, 245
Truman-Douglas letter, 216, 219, 223, 229, 230
Tugwell, Rexford Guy, 176
Tully, Grace, 216, 223
Tumulty, Joseph, role of, during Wilson's illness, 132, 135–136, 140
two-thirds rule, 37, 38
Tyler, John
attempt by, to win full term, 50–51, 64
attitude of, toward Presidential succession, 45–46, 390
family of, 50
impeachment of, threatened, 49–50
narrow escape of, from death, 385
President, 45, 50
resignation of, demanded, 48
Senator, 25
vetoes by, 48–49
Vice President, 44
Vice-Presidential nominee, 43

Un-American Activities, House Committee on
Dies, Chairman of, 192
Hiss appearance before, 253
Union, preservation of, 56, 59, 62, 64, 68
Union Pacific Railroad, 85, 86
Upshur, Abel P., 325
Urban Transportation Act, 300

vacancies in Presidential and Vice-Presidential offices, 384–385, 389–390
Van Buren, Martin
attitude of, toward Eaton affair, 27, 28–29
background of, 26
Free Soil Presidential candidate, 64
minister to England, 35–36
nicknames of, 26, 32, 38
President, 40, 52
resignation of, as Secretary of State, 34
Secretary of State, 26, 33, 35
Senator, 25
Texas statehood opposed by, 52
Vice President, 6, 24, 38
Vice-Presidential nominee, 36, 279
Versailles, Treaty of, 55, 134, 139
Vice Presidency, 372–383
assessment of, 380
a consolation prize, 123, 280
future of, 382–383
multiple, suggested, 388

Vice Presidency (*continued*)
prestige of, 373
strengthening of, 174–175
upgrading of, 267
weakness of, 156
Vice President
oldest, 249
seven years without a, 63
working, 174, 259
youngest, 63
Vice-Presidential nominees, methods of choosing, 123, 373–375
Vice Presidents, 372–383
advanced to Presidency, 83
agreements with Presidents on succession, 382–383
duties of, 7–9, 299, 322–323, 353, 378–380, 382
elected to Presidency, 6
elected twice, 375
official residence recommended for, 373
relations of, with Senate, 379–380
Villard, Oswald Garrison, 161
Volpe, John, contender for Vice President in 1968, 342–343

Wade, Benjamin, 82, 83
Wagner, Robert, 289
Walker, Frank, role of, in picking FDR's fourth-term running mate, 212, 214, 218, 219, 224, 229
Walker, Robert J., 53
Wallace, George, Independent Presidential candidate, 1968, 341, 351–353
Wallace, Henry A.
attitude of, toward Communists, 188–189, 246
background of, 175
books by, 178, 183
characterizations of, 177, 180, 186
FDR's attitude toward, 181–182
most memorable speech by, 187–188
Progressive party candidate, 64, 246
second-term Vice-Presidential nomination sought by, 197, 198–238, 270
Secretary of Agriculture, 176
Secretary of Commerce, 241, 244, 245
strange theories of, 177, 184–186
switch of, from Republicans to Democrats, 176
Vice President, 174–175, 186
wartime activities of, 189–194
Warren, Charles, 58
Warren, Earl, Vice-Presidential candidate (1948), 248
Washington, George, 9–11, 16
Watson, General Edwin M. (Pa)
attitude of, toward FDR's third term, 182
opposition of, to Wallace, 205
Webster, Daniel
Clay supported by, in Compromise of 1850 debate, 58–59
death of, 62
debate with Calhoun, 39
debate with Hayne, 30
foe of Van Buren, 35, 36
a leading Whig, 43
Presidential nomination sought by, 62
Secretary of State, 47, 49, 61
Senator, 24, 25
Weed, Thurlow, 56, 62
Wehle, Louis B., 210
Welles, Gideon, 71, 78
Westmoreland, William, 329
Wheeler, William A., Vice President under Hayes, 88
Whigs, 40, 41, 43, 44, 47–51, 54, 56, 57, 61, 62
White, Dr. Paul Dudley, 265
White, Theodore H.
Nixon described by, 284
quoted on Humphrey, 383
White, William Allen, comment by, on FDR, 194
White, William H., 359
White, William S., 298
White House Office of Intergovernmental Relations, 9, 353, 380
Willkie, Wendell
death of, 325
Presidential ambition of, 208
Presidential candidate (1940), 184
Wilson, Edith (Mrs. Woodrow), "regency" of, 132, 134, 137–138, 266, 334
Wilson, Henry ("Cobbler of Natick")
Crédit Mobilier, involvement of, 86

Wilson, Henry (*continued*)
death of, 87
Vice President (1872), 85
Wilson, Woodrow
false report of death of, 138
illness of, 132–138, 143, 272, 332
Lansing resignation requested by, 136, 394
Marshall's relationship with, 126, 127, 128, 143
nomination of, first-term, 38, 125
in Paris, 130, 131
second-term, 129
third-term hopes of, 143
See also League of Nations; Versailles, Treaty of
Winant, John G., potential 1944 Vice-Presidential nominee, 203, 213
Wolcott, Oliver, 12, 13
Wood, General Leonard, 145
Woodrow Wilson and the Great Betrayal, 142
Wright, Robert, 18
Wright, Silas, Vice-Presidential nomination refused by, 52–53, 113, 155

Yarborough, Ralph, 304
Youngblood, Rufus, 373

Zangara, Guiseppe, would-be FDR assassin, 166